Troubleshooting and Repairing PC Drives and Memory Systems

TAB Electronics Technician Library

BIGELOW • *Troubleshooting and Repairing Computer Monitors, 2/e*

BIGELOW • *Troubleshooting and Repairing Computer Printers, 2/e*

DAVIDSON • *Troubleshooting and Repairing Audio Equipment*

DAVIDSON • *Troubleshooting and Repairing Camcorders*

DAVIDSON • *Troubleshooting and Repairing Compact Disc Players*

DAVIDSON • *Troubleshooting and Repairing Consumer Electronics without a Schematic, 2/e*

DAVIDSON • *Troubleshooting and Repairing Microwave Ovens, 4/e*

GOODMAN • *Maintaining and Repairing VCRs*

GOODMAN • *Troubleshooting and Repairing Color Television Systems*

HORDESKI • *Troubleshooting and Repairing PCs: Beyond the Basics, 3/e*

KLEINART • *Troubleshooting and Repairing Major Appliances*

MCCOMB • *Troubleshooting and Repairing VCRs, 3/e*

Other Books by Stephen J. Bigelow

Bigelow's Computer Repair Toolkit

The PC Technician's Pocket Reference

The TAB Electronics Technician's On-Line Resource Reference

Troubleshooting, Maintaining, and Repairing Personal Computers: A Technician's Guide

To order or receive additional information on these or any other McGraw-Hill titles, in the United States please call 1-800-722-4726. In other countries, contact your local McGraw-Hill representative.

Troubleshooting and Repairing PC Drives and Memory Systems

Stephen J. Bigelow

Second Edition

McGraw-Hill

New York   San Francisco   Washington, D.C.   Auckland   Bogotá
Caracas   Lisbon   London   Madrid   Mexico City   Milan
Montreal   New Delhi   San Juan   Singapore
Sydney   Tokyo   Toronto

Library of Congress Cataloging-in-Publication Data

Bigelow, Stephen J.
    Troubleshooting and repairing PC Drives and memory systems /
Stephen J. Bigelow.—2nd ed.
        p.   cm.
    Includes index.
    ISBN 0-07-006384-2 (cloth).—ISBN 0-07-006385-0 (paper)
    1. Computer storage devices—Repairing.   2. Data disk drives—
Repairing.   I. Title.
TK7895.M4B5   1997
621.39'7'0287—dc21   97-26278
                                                            CIP

McGraw-Hill

*A Division of The **McGraw·Hill** Companies*

1 2 3 4 5 6 7 8 9 0   DOC/DOC   9 0 2 1 0 9 8 7 (HC)
1 2 3 4 5 6 7 8 9 0   DOC/DOC   9 0 2 1 0 9 8 7 (PBK)

ISBN 0-07-006384-2 (HC)
ISBN 0-07-006385-0 (PBK)

*The sponsoring editor for this book was Scott Grillo, the editing
supervisor was Jane Palmieri, and the production supervisor was
Tina Cameron. It was set in ITC Century Light per the EL1 Specs by
Kim Sheran of McGraw-Hill's Professional Book Group composition
unit, Hightstown, N.J.*

Printed and bound by R. R. Donnelley & Sons Company.

McGraw-Hill books are available at special quantity discounts to use as
premiums and sales promotions, or for use in corporate training programs. For
more information, please write to the Director of Special Sales, McGraw-Hill,
11 West 19th Street, New York, NY 10011. Or contact your local bookstore.

 This book is printed on recycled, acid-free paper containing a
minimum of 50% recycled, de-inked fiber.

Contents

Preface

My father introduced me to electronics when I was in my early teens. Through the GI bill and a lot of hard work, he made his way through an array of home-study courses. It didn't take long before he could follow just about any circuit. The cellar was his shop. A small arsenal of home-built test equipment took up a better part of the work-bench. Any sick or dying television, radio, or tape deck was considered fair game for his soldering iron. I can remember long evenings assisting Dad in "emergency surgery," trying to save ailing home electronics from certain destruction. Some were rescued, others simply went on to "hardware heaven." Although I was too young to understand the math and science of electronics at the time, I caught the bug—troubleshooting and repairing were fun.

In the years that followed, I've learned a lot about electronics and trouble-shooting. Perhaps the most important thing of all is the need for *information*. With a clear understanding of how and why circuits and systems work, tracking down trouble becomes much less difficult. That is why I wrote this book. Since computers and peripherals have become so prevalent in our everday lives, it seemed only natural to provide a thorough, comprehensive text on computer technology and repair for personal computers. It is written for electronics enthusiasts and technicians who want to tackle their own computer problems as quickly and painlessly as possible.

After all, troubleshooting and repairing should be fun.

Thanks Dad!

Stephen J. Bigelow

Acknowledgments

It is simply impossible to prepare a state-of-the-art troubleshooting and repairing text such as this without the encouragement, cooperation, and support of a great many talented and generous individuals. I would like to thank the following individuals and organizations for their gracious contributions to this book.

May Adachi; Teac Coordinator.

Karen J. Baker; PACE Incorporated.

Lea Baker; Simon/McGarry Public Relations.

Debbie Beech; Hewlett-Packard Limited (U.K.)

Randi Braunwalder; Hewlett-Packard Company (Boise Division).

Jim Ciraulo; Adtron Corporation.

Deirdre D'Amico; OK Industries, Incorporated.

Elizabeth R. Dessuge; Accurite Technologies Incorporated.

Gregg Elmore; B+K Precision (a division of Maxtec International).

David Y. Feinstein; Innoventions, Incorporated.

Mark Fisher; ITT Pomona.

Paula Fisher; NEC Technologies, Incorporated.

Elizabeth Foley; Graseby Plastic Systems.

Sandy Garcia; Mountain Network Solutions, Incorporated.

Howie Greenhalgh; Lynx Technology, Incorporated.

Sharon Gregory; SunDisk Corporation.

Traci Hayes; Hill and Knowlton (for Toshiba America Information Systems, Inc).

Jennifer B. Hennigan; AMP Incorporated.

Susan Johnson; National Labnet Company.

Steve Hire; Cooper Hand Tools.

Andrea Mace; Maxtor Corporation.

Fran McGehee; Tandy Corporation/Radio Shack.

Cara O'Sullivan; Iomega.

Karrin L. Pate; Quantum Corporation.

Rickie Rosenberg; Texas Instruments, Incorporated.

Todd Schreibman; Link Computer Graphics, Incorporated.

Mike Siewruk; Landmark Research International, Incorporated.

Stephanie Smith; Sony Corporation of America.

Daniel Sternglass; Databook Incorporated.

William B. White; Elan Systems, Incorporated.

How to Contact the Author

Your comments and questions can be sent directly to the author. Feel free to share your personal troubleshooting experiences or test equipment techniques, and let him know what you want to see in future editions. Contact the author by mail, fax, or e-mail:

Stephen J. Bigelow
Dynamic Learning Systems
P. O. Box 282
Jefferson, MA 01522
Fax: (508) 829-6819
E-mail: sbigelow@cerfnet.com
WWW: http://www.dlspubs.com

Be sure to include your full name, address, and a complete telephone number where you can be reached or faxed. Although the author cannot provide full-time troubleshooting support, every message *will* be answered by mail or fax.

1
CHAPTER

Mass-Storage Devices

The ability to retain information is as important to a computer as its microprocessor. Computers must have immediate access to program instructions and data during processing. Programs and data must also be retained while the computer is turned off. Otherwise, a human operator would have to manually enter each instruction and data item by hand as the program executes. As you might imagine, the computer as we know it would simply not exist without some type of storage mechanism (Fig. 1-1).

Since the introduction of the earliest computers, the insatiable demand for more and faster storage has given rise to several families of powerful storage devices. Each family is capable of retaining substantial amounts of information, and they have become known collectively as *mass-storage devices*. With today's storage-hungry application programs and operating systems such as Windows 95, Windows NT, and OS/2, the need for large, fast storage is more acute then ever. The need for even more storage will likely be a driving force behind computer development for many years to come. This book is devoted to the study and repair of PC drives and memory systems.

There are three major technologies at work in modern mass-storage systems: *electronic, magnetic,* and *optical.* Electronic mass storage uses semiconductor devices (primarily integrated circuits). Magnetic mass storage employs a delicate interaction of magnetic material, mechanics, and electronics to hold its data. Optical mass storage employs electronics and mechanics in conjunction with optical materials and principles to access vast quantities of information. These three mass-storage technologies enjoy their own unique advantages and suffer their own particular limitations, but each has secured an important place in computer applications. You will learn about these technologies in detail throughout the course of this book.

Before we jump right into the particulars of mass-storage devices, however, you should know a bit about computers in general. If you already have a good knowledge of computer basics, feel free to skip these sections. For those of you whose computer background may be a bit weak, the following material can give you an appreciation of today's IBM-compatible computers, and a better understanding of where mass-storage devices fit in the overall scheme of computer operations.

Toshiba America Information Systems.

1-1 A Toshiba T100X Dynapad pen computer.

Computer Primer

In order to understand a computer, there are two important concepts that you must grasp: digital logic and number systems. These concepts are absolutely fundamental to the operation of every computer system ever made, since they define the ways in which information is interpreted and represented by electronic circuitry. Let's start at the beginning.

Digital logic

The lineage of modern digital logic can be traced back to 1854. George Boole developed a new way of thinking by substituting symbols instead of words to reach logical conclusions. This symbolic logic became known as *boolean logic* or *boolean algebra*. The interesting feature of boolean logic is that input and output conditions can only be expressed as true or false (yes or no). While boolean concepts had little practical application during the mid-nineteenth century, they would form the basis for electronic logic devices less than 100 years later.

With the advent of electron tubes, it became possible to implement boolean logic in the form of electronic circuits which could "automatically" solve the simple addition and multiplication relationships envisioned by Boole. Since logic circuits only dealt with two conditions (on/off or 1/0), they were dubbed *binary* logic circuits. As electron tubes gave way to semiconductor components such as diodes and transistors, additional logic functions appeared which took their roots in Boole's principles (i.e., NAND, NOR, INVERTER, BUFFER, XOR, XNOR). Each logic function was implemented using fairly standard electronic circuitry, so they became known as logic *gates*. Logic also became known as digital logic due to the use of logic circuits to perform mathematical computations. When discrete logic circuits were finally fabricated as integrated circuits, the gate concept stuck, and it remains in use to this day. For the purposes of this book, the terms "boolean logic," "binary logic," and "digital logic" are all identical.

For an electronic circuit to deal with binary logic, there must be a direct relationship between logic states and electrical signals. This relationship is critical because logic circuits perform operations based upon the voltage signals existing at each input. As you might imagine, an incorrect signal voltage may result in an erroneous logic output. A binary *true* (or on) condition usually indicates the *presence* of a voltage, while a binary *false* (or off) indicates the *absence* of a voltage. This is generally known as conventional or *active-high* logic. In some cases, however, the active-high convention is reversed, where an on state is represented by an absence of voltage and an off state is shown by a presence of a voltage. This is called *active-low logic*. Active-low logic signals are represented with a solid bar over the signal label. Occasionally, active-low signals are also shown with a minus (−) sign or apostrophe (') after the label.

For the example of Fig. 1-2, the label "Error" is an active-high signal. When a logic 1 signal voltage is present, the condition is true. When a logic 0 signal voltage is present, the condition is false. If the label were marked "Error," an active-low signal would be indicated. Here, a logic 1 signal voltage would be considered false, so there would be no error condition. A logic 0 signal voltage would represent a true state, so an error condition would exist. Active-low logic is used because it is often faster to make a signal logic 0 than logic 1. Thus, active-low signals help to boost logic system performance at the hardware level. From a troubleshooting standpoint, however, you need only realize the difference between active-high and active-low signals during your testing. Some schematics and block diagrams may also accent active-low signal lines using small circles (called *bubbles*) at the circuit's output.

Binary numbers

You are already familiar with the decimal number system. It consists of ten characters—0 through 9. Each character (or digit) represents a discrete quantity that we

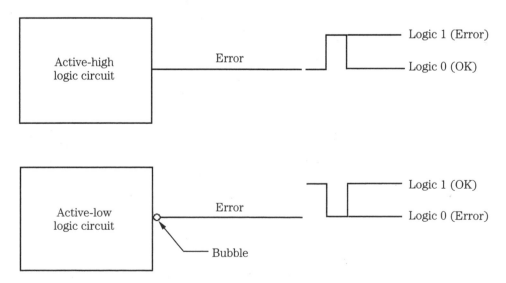

1-2 An example of active-high vs. active-low logic.

all can associate with. By combining digits using basic rules of place values, you can represent virtually any quantity. The same is true of binary logic.

Binary logic uses a number system of only 2 characters instead of 10. A true condition is considered to be a logic 1, and a false condition is considered to be a logic 0. These binary digits (or *bits*) can also be combined to represent almost any quantity. Where a decimal digit can be 0 through 9, a binary digit can only be 0 or 1.

In the decimal number system, a single digit alone can express 10 discrete levels or magnitudes (0 to 9). When the quantity to be expressed exceeds the capacity of a single digit, the number carries over into the next higher place value. Decimal place values are based on the power of 10, since there are 10 digits in the decimal system. As you may remember, the decimal place values are ones, tens, hundreds, thousands, ten-thousands, etc. As an example, the number 35 has a 3 in the tens place and a 5 in the ones place. The number would be resolved as (3×10) + (5×1). You have done this subconsciously since early grammar school. The number 256 has a 2 in the hundreds place, a 5 in the tens place, and a 6 in the ones place $(2 \times 100) + (5 \times 10) + (6 \times 1)$, and so on.

Since the binary number system uses only 2 digits instead of 10, each place value is to the power of 2. This would create a place value system as shown in Fig. 1-3; ones, twos, fours, eights, sixteens, thirty-twos, sixty-fours, etc. The binary number 100110 (pronounced one, zero, zero, one, one, zero) uses a 1 in the 32s, 4s, and 2s places. To convert the binary number to a decimal equivalent, simply add up the associated place values wherever 1s are present. The number 100110 is equivalent to the decimal number 38. The number of quantities that can be expressed by a binary number is equal to the twos power (2^n) of the number of available bits. For instance, 4 bits can express 16 (2^4) quantities, 8 bits can express 256 (2^8) quantities, and so on.

Binary-coded decimal

Binary-coded decimal (BCD) is a common technique of representing decimal digits with their binary equivalent numbers. For example, the decimal number 25 would be represented as 1010 0101 in BCD (in straight binary, a decimal 25 would be represented as 11001). Since each decimal number is directly replaced by its 4-bit binary

2^7	2^6	2^5	2^4	2^3	2^2	2^1	2^0	
128s	64s	32s	16s	8s	4s	2s	1s	
		1	0	0	1	1	0	Binary number
		1	x	32	=	32		
		0	x	16	=	0		
		0	x	8	=	0		
		1	x	4	=	4		
		1	x	2	=	2		
		0	x	1	=	0		
						38		Decimal equivalent

100110 binary = 38 decimal

1-3 An example of binary number formation.

equivalent, BCD offers a fast and easy conversion from BCD to decimal, and vice versa. BCD has historically found use with variable-state input devices such as thumbwheel switches and as raw data to drive seven-segment LEDs. Today, BCD is typically used for data coding in certain optical disk systems. You will see more about optical disks later in this book.

Hexadecimal numbers

While the decimal number system uses 10 digits and the binary number system uses 2 digits, the hexadecimal (or *hex*) number system uses 16 digits. The characters 0 to 9 are used, along with the letters A, B, C, D, E, and F to represent the quantities 10 to 15. The place-value technique used to form hexadecimal numbers is the same used with decimal or binary numbers, but each place value is now to the power of 16 instead of 10 or 2. Figure 1-4 illustrates two hexadecimal examples. First, the hexadecimal number 3C uses a 3 in the 16ths place and a C (12) in the 1s place. This results in a decimal equivalent of (3 × 16) + (12 × 1) or 60. The second hexadecimal example uses an F (15) in the 16ths place and an F (15) in the 1s place. A hex FF represents a decimal 255.

It is interesting to note that there are exactly four binary bits in every hexadecimal character. For example, the hexadecimal number 5 can be represented with a binary number 0101, while the hexadecimal number F equals a binary 1111. This relationship makes it very easy to translate between hexadecimal and binary numbers, and is the main reason why hexadecimal notation has been embraced so thoroughly in the computer field. A 16-digit binary address can be represented with only 4 hex characters.

Octal numbers

Octal numbers are yet another way of expressing quantities using a number system of 8 digits. The characters 0 to 7 are used to represent the 8 digits. Octal place values, however, utilize powers of 8 instead of powers of 10, 2, or 16. Figure 1-5 shows how a typical octal number is formed. Once an actual number counts from 0 to 7, the next numbers are 10 to 17, 20 to 27, and so on. The octal number 170 uses a 1 in the 64ths place, a 7 in the 8ths place, and a 0 in the 1s place. The equivalent decimal number is 120.

You may note that with 8 digits, only 3 binary digits are needed to represent each octal digit. An octal 1 would equate to a binary 001, an octal 4 would be a binary 100, and an octal 7 would be a binary 111, and so on. This relationship also makes it very convenient to translate between octal and binary number systems. Like hexadecimal, the octal system was developed to facilitate fast back-and-forth conversion. However, octal is used less than hex since hex can represent more bits with fewer characters. The relationship between decimal, hexadecimal, octal, and binary numbers is illustrated in Table 1-1.

A Basic Computer

In the broadest sense, a *digital computer* is an electronic device utilizing the rules of boolean logic to input, store, manipulate, and output binary information—nothing

16^4	16^3	16^2	16^1	16^0
65.536s	4096s	256s	16s	1s

3C hex

3	x	16	=	48
12	x	1	=	12
				60 Decimal

3C = 0011 1100 Binary

FF hex

15	x	16	=	240
15	x	1	=	15
				255 Decimal

FF = 1111 1111 Binary

1-4 An example of hexadecimal number formation.

8^4	8^3	8^2	8^1	8^0
4096s	512s	64s	8s	1s
		1	7	0

170 Octal

1	x	64	=	64
7	x	8	=	56
0	x	1	=	0
				120 Decimal

170 Octal = 001 111 000 Binary

1-5 An example of octal number formation.

Table 1-1. Relationship Between Decimal, Binary, Hexadecimal, and Octal Numbers

Decimal	Binary	Hexadecimal	Octal
0	0	0	0
1	1	1	1
2	10	2	2
3	11	3	3
4	100	4	4
5	101	5	5
6	110	6	6
7	111	7	7
8	1000	8	10
9	1001	9	11
10	1010	A	12
11	1011	B	13
12	1100	C	14
13	1101	D	15
14	1110	E	16
15	1111	F	17

more. Every computer ever made finds its foundations in this fundamental concept. To fulfill such a broad definition, a computer must contain at least four major functional elements as illustrated in Fig. 1-6; a processing unit, memory, input devices, and output devices. While a modern full-featured computer can contain many specialized functions, each function can generally be categorized as one of these four elements.

Central processing unit

The central processing unit (also called a CPU, μP, or microprocessor) is at the heart of every modern computer system. It is the CPU which provides a computer with much of its processing power. Strangely, a CPU is only capable of three types of operations: *arithmetic, logic,* and *control*—that's it. Arithmetic operations allow the CPU to add, subtract, multiply, and divide. Logical operations let the CPU make comparisons and conditional decisions about various pieces of data. Control operations allow a CPU to access ports and data anywhere within the computer and move information from one place to another. Even the hundreds of unique and powerful instructions found in sophisticated CPUs can be grouped into these three categories.

The great advantage to a CPU is not in its internal design. In fact, CPUs make use of very generalized internal designs which actually tend to be much slower than streamlined ICs that are dedicated to performing one particular function. What CPUs may lack in speed performance, they make up for in flexibility—the ability to carry out operations in any order as instructed. The instructions which direct a microprocessor's operations are called a *program.* Programs are held in mass-storage areas outside of the CPU (typically in a bank of memory ICs). The CPU accesses its instructions and data from the program in storage, then executes each operation as the particular instruction specifies. Thus, by altering the pattern of instructions and data in storage, the same CPU can perform an entirely different set of operations.

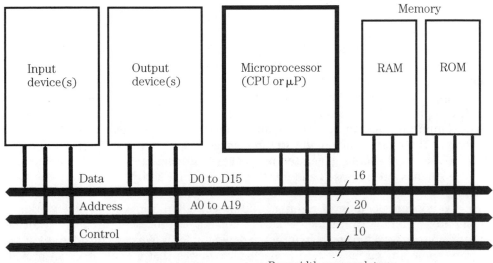

1-6 Diagram of a simple computer system.

Even though today's computers utilize an assortment of powerful integrated circuits (ICs) to achieve high-level control over drives, displays, and keyboards, the actual program instructions which make those parts work together are still executed exclusively by the CPU.

Storage

A CPU functions through the use of instructions contained in a program. However, the CPU is merely a processing tool. Aside from a few internal registers used to store temporary information, microprocessors offer no way to retain the program that they are supposed to run. This limitation requires the program (and any associated program data) to be held *outside* of the CPU. The CPU can then simply access the stored program and execute it as directed. Computers use solid-state memory ICs to retain current program information. Temporary memory (random access memory, or RAM) holds the current application program (i.e., a word processor or spreadsheet) as well as the computer's operating system (i.e., DOS, Windows 95, or OS/2). Permanent memory (read-only memory, ROM) holds the computer's power-on self-test (POST) routines and its basic input/output system (BIOS).

Over the last few years, memory ICs have undergone some dramatic improvements in speed and capacity. Many commercial computers now come with 16 to 32 MB of RAM as standard equipment. The next few years will probably see those figures double. With so much inexpensive memory available, solid-state memory ICs have become an important branch on the mass-storage family tree. You will see more about memory ICs later in this chapter. Chapter 4 covers memory devices in detail, and Chap. 5 discusses a powerful new application of memory ICs in self-contained solid-state memory cards.

Input and output devices

Although a CPU and memory together can technically constitute a working "computer," such a computer would have very little practical value since the device would have absolutely no interaction with the outside world. In order to be useful, a computer *must* be able to carry information to or from the outside world. For our purposes here, we can consider the "outside world" to be any component or mechanism outside of the CPU or its memory devices.

Input devices are a huge category of circuits and electromechanical systems that can provide information to the CPU and its memory. The CPU can then make use of input information to adapt to any changes in the outside world. A *keyboard* is one of the most common and well-recognized input devices. When you press a key, a numerical code is generated by the keyboard circuitry. The CPU recognizes that a key has been pressed and interrupts its current activity to acquire the key's numerical code.

Even when a computer can read and process data from the outside world, no computer is complete until the results of a computer's processing are made available to the outside world in some coherent, meaningful form. We can consider an output device to be any circuit or electromechanical device that a computer can provide data to. A computer monitor and flat-panel display are two typical output devices. The CPU can output numerical codes representing commands, text, or graphics to a video controller IC. The video controller IC stores and processes those codes and generates the information needed to form the display image.

Many other circuits and electromechanical devices are capable of acting as both input and output devices. A serial communication port is a popular input/output (I/O) circuit which allows data to flow into and out of a computer under program control. Many I/O devices are the mass-storage systems that are covered in this book: floppy disk drives, hard disk drives, CD-ROM drives, tape drives, and solid-state memory cards. Each of these devices can receive data output from the CPU (except for the CD-ROM), and provide data input to the CPU as well.

Buses

As you look over the simple computer diagram of Fig. 1-6, you will see that each part of the classical computer is interconnected using three major sets of signals called *buses.* It is important for you to realize that even though the bus may appear as a single solid line, it represents a collection of individual signals all traveling together. The exact number of lines in a bus depends on the particular microprocessor and memory arrangement being used, but the number of lines is usually marked on the bus line with a slash, or indicated discretely with labels (i.e., D0 to D7 would suggest an 8-bit bus).

There are three major buses in a computer: the address bus, the data bus, and the control bus. Some designers and technicians like to consider the distribution of system power (+Vcc) and ground (Vss) as a fourth bus. The *address bus* is controlled exclusively by the CPU. Binary information placed on the address bus defines the precise location in the computer where information can be read or written by the CPU. Microprocessors typically offer more than 20 address lines (A0 to A19), but advanced addressing techniques allow CPUs to access more than 1 billion (theoretical) locations.

A *data bus* carries binary information to or from the unique locations specified by the address bus. Such binary information may be an instruction needed by the CPU, the result of a calculation or comparison, the destination address of a program subroutine or jump, etc. A CPU can either input or output data on the data bus.

The *control bus* carries a selection of digital signals that are used to direct system operations. Control signals can vary quite a bit between computer models and manufacturers, so it is difficult to define one bus that is common to all computers. The number and purpose of control signals will depend on the CPU being used and the overall complexity of the system. One common control is the read/write (R/W) signal generated by the CPU. If the R/W signal indicates a "read," the CPU inputs the contents of the data bus at the location specified by the address bus. If a "write" is directed by the R/W line, the CPU will output data to the address specified by the address bus. Buses are extremely important for this book because most mass-storage devices are interfaced to a computer through its major buses.

Motherboards and Bus Architecture

The circuitry required to implement a working computer is fabricated onto printed circuit boards that are mounted in a desktop case. It is a simple matter to provide a complete computer on a single PC board. This is how notebook and laptop computers are manufactured today. In fact, early computers such as Commodore's VIC-20 utilized a single-board design.

However, when IBM designed their personal computers in the early 1980s, they cut costs by providing only the essential (or core) components on the motherboard. Core components include the microprocessor, a socket for an optional math co-processor, base memory (now exceeding 4 MB in many desktop systems), BIOS memory (ROM), and support circuitry supplying clocks, system controllers, and signal converters. Other computer functions such as video controllers, drive controllers, and communication circuits must be added to the computer as plug-in expansion boards.

Active backplanes

Classical desktop systems incorporate the core components on a main system PC board (also called a *motherboard* or *backplane*) as shown in Fig. 1-7. The major signal buses are provided to a series of large card-edge connectors. Each card-edge connector can accept a standard-sized expansion board. When a new feature is plugged in to upgrade the computer, it interfaces directly to the main system buses. This approach is known as an *active backplane* system. The term "active" indicates that active semiconductor components are at work on the backplane PC board.

Expansion
slot

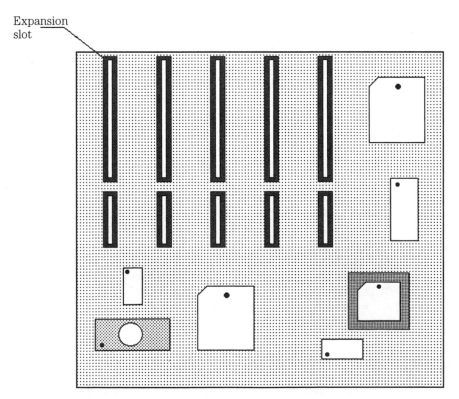

1-7 An "active backplane" motherboard.

Passive backplanes

The disadvantage of active backplane systems is that of large physical size—a substantial amount of motherboard area (or real estate) is needed to hold the active components as well as the expansion board connectors. With so many computer systems struggling to reduce the overall case size (or footprint), active backplanes are often too large. Another problem with active backplane systems is the fixed nature of core components—everything can be changed in an active backplane system except for the core components. To overcome the limitations imposed by active backplane systems, computer designers have introduced the *passive backplane* architecture.

A "passive" backplane uses no active components. This results in a simple, much more petite PC board as shown in Fig. 1-8. The CPU, BIOS, core memory, math coprocessor, and support circuitry are removed from the motherboard and placed on a plug-in board of their own. Such a CPU board would then occupy its own expansion slot. You could also upgrade or repair the computer's core functions simply by removing the old CPU board and installing the new CPU board. All other expansion boards such as video controllers and drive controllers are exactly the same as for active backplane systems. Since you will probably have to deal with expansion boards and computer backplanes during mass-storage troubleshooting, you should be familiar with PC buses as well. This book shows you five popular IBM PC buses, the PC/XT bus, the PC/AT bus, the PC/MicroChannel bus, the Video Local (VL) bus, and the Peripheral Component Interconnect (PCI) bus. Although the classical IBM PC/XT bus has certainly been obsolete for quite some time now, XTs will still appear in homes and schools for years to come.

PC/XT bus

The original backplane bus for the IBM PC/XT uses a card-edge connector with 62 pins marked A1 to A31 and B1 to B31 as illustrated in Fig. 1-9. There are 3 ground lines, 5 power lines, 20 address lines, 8 data lines, 10 interrupt lines, and 16 control signals. The labels for each bus pin are described in Table 1-2.

The oscillator signal (pin B30) is a multipurpose clock generated directly by a crystal oscillator. The 14.31818-MHz clock is precisely three times the frequency needed by the CPU and four times the frequency at which TVs and monitors achieve a color signal lock. This way, the oscillator not only drives the CPU, but the display system as well. The oscillator signal can also be used by any expansion circuit requiring synchronization with the CPU. The clock signal (pin B20) is a 4.77-MHz square wave derived by dividing the oscillator signal by 3, and is used to drive the CPU directly. It can also be used to operate other expansion boards in the system.

An I/O Channel Check (pin A1) is a check of memory and devices attached to the system bus. When the signal is logic 1, parity check is correct, and the CPU knows that processing is continuing normally. When a parity check error occurs, the signal becomes logic 0. This effectively crashes the computer. When a pulse is applied to the Reset Driver line (pin B2), the entire system will be reinitialized (also known as a *warm boot* or *warm start*).

When the CPU places an address on its address bus (pins A12 to A31), a brief pulse is placed on the Address Latch Enable (ALE pin B28) to indicate that the address is valid. External circuitry uses the ALE to address the address while the CPU goes on to other

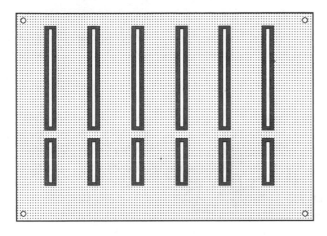

1-8 A "passive backplane" motherboard.

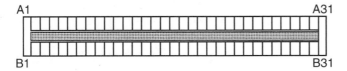

1-9 Pinout diagram of an IBM PC/XT bus connector.

work. During a memory read, the CPU activates the Memory Read Command (pin B12), which inputs data on the data lines (pins A2 to A9) from the specified address. Conversely, the CPU activates its Memory Write Command (pin B11) during a write operation. This causes data to be output to the specified address. If the CPU is working with an I/O port instead of memory, the CPU can input data from an I/O port address by activating the I/O Read Command (pin B14), or output data to an I/O port address by activating the I/O Write Command (pin B13). Since a microprocessor can access I/O much faster than I/O devices can respond, the I/O Channel Ready line (pin A10) can cause the CPU to wait until the I/O circuit has caught up.

IBM bus architectures also allow for data transfers under Direct Memory Access (DMA) control. DMA transfers can be accomplished much faster than working through a microprocessor, but a DMA controller circuit must take control of the address and data bus lines. An Address Enable signal (pin A11) tells the DMA controller when to take charge of the system and begin its data transfer. The number of bytes to be moved is declared, and the controller counts each byte as it is transferred. When all bytes have been moved, the Terminal Count signal (pin B27) is asserted to indicate that the data transfer has been completed.

Devices requiring direct memory access make their requests by asserting one of three DMA Request lines (pins B18, B6, and B16), where DMA request level 1 is the highest system priority, and DMA request level 3 is the lowest system priority. When a DMA request is accepted, the DMA controller confirms the request by asserting the appropriate DMA Acknowledge line (pins B19, B17, B26, and B15). Only

Table 1-2. Expansion Board Pinout for the PC/XT Bus

Signal	Label	Signal	Label
B1	Ground	A1	I/O Channel Check
B2	Reset Driver	A2	Data 7
B3	+5 Vdc	A3	Data 6
B4	Interrupt Request 2	A4	Data 5
B5	−5 Vdc	A5	Data 4
B6	DMA Request 2	A6	Data 3
B7	−12 Vdc	A7	Data 2
B8	Card Selected (XT Only)	A8	Data 1
B9	+12 Vdc	A9	Data 0
B10	Ground	A10	I/O Channel Ready
B11	Memory Write	A11	Address Enable
B12	Memory Read	A12	Address 19
B13	I/O Write	A13	Address 18
B14	I/O Read	A14	Address 17
B15	DMA Acknowledge 3	A15	Address 16
B16	DMA Request 3	A16	Address 15
B17	DMA Acknowledge 1	A17	Address 14
B18	DMA Request 1	A18	Address 13
B19	DMA Acknowledge 0	A19	Address 12
B20	Clock	A20	Address 11
B21	Interrupt Request 7	A21	Address 10
B22	Interrupt Request 6	A22	Address 9
B23	Interrupt Request 5	A23	Address 8
B24	Interrupt Request 4	A24	Address 7
B25	Interrupt Request 3	A25	Address 6
B26	DMA Acknowledge 2	A26	Address 5
B27	Terminal Count	A27	Address 4
B28	Address Latch Enable	A28	Address 3
B29	+5 Vdc	A29	Address 2
B30	Oscillator	A30	Address 1
B31	Ground	A31	Address 0

acknowledge lines 1, 2, and 3 are available to the system for general use. DMA acknowledge line 0 (pin B19) is the highest-priority acknowledge signal used to handle memory refresh operations.

Another way to obtain the microprocessor's attention is to assert one of the CPU's Interrupt lines (pins B4, B25, B24, B23, B22, and B21). There are six interrupts available to the bus (labeled Interrupt 2 to Interrupt 7) where level 2 is the highest-priority interrupt, and level 7 is the lowest priority. Interrupt 0 is a system timer interrupt, and Interrupt 1 is devoted to servicing the keyboard. After an interrupt routine is serviced, the CPU returns to its original program.

There is no doubt that the IBM PC/XT and all XT-compatible computers have been entirely obsolete for years now, yet the many XTs that were sold during the early 1980s will have a place in homes, offices, and schools for years to come. As a result, you should at least be familiar with the XT bus architecture.

PC/AT bus

It did not take long before the limitations of XT computers became painfully apparent. The XT proved far too limited in its memory capacity, its Intel 8088 microprocessor could only support an 8-bit data bus, and its system services (i.e., interrupts and DMA) were inadequate for all but simple processing applications. Computer designers had to upgrade the XT without making obsolete the broad base of XT expansion products that had been created. The next generation of computers from IBM was dubbed the PC/AT. An AT computer is centered around the 16-bit Intel 80286 microprocessor, but retains compatibility with just about all 8-bit XT expansion products.

Instead of redesigning the XT bus, the AT bus simply added a second connector along with the original 62-pin card-edge connector. This supplemental connector is a 36-pin card-edge connector marked C1 to C18 and D1 to D18 as shown in Fig. 1-10. The AT extension adds five interrupts, eight data lines (D8 to D15), four DMA request/acknowledge pairs, four extra address lines (A20 to A23), and some additional control lines. Table 1-3 lists the labels for each AT pin. The AT bus has proved to be so versatile and resilient that the Institute of Electrical and Electronic Engineers (IEEE) adopted the bus as an industry standard called the Industry Standard Architecture (ISA) bus.

Since the AT bus allows both 8-bit and 16-bit expansion boards to be used in the same computer, the System Bus High Enable (pin C1) must be asserted for a 16-bit data transfer to occur. An expansion board uses the Memory 16-bit Chip Select (pin D1) or the I/O 16-bit Chip Select (pin D2) to request data transfer to or from memory or an I/O port. The Zero Wait State signal (pin B8) allows an expansion board essentially to speed up bus operation by eliminating wait states between bus cycles.

Addressing in the 16-bit range is facilitated with supplemental Memory Read (pin C9) and Memory Write (pin C10) signals. Any addressing below the 1-MB real addressing range uses the memory read and memory write lines on the original 62-pin connector, while any addressing performed above 1 MB will use the additional read and write signals.The AT bus also allows a limited amount of bus sharing (similar to DMA) with other microprocessors. A new CPU can take control of the system for a few milliseconds by asserting the Master line (pin D17). When the original CPU must resume bus control, a Refresh signal (pin B19) is asserted which warns the "visiting" CPU to relinquish control so the original CPU can refresh its local memory.

PC MicroChannel Bus

The IBM MicroChannel Architecture (MCA) bus created in 1987 is a rethinking of computer expansion slot capabilities which have been extended into the realm of

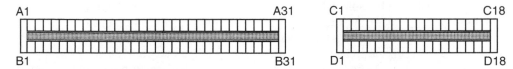

1-10 Pinout diagram of an IBM PC/AT bus connector.

Table 1-3. Expansion Board Pinout for the PC/AT Bus

Signal	Label	Signal	Label
B1	Ground	A1	I/O Channel Check
B2	Reset Driver	A2	Data 7
B3	+5 Vdc	A3	Data 6
B4	Interrupt Request 9	A4	Data 5
B5	−5 Vdc	A5	Data 4
B6	DMA Request 2	A6	Data 3
B7	−12 Vdc	A7	Data 2
B8	Zero Wait State	A8	Data 1
B9	+12 Vdc	A9	Data 0
B10	Ground	A10	I/O Channel Ready
B11	Real Memory Write	A11	Address Enable
B12	Real Memory Read	A12	Address 19
B13	I/O Write	A13	Address 18
B14	I/O Read	A14	Address 17
B15	DMA Acknowledge 3	A15	Address 16
B16	DMA Request 3	A16	Address 15
B17	DMA Acknowledge 1	A17	Address 14
B18	DMA Request 1	A18	Address 13
B19	Refresh	A19	Address 12
B20	Clock	A20	Address 11
B21	Interrupt Request 7	A21	Address 10
B22	Interrupt Request 6	A22	Address 9
B23	Interrupt Request 5	A23	Address 8
B24	Interrupt Request 4	A24	Address 7
B25	Interrupt Request 3	A25	Address 6
B26	DMA Acknowledge 2	A26	Address 5
B27	Terminal Count	A27	Address 4
B28	Address Latch Enable	A28	Address 3
B29	+5 Vdc	A29	Address 2
B30	Oscillator	A30	Address 1
B31	Ground	A31	Address 0
D1	Memory 16-bit Chip Select	C1	System Bus High Enable
D2	I/O 16 bit Chip Select	C2	Unlatched Address 23
D3	Interrupt Request 10	C3	Unlatched Address 22
D4	Interrupt Request 11	C4	Unlatched Address 21
D5	Interrupt Request 12	C5	Unlatched Address 20
D6	Interrupt Request 15	C6	Unlatched Address 19
D7	Interrupt Request 14	C7	Unlatched Address 18
D8	DMA Acknowledge 0	C8	Unlatched Address 17
D9	DMA Request 0	C9	Memory Read
D10	DMA Acknowledge 5	C10	Memory Write
D11	DMA Request 5	C11	Data 8
D12	DMA Acknowledge 6	C12	Data 9
D13	DMA Request 6	C13	Data 10

Table 1-3. *Continued*

Signal	Label	Signal	Label
D14	DMA Acknowledge 7	C14	Data 11
D15	DMA Request 7	C15	Data 12
D16	+5 Vdc	C16	Data 13
D17	Master	C17	Data 14
D18	Ground	C18	Data 15

32-bit data processing. MCA expansion boards are physically smaller than full-slot AT boards, and use smaller, denser connectors, but the differences are more than physical. An MCA bus is designed to be faster and more powerful than the AT bus. With 32 bits of data, 32 address lines capable of addressing 4 GB of memory, a built-in audio channel carrying signals from 50 Hz to 10 kHz, and a built-in Video Graphics Array (VGA) capacity, the MCA bus is intended for high-performance computing. The MCA bus is also designed to handle *bus arbitration*—the ability of various CPUs to take control of the bus. Figure 1-11 illustrates the pinout for a typical MCA card slot, and each pin is labeled in Table 1-4.

Although the MCA architecture offers some performance advantages over the AT bus, it is not widely accepted. As a result, this edition of the book will not look at the MCA bus any further.

Video Local (VL) bus

The path to a "standard" local bus was not an easy one. In 1991 and 1992, a few chip set suppliers and manufacturers implemented nonstandard high-performance I/O buses. For example, some OPTi chip sets were designed to support an OPTi local bus. Unfortunately, the OPTi local bus was supported by only a small handful of manufacturers, and since the OPTi approach was specific to their chip sets, few (if any) I/O cards were ever actually developed for these buses and few manufacturers provided them. Thus, OPTi and other proprietary buses met the same fate as all other nonstandardized approaches in the PC industry—they disappeared. However, the failure of proprietary local bus designs did not prevent industry acceptance of a "standard" VL bus design developed by the VESA (Video Electronics Standards Association) in late 1992. By placing the VL extension connectors in-line with standard ISA connectors, the VL board can also serve as an ISA board—only with far higher data throughput.

The essential advantage of a VL bus is direct access to the CPU's main buses. This allows a VL device to transfer rapidly the large quantities of data that are vital for high-performance video under Windows. Further, there is no limit on the clock speed of a VL bus. With such close interaction between the bus and CPU, the bus speed is linked to that of the CPU. As a result, faster CPU speed will result in faster bus speed. Unfortunately, this is where the advantages end.

While virtually direct connection to the CPU may seem like a real asset, there are also some serious drawbacks that you should understand. Processor dependence can ultimately become a disadvantage for the VL bus. Since higher processor

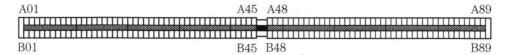

1-11 Pinout diagram of an IBM MicroChannel bus connector.

Table 1-4. Expansion Board Pinout for the PC MicroChannel Bus

Signal	Label	Signal	Label
A01	Card Setup	B01	Audio Ground
A02	Make 24	B02	Audio Signal
A03	Ground	B03	Ground
A04	Address 11	B04	14.3-MHz Oscillator
A05	Address 10	B05	Ground
A06	Address 09	B06	Address 23
A07	+5 Vdc	B07	Address 22
A08	Address 08	B08	Address 21
A09	Address 07	B09	Ground
A10	Address 06	B10	Address 20
A11	+5 Vdc	B11	Address 19
A12	Address 05	B12	Address 18
A13	Address 04	B13	Ground
A14	Address 03	B14	Address 17
A15	+5 Vdc	B15	Address 16
A16	Address 02	B16	Address 15
A17	Address 01	B17	Ground
A18	Address 00	B18	Address 14
A19	+12 Vdc	B19	Address 13
A20	Address Decode Latch	B20	Address 12
A21	Preempt	B21	Ground
A22	Burst	B22	Interrupt 09
A23	−12 Vdc	B23	Interrupt 03
A24	Arbitration 00	B24	Interrupt 04
A25	Arbitration 01	B25	Ground
A26	Arbitration 02	B26	Interrupt 05
A27	−12 Vdc	B27	Interrupt 06
A28	Arbitration 03	B28	Interrupt 07
A29	Arbitration Grant	B29	Ground
A30	Terminal Count	B30	Reserved
A31	+5 Vdc	B31	Reserved
A32	Status Bit 0	B32	Channel Check
A33	Status Bit 1	B33	Ground
A34	Memory I/O	B34	Command
A35	+12 Vdc	B35	Channel Ready Return
A36	Card Ready	B36	Card Selected Feedback
A37	Data Line 00	B37	Ground

Table 1-4. *Continued*

Signal	Label	Signal	Label
A38	Data Line 02	B38	Data Line 01
A39	+5 Vdc	B39	Data Line 03
A40	Data Line 05	B40	Data Line 04
A41	Data Line 06	B41	Ground
A42	Data Line 07	B42	Channel Reset
A43	Ground	B43	Reserved
A44	Data Size 16 Return	B44	Reserved
A45	Refresh	B45	Ground
A46	KEY (empty position)	B46	KEY (empty position)
A47	KEY (empty position)	B47	KEY (empty position)
A48	+5 Vdc	B48	Data Line 08
A49	Data Line 10	B49	Data Line 09
A50	Data Line 11	B50	Ground
A51	Data Line 13	B51	Data Line 12
A52	+12 Vdc	B52	Data Line 14
A53	Reserved	B53	Data Line 15
A54	Status Byte High Enable	B54	Ground
A55	Card Data Size 16	B55	Interrupt 10
A56	+5 Vdc	B56	Interrupt 11
A57	Interrupt 14	B57	Interrupt 12
A58	Interrupt 15	B58	Ground
A59	Reserved	B59	Reserved
A60	Reserved	B60	Reserved
A61	Ground	B61	Reserved
A62	Reserved	B62	Reserved
A63	Reserved	B63	Ground
A64	Reserved	B64	Data Line 16
A65	+12 Vdc	B65	Data Line 17
A66	Data Line 19	B66	Data Line 18
A67	Data Line 20	B67	Ground
A68	Data Line 21	B68	Data Line 22
A69	+5 Vdc	B69	Data Line 23
A70	Data Line 24	B70	Reserved
A71	Data Line 25	B71	Ground
A72	Data Line 26	B72	Data Line 27
A73	+5 Vdc	B73	Data Line 28
A74	Data Line 30	B74	Data Line 29
A75	Data Line 31	B75	Ground
A76	Reserved	B76	Byte Enable 0
A77	+12 Vdc	B77	Byte Enable 1
A78	Byte Enable 3	B78	Byte Enable 2
A79	Data Size 32 Return	B79	Ground
A80	Card Data Size 32	B80	Translate 32
A81	+12 Vdc	B81	Address 24
A82	Address 26	B82	Address 25

Table 1-4. *Continued*

Signal	Label	Signal	Label
A83	Address 27	B83	Ground
A84	Address 28	B84	Address 29
A85	+5 Vdc	B85	Address 30
A86	Reserved	B86	Address 31
A87	Reserved	B87	Ground
A88	Reserved	B88	Reserved
A89	Ground	B89	Reserved

speed results in higher bus capacitance, VL signals can lose reliability at high CPU clock frequencies. Further, the processor signals were intended to attach to only a few chips (like the RAM controller) and have very precise timing rules. In fact, each type of Intel i486 chip (i.e., i486SX, i486DX, and i486DX/2) has slightly different timing requirements. When additional capacitance loads are added by adding multiple connectors and multiple local-bus chips, all sorts of undesirable things can happen. The two most likely problems are: (1) data "glitches" due to slowed processor bus signals, and (2) out-of-spec timing for different I/O cards with different loading characteristics.

Although the VL specification does not list an upper frequency limit, the potential load problems discussed above dictate a practical limit. With a clock speed of 33 MHz, a VL motherboard should be able to support two VL devices reliably. At 40 MHz, only one VL device should be used. Above 40 MHz, the chances of unreliable operation with even one VL device become substantial. If you find yourself working on a fast VL system with random system errors, see if the problem goes away when the VL device(s) are removed (and replaced with ISA equivalents if necessary).

Another problem is the lack of *concurrency*. For a PCI bus, the CPU can continue operating when a PCI device takes control of the system buses. VL architecture also allows for bus mastering operation, but when a VL device takes control of the bus, the CPU must be stopped. While this is technically not a defect, it clearly limits the performance of high-end devices (i.e., SCSI controllers) that might attempt to use a VL architecture. Finally, there are several other disadvantages to the VL bus. It is a +5-Vdc architecture (where PCI can support +3.3 Vdc). Unlike PCI, there is no "autoconfiguration" capability in the VL bus (jumpers and DIP switches are required).

The VL bus uses a 116-pin card-edge connector with small contacts (similar in appearance to MicroChannel contacts) as shown in Fig. 1-12. The current VL bus release (2.0) offers a 32-bit data path with a maximum data throughput of about 130 MB/s, while the full 64-bit implementation provides a 64-bit data path (Data 0 to Data 63) with a maximum rated data throughput of about 260 MB/s. The pinout for a VL bus is illustrated in Table 1-5. One of the most interesting things to note about the VL bus is that it is an extension to the standard ISA/EISA bus. The two right connectors are 16-bit ISA bus connectors. It is the two left connectors that provide the VL compatibility. The long VL connector portion provides the 32-bit VL support, and the left-most connector handles 64-bit support.

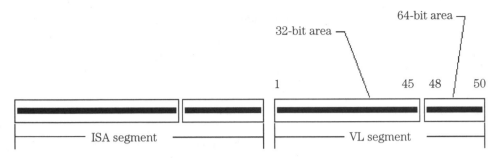

1-12 Pinout diagram of a Video Local (VL) bus connector.

The Data/−Command (D/−C) signal tells whether information on the bus is data or a command. Clock signals from the CPU are provided through the Local Bus Clock (LCLK) line. Memory/−I/O (M/−I/O) distinguishes between memory and I/O access, while the Write/−Read (W/−R) signal differentiates between read or write operations. Since the VL bus is 64 bits wide, the − Byte Enable lines (−BE0 to −BE7) indicate which 8-bit portions of the 64-bit bus are being transferred. A −Reset signal (−RESET) will initialize the VL device. The −Ready Return (−RDYRTN) line indicates that the VL bus is free for access. Data bus width is determined by the −Local Bus Size 16 (−LBS16) or −Local Bus Size 64 (−LBS64) signals. If a 64-bit bus width is used, the −Acknowledge 64 Bit (−ACK64) signal is true.

Accessing the VL bus is a process of arbitration—much like the arbitration that takes place on an MCA or EISA bus. Each VL device is defined by its own ID number (ID0 to ID4). The −Local Bus Ready (−LRDY), −Local Bus Device (−LDEV), −Local Bus Request (−LREQ), and −Local Bus Grant (−LGNT) lines are used to negotiate for control of the VL bus. In most cases, there is only one VL device on the bus, but arbitration must be performed to ensure proper access to memory.

Peripheral Component Interconnect (PCI) bus

By the late 1980s, the proliferation of 32-bit CPUs and graphics-intensive operating systems made it painfully obvious that the 8.33-MHz ISA bus was no longer satisfactory. The PC industry began to develop alternative architectures for improved performance, namely VL and PCI. While the VL bus seems ideal, there are some serious limitations that must be overcome. In mid 1992, Intel Corporation and a comprehensive consortium of manufacturers introduced the *Peripheral Component Interconnect* (PCI) bus. Where the VL bus was designed specifically to enhance PC video systems, the 188-pin PCI bus provides a bus architecture that also supports peripherals such as hard drives and networks.

The PCI architecture is capable of transferring data at 132 MB/s—a great improvement over the 5 MB/s transfer rate of the standard ISA bus. Another key advantage of the PCI bus is that it will have automatic configuration capabilities for switchless/jumperless peripherals. Autoconfiguration (the heart of "plug-and-play") will take care of all addresses, interrupt settings, and DMA assignments used by a PCI peripheral.

Table 1-5. VL Bus Pinout (Rev. 2.0)

64 bit	32 bit	Pin	Pin	32 bit	64 bit
—	Data 00	A01	B01	Data 01	—
—	Data 02	A02	B02	Data 03	—
—	Data 04	A03	B03	Ground	—
—	Data 06	A04	B04	Data 05	—
—	Data 08	A05	B05	Data 07	—
—	Ground	A06	B06	Data 09	—
—	Data 10	A07	B07	Data 11	—
—	Data 12	A08	B08	Data 13	—
—	+Vcc	A09	B09	Data 15	—
—	Data 14	A10	B10	Ground	—
—	Data 16	A11	B11	Data 17	—
—	Data 18	A12	B12	+Vcc	—
—	Data 20	A13	B13	Data 19	—
—	Ground	A14	B14	Data 21	—
—	Data 22	A15	B15	Data 23	—
—	Data 24	A16	B16	Data 25	—
—	Data 26	A17	B17	Ground	—
—	Data 28	A18	B18	Data 27	—
—	Data 30	A19	B19	Data 29	—
—	+Vcc	A20	B20	Data 31	—
Data 63	Address 31	A21	B21	Address 30	Data 62
—	Ground	A22	B22	Address 28	Data 60
Data 61	Address 29	A23	B23	Address 26	Data 58
Data 59	Address 27	A24	B24	Ground	—
Data 57	Address 25	A25	B25	Address 24	Data 56
Data 55	Address 23	A26	B26	Address 22	Data 54
Data 53	Address 21	A27	B27	+Vcc	—
Data 51	Address 19	A28	B28	Address 20	Data 52
—	Ground	A29	B29	Address 18	Data 50
Data 49	Address 17	A30	B30	Address 16	Data 48
Data 47	Address 15	A31	B31	Address 14	Data 46
—	+Vcc	A32	B32	Address 12	Data 44
Data 45	Address 13	A33	B33	Address 10	Data 42
Data 43	Address 11	A34	B34	Address 8	Data 40
Data 41	Address 9	A35	B35	Ground	—
Data 39	Address 7	A36	B36	Address 6	Data 38
Data 37	Address 5	A37	B37	Address 4	Data 36
—	Ground	A38	B38	−WBAK	—
Data 35	Address 3	A39	B39	−BE 0	−BE 4
Data 34	Address 2	A40	B40	+Vcc	—
−LBS64	n/c	A41	B41	−BE 1	−BE 5
—	−RESET	A42	B42	−BE 2	−BE 6
—	D/−C	A43	B43	Ground	—
—	M/−I/O	A44	B44	−BE 3	−BE 7

Table 1-5. *Continued*

64 bit	32 bit	Pin	Pin	32 bit	64 bit
—	W/−R	A45	B45	−ADS	—
Key	Key	Key	Key	Key	Key
Key	Key	Key	Key	Key	Key
—	−RDYRTN	A48	B48	−LRDY	—
—	Ground	A49	B49	−LDEV	—
—	IRQ 9	A50	B50	−LREQ	—
—	−BRDY	A51	B51	Ground	—
—	−BLAST	A52	B52	−LGNT	—
Data 32	ID 0	A53	B53	+Vcc	—
Data 33	ID 1	A54	B54	ID 2	—
—	Ground	A55	B55	ID 3	—
—	LCLK	A56	B56	ID 4	−ACK64
—	+Vcc	A57	B57	n/c	—
—	−LBS16	A58	B58	−LEADS	—

The PCI bus supports *linear bursts,* which is a method of transferring data that ensures the bus is continually filled with data. The peripheral devices expect to receive data from the system main memory in a linear address order. This means that large amounts of data are read from or written to a single address, which is then incremented for the next byte in the stream. The linear burst is one of the unique aspects of the PCI bus, since it will perform both burst reads and burst writes. In short, it will transfer data on the bus *every* clock cycle. This doubles the PCI throughput compared to buses without linear burst capabilities.

The devices designed to support PCI have low *access latency,* reducing the time required for a peripheral to be granted control of the bus after requesting access. For example, an Ethernet controller card connected to a local area network (LAN) has large data files from the network coming into its buffer. Waiting for access to the bus, the Ethernet is unable to transfer the data to the CPU quickly enough to avoid a buffer overflow—forcing it to temporarily store the file's contents in extra RAM. Since PCI-compliant devices support faster access times, the Ethernet card can promptly send data to the CPU.

The PCI bus supports *bus mastering,* which allows one of a number of intelligent peripherals to take control of the bus in order to accelerate a high-throughput, high-priority task. PCI architecture also supports *concurrency*—a technique that ensures the microprocessor operates simultaneously with these masters instead of waiting for them. As one example, concurrency allows the CPU to perform floating-point calculations on a spreadsheet while an Ethernet card and the LAN have control of the bus. Finally, PCI was developed as a dual-voltage architecture. Normally, the bus is a +5-Vdc system like other buses. However, the bus can also operate in a +3.3 Vdc (low-voltage) mode.

The layout for a PCI bus slot is shown in Fig. 1-13. Note that there are two major segments to the +5-Vdc-version connector. A +3.3-Vdc-version connector adds a key in the 12/13 positions to prevent accidental insertion of a +5-Vdc PCI board into a +3.3-Vdc slot. Similarly, the +5-Vdc slot is keyed in the 50/51 position to prevent placing a +3.3-Vdc board into a +5-Vdc slot. The pinout for a PCI bus is shown in Table 1-6.

To reduce the number of pins needed in the PCI bus, data and address lines are multiplexed together (Adr./Dat 0 to Adr./Dat 63). It is also interesting to note that PCI is the first bus standard designed to support a low-voltage (+3.3 Vdc) logic implementation. On inspection, you will see that +5 Vdc and +3.3 Vdc implementations of the PCI bus place their physical key slots in different places so that the two implementations are *not* interchangeable. The Clock (CLOCK) signal provides timing for the PCI bus only, and can be adjusted from DC (0Hz) to 33MHz. Asserting the −Reset (−RST) signal will reset all PCI devices. Since the 64-bit data path uses 8 bytes, the Command/−Byte Enable signals (C/−BE0 to C/−BE7) define which bytes are transferred. Parity across the Address/Data and Byte Enable lines is represented with a Parity (PAR) or 64-Bit Parity (PAR64) signal. Bus mastering is initiated by the −Request (−REQ) line and granted after approval using the −Grant (−GNT) line.

When a valid PCI bus cycle is in progress, the −Frame (−FRAME) signal is true. If the PCI bus cycle is in its final phase, −Frame will be released. The −Target Ready (−TRDY) line is true when an addressed device is able to complete the data phase of its bus cycle. An − Initiator Ready (−IRDY) signal indicates that valid data are present on the bus (or the bus is ready to accept data). The −Frame, −Target Ready, and −Initiator Ready signals are all used together. A −Stop (−STOP) signal is asserted by a target asking a master to halt the current data transfer. The ID Select (IDSEL) signal is used as a chip select signal during board configuration read and write cycles. The −Device Select (−DEVSEL) line is both an input and an output. As an input, −DEVSEL indicates if a device has assumed control of the current bus transfer. As an output, −DEVSEL shows that a device has identified itself as the target for the current bus transfer.

There are four *interrupt* lines (−INTA to −INTD). When the full 64-bit data mode is being used, an expansion device will initiate a −64-Bit Bus Request (−REQ 64) and await a −64-Bit Bus Acknowledge (−ACK64) signal from the bus controller. The −Bus Lock (−LOCK) signal is an interface control used to ensure use of the bus by a selected expansion device. Error reporting is performed by −Primary Error (−PERR) and −Secondary Error (−SERR) lines. Cache memory support is also provided on the PCI bus.

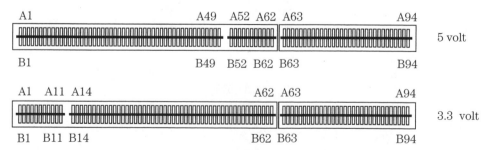

1-13 Pinout diagram of a Peripheral Component Interconnect (PCI) bus connector.

Table 1-6. PCI Bus Pinout—5 V and 3.3 V (Rev. 2.0)

5 V	3.3 V	Pin	Pin	3.3 V	5 V
−12 Vdc	−12 Vdc	B1	A1	−TRST	−TRST
TCK	TCK	B2	A2	+12 Vdc	+12 Vdc
Ground	Ground	B3	A3	TMS	TMS
TDO	TDO	B4	A4	TDI	TDI
+5 Vdc	+5 Vdc	B5	A5	+5 Vdc	+5 Vdc
+5 Vdc	+5 Vdc	B6	A6	−INTA	−INTA
−INTB	−INTB	B7	A7	−INTC	−INTC
−INTD	−INTD	B8	A8	+5 Vdc	+5 Vdc
−PRSNT1	−PRSNT1	B9	A9	Reserved	Reserved
Reserved	Reserved	B10	A10	+3.3 Vdc (I/O)	+5 Vdc
−PRSNT2	−PRSNT2	B11	A11	Reserved	Reserved
Ground	Key	B12	A12	Key	Ground
Ground	Key	B13	A13	Key	Ground
Reserved	Reserved	B14	A14	Reserved	Reserved
Ground	Ground	B15	A15	−RST	−RST
Clock	Clock	B16	A16	+3.3 Vdc	+5 Vdc
Ground	Ground	B17	A17	−GNT	−GNT
−REQ	−REQ	B18	A18	Ground	Ground
+5 Vdc	+3.3 Vdc	B19	A19	Reserved	Reserved
Adr/Dat 31	Adr/Dat 31	B20	A20	Adr/Dat 30	Adr/Dat 30
Adr/Dat 29	Adr/Dat 29	B21	A21	+3.3 Vdc	+5 Vdc
Ground	Ground	B22	A22	Adr/Dat 28	Adr/Dat 28
Adr/Dat 27	Adr/Dat 27	B23	A23	Adr/Dat 26	Adr/Dat 26
Adr/Dat 25	Adr/Dat 25	B24	A24	Ground	Ground
+5 Vdc	+3.3 Vdc	B25	A25	Adr/Dat 24	Adr/Dat 24
C/−BE3	C/−BE3	B26	A26	IDSEL	IDSEL
Adr/Dat 23	Adr/Dat 23	B27	A27	+3.3 Vdc	+5 Vdc
Ground	Ground	B28	A28	Adr/Dat 22	Adr/Dat 22
Adr/Dat 21	Adr/Dat 21	B29	A29	Adr/Dat 20	Adr/Dat 20
Adr/Dat 19	Adr/Dat 19	B30	A30	Ground	Ground
+5 Vdc	+3.3 Vdc	B31	A31	Adr/Dat 18	Adr/Dat 18
Adr/Dat 17	Adr/Dat 17	B32	A32	Adr/Dat 16	Adr/Dat 16
C/−BE2	C/−BE2	B33	A33	+3.3 Vdc	+5 Vdc
Ground	Ground	B34	A34	−FRAME	−FRAME
−IRDY	−IRDY	B35	A35	Ground	Ground
+5 Vdc	+3.3 Vdc	B36	A36	−TRDY	−TRDY
−DEVSEL	−DEVSEL	B37	A37	Ground	Ground
Ground	Ground	B38	A38	−STOP	−STOP
−LOCK	−LOCK	B39	A39	+3.3 Vdc	+5 Vdc
−PERR	−PERR	B40	A40	SDONE	SDONE
+5 Vdc	+3.3 Vdc	B41	A41	−SBO	−SBO
−SERR	−SERR	B42	A42	Ground	Ground
+5 Vdc	+3.3 Vdc	B43	A43	PAR	PAR
C/−BE1	C/−BE1	B44	A44	Adr/Dat 15	Adr/Dat 15

Table 1-6. *Continued*

5 V	3.3 V	Pin	Pin	3.3 V	5 V
Adr/Dat 14	Adr/Dat 14	B45	A45	+3.3 Vdc	+5 Vdc
Ground	Ground	B46	A46	Adr/Dat 13	Adr/Dat 13
Adr/Dat 12	Adr/Dat 12	B47	A47	Adr/Dat 11	Adr/Dat 11
Adr/Dat 10	Adr/Dat 10	B48	A48	Ground	Ground
Ground	Ground	B49	A49	Adr/Dat 9	Adr/Dat 9
Key	Ground	B50	A50	Ground	Key
Key	Ground	B51	A51	Ground	Key
Adr/Dat 8	Adr/Dat 8	B52	A52	C/−BE0	C/−BE0
Adr/Dat 7	Adr/Dat 7	B53	A53	+3.3 Vdc	+5 Vdc
+5 Vdc	+3.3 Vdc	B54	A54	Adr/Dat 6	Adr/Dat 6
Adr/Dat 5	Adr/Dat 5	B55	A55	Adr/Dat 4	Adr/Dat 4
Adr/Dat 3	Adr/Dat 3	B56	A56	Ground	Ground
Ground	Ground	B57	A57	Adr/Dat 2	Adr/Dat 2
Adr/Dat 1	Adr/Dat 1	B58	A58	Adr/Dat 0	Adr/Dat 0
+5 Vdc	+3.3 Vdc	B59	A59	+3.3 Vdc	+5 Vdc
−ACK64	−ACK64	B60	A60	−REQ64	−REQ64
+5 Vdc	+5 Vdc	B61	A61	+5 Vdc	+5 Vdc
+5 Vdc	+5 Vdc	B62	A62	+5 Vdc	+5 Vdc
Key	Key	Key	Key	Key	Key
Key	Key	Key	Key	Key	Key
Reserved	Reserved	B63	A63	Ground	Ground
Ground	Ground	B64	A64	C/−BE7	C/−BE7
C/−BE6	C/−BE6	B65	A65	C/−BE5	C/−BE5
C/−BE4	C/−BE4	B66	A66	+3.3 Vdc	+5 Vdc
Ground	Ground	B67	A67	PAR64	PAR64
Adr/Dat 63	Adr/Dat 63	B68	A68	Adr/Dat 62	Adr/Dat 62
Adr/Dat 61	Adr/Dat 61	B69	A69	Ground	Ground
+5 Vdc	+3.3 Vdc	B70	A70	Adr/Dat 60	Adr/Dat 60
Adr/Dat 59	Adr/Dat 59	B71	A71	Adr/Dat 58	Adr/Dat 58
Adr/Dat 57	Adr/Dat 57	B72	A72	Ground	Ground
Ground	Ground	B73	A73	Adr/Dat 56	Adr/Dat 56
Adr/Dat 55	Adr/Dat 55	B74	A74	Adr/Dat 54	Adr/Dat 54
Adr/Dat 53	Adr/Dat 53	B75	A75	+3.3 Vdc	+5 Vdc
Ground	Ground	B76	A76	Adr/Dat 52	Adr/Dat 52
Adr/Dat 51	Adr/Dat 51	B77	A77	Adr/Dat 50	Adr/Dat 50
Adr/Dat 49	Adr/Dat 49	B78	A78	Ground	Ground
+5 Vdc	+3.3 Vdc	B79	A79	Adr/Dat 48	Adr/Dat 48
Adr/Dat 47	Adr/Dat 47	B80	A80	Adr/Dat 46	Adr/Dat 46
Adr/Dat 45	Adr/Dat 45	B81	A81	Ground	Ground
Ground	Ground	B82	A82	Adr/Dat 44	Adr/Dat 44
Adr/Dat 43	Adr/Dat 43	B83	A83	Adr/Dat 42	Adr/Dat 42
Adr/Dat 41	Adr/Dat 41	B84	A84	+3.3 Vdc	+5 Vdc
Ground	Ground	B85	A85	Adr/Dat 40	Adr/Dat 40
Adr/Dat 39	Adr/Dat 39	B86	A86	Adr/Dat 38	Adr/Dat 38
Adr/Dat 37	Adr/Dat 37	B87	A87	Ground	Ground

Table 1-6. *Continued*

5 V	3.3 V	Pin	Pin	3.3 V	5 V
+5 Vdc	+3.3 Vdc	B88	A88	Adr/Dat 36	Adr/Dat 36
Adr/Dat 35	Adr/Dat 35	B89	A89	Adr/Dat 34	Adr/Dat 34
Adr/Dat 33	Adr/Dat 33	B90	A90	Ground	Ground
Ground	Ground	B91	A91	Adr/Dat 32	Adr/Dat 32
Reserved	Reserved	B92	A92	Reserved	Reserved
Reserved	Reserved	B93	A93	Ground	Ground
Ground	Ground	B94	A94	Reserved	Reserved

Mass-Storage Overview

The ability to store large amounts of information is a critical aspect of all computer systems. Storage allows programs and data to become a working part of the computer. Without storage ability, program instructions and data would have to be entered manually as the computer runs—an unfeasible option. In addition to existing programs and data, storage devices often serve as a repository for the results of program operations. For example, you can load and run a word processor, then save the created document back to a storage device as a unique computer file. Clearly, computers as we know them, would be absolutely useless without mass-storage devices.

As you may expect, there are many varied ways to store digital information. Some of the earliest methods utilized punched paper cards or tape. While punched paper storage has long since disappeared into history, other technologies have evolved to serve the needs of today's computers. This book discusses the three major storage technologies currently in use: solid-state ICs, magnetic media, and optical media. You will also learn about some hybrid storage devices that incorporate features from more than one storage technology.

Memory ICs

Solid-state storage technology uses memory ICs to retain information. Classical memory serves two very important uses in a computer. First, memory ICs provide the computer's *working storage*—where programs are stored while the system executes its instructions. Working memory allows the CPU to access current instructions and hold variables developed during run time. For example, a program must be loaded from some other mass-storage device into working memory before the CPU can run the program. Most computers today offer at least 16 MB of memory, but 32 MB will probably be more common by the time you read this book. Working memory is typically *temporary*—that is, its contents are only valid as long as computer power is available. If the computer is turned off or power should fail, the contents of working memory will be lost. When power is restored, the program will have to be reloaded and run from scratch.

Second, memory ICs are used to hold the computer's power-on self-test (POST) and basic input/output system (BIOS) routines. The POST is invoked to test and initialize the computer during startup. BIOS is a set of short routines that let the computer handle its key operations. BIOS routines can be called by the computer's operating system (OS) or applications program. BIOS memory is *permanent*—the IC will retain its contents even when power is turned off. Permanent memory guarantees that the routines will be immediately available whenever the system is on. Since memory ICs operate directly with electronic signals, an IC provides very high performance with access times lower than 100 nanoseconds (ns). Memory devices are detailed in Chap. 4.

PC cards

Memory ICs have come a long way in the last decade. Today, several megabytes can be stored with only a few ICs. High capacity combined with fast speed and moderately low power requirements have opened a new demand for PC card mass storage (also called memory cards). A memory card is basically a bank of temporary or permanent memory ICs which are self-contained in a small credit-card module.

There are now a substantial number of memory card designs, but the choice of temporary or permanent memory type depends on the particular card's intended applications. Laptop/notebook, palmtop, and pen-based computer systems are beginning to integrate memory cards as standard equipment. Card capacities range from several hundred kilobytes to 16 MB or more. Chapter 7 presents a detailed discussion of memory card types, interfaces, and troubleshooting techniques.

Floppy disk drives

Magnetic storage is nothing new to computer systems. Reel-to-reel tape and magnetic drum storage systems have been used for decades with old mainframe computers. Although reel and drum storage are obsolete today, the principles and characteristics of magnetic storage technology continue to be refined. The floppy disk drive system is one of the most popular and enduring mass-storage systems. Floppy drives are not fast (with access times on the order of milliseconds) and they cannot store huge volumes of information (up to 1.44 MB), but the medium itself is removable and very inexpensive.

Floppy drives had existed before IBM's entry into the personal computer industry, but the phenomenal success of IBM's XT catapulted the floppy drive into standardization. With standard drives and diskettes, software manufacturers found a perfect medium for distributing commercial software packages. Computer users could also transfer files between machines in a quick and easy fashion. There is little doubt that the universal appeal and convenience of floppy drives, combined with the rapid introduction of utility software (i.e., spreadsheets and word processors) were key factors in the acceptance of personal computers—not to mention the birth of the commercial software industry.

Not long after 5.25-in (13.34-cm) became established, 3.5-in (8.89-cm) drives made their debut. In spite of their smaller physical size and simplified mechanics, 3.5-in drives could fit more information on a disk than their 5.25-in predecessors. Both drive sizes are still commonly in use today, and in both normal (or double) density and high-density versions. Chapter 5 shows you the components, technologies, and troubleshooting techniques needed to repair 5.25-in and 3.5-in floppy disk drives.

Hard disk drives

Of all the peripheral devices that have evolved for personal computers over the last decade, few have been embraced as completely as the hard disk drive. Hard drives have rapidly evolved from an expensive luxury into an *absolute* necessity. Virtually all application programs today require so much storage space for interrelated programs and files that it would literally be impossible to run such programs from the floppy drive alone. Hard drives utilize all of the magnetic recording principles just as floppy drives do, but hard drives have been optimized and refined to offer startling performance and storage capacity that are orders of magnitude above what a floppy drive can provide.

Hard disks are perhaps the most adept of today's mass-storage devices. They provide gigabytes (thousands of megabytes) of capacity for programs and data. In only a few moments, the drive is able to access and read (or write) the equivalent of a textbook or novel. Fast hard drive operation can actually make your entire system appear to operate faster—not a bad track record for devices that are now smaller than a deck of playing cards and using less power than most night lights. Chapter 6 explains hard drive technology and troubleshooting in detail.

Tape drives

Tape systems are another species of magnetic mass storage designed exclusively for creating a backup copy of your entire hard disk. True, you could back up your hard disk onto floppy disks, but it would require dozens of floppy disks to completely back up today's large hard drives. Also, the tedium and inconvenience of diskette swapping can lead to wasteful operator errors. Tape drives can copy the contents of your hard drive onto a single high-capacity cassette. It has been said that a tape cartridge is the floppy disk in an age of gigabytes.

There are a few disadvantages to tape drive systems. They have changed very little in principle since the days of reel-to-reel tapes. A tape drive is a painfully slow device—in part because of the nature of magnetic tape technology, and in part because of the huge volume of data that must be transferred. Tapes are also *sequential* storage devices, so you cannot back up or restore a single file or files at random. You must start from the beginning and save (or restore) everything at once—it's usually an all or nothing proposition.

As distasteful as it may be to purchase and use a tape drive system, the ability to back up and protect a large volume of data on a regular basis is remarkably important (especially in a business environment). Backup is protection against the many ills that can plague a hard drive. The proven integrity and reliability of a tape backup has ensured that tape drives will be around for quite some time. Chapter 8 deals with the mechanisms and troubleshooting of tape drive systems.

Optical drives

Optical storage techniques are now well established in the computer industry. By using beams of coherent (laser) light, digital information can be deciphered from reasonably simple plastic disks. Capacities of 500 MB to 1 GB or more are not uncommon. Data integrity is rated to last for centuries with some optical media—

much longer than even the best magnetic media. Ruggedness is another key concern. After all, there is no need for low-flying read/write heads, and there is no contact between the head and medium. Even if the medium's surface becomes slightly damaged, optical systems can "look past" many surface imperfections. With such high data capacity and inherently reliable operation, optical mass-storage systems such as CD-ROM drives are now as integral to normal computer operations as the hard drive. Chapter 9 explains optical drive technology and presents a series of troubleshooting procedures.

DVD drives

One of the original advantages of the CD-ROM drive was its capacity—CDs offered 600 MB of storage at a time when hard drives were 200 to 300 MB. Now that 2.1-GB hard drives are considered cheap, and drives over 5 GB are now available, CD-ROM drives face some major changes. The dream of placing feature-length video data and high-quality audio onto the CD was never realized, but technology may offer an alternative storage medium in the form of a Digital Video Disk (or DVD).

The DVD looks just like an ordinary CD, but can hold anywhere from 4 to 17 GB! Just consider what this means to the entertainment industry—DVDs will bring you feature-length films of unbelievable quality in 5.1-channel surround sound that can be shuttled through like a standard CD. You're also able to choose from eight different language tracks and 32 subtitled languages. DVD-ROM discs can also dramatically transform multimedia applications. Their extremely high storage capacity will allow high-quality full-motion video to be fully realized in entertainment and interactive design. This will enhance the "virtual reality" feeling of software products and provide the consumer with a better overall interactive experience.

Eventually, DVD will also offer a rewritable storage technology (DVD-R) that can be recorded and erased. And DVD technology offers backward read capability with existing audio CDs and CD-ROMs, so your current software will not be rendered obsolete. Companies like Toshiba and Diamond Multimedia are already releasing the first generation of DVD products. While these drives are far too new to be covered properly here, you can expect future editions of this book to cover DVD technology in much more detail.

2
CHAPTER

Tools and
Test Equipment

You need a selection of basic tools and test equipment before trying to tackle a storage system repair (Fig. 2-1). Test equipment allows you to measure important circuit parameters such as voltage, current, resistance, capacitance, and semiconductor junction conditions. Additional test equipment can let you follow logic conditions and view complex waveforms at critical points in the circuit. This chapter introduces the background and testing methods for multimeters, component checkers, logic probes, and oscilloscopes. This chapter also gives you an advance look at some of the more specialized test instruments that you may encounter in mass-storage repair, and introduces some handy diagnostic software for memory and drive diagnostics.

Tools and Materials

If you don't have a well-stocked toolbox yet, now is the time to consider the things you need. Before you begin a repair, gather a set of small hand tools and some inexpensive materials. *Never* underestimate the value of having the proper tools— they can often make or break your repair efforts.

Hand tools

Hand tools are basically used to disassemble and reassemble your housings, enclosures, mounting brackets, and expansion card rail guides. It is not necessary to stock top-quality tools, but your tools should be of the proper size and shape to do the job. Since many of today's computers and peripheral devices are extremely small and tightly packaged assemblies, you should select tools that are small and thin wherever possible.

Screwdrivers should be the first items on your list. Computer assemblies are generally held together with small or medium-sized Phillips-type screws. Once you are able to remove the outer housings, you will probably find that most other internal

Iomega Corp.

2-1 An Iomega Bernoulli MultiDisk storage system.

parts are also held in place with Phillips screws. Consider obtaining one or two small Phillips screwdrivers, as well as one medium-sized version. You will almost *never* need a large screwdriver. Each screwdriver should be about 4-in (10.16-cm) to 6-in (15.24-cm) long with a wide handle for a good grip. Jewelers screwdrivers are recommended for very fine or delicate assemblies. Round out your selection of screwdrivers by adding one small and one medium regular (flat-blade) screwdriver. You won't use them as often as Phillips screwdrivers, but regular screwdrivers *will* come in handy.

There are three specialized types of screw heads that you should be aware of. *Allen screws* use a hex (six-sided) hole instead of a regular or Phillips-type blade. *Torx* and *spline screws* use specially shaped holes that only accept the corresponding size and shape of driver. It is a good idea to keep a set of small hex keys on hand, but you will rarely find specialized screw heads. Torx and spline screws are almost never encountered.

Wrenches are used to hold hex-shaped bolt heads or nuts. There are not many instances where you need to remove nuts and bolts, but an inexpensive set of small electronics-grade open-ended wrenches is recommended. If you prefer, a small adjustable wrench can be used instead.

Needlenose pliers are valued additions to your toolbox. Not as bulky and awkward as ordinary mechanic's pliers, needlenose pliers can be used to grip or bend both mechanical and electronic parts. Needlenose pliers can also serve as heat sinks during desoldering or soldering operations. Chapter 3 discusses soldering and desoldering in more detail. Obtain a short-nose and long-nose set of needlenose pliers. Short-nose pliers make great heat sinks and can grasp parts securely. Long-nose pliers are excellent for picking up and grasping parts lost in the tight confines of a computer or peripheral. All sets of needlenose pliers should be small, good-quality electronics-grade tools.

Diagonal cutters are also an important part of your tool collection. Cutters are used to cut wire and component leads when working with a small computer's electronics. You really only need one good set of cutters, but the cutters should be small, good-quality electronics-grade tools. Cutters should also have a low profile and a small cutting head to fit in tight spaces. *Never* use cutters to cut plastic, metal, or PC board material.

Add a pair of *tweezers* to your tool kit. The tweezers should be small, long, and made from antistatic plastic material. Metal tweezers should be avoided wherever possible to prevent accidental short circuits (as well as a shock hazard) if they come into contact with operating circuitry. Metal tweezers can also conduct potentially damaging static charges into sensitive ICs.

Soldering tools

You need a good-quality, general-purpose *soldering iron* to repair wiring and other basic electrical circuits (Fig. 2-2). A low-wattage (20 to 25 W) iron with a fine tip is usually best. You can obtain a decent soldering iron from any local electronics store. Most soldering irons are powered directly from AC, and these are just fine for general touch-ups and heavier work. However, you should consider a DC-powered or gas-fueled iron for desoldering delicate, static-sensitive ICs. No matter what iron you buy, try to ensure that it is recommended as "static-safe."

Note: A soldering iron *absolutely must* have its *own metal stand! Never,* under *any* circumstances, allow a soldering iron to rest on a counter or table top unattended. The potential for nasty burns or fire is simply too great. Keep a wet sponge handy to wipe the iron's tip periodically. Invest in a roll of good-quality electronics-grade rosin-core solder.

Desoldering tools are necessary to remove faulty components and wires. Once the solder joint is heated with the soldering iron, a desoldering tool can remove the molten solder to free the joint. A solder vacuum uses a small, spring-loaded plunger mounted in a narrow cylinder. When triggered, the plunger recoils and generates a vacuum which draws up any molten solder in the vicinity. Solder wick is little more than a fine copper braid. By heating the braid against a solder joint, molten solder wicks up into the braid through capillary action. Such conventional desoldering tools are most effective on through-hole components.

Surface-mounted components can also be desoldered with conventional desoldering tools, but there are more efficient techniques for surface-mount parts. Specially shaped desoldering tips (Fig. 2-3) can ease surface-mount desoldering by heating all of the component's leads simultaneously. Powered vacuum pumps (Fig. 2-4) can also be used to remove molten solder much more thoroughly then spring-loaded versions.

2-2 A Weller MC5000 soldering station.

2-3 A surface-mount desoldering tip.

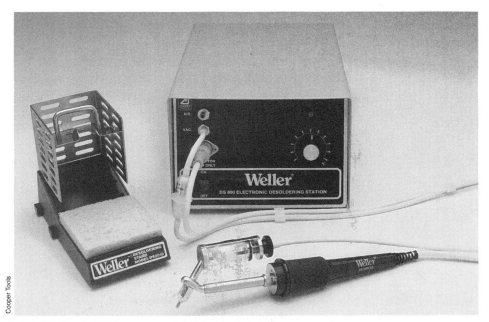

2-4 A Weller DS800 vacuum desoldering station.

Miscellany

A hand-held, battery-powered vacuum cleaner will be helpful in your routine maintenance operations. Periodically removing dust and debris from your keyboard can prevent intermittent key operation. You should also brush or vacuum any dust that may be accumulating in your computer's vent holes. Clear vent holes help to keep computers and peripherals running cooler.

Most computer systems now use surface-mount ICs and components, so you rarely have need of IC inserters and extractors. The exceptions to this rule are for PLCCs (plastic-leaded chip carriers) and PGAs (pin grid arrays). Once a PLCC or PGA has been inserted into its socket, there is virtually no way to remove it without the use of a specialized extraction tool. The extractor tool's tips either grasp the PGA IC's edges directly, or are inserted into slots at either set of opposing corners on a PLCC socket. Squeeze the extractor *gently* to push the tips under the IC, then wiggle the IC to pull it free. Once an IC is free, be certain to keep it on an antistatic mat, or on a piece of antistatic foam.

You may also use a selection of appropriate test clips. Test clips fit over ICs of virtually every description and allow you to attach test leads for hands-free testing. Figure 2-5 shows a simple PLCC test clip for 32-pin PLCC ICs. The clip is squeezed gently and pushed over the IC. Spring action then holds the clip in place. You can place logic analyzer or oscilloscope leads on the bare pins available from the clip. Figure 2-6 shows somewhat larger test clips designed to fit QFP (quad flat pack) ICs. The exact size of a test clip varies with the number of pins and pin spacing (pitch) of the particular IC under test.

Your tool kit should always have a supply of antistatic materials to help prevent accidental damage to your expensive electronics. An *antistatic wrist strap* connects your body to ground in order to remove any static charge buildup from your body. Whenever working with PC boards and ICs, use *antistatic foam* to hold ICs and *antistatic bags* to hold PC boards. Avoid Styrofoam and other plastics that hold static charges. You might also like to invest in an *antistatic mat*. A mat rolls out onto

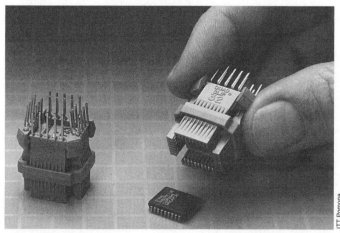

2-5 A PLCC test clip.

2-6 A quad flat pack (QFP) test clip.

a desk or workbench and connects to ground much like a wrist strap. An antistatic mat will allow you to place delicate PC boards and chassis on your workbench while you work with them.

Keep an assortment of solid and stranded *hookup wire* in your toolbox. Wire should be between 18 to 24 AWG (gauge)—preferably above 20 AWG. *Heat shrink tubing* is another handy material for your repairs. Tubing can be cut to length as needed, then positioned and shrunk to insulate wire splices and long component leads. You may wish to buy a specialized heat gun to shrink the tubing, but an ordinary blow drier for hair will usually work just as well. When heating tubing, be certain to direct hot air *away* from ICs and PC boards.

Multimeters

Multimeters are by far the handiest and most versatile pieces of test equipment that you will ever use (Fig. 2-7). If your toolbox does not contain a good-quality multimeter already, now would be a good time to consider purchasing one. Even the most basic digital multimeters are capable of measuring resistance, ac and dc voltage, and ac and dc current. For under $150, you can buy a digital multimeter that includes handy features like a capacitance checker, a frequency meter, an extended current measuring range, a continuity buzzer, and even a diode and transistor checker. These are features that will aid you not only in computer and peripheral repairs, but in many other types of electronic repairs as well. Digital multimeters are easier to read, more tolerant of operator error, and more precise then their analog predecessors.

Meter setup

For most multimeters, there are only three considerations during setup and use. First, turn the meter ON. Unlike analog multimeters, digital multimeters require power to operate liquid crystal or light-emitting diode (LED) displays. Make sure that you turn meter power OFF again when you are done with your testing. Power awareness will help you conserve battery life. Second, your meter must be set to its desired function or mode. The *function* may be frequency, voltage, capacitance, resistance, etc., depending on the particular physical parameter that you wish to measure.

Finally, you must select the meter's *range* for its selected function. Ideally, you should choose the range that is nearest to (but above) the level you expect to measure. For example, suppose you are measuring a 9-V battery. You would set your meter to the dc voltage function, then set your range as close to (but greater than) 9 V as possible. If your voltage ranges are 0.2, 2.0, 20.0, and 200 Vdc, selecting the 20.0-Vdc range is the best choice. If your reading exceeds the meter's current range, an *overrange* warning will be displayed until you increase the meter's range above the measured value. Some digital multimeters are capable of automatically selecting the appropriate range setting once a signal is applied.

Note: If you are unsure about just which range to use, start by choosing the *highest* possible range. Once you actually take some measurements and get a better idea of the actual reading, you can then adjust the meter's range "on the fly" to achieve a more precise reading.

Checking test leads

It is usually a good idea to check the integrity of your test leads from time to time. Since test leads undergo a serious amount of tugging and general abuse, you should be able to confirm that the probes are working as expected. There are few experiences more frustrating than to invest time and money replacing parts that your meter suggested were faulty, only to discover that meter leads had an internal fault.

To check your probes, set your meter to the "resistance" function, then select the *lowest* scale (i.e., 0.10 ohms). You will see an "overrange" condition. This is expected when setting up for resistance measurements. Check to be sure that both test probes are inserted into the meter properly, then touch the probe tips together. The resistance reading should drop to about 0 ohms to indicate that your meter probes are intact. If you do not see roughly 0 ohms, check your probes carefully. After you have proven out your test probes, return the multimeter to its original function and range so that you can continue testing.

2-7 A B+K Model 2707 multimeter.

You may see other terms related to multimeter testing, such as static and dynamic. *Static* tests are usually made on components (either in or out of a circuit) with power removed. Resistance, capacitance, and semiconductor junction tests are all static tests. *Dynamic* tests typically examine circuit conditions, so power must be applied to the circuit, and all components *must* be in place. Voltage, current, and frequency are the most common dynamic tests.

Measuring voltage

Every signal in your small computer has a certain amount of voltage associated with it. By measuring signal voltages with a multimeter (or other test instrument), you can usually make a determination as to whether or not the signal is correct. Supply voltages which provide power to your circuits can also be measured to ensure that components are receiving enough energy to operate. Voltage tests are the most fundamental (and the most important) dynamic tests in electronic troubleshooting.

Multimeters can measure both dc voltages (marked DCV or Vdc) and ac voltages (marked ACV or Vac) directly. Remember that *all* voltage measurements are taken *in parallel* with the desired circuit or component. *Never* interrupt a circuit and attempt to measure voltage in series with other components. Any such reading would be meaningless, and your circuit will probably not even function.

Follow your setup guidelines and configure your meter to measure ac or dc voltage as required, then select the proper range for the voltages you will be measuring. If you are unsure just what range to use, always start with the largest possible range. An autoranging multimeter will set its own range once a signal is applied. Place your test leads across (*in parallel* with) the circuit or part under test (or PUT) as shown in Fig. 2-8, then read voltage directly from the meter's digital display. DC voltage readings are polarity-sensitive, so if you read +5 Vdc and reverse the test leads, you will see a reading of −5 Vdc; ac voltage readings are *not* polarity sensitive.

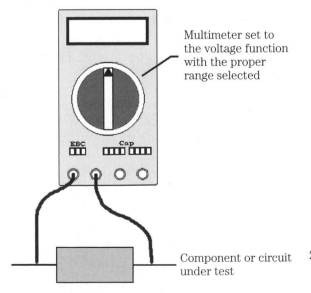

Multimeter set to the voltage function with the proper range selected

Component or circuit under test

2-8 Measuring voltage.

Measuring current

Most general-purpose multimeters allow you to measure ac current (marked ACA or Iac) and dc current (marked DCA or Idc) in an operating circuit, although there are typically fewer ranges to choose from. As with voltage measurements, current is a dynamic test, so the circuit or component being tested must be under power. However, current *must* be measured *in series* with a circuit or component.

Unfortunately, inserting a meter in series is not always a simple task. In many cases, you must interrupt a circuit at the point you wish to measure, then connect your test leads across the break. While it may be quite easy to interrupt a circuit, remember that you must also put the circuit back together, so use care when choosing a point to break. *Never* attempt to measure current in parallel across a component or circuit. Current meters, by their very nature, exhibit a very low resistance across their test leads (often below 0.1 ohm). Placing a current meter in parallel can cause a short circuit across a component that can damage the component, the circuit under test, or the meter itself.

Set your multimeter to the desired function (DCA or ACA) and select the appropriate range. If you are unsure about the proper range, set the meter to its *largest* possible range. It is usually necessary to plug your positive test lead into a "current input" jack on the multimeter. Unless your multimeter is protected by an internal fuse (most meters *are* protected), its internal current measurement circuits can be damaged by excessive current. Make sure that your meter can handle the maximum amount of current you are expecting.

Turn off all power to a circuit before inserting a current meter. Deactivation prevents any unpredictable or undesirable circuit operation when you actually interrupt the circuit. If you wish to measure power supply current feeding a circuit such as in Fig. 2-9, break the power supply line at any convenient point, insert the meter carefully, then reapply power. Read current directly from the meter's display. This procedure can also be used for taking current measurements within a circuit.

Measuring frequency

Some multimeters offer a frequency counter (marked f or Hz) that can read the frequency of a sinusoidal signal. The ranges that are available will depend on your particular meter. Simple handheld meters can often read up to 100 kHz, while benchtop models can handle 10 MHz or more. Frequency measurements are dynamic readings made with circuit power applied.

Set your multimeter to its frequency counter function and select the appropriate range. If you are unsure just what range to use, start your measurements at the highest possible range. Place your test leads *in parallel* across the component or circuit to be tested as shown in Fig. 2-10, and read frequency directly from the meter's display. An autoranging multimeter will select the proper range after the signal is applied.

Note: Analog frequency measurements have little practical use in computer repair since most signals you encounter will be square instead of sinusoidal. Square waves usually yield false readings unless the meter is designed specifically for square wave readings. A digital frequency counter and an oscilloscope can be used to measure square waves instead.

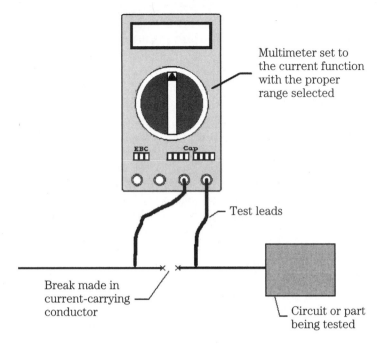

Multimeter set to
the current function
with the proper
range selected

Test leads

Break made in
current-carrying
conductor

Circuit or part
being tested

2-9 Measuring current.

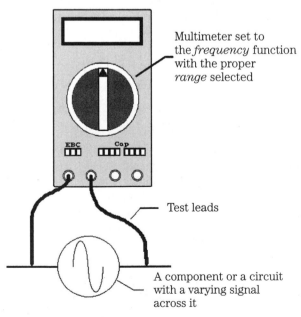

Multimeter set to
the *frequency* function
with the proper
range selected

Test leads

A component or a circuit
with a varying signal
across it

2-10 Measuring frequency.

Measuring resistance

Resistance (ohms) is the most common static measurement that your multimeter is capable of. This is a handy function, not only for checking resistors themselves, but for checking other resistive elements like wires, solenoids, motors, connectors, and some basic semiconductor components. Resistance is a static test, so all power to the component or circuit must be removed. It is usually necessary to remove at least one component lead from the circuit to prevent interconnections with other components from causing false readings.

Ordinary resistors, coils, and wires can be checked simply by switching to a resistance function (often marked OHMS, or with the Greek symbol omega (Ω) and selecting the appropriate range. Autoranging multimeters will select the proper range after the meter's test leads are connected. Many multimeters can reliably measure resistance up to about 20 Mohms. Place your test leads *in parallel* across the component as shown in Fig. 2-11, and read resistance directly from the meter's display. If resistance exceeds the selected range, the display will indicate an overrange (or infinite resistance) connection.

Continuity checks are made to ensure a reliable, low-resistance connection between two points. For example, you could check the continuity of a cable between two connectors to ensure that both ends are connected properly. Set your multimeter to a low resistance scale, then place your test leads across both points to measure. Ideally, good continuity should be about 0 ohms. Continuity tests can also be taken to show that a short circuit has not occurred between two points.

Measuring capacitors

There are two methods of checking a capacitor using your multimeter: by *exact measurement,* and by a *quality check.* The exact measurement test determines

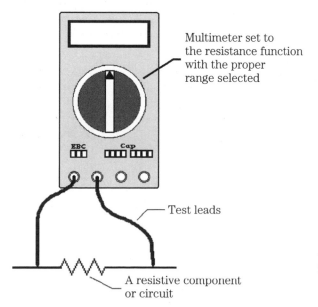

Multimeter set to
the resistance function
with the proper
range selected

Test leads

A resistive component
or circuit

2-11 Measuring resistance.

the actual value of a capacitor. If the reading is close enough to the value marked on the capacitor, you know the device to be good. If not, you know the device is faulty and should be replaced. Exact measurement requires your multimeter to be equipped with a built-in capacitance checker. If your meter does not have a built-in capacitance checker, you can measure a capacitor directly on any other type of specialized component checker such as the B+K Precision Model 390 Test Bench shown in Fig. 2-12. You could also use your multimeter to perform a simple quality check of a suspect capacitor.

Capacitor checkers, whether built into your multimeter or part of a stand-alone component checker, are extremely simple to use. Turn off all circuit power. Set the function to measure capacitors, select the range of capacitance to be measured, then place your test probes *in parallel* across the capacitor to be measured. You should remove at least one of the capacitor's leads from the circuit being tested in order to prevent the interconnections of other components from adversely affecting the capacitance reading. In some cases, it may be easier to remove the suspect part entirely before measuring it. Some meters provide test slots that let you insert the component directly into the meter's face. Once in place, you can read the capacitor's value directly from the meter display.

If your multimeter is not equipped with an internal capacitor checker, you could still use the resistance ranges of your ohmmeter to approximate a capacitor's quality. This type of check provides a "quick-and-dirty" judgment of whether the capacitor is good or bad. The principle behind this type of check is simple; all ohmmeter ranges use an internal battery to supply current to the component under test. When that current is applied to a working capacitor as shown in Fig. 2-13, it will cause the capacitor to charge. Charge accumulates as the ohmmeter is left connected. When first connected, the uncharged capacitor draws a healthy amount of current—this reads as low resistance. As the capacitor charges, its rate of charge slows down and less and less current is drawn as time goes on. This results in a gradually increasing resistance level. Ideally, a fully charged capacitor stops drawing current; this results in an overrange or infinite resistance display. When a capacitor behaves in this way, it is probably good.

2-12 A B+K Model 390 multimeter.

B+K Precision

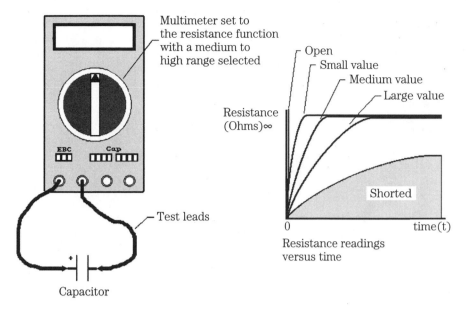

2-13 Measuring the quality of a capacitor using the multimeter resistance function.

Understand that you are not actually measuring resistance *or* capacitance here, but only the profile of a capacitor's charging characteristic. If the capacitor is extremely small (in the picofarad range), or is open-circuited, it will not accept any substantial charge, so the multimeter will read infinity almost immediately. If a capacitor is partially (or totally) short-circuited, it will not hold a charge, so you may read 0 ohms, or resistance may climb to some value below infinity and remain there. In either case, the capacitor is probably defective. If you doubt your readings, check several other capacitors of the same value and compare readings. Be sure to make this test on a moderate- to high-resistance scale. A low-resistance scale may over-range too quickly to achieve a clear reading.

Diode checks

Many multimeters provide a special "diode" resistance scale that is used to check the static resistance of common diode junctions. Since working diodes only conduct current in one direction, the diode check lets you determine whether a diode is open- or short-circuited. Remember that diode checking is a static test, so all power must be removed from the part under test. Before making measurements, be certain that at least one of the diode's leads has been removed from the circuit. Isolating the diode prevents interconnections with other circuit components from causing false readings.

Select the "diode" option from your multimeter's resistance functions. You generally do not have to bother with a range setting while in the diode mode. Connect your test leads *in parallel* across the diode in the *forward-bias* direction as shown in Fig. 2-14. A working silicon diode should exhibit a static resistance between about 450 and 700 ohms, which will read directly on the meter's display. Reverse

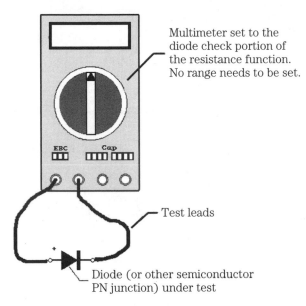

Multimeter set to the
diode check portion of
the resistance function.
No range needs to be set.

Test leads

Diode (or other semiconductor
PN junction) under test

2-14 Making a forward-bias diode check.

the orientation of your test probes to reverse-bias the diode as in Fig. 2-15. Since a
working diode will not conduct at all in the reverse direction, you should read infinite resistance.

A short-circuited diode will exhibit a very low resistance in the forward- *and*
reverse-biased directions. This indicates a shorted semiconductor junction. An
open-circuited diode will exhibit very high resistance (usually infinity) in both its
forward- and reverse-biased directions. A diode that is opened or shorted must be
replaced. If you feel unsure how to interpret your measurements, test several other
comparable diodes and compare readings.

Transistor checks

Transistors are slightly more sophisticated semiconductor devices that can be tested
using a transistor checking function on your multimeter or component checker.
Transistor junctions can also be checked using a multimeter's diode function. The
following procedures show you both methods of transistor checking.

Some multimeters feature a built-in transistor checker that measures a bipolar
transistor's gain (called *Beta* or *hfe*) directly. By comparing measured gain to the
gain value specified in manufacturer's data (or measurements taken from other identical parts), you can easily determine whether the transistor is operating properly.
Multimeters with a transistor checker generally offer a test fixture right on the meter's face. The fixture consists of 2, three-hole sockets; one socket for NPN devices,
and another hole for PNP devices. If your meter offers a transistor checker, insert
the transistor into the test fixture on the meter's face.

Since all bipolar transistors are three-terminal devices (emitter, base, collector),
they must be inserted into the meter in their proper lead orientation before you can
achieve a correct reading. Manufacturer's data sheets for a transistor will identify

each lead and tell you the approximate gain reading that you should expect to see. Once the transistor is inserted appropriately in its correct socket, you can read gain directly from the meter's display.

Set the meter to its transistor checker function. You should not have to worry about selecting a range when checking transistors. Insert the transistor into its test fixture. An unusually low reading (or zero) suggests a short-circuited transistor, while a high (or infinite) reading indicates an open-circuited transistor. In either case, the transistor is probably defective and should be replaced. If you are uncertain of your readings, test several other identical transistors and compare your readings.

If your particular multimeter or parts tester only offers a diode checker, you can approximate the transistor's condition by measuring its semiconductor junctions individually. Figure 2-16 illustrates the transistor junction test method. Although structurally different from conventional diodes, the base-emitter and base-collector junctions of bipolar transistors behave just like diodes. As a general rule, you should remove the transistor from its circuit to prevent false readings caused by other interconnected components. Junction testing is also handy for all varieties of surface-mount transistors which will not fit into conventional multimeter test sockets.

Set your multimeter to its diode resistance function. If your suspect transistor is NPN type (manufacturer's data or a corresponding schematic symbol will tell you), place your *positive* test lead at the transistor's base, and place your *negative* test lead on the transistor's emitter. This test lead arrangement should forward-bias the transistor's base-emitter junction and result in a normal amount of diode resistance (450 to 700 ohms). Reverse your test leads across the base-emitter junction. The junction should now be reverse-biased showing infinite resistance. Repeat this entire procedure for the base-collector junction.

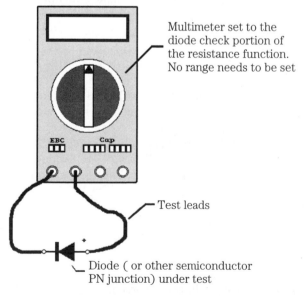

Multimeter set to the diode check portion of the resistance function. No range needs to be set

Test leads

Diode (or other semiconductor PN junction) under test

2-15 Making a reverse-bias diode check.

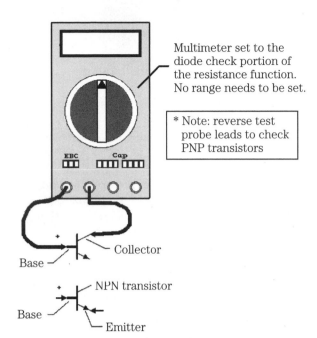

Multimeter set to the diode check portion of the resistance function. No range needs to be set.

* Note: reverse test probe leads to check PNP transistors

Collector
Base

NPN transistor
Base
Emitter

2-16 Testing the junction of a bipolar transistor.

If your suspect transistor is the PNP type, the placement of your test leads will have to be reversed from the procedure described above. In other words, a junction that is forward-biased in an NPN transistor will be reverse-biased in a PNP device. To forward-bias the base-emitter junction of a PNP transistor, place your positive test lead on the emitter, and your negative test lead on the base. The same concept holds true for the base-collector junction.

Once both junctions are checked, measure the diode resistance from collector to emitter. You should read infinite resistance in *both* test lead orientations. Although there should be no connection from collector to emitter while the transistor is un-powered, a short circuit can sometimes develop during a failure.

If any of your junctions read an unusually high (or infinite) resistance in both directions, the junction is probably open-circuited. An unusually low resistance (or 0 ohms) in either direction suggests that the junction is short-circuited. Any resistance below infinity between the collector and emitter suggests a damaged transistor. In any case, the transistor should be replaced. The B+K Model 540 Component Checker displays the dynamic performance of bipolar and field-effect transistors (FETs) as a graphic representation on a cathode ray tube (CRT) (Fig. 2-17). By observing the graphic curve characteristic of each unique transistor, you can determine whether or not the device is faulty. Some graphic analyzers also provide an output that allows the curve to be plotted or printed for future reference.

IC checks

There are very few *conclusive* ways to test ICs without resorting to complex logic analyzers and expensive IC testing equipment. ICs are so incredibly diverse, there is simply no one universal test that will pinpoint every possible failure. The one IC testing technique that appears to find a large percentage of IC faults is the "comparison" approach. By comparing the performance of a suspect IC against that of a known good (or reference) IC, any differences can be quickly identified and reported. The B+K Precision Model 541 shown in Fig. 2-18 is an IC comparator capable of checking DIP ICs up to 40 pins. A reference IC is inserted into the left socket, while the suspect component is placed into the right socket. Each IC pin is signaled individually by selecting the corresponding button along the tester's front. Although the testing process is somewhat redundant, there is usually good confidence in the test results.

Note: You can also make extensive use of IC service charts (sometimes called service checkout charts). IC service charts show the logic (or voltage) level for each pin of an IC. By checking the actual state of each pin against the chart, you can often identify faulty devices.

Circuit Analyzer

If you are a technician or working in a professional computer repair environment, it may be faster and more helpful to test components while still inserted in the circuit, or even test the entire circuit. Circuit analyzers such as the Model 545 from B+K Precision

2-17 A B+K Model 540 Component Tester.

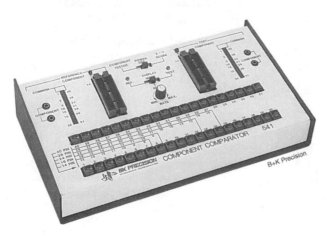

2-18 A B+K Model 541 Component Comparator.

(Fig. 2-19) use an *impedance signature* test technique. An impedance signature is obtained by applying a very low current sine-wave signal across a component or circuit, then displaying the voltage-to-current (VI) curve on a CRT or flat-panel display. Every component or circuit offers a unique, repeatable VI curve, so any differences at all are easily recognized. The Model 545 offers two input channels, which allows the suspect component or circuit to be compared against a known-good reference.

The displays illustrated in Fig. 2-20 show the typical output of a circuit analyzer. Test systems such as the Model 545 will test resistors, capacitors, inductors, diodes

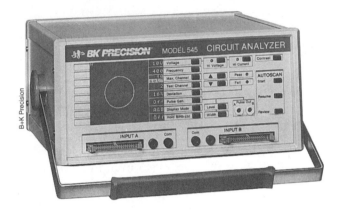

2-19 A B+K Model 545 Circuit Analyzer.

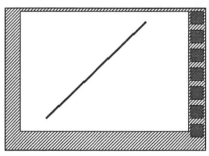

Resistor (straight line)

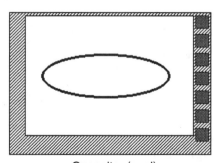

Capacitor (oval)

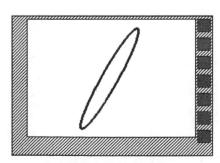

Inductor (slanted oval)

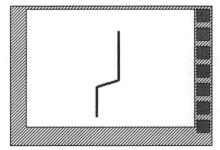

PNP transistor

2-20 Typical circuit analyzer traces.

(and diode bridges), LEDs, zener diodes, bipolar transistors, FETs, optoisolators, and silicon controlled rectifiers (SCRs). It is also interesting to note that the analyzer will also test simple analog and digital ICs, as well as a broad array of components in combination. The B+K analyzer offers a serial communication interface that allows images presented on the display to be downloaded to any computer or printer. While the actual testing procedures are different for every type of system, circuit analyzers are powerful additions to your professional test bench.

Logic Probes

The problem with multimeters is that they do not relate very well at all to the fast-changing signals found in digital logic circuits. A multimeter can certainly measure whether a logic voltage is on or off, but if that logic signal changes quickly (i.e., a clock or bus signal), a DC voltmeter will only show the *average* signal. A logic probe is little more than an extremely simple voltage sensor, but it can precisely and conveniently detect digital logic levels, clock signals, and digital pulses. Some logic probes can operate at speeds greater than 50 MHz.

Logic probes are rather simple-looking devices, as shown in Fig. 2-21. Indeed, logic probes are perhaps the simplest and least-expensive test instruments that you will ever use, but they provide valuable and reliable information when you are troubleshooting digital logic circuitry. Logic probes are usually powered from the circuit under test, and they must be connected into the common (ground) of the circuit being tested to ensure a proper reference level. Attach the probe's power lead to any *logic* supply voltage source in the circuit. Logic probes are capable of working from a wide range of supply voltages (typically +4 to +18 Vdc).

Reading the logic probe

Logic probes use a series of LED indicators to display the measured condition; a logic "high" (or 1), a logic "low" (or 0), or a "pulse" (or clock) signal. Many models offer a switch that allows the probe to operate with two common logic families: transistor-transistor logic (TTL) or complementary metal oxide semiconductor (CMOS). You may sometimes find TTL and CMOS devices mixed in the same circuit, but one family of logic devices will usually dominate.

In order to use a logic probe, touch its metal tip to the desired IC or component lead. Be certain that the point you wish to measure is, in fact, a logic point. High-voltage signals can damage your logic probe. The logic state is interpreted by a few simple gates within the probe, then displayed on the appropriate LED (or combination of LEDs). Table 2-1 illustrates the LED sequences for one particular type of logic probe. By comparing the probe's measurements to the information contained in an IC service chart or schematic diagram, you can determine whether or not the signal (or suspect IC) is behaving properly.

Reading low-voltage logic

For many years now, conventional digital logic ICs have been powered by a supply voltage of +5 Vdc. If you have any experience at all with digital logic, you probably recognize the +5 Vdc standard. However, the +5 Vdc standard is quickly

2-21 A typical logic probe.

Table 2-1. Typical Logic Probe LED Patterns

Input signal	High LED	Low LED	Pulse LED
Logic 1 (TTL or CMOS)	On	Off	Off
Logic 0 (TTL or CMOS)	Off	On	Off
Bad logic level or open circuit	Off	Off	Off
Square wave <200 kHz	On	On	Blink
Square wave >200 kHz	On/Off	On/Off	Blink
Narrow "high" pulse	Off	On/Off	Blink
Narrow "low" pulse	On/Off	Off	Blink

being replaced by a new, low-voltage standard; +3.3 Vdc. A lower supply voltage means that ICs will draw significantly less power. For battery-powered equipment, this means fewer battery changes and longer charge life. With ICs running at around +3 V what happens to logic signal levels?

Fortunately, the family of new 3-V ICs still operate within the accepted conventions of 5-V logic levels. For example, a 5-V logic IC provides a *minimum* logic 1 output of +2.4 Vdc, and a *maximum* logic 0 output of +0.4 Vdc, while accepting a minimum logic 1 input of +2.0 Vdc and a maximum logic 0 input of +0.8 Vdc. The new 3-V logic tends to "ride the rails" by providing a logic 1 at about +3.0 Vdc and a logic 0 of roughly 0 Vdc, yet it accepts a minimum logic 1 input of +2.0 Vdc and a maximum logic 0 input of +0.8 Vdc. As you might see, the two logic families use compatible logic levels. The only problem arises when a logic 1 from a 5-V gate (which can be as high as +4.9 Vdc) drives a 3-V logic input. When an input voltage exceeds supply voltage in this way, the low-voltage logic can be damaged. Low-voltage logic designers are investing a great deal of effort to overcome this voltage incompatibility problem. The relationship of logic levels to voltage levels is illustrated graphically in Fig. 2-22.

As far as your troubleshooting effort is concerned, be aware that mobile computers (notebook, palmtop, and pen computers) probably utilize many (if not all) low-voltage logic components. Desktop systems are only beginning to utilize low-voltage logic. Since the logic levels are at least compatible in principle, your logic probe should be able to provide correct readings as long as it is being powered and grounded correctly.

Oscilloscopes

Oscilloscopes offer a tremendous advantage over multimeters and logic probes. Instead of reading signals in terms of numbers or lighted indicators, an oscilloscope will show voltage versus time on a graphical display. Not only can you observe ac and dc voltages, but oscilloscopes enable you to watch any other unusual signals occur in real time. When used correctly, an oscilloscope allows you to witness signals and events occurring in terms of microseconds or less. If you have used an oscilloscope (or seen one used), then you probably know just how useful they can be. Oscilloscopes such as the one shown in Fig. 2-23 may appear somewhat overwhelming at first, but many of their operations work the same way regardless of what model you are working with.

Oscilloscope start-up procedure

Before you begin taking measurements, a clear, stable trace must be obtained (if not already visible). If a trace is not already visible, make sure that any CRT screen

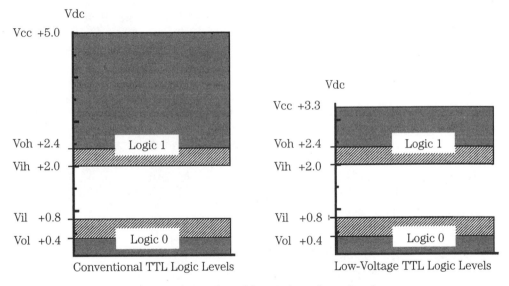

2-22 A graphic comparison of +5 volt and low-voltage logic levels.

2-23 A B+K Model 2160 oscilloscope.

storage modes are turned off, and that trace intensity is turned up to at least 50%. Set trace triggering to its automatic mode and adjust the horizontal and vertical offset controls to the center of their ranges. Be sure to select an *internal* trigger source from the channel your probe is plugged in to, then adjust the trigger *level* until a stable trace is displayed. Vary your vertical offset if necessary to center the trace in the CRT.

If a trace is not yet visible, use the *beam finder* to reveal the beam's location. A beam finder simply compresses the vertical and horizontal ranges to force a trace onto the display. This gives you a rough idea of the trace's relative position. Once you are able to finally move the trace into position, adjust your focus and intensity controls to obtain a crisp, sharp trace. Keep intensity at a moderately low level to improve display accuracy and preserve the CRT phosphors.

Your oscilloscope should be calibrated to its probe before use. A typical oscilloscope probe is shown in Fig. 2-24. Calibration is a quick and straightforward operation which requires only a low-amplitude, low-frequency square wave. Many models have a built-in "calibration" signal generator (usually a 1-kHz, 300-mV square wave with a duty cycle of 50%). Attach your probe to the desired input jack, then place the probe tip across the calibration signal. Adjust your horizontal (TIME/DIV) and vertical (VOLTS/DIV) controls so that one or two complete cycles are clearly shown on the CRT.

Observe the visual characteristics of the test signal as shown in Fig. 2-25. If the square wave's corners are rounded, there may not be enough probe capacitance (sometimes denoted with the label "Cprobe"). Spiked square wave corners suggest too much capacitance in the probe. Either way, the scope and probe are not matched properly. You must adjust the probe capacitance to establish a good electrical match—otherwise, signal distortion will result during your measurements. Slowly adjust the variable capacitance of your probe until the corners shown on the

2-24 A B+K Model PR-46 oscilloscope probe.

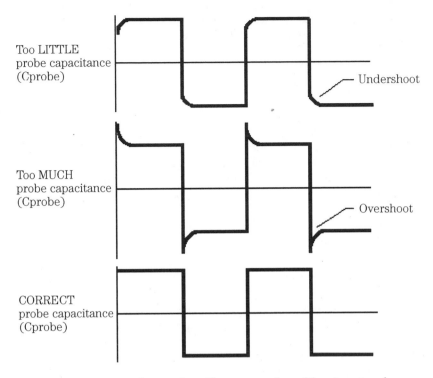

Too LITTLE probe capacitance (Cprobe)

— Undershoot

Too MUCH probe capacitance (Cprobe)

— Overshoot

CORRECT probe capacitance (Cprobe)

2-25 A comparison of typical oscilloscope probe calibration signals.

calibration signal are as square as possible. If you are not able to achieve a clean square wave, try a different probe.

Voltage measurements

The first step in any voltage measurement is to set your normal trace (called the *baseline*) where you want it. Normally, the baseline is placed along the center of the graticule during start-up, but it can be placed anywhere along the CRT, as long as the trace is visible. To establish a baseline, switch your input coupling control to its ground position. Grounding the input disconnects any existing input signal and ensures a zero reading. Adjust the vertical offset control to shift the baseline wherever you want the zero reading to be (usually in the display center). If you have no particular preference, simply center the trace in the CRT.

To measure dc, set your input coupling switch to its dc position, then adjust the VOLTS/DIV control to provide the desired amount of sensitivity. If you are unsure just which sensitivity is appropriate, start with a very low sensitivity (a large VOLTS/DIV setting), then carefully increase sensitivity (reduce the VOLTS/DIV setting) after your input signal is connected. This procedure prevents a trace from simply jumping off the screen when an unknown signal is first applied. If your signal does happen to leave the visible portion of the display, you could reduce the sensitivity (increase the VOLTS/DIV setting) to make the trace visible again.

For example, suppose you were measuring a +5 Vdc power supply output. If VOLTS/DIV is set to 5 VOLTS/DIV, each major vertical division of the CRT display represents 5 Vdc, so your +5-Vdc signal should appear 1 full division above the baseline (5 VOLTS/DIV ×1 DIV = 5 Vdc) as shown in Fig. 2-26. At a VOLTS/DIV setting of 2 VOLTS/DIV, the same +5-Vdc signal would now appear 2.5 divisions above your baseline (2 VOLTS/DIV × 2.5 DIV = 5 Vdc). If your input signal were a negative voltage, the trace would appear *below* the baseline, but it would be read the same way.

AC signals can also be read directly from the oscilloscope. Switch your input coupling control to its ac position, then set a baseline just as you would for dc measurements. If you are unsure about how to set the vertical sensitivity, start with a low sensitivity (a large VOLTS/DIV setting), then slowly increase the sensitivity (reduce the VOLTS/DIV setting) once your input signal is connected. Keep in mind that ac voltage measurements on an oscilloscope will *not* match ac voltage readings on a multimeter. An oscilloscope displays instantaneous *peak* values for a waveform, while ac voltmeters measure in terms of RMS (root mean square) values. To convert a peak voltage reading to RMS, divide the peak reading by 1.414. Another limitation of multimeters is that they can only measure sinusoidal ac signals. Square, triangle, or other unusual waveforms will be interpreted as an average value by a multimeter.

When actually measuring an ac signal, it may be necessary to adjust the oscilloscope's trigger level control to obtain a stable (still) trace. As Fig. 2-27 illustrates, signal voltages can be measured directly from the display. For example, the sinusoidal waveform of Fig. 2-27 varies from −10 to +10 V. If oscilloscope sensitivity were set to 5 VOLTS/DIV, signal peaks would occur 2 divisions above and 2 divisions below the baseline. Since the oscilloscope provides peak measurements, an ac voltmeter would show the signal as peak/1.414 [10/1.414] or 7.07 V RMS.

Time and frequency measurements

An oscilloscope is an ideal tool for measuring critical parameters such as pulse width, duty cycle, and frequency. It is the horizontal sensitivity control (TIME/DIV) which comes into play with time and frequency measurements.

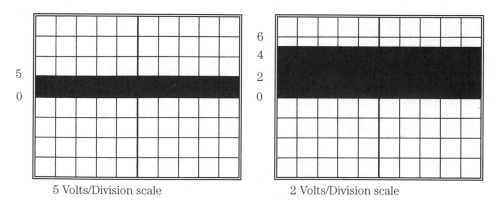

5 Volts/Division scale   2 Volts/Division scale

2-26 Measuring dc voltages with an oscilloscope.

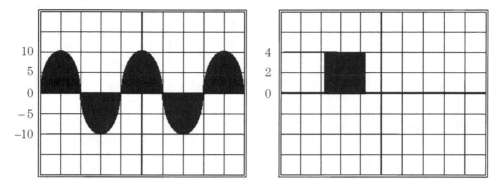

2-27 Measuring ac voltages with an oscilloscope.

Before making any measurements, you must first obtain a clear baseline as you would for voltage measurements. When a baseline is established and a signal is finally connected, adjust the TIME/DIV control to display one or two complete signal cycles.

Typical period measurements are illustrated in Fig. 2-28. With VOLTS/DIV set to 5 ms/DIV, the sinusoidal waveform shown repeats every 2 divisions. This represents a period of [5 ms/DIV × 2 DIV] 10 ms. Since frequency is simply the reciprocal of time, it can be calculated by inverting the time value. A period of 10 ms would represent a frequency of [1/10 ms] 100 Hz. This also works for square waves and regularly repeating nonsinusoidal waveforms. The square wave shown in Fig. 2-28 repeats every 4 divisions. At a TIME/DIV setting of 1 ms/DIV, its period would be 4 ms. This corresponds to a frequency of [1/4 ms] 250 Hz.

Instead of measuring the entire period of a pulse cycle, you can also read the time *between* any two points of interest. For the square wave of Fig. 2-28, you could read the pulse width to be 1 ms. You could also read the low portion of the cycle as a duration of 3 ms (added together for a total signal period of 4 ms). A signal's *duty cycle* is simply the ratio of a signal's ON time to its total period expressed as a percentage. For example, a square wave that is ON for 2 ms and OFF for 2 ms would have a duty cycle of [2 ms/(2 ms + 2 ms) × 100%] 50%. For an ON time of 1 ms and an OFF time of 3 ms, its duty cycle would be [1 ms/(1 ms + 3 ms) × 100%] 25%, and so on.

Diagnostic Software

So far, this chapter has focused on physical tools and test equipment used for troubleshooting. As a technician, you must realize that it is not always cost-effective (or even feasible) to apply test equipment in drive repairs. The labor may easily exceed the cost of another drive. Instead, technicians often apply software tools to test and diagnose drive problems. Typical software tools include the commercial standards like Norton Utilities, or DOS standbys like DEFRAG, SCANDISK, and CHKDSK, but this part of the chapter outlines some of the more popular shareware tools available for drive troubleshooting.

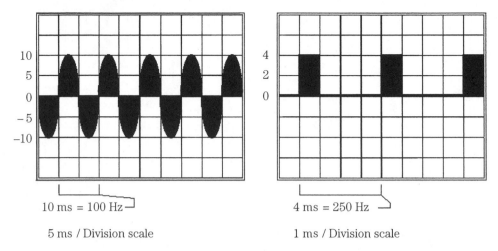

10 ms = 100 Hz

5 ms / Division scale

4 ms = 250 Hz

1 ms / Division scale

2-28 Measuring time on an oscilloscope.

Note: You can find all of these tools (and many more) in the book *Bigelow's Computer Repair Toolkit* published by McGraw-Hill, and available at your favorite bookstore, or from 800-722-4726.

DATA_REC.ZIP

A hard drive crash is frustrating and frightening. Even with your work fully backed up, the time and expense of troubleshooting and drive replacement can be an expensive proposition. If caught unprepared, a drive crash can destroy weeks (or months) of invaluable hard work. Recovering data from a crashed hard drive is more of an art than a science, and there are few tools that are actually up to the task, but Tiramisu is one of the only shareware tools available that can reconstruct data from failed drives. Tiramisu is designed to help drives that have been hit by a virus, scratched by a head crash, accidentally formatted or partitioned, corrupted by a power failure, or damaged by buggy applications. Tiramisu scans the drive even when there are physical damages—the found data are analyzed and reconstructed. The program works on drives without a readable boot sector, readable FAT, or readable directory entries. Tiramisu can handle drives that are no longer recognized by DOS.

DUGIDE.ZIP

Every hard drive ever manufactured has its own "geometry"—the number of cylinders, heads, sectors, and so on which define the way a drive retains data. When a new drive is installed, an old drive is replaced, or the contents of CMOS are lost, a technician is faced with the prospect of tracking down and restoring the geometry figures for each hard drive. While most hard drive manufacturers make their data readily available through on-line and fax-back services, it still takes time and effort to perform that research. On the other hand, programs like DUG_IDE.EXE interrogate a hard drive and display the resulting details for quick reference.

AUTOTEST.ZIP

Part of drive testing often involves measuring performance. While performance is not a critical factor with floppy drives, poor performance (usually in conjunction with other DOS errors) may suggest a failing drive, or the presence of a hardware conflict. The AUTOTEST.EXE diagnostic is designed to measure floppy drive performance by putting the drive through a series of random and sequential reads. Unusually long read times may suggest problems with the R/W heads, track stepping motor, or spindle motor.

DFR.ZIP

There are some occasions where the data on a floppy disk is just as valuable as the data on a hard drive. When the floppy diskette fails, the loss of data or programs on it may be catastrophic. The DFR package from Mark Vitt is a highly automated recovery tool that specializes in recovering files from floppy disks. DFR can recover files to a hard drive, or another floppy disk.

CDSPEED.ZIP

As a technician, you will eventually need to measure and evaluate the performance of a CD-ROM drive during the course of your troubleshooting or upgrade procedure. The CDSPEED.ZIP package provides you with a tool that measures the sustained data transfer rate of a CD-ROM drive, the efficiency of the CD-ROM device driver in service, and the overall utilization of CPU processing power (which helps you determine just how much of a load the CD-ROM drive actually is on your system).

CDTA.ZIP

Timing and performance are vital aspects of all drives, so as a technician, you will eventually need to measure the performance and data throughput of new or replacement CD-ROM drives. The CDTA.ZIP package is designed to test the data throughputs and access times for most CD-ROM drives using conventional low-level drivers and MSCDEX.

CHECK136.ZIP

Some technicians simply do not like the idea of menus and report screens. CHECKSYS is a basic system diagnostic that abandons the use of menu screens and windows in favor of a command-line system. When CHECKSYS is executed, it will return a description of the whole PC system (or an error level if necessary). CHECKSYS can also be used to inspect specific subsystems and return one-line descriptions of system status. The command-line architecture of CHECKSYS also makes it possible to add routine diagnostic functions in the system startup files (i.e., AUTOEXEC.BAT), or other batch files.

CONF810E.ZIP

Information is the technician's most vital resource whenever repairing, testing, or examining a PC prior to an upgrade. Success often lies in knowing "what's in the box."

Rather than the time-consuming process of disassembling the computer and examining each item by eye, a well-written, up-to-the-minute system information utility can tell a technician everything he or she needs to know before even picking up a screwdriver. The long-running PC-Config series of utilities by Michael Holin is one of the most recognized and respected shareware system information utilities/benchmarking programs available. With version 8.10E now in the field, PC-Config retains its leadership as a thorough and reliable system utility.

3
CHAPTER

Service Guidelines

Electronic troubleshooting is a unique pursuit—an activity that falls somewhere between art and science. Your success depends not only on the right documentation and test equipment, but on intuition and a thorough, careful troubleshooting approach. This chapter shows you how to evaluate and track down problems in your system and locate technical data, and offers a series of service guidelines that can ease your work.

The Troubleshooting Process

Regardless of how complex your particular computer or peripheral device may be, a dependable troubleshooting procedure can be broken down into four basic steps as illustrated in Fig. 3-1: define your symptoms, identify and isolate the potential source (or location) of your problem, repair or replace the suspected component or assembly, and retest the unit thoroughly to be sure that you have solved the problem. If you have not solved the problem, start again from step 1. This is a universal procedure that you can apply to *any* sort of computer troubleshooting, not just for PC drives or memory systems.

Define your symptoms

Sooner or later, your floppy drive, tape backup, or other storage device is going to break down. In many cases, the cause may be as simple as a loose wire or connector, or as complicated as an IC failure. Before you open your tool box, you *must* have a firm understanding of *all* the symptoms. Think about the symptoms carefully. Is the disk or tape inserted properly? Is the power or access LED lit? Does this problem occur only when the computer is tapped or moved? By recognizing and understanding your symptoms, it can be much easier to trace a problem to the appropriate assembly or component.

Take the time to write down as many symptoms as you can. This note taking may seem tedious now, but once you have begun your repair, a written record of symptoms and circumstances will help to keep you focused on the task at hand. It will also

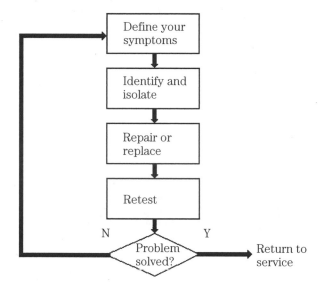

3-1 Flowchart for the universal troubleshooting process.

help to jog your memory if you must explain the symptoms to someone else at a later date. As a professional troubleshooter, you must often log problems or otherwise document your activities anyway.

Identify and isolate

Before you try to isolate a problem within a piece of computer hardware, you must *first* be sure that it is the equipment itself that is causing the problem. In many circumstances, this will be fairly obvious, but there may be situations that appear ambiguous (i.e., there is no power, no DOS prompt, etc.). Always remember that your storage devices work because of an intimate mingling of hardware and software. A faulty or improperly configured piece of software can cause confusing system errors.

When you are confident that the failure lies in your system's hardware, you can begin to identify possible problem areas. Start your search at the subsection level. The troubleshooting procedures throughout this book will guide you through the major sections of today's popular storage systems and aid you in deciding which subsection may be at fault. When you have identified a potential problem area, you can begin the actual repair process, and possibly even track the fault to a component level.

Repair or replace

Once you have an understanding of what is wrong and where to look, you may begin the actual repair process that you feel will correct the symptoms. Most storage devices are a mix of both electronic circuitry and electromechanical devices, so most procedures will require the exchange of electronic or electromechanical parts. As a general rule, all procedures should be considered important and should be followed carefully.

Parts are usually classified as components or subassemblies. A *component* part is the smallest possible individual part that you can work with. Components can serve many different purposes in a computer. Resistors, capacitors, transformers, motors, and ICs are just a few types of component parts. Components contain no serviceable parts within themselves—a defective component *must* be replaced. A *subassembly* can be composed of many individual components. Unlike components, subassemblies serve a single specific purpose in a storage device (i.e., a read/write head or amplifier PC board), but it can usually be repaired by locating and replacing any faulty components.

Note: In today's highly competitive world of PC repair, it is often more economical for you to focus on replacing defective subassemblies (i.e., replace a suspect CD-ROM drive) rather than trace down defective components.

Mail-order component companies listed at the back of this book can provide you with general-purpose electronic components and equipment to aid in your repair. Most will send along their complete catalogs or product listings at your request. Keep in mind, however, that computers and their peripheral devices make extensive use of specialized ICs and physical assemblies. For specialized parts, you will often have to deal directly with the manufacturer. Going to a manufacturer is always somewhat of a calculated risk. They may choose to do business *only* with their affiliated service centers, or just refuse to sell parts to consumers outright. If you do find a manufacturer willing to sell you parts, you should know the *exact* code or part number used by that manufacturer (often available right from the manufacturer's technical data if you have it). Keep in mind that many manufacturers are ill-equipped to deal directly with individual consumers, so be patient and prepared to make several different calls.

During a repair, you may reach a roadblock that requires you to leave your equipment for a day or two (maybe longer). Make it a point to reassemble your system as much as possible before leaving it. Gather any loose parts in plastic bags, seal them shut, and mark them clearly. If you are working with electronic circuitry, make sure to use good-quality antistatic boxes or bags for storage. Partial reassembly (combined with careful notes) will help you remember how the unit goes together later on.

Retest

When a repair is finally complete, the system must be reassembled carefully before testing it. Guards, housings, cables, and shields *must* be restored before final testing. If symptoms persist, you will have to reevaluate the symptoms and narrow the problem to another part of the equipment. If normal operation is restored (or greatly improved), test the computer's various functions. When you can verify that your symptoms have stopped during actual operation, the equipment may be returned to service.

Do not be discouraged if the equipment still malfunctions. Simply walk away, clear your head, and start again by defining your current symptoms. *Never* continue with a repair if you are tired or frustrated—tomorrow is another day. Even the most experienced troubleshooters get overwhelmed from time to time. You should also realize that there may be more than one bad part to deal with. Remember that storage devices are just a collection of assemblies, and each assembly is a collection of parts. Normally, everything works together, but when one part fails, it may cause one or more interconnected parts to fail as well. When repairing a computer, be prepared to make several repair attempts before the computer is repaired completely. Experience will show you which shortcuts are most effective.

Postrepair testing

You should also be familiar with the idea of "burn-in" testing once your repair is complete. In modern electronics, the general rule of reliability suggests that a device will fail *very* quickly or will last a long time. With this rule in mind, it is usually desirable to run the PC for at least 24 hours after the repair is done. This will "stress" the new part or drive, and (hopefully) any marginal part will fail right there while you still have the system on your workbench. The part is still under warranty, and you can replace the weak part again. This kind of testing improves the reliability of your repair, and makes you look better to your customer.

Note: Always suspect a potential for premature failures when installing replacement devices.

Notes on technical information

Information is perhaps your most valuable tool when repairing any piece of electronic equipment. Highly involved electronic troubleshooting will generally require a complete set of schematics and a parts list. Some peripheral manufacturers do sell technical information for their products (or at least their older products). Tandy Corporation (a.k.a. Radio Shack), Sony, Teac, and Sharp are just a just a few manufacturers that make their technical data available to consumers and independent technicians. Contact the literature or customer service department of your particular manufacturer for specific data prices and availability; be sure to request a service manual or maintenance manual (not an owner's or user's manual). Keep in mind that some technical data (when you can get it) can be extremely expensive. Unless you regularly work on particular devices, it is sometimes more economical to forego detailed repair efforts and simply replace the suspect device outright.

If you are able to obtain technical information, it is strongly recommended that you have the data on hand *before* starting your repair. Service manuals often contain important information on custom or application-specific ICs (ASICs) that you will be unable to obtain elsewhere.

Static Electricity

As with any type of electronic troubleshooting activity, there is always a risk of further damage being caused to equipment accidentally during the repair process. With sophisticated computer electronics, that damage hazard comes in the form of *electrostatic discharge* (or ESD) that can destroy sensitive electronic parts. If you have ever walked across a carpeted floor on a cold, dry winter day, you have probably experienced the effects of ESD firsthand while reaching for a metal object (such as a door knob). Under the right conditions, your body can accumulate static charge potentials that exceed 20,000 V!

When you provide a conductive path for electrons to flow, that built-up charge rushes away from your body at the point closest to the metal object. The result is often a brief, stinging shock. Such a jolt can be startling and annoying, but it is generally harmless to people. Semiconductor devices, on the other hand, are *highly* susceptible to real physical damage from ESD when you handle or replace circuit boards and ICs. This section will introduce you to static electricity and show you how to prevent ESD damage during your repairs.

Static formation

When two dissimilar materials are rubbed together (such as a carpet and the soles of your shoes), the force of friction causes electrons to move from one material to another. The excess (or lack) of electrons causes a charge of equal but opposite polarities to develop on each material. Since electrons are not flowing, there is no current, so the charge is said to be *static*. However, the charge does exhibit a voltage potential. As materials continue to rub together, their charge increases—sometimes to potentials of thousands of volts.

In a human, static charges are often developed by normal, everyday activities such as combing your hair. Friction between the comb and your hair causes opposing charges to develop. Sliding across a vinyl car seat, pulling a sweater on or off, or taking clothes out of a dryer are just some of the ways static charges can develop in the body. It is virtually impossible to avoid. ESD is more pronounced in winter months because dry (low-humidity) air allows a greater accumulation of charge. In the summer, humidity in the air tends to bleed away (or short circuit) most accumulated charges before they reach shock levels that you can physically feel. Regardless of the season, though, ESD is always present to some degree, and always a danger to sensitive electronics.

Device damage

ESD poses a serious threat to most advanced ICs. ICs can easily be destroyed by static discharge levels of just a few hundred volts—well below your body's ability to even feel a static discharge. Static discharge at sufficient levels can damage bipolar transistors, transistor-transistor logic (TTL) gates, emitter-coupled logic (ECL) gates, operational amplifiers (op-amps), silicon-controlled rectifiers (SCRs), and junction field-effect transistors (JFETs), but certainly the most susceptible components to ESD are those ICs fabricated using metal-oxide semiconductor (MOS) technology.

The MOS family of devices (PMOS, NMOS, HMOS, CMOS, etc.) has become the cornerstone of high-performance ICs such as memories, high-speed logic processors, and microprocessors, and other advanced components that can be found in today's small computers. Today's CPUs can fit millions of transistors onto a single IC die. Every part of these transistors must be made continually smaller to keep pace with the constant demand for ever-higher levels of IC complexity. As each part of the transistor shrinks, however, their inherent breakdown voltage drops, and their susceptibility to ESD damage escalates.

A typical MOS transistor breakdown is illustrated in Fig. 3-2. Notice the areas of positive and negative semiconductor material which forms its three terminals:

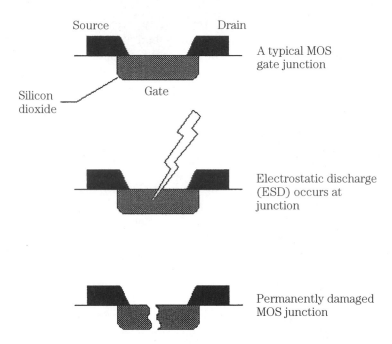

3-2 The sequence of electrostatic breakdown in a MOS device.

(1) source, (2) gate, and (3) drain. The gate is isolated from the other parts of the transistor by a thin film of silicon dioxide (sometimes called the *oxide layer*). Unfortunately, this layer is extremely thin. High voltages, like those voltages from ESDs, can easily overload the oxide layer. This results in a puncture through the gate. Once this happens, the transistor (and therefore the entire IC) is permanently defective and must be replaced.

Controlling static electricity

Never underestimate the importance of static control during your repairs. Without realizing it, you could destroy a new IC or circuit board before you even have the chance to install it, and you would never even know that static damage has occurred. All it takes is the careless touch of a charged hand or a loose piece of clothing. Take the necessary steps to ensure the safe handling and replacement of your sensitive (and expensive) electronics.

One way to control static is to keep charges away from boards and ICs to begin with. This is often accomplished as part of a device's packaging and shipping container. ICs are typically packed in a specially made conductive foam. Carbon granules are compounded right into the polyethylene foam to achieve conductivity (about 3,000 ohms per centimeter). Foam support helps to resist IC lead bending, absorb vibrations, and keeps every lead of the IC at the same potential (known as *equipotential bonding*). Conductive plastics are used to manufacture antistatic boxes as shown in Fig. 3-3. Antistatic boxes may be used with or without conductive foam. Conductive foam and antistatic boxes are reusable, so you can insert ICs for safe keeping, then remove them as needed. You can purchase conductive foam from just about any electronics retail store.

Circuit boards are normally held in conductive plastic bags that dissipate static charges before damage can occur. Antistatic bags (Fig. 3-4) are made up of different material layers—each material exhibiting different amounts of conductivity. The bag acts as a *faraday cage* for the device it contains. Electrons from an ESD will dissipate along a bag's surface layers instead of passing through the bag wall to its contents. Antistatic bags are also available through many electronics retail stores.

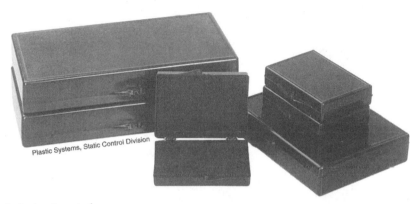

3-3 Antistatic boxes.

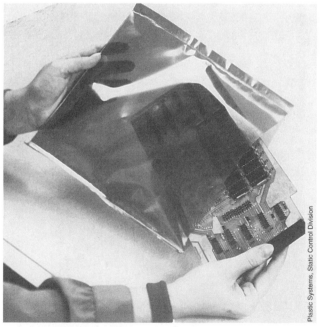

3-4 An antistatic bag.

Whenever you work with sensitive electronics, it is a good idea to dissipate charges that may have accumulated on your body. A conductive fabric wrist strap (Fig. 3-5) which is soundly connected to an earth ground will slowly bleed away any charges from your body. Avoid grabbing hold of a ground directly. Although this will discharge you, it can result in a nasty jolt if you have picked up a large electrostatic charge.

Even the action of wiping a plastic cabinet or video monitor can produce a large electrostatic field. Antistatic chemical agents added to lint-free cleaning wipes (Fig. 3-6) allow cleaning to be performed without the fear of excessive ESD accumulation. Wipes are typically pretreated and sealed in small pouches for convenience.

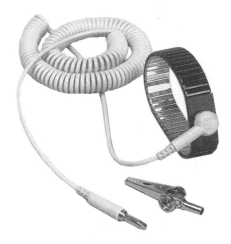

3-5 An antistatic wrist strap. (*Plastic Systems, Static Control Division*)

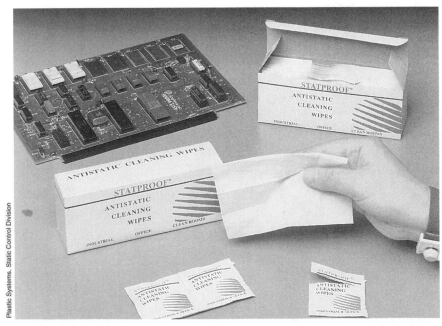

Plastic Systems, Static Control Division

3-6 Antistatic chemical wipes.

Work surfaces must also be as static free as possible. This is very important! When circuit boards or chassis are removed from their systems and brought to your workbench, use an antistatic mat (Fig. 3-7) to protect your delicate electronics. The antistatic mat is essentially a conductive layer that is unrolled onto desks or benches, and it connects to earth ground rather like an ordinary wrist strap.

There are instruments that can be used to measure the level of electrostatic fields on any surface or object. Electrostatic meters (Fig. 3-8) are relatively inexpensive and easy to use—just bring the meter within an inch or so of the item to be measured, press the "read" button, and read the static level in kilovolts (kV, or thousands of volts) directly from the meter display. Electrostatic meters are generally powered from one or more AA-type batteries.

Remember to make careful use of your static controls. Keep ICs and circuit boards in their antistatic containers at all times. *Never* place parts onto or into synthetic materials (such as nonconductive plastic cabinets or fabric coverings) that could hold a charge. Handle static sensitive parts carefully. Avoid touching IC pins if at all possible. Be sure to use a conductive wrist strap and mat connected to a reliable earth ground.

Electricity Hazards

No matter how harmless your storage device may appear, always remember that potential shock hazards *can* exist. Although internally mounted storage devices operate from dc voltages produced by the computer, external storage devices are sometimes powered by ac line voltage. When an ac-powered storage device is disassembled, there can be several locations where live ac voltage is exposed and easily accessible. Electronic equipment operates from 120 V ac at 60 Hz. Many European countries use 240 V ac at 50 Hz. When this kind of voltage potential establishes a path through your body, it can cause a flow of current that may be large enough to stop your heart. Since it only takes about 100 mA to trigger a cardiac arrest, and a typical power supply fuse is rated for 1 or 2 A, fuses and circuit breakers will *not* protect you.

It is your skin's resistance that limits the flow of current through the body. Ohm's law states that for any voltage, current flow increases as resistance drops (and vice versa). Dry skin exhibits a high resistance of several hundred thousand ohms, while moist, cut, or wet skin can drop to only several hundred ohms. This means that even comparatively low voltages can produce a shock if your skin resistance is low enough. Take the following steps to protect yourself from injury:

- Keep the device under repair *unplugged* (not just turned off) as much as possible during disassembly and repair. When you must perform a service procedure that requires power to be applied, plug the supply into an isolation transformer just long enough to perform your procedure, then unplug it again. This makes the repair safer for you, as well as for anyone else that may happen along.
- Whenever you must work on a power supply, try to wear rubber gloves. These will insulate your hands just like insulation on a wire. You may think that rubber gloves are inconvenient and uncomfortable, but they are far

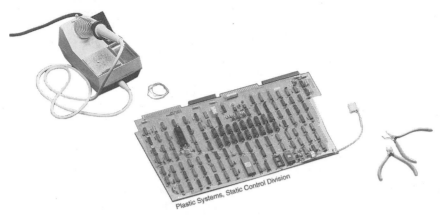

3-7 An antistatic work surface mat.

3-8 An electrostatic field meter.

better than the inconvenience and discomfort of an electric shock. Make it a point to wear a long-sleeved shirt with sleeves rolled down and buttoned; this will insulate your forearms.

- If rubber gloves are absolutely out of the question for one reason or another, remove all metal jewelry and work with one hand behind your back. The metals in your jewelry are excellent conductors. Should your ring or watchband hook onto a "live" ac line, it can conduct current directly to your skin. By keeping one hand behind your back, you cannot grasp both ends of a live ac line to complete a strong current path through your heart.
- Work dry! Do *not* work with wet hands or clothing. Do *not* work in wet or damp environments. Make sure that any nearby fire extinguishing equipment is suitable for electrical fires.
- Treat electricity with tremendous respect. Whenever electronic circuitry is exposed (especially power supply circuitry), a shock hazard *does* exist. Remember that it is the flow of current through your body, not the voltage

potential, that can injure you. Insulate yourself as much as possible from any exposed wiring.

Conventional Soldering Technology

Soldering is the most commonly used method of connecting wires and components within an electrical or electronic circuit (Fig. 3-9). Metal surfaces (in this case, component leads, wires, or printed circuit boards) are heated to high temperatures, then joined together with a layer of compatible metal in its molten state. When performed correctly with the right materials, soldering forms a lasting, corrosion-proof, intermolecular bond that is mechanically strong and electrically sound. All that is required is the appropriate soldering iron and electronics-grade (called 60/40) solder. This section explains the tools and techniques for both regular and surface-mount soldering.

Soldering background

By strict definition, *soldering* is a process of bonding metals together. There are three distinct types of soldering: (1) brazing, (2) silver soldering, and (3) soft soldering. Brazing and silver soldering are used when working with hard or precious metals, but soft soldering is the technique of choice for electronics work.

In order to bond wires or component leads (typically made of copper), a third metal must be added while in its molten state. The bonding metal is known simply as "solder." Several different types of solder are available to handle each soldering technique, but the chosen solder *must* be compatible with the metals to be bonded— otherwise, a bond will not form. Lead and tin are two common and inexpensive metals that adhere very well to copper. However, neither metal by itself has the strength, hardness, and melting point characteristics to make them practically useful. Therefore, lead and tin are combined into an alloy. A ratio of approximately 60% tin and 40% lead yields an alloy that offers reasonable hardness, good pliability, and

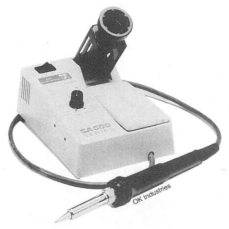

3-9 An adjustable temperature soldering station.

a relatively low melting point that is ideal for electronics work. This is the solder that must be used.

While solder adheres very well to copper, it does not adhere well at all to the natural oxides that form on a conductor's surface. Even though conductors may appear clean and clear with the unaided eye, some amount of oxidation is always present. Oxides must be removed before a good bond can be achieved. A resin cleaning agent (called *flux*) can be applied to conductors before soldering. Resin is chemically inactive at room temperature, but it becomes extremely active when heated to soldering temperatures. Activated flux bonds with oxides and strips them away from copper surfaces. As a completed solder joint cools, residual resin also cools and returns safely to an inactive state.

Never under *any* circumstances should you use an acid or solvent-based flux to prepare conductors. Acid fluxes can clean away oxides as well as resin, but acids and solvents remain active after the joint cools. Over time, active acid flux continues to dissolve copper wires and eventually causes a circuit failure. Resin flux can be purchased as a paste that is brushed onto conductors before soldering, but most electronic solders have a core of resin manufactured right into the solder strand itself. Prefabricated flux eliminates the mess of flux paste, and cleans the joint as solder is applied. The paste solder used in surface-mount soldering usually contains chemical agents also.

Irons and tips

A soldering iron is little more than a resistive heating element built into the end of a long steel tube as shown in the cross-sectional diagram of Fig. 3-10. When voltage is applied to the heater, it warms the base of a metal tip. Any heat conducted down the cooldown tube (toward the handle) is dissipated harmlessly to the surrounding air. This keeps the handle temperature low enough to hold comfortably. Even the larger professional soldering stations operate using this general approach.

Although some heat is wasted along the cooldown tube, most heat is channeled into a soldering tip similar to the one shown in Fig. 3-11. Tips generally have a core of solid copper that is plated with iron. The plated core is then coated with a layer of nickel to stop high-temperature metal corrosion. The entire assembly (except for the tip's very end) is finally plated with chromium, which gives a new tip its shiny chrome appearance. A chromium coating renders the tip *nonwettable* (solder will not stick to it). Since solder must stick at the tip's end, that end is plated with tin. A tin coating (a basic component of solder) makes the tip *wettable* so that molten solder will adhere. Tips can be manufactured in a wide variety of shapes and sizes to handle different soldering tasks. Before you select the best tip for the job, you must understand ideal soldering conditions.

The very best soldering connections are made within only a narrow window of time and temperature. A solder joint heated between 260 to 288°C (500 to 550°F) for 1 to 2 s will make the best connections. You should select a soldering iron wattage and tip shape to achieve these conditions. For very precise work, use a tip temperature sensor (Fig. 3-12) to verify the tip's actual temperature. The purpose of soldering irons is *not* to melt solder. Instead, a soldering iron is supposed to deliver heat to a joint; the *joint* should melt the solder. A large solder joint (with larger or

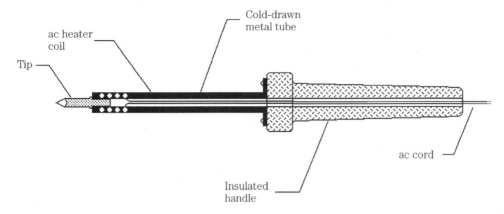

3-10 Cross-sectional diagram of a simple soldering iron.

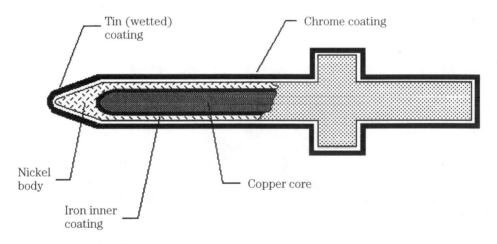

3-11 Cross-sectional diagram of a typical soldering iron tip.

more numerous connections) requires a larger iron and tip than a small joint (with fewer or smaller connections). If you use a small iron to heat a large joint, the joint may dissipate heat faster than the iron can deliver it, so the joint may not reach an acceptable soldering temperature. Conversely, using a large iron to heat a small joint will overheat the joint. Overheating can melt wire insulation and damage printed circuit board traces. This is the reason why temperature-controlled soldering stations (Fig. 3-13) or multiiron stations are so popular. Match wattage to the application. Most general-purpose electronics work can be accomplished using a 25- to 30-W soldering iron.

Since the end of a tip actually contacts the joint to be soldered, the tip's shape and size can assist heat transfer greatly. When heat must be applied across a wide area (such as a wire splice), a wide-area tip should be used. A screwdriver (or flat-blade) tip is a good choice. If heat must be directed with pinpoint accuracy for small, tight joints or printed circuits, a narrow blade or conical tip is best. Figure 3-14 illustrates

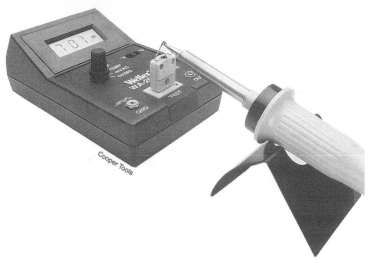

3-12 A soldering iron tip temperature sensor.

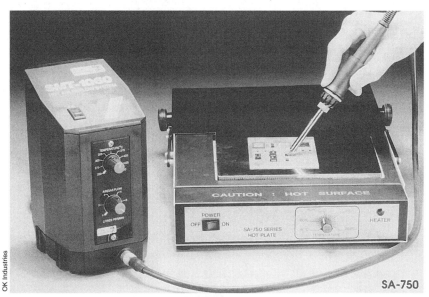

3-13 A surface-mount hot-plate desoldering/rework station.

a selection of conventional Weller soldering iron tips, and Fig. 3-15 shows a selection of surface-mount tips. More information on surface-mount soldering is presented later in this chapter.

Soldering

Always keep your soldering iron parked in a secure holder while it is on! *Never* allow a hot iron to sit freely on a table top or on anything that may be flammable. *Make it*

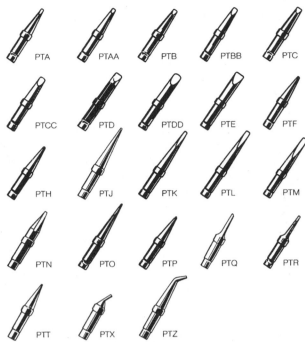

3-14 Conventional Weller soldering tips. (*Cooper Tools*)

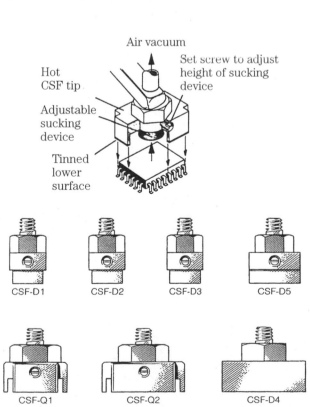

3-15 Desoldering tips for quad flat pack ICs. (*Cooper Tools*)

a rule to always wear safety glasses when soldering. Active resin or molten solder can easily flick off the iron or joint and do permanent damage to the tissue in your eyes.

Give your iron plenty of time to warm up. Five minutes of warming time is usually adequate, but small-wattage irons (or irons with larger tips) may need even more time. Once the iron is at its working temperature, you should coat the wettable portion of the tip with a layer of fresh solder—a process known as *tinning* the iron. Rub the tip into a sponge soaked in clean water to wipe away any accumulations of debris and carbon that may have formed, then apply a thin coating of fresh solder to the tip's end. Solder penetrates the tip to a molecular level and forms a cushion of molten solder that aids in heat transfer. Retin the iron whenever its tip becomes blackened—perhaps every few minutes or after several joints.

It is often helpful to tin each individual conductor before actually making the complete joint. To tin a wire, prepare it by stripping away $3/16$ to $1/4$ in of insulation. As you strip insulation, be sure not to nick or damage the conductor. Heat the exposed copper for about 1 s, then apply solder into the *wire*—not into the iron! If the iron and tip are appropriate, solder should flow evenly and smoothly into the conductor. Apply just enough solder to bond each of a stranded wire's exposed strands. You will find that conductors heat faster and solder flows better when all parts of a joint are tinned in advance.

Making a complete solder joint is just as easy. Bring together each of your conductors as necessary to form the joint. For example, if you are soldering a component into a printed circuit board, insert the component's leads into their appropriate PC board holes. Place the iron against *all* conductors to be heated at the joint. For a printed circuit board, heat the printed trace and component lead together (Fig. 3-16). After about 1 s, flow solder gently into the hot *conductors* (not the iron). Be sure that solder flows cleanly and evenly into the joint. Apply solder for another 1 or 2 s, then remove both solder and iron. Do *not* attempt to touch or move the joint for several seconds. Wait until the solder cools and sets. If the joint requires additional solder, reheat the joint and flow in a bit more solder. You can identify a good solder joint

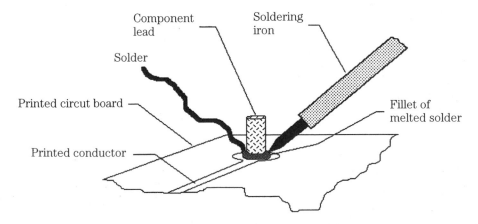

3-16 Forming a basic solder connection.

by its smooth, even, silvery-gray appearance. Any charred or carbonized flux on the joint indicates that your soldering temperature is too high (or heat is being applied for too long). Remember that solder cannot flow unless the joint is hot. If the joint is not hot, solder will cool before it bonds. The result is a rough, built-up, dull gray or blackish mound that does not adhere to the joint very well. This is known as a *cold* solder joint. A cold joint can often be corrected by reheating the joint properly and applying fresh solder. If you are uncomfortable with soldering techniques, it is highly recommended that you practice on scrap wire or printed circuit (PC) boards until you become proficient.

Conventional desoldering

When desoldering an electronic connection, you must remove the intermolecular bond that has formed during the soldering process. In reality, however, this is virtually impossible to achieve completely. The best that you can hope for is to remove enough solder to gently break the connection apart without destroying the component or damaging the associated PC trace. Desoldering is basically a game of removing as much solder as possible—the more solder, the better.

You will find that some connections are very easy to remove. For instance, a wire inserted into a PC board may be removed easily just by heating the joint and gently withdrawing the wire from its hole once solder is molten. Use *extreme* caution when desoldering wires and components. Leads and wires under tension may spring free once solder is molten. A springing wire can launch a bead of hot solder into the air. *Always use safety glasses or goggles to protect your eyes from flying solder.*

Desoldering other types of connections, such as through-hole components, is usually more difficult. When desoldering a part with more than one wire, it is virtually impossible to heat all of its leads simultaneously while withdrawing the part. As a result, it becomes necessary to remove as much solder as possible from each lead, then gently break each lead free as shown in Fig. 3-17. Grab hold of each lead with a pair of needlenose pliers and wiggle the lead back and forth gently until it breaks free. Solder can be removed using regular desoldering tools such as a solder vacuum or solder wick.

Surface-mount technology

Conventional printed circuits make use of through-hole components. Leaded parts are inserted on one side of the PC board, while their leads are soldered to printed wiring traces on the other side. Through-hole PC board assembly had been the premier method of circuit mass production since the 1960s. With the ever-increasing need to pack more circuitry into ever-less board space, through-hole circuit assembly is rapidly being made obsolete by the technique known as surface-mount (SM) fabrication. A SM PC board uses specially miniaturized components that are mounted and soldered to one side of the PC board only (Fig. 3-18). There are no leads to protrude through the board. In the last few years, just about every electronic component has become available in one or more SM package versions. While SM assemblies are growing in popularity, it is not uncommon to find "hybrid" assemblies containing both SM and through-hole components.

There are many real advantages to using SM PC boards. Components are changed significantly. For example, SM components are cheaper, lighter, and smaller

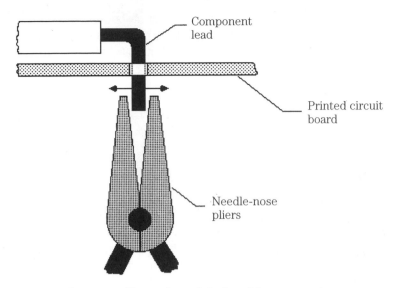

3-17 Breaking a stubborn through-hole solder connection.

3-18 View of surface-mount components on a printed circuit board.

than leaded components. This holds true for all SM components. The absence of long leads allows SM components to resist high shock and vibration (there is also no need to bend or cut component leads during PC board assembly). Removing long component leads also reduces parasitic circuit inductance and capacitance, making SM circuits especially useful in high-frequency or radiofrequency (RF) applications. SM components are ideal for use in automatic PC board assembly machinery.

Such broad changes in component designs have had equally important effects on the PC boards themselves. Smaller individual components allow PC boards to be made smaller. Since SM components only attach to one side of the PC board, it is possible to mount SM components on *both* sides of the board—the same-sized PC board could therefore hold twice as many SM components as a similar board for through-hole components. PC board materials are exactly the same for SM circuits—no special board materials are needed. Eliminating through-hole components also eliminates many plated through-holes that are needed to connect board sided via component leads. Reduced drilling and plating can cut manufacturing costs even further.

Surface-mount desoldering

During a repair, you can use a conventional low-wattage soldering iron to install replacement parts one lead at a time. Desoldering SM components, however, is a delicate and intricate task. As with conventional desoldering, it is virtually impossible to remove every molecule of solder from two mated surfaces. Even with the best solder wick or solder vacuum, a part will remain lightly bonded to its PC traces. You cannot heat and withdraw individual component leads, and any attempt to pull them from the board will certainly damage the PC traces. SM desoldering presents some unique and perplexing problems for troubleshooters.

Perhaps the only truly effective way to desolder an SM component is to use a soldering pencil fitted with a SM desoldering tip (Fig. 3-19). SM tips are designed to heat every joint of a part simultaneously (instead of conventional tips that only direct heat to one joint at a time). By heating each joint together, the part becomes free and can be withdrawn from the board cleanly with a small vacuum nozzle or tweezers. You could also "sweep" the freed part right off the board in one quick motion, then clean up any residual solder with conventional desoldering tools.

Figure 3-20 shows a dual soldering station with a "tweezer" iron and QFP (quad flat pack) iron. *Make it a point to ALWAYS wear safety glasses when soldering or desoldering.* Some full-featured solder rework stations offer an adjustable temperature control, along with a vacuum attachment for solder or component removal. Keep in mind that most SM tips are physically much larger than conventional tips. Larger tips typically need more power (25 to 35 W) to achieve temperatures that will

3-19 SMT desoldering with an SOIC tip.

OK Industries

3-20 Desoldering equipment for SMT rework.

melt solder. If you are outfitting to perform SM repairs, it is very worthwhile to invest in a solder station and tip set designed for SM work. For the budget-conscious enthusiast, a handheld soldering pencil can be fitted with SM tips for relatively little money.

There is a large selection of SM desoldering tips to choose from depending on the type of SM device that you must remove. Figure 3-21 shows a close-up view of a hot-air SM tip with a built-in vacuum nozzle. Hot air is used to melt the solder at each QFP lead. When solder is molten, the IC will be withdrawn from the PC board by a small vacuum line within the iron.

Printed Circuits

In the very early days of consumer electronics, circuit assemblies were manufactured by hand on bulky, metal frames. Each component was then wired together by hand. If you have ever seen a chassis from an old tube-driven television or radio, you have probably seen this type of construction. Eventually, the costs of hand-building electronic chassis became so high, a new technique was introduced that used photographic processes to actually print wiring patterns onto copper-clad boards. Excess copper was then chemically stripped away leaving only the desired wiring patterns. Parts could then be inserted and soldered quickly, easily, and accurately.

Before long, manufacturers realized that these printed circuits appeared more uniform, were easier to inspect and test, required much less labor to assemble, and were lighter and less bulky than metal chassis assembly. Today, virtually all electronic equipment incorporates some type of printed circuit (PC) board. The size and complexity of the board will depend largely on the particular circuit's job. This section will describe the major types of PC boards that you may encounter, and present a selection of PC board troubleshooting and repair techniques that you can use.

Types of printed circuits

Printed circuits are available as single-sided, double-sided, or multilayer boards. Computer equipment typically uses multilayer boards. Each type of board can hold surface-mount and/or through-hole components. Single-sided PC boards are the simplest and least-expensive type of printed circuit. Copper traces are etched only on one side of the board. Holes can then be drilled through the board to accommodate component leads if necessary. Through-hole components are inserted from the blank side of the board (the "component" side) so that their leads protrude on the copper trace side (the "solder" side). Component leads can then be soldered to their copper traces to complete the printed circuit. Single-sided PC boards support SM components.

When circuits become too complex to route all traces on one side of the PC board, traces can be etched onto both sides of a printed circuit. This is called a double-sided PC board. Plated (electrically conductive) holes are used to interconnect both sides of the board as needed. Such plated holes are also used to hold through-hole component leads. Solder conducts up the plated hole through capillary action and ensures that a component lead is properly connected to both sides of the board. This allows the board to be soldered from one side only during manufacture. However, desoldering leads in plated holes can become somewhat difficult since solder adheres all the way through

3-21 A QFP desoldering tip.

the hole. All internal solder must be removed before a lead can be withdrawn. If you pull out a wire or component lead before solder is removed, you stand a good chance of ripping the plating right out of the hole. Double-sided PC boards are excellent for SM components since components can be soldered on both sides of the board.

Even more complex circuit designs can be fabricated on multilayer PC boards. Not only will you find traces on both external sides of the PC board, but there can be even more layers of etched traces sandwiched and interconnected between these two faces (each layer is separated by a thin insulating layer). As with double-sided boards, multilayer boards use plated through-holes to hold component leads and bond various layers together.

Typical printed circuits use etched copper traces on a base material of paper-based phenolic or epoxy. Other printed circuits incorporate a base of glass-fabric epoxy, or some similar plastic-based substance. These materials offer a light, strong, rigid base for printed circuits. A fourth (but less commonly used) type of printed circuit is known as the "flexible" printed circuit. Copper traces are deposited onto a layer of plastic. Traces can be included on both sides of this base layer to form a single or double-sided circuit. Traces are then covered by an insulating layer of plastic. Using alternate layers of copper traces and flexible insulation, it is possible to form multilayer flexible printed circuits.

Flexible circuits have the ability to fold and conform to tight or irregular spaces. As a result, flexible circuits are often used as wiring harnesses—that is, components are placed as needed, then a flexible circuit is inserted and attached by screws or solder to interconnect each component. Individual components are rarely soldered to a flexible PC as they are with a rigid PC board.

Printed circuit repairs

Printed circuits are generally very reliable structures, but instances of physical abuse can easily damage the rigid phenolic or glass base, as well as any printed traces. If damage occurs to a PC board, you should know what signs of damage to look for, and what steps you can take to correct any damage. There are four general PC board problems that you should know about: lead failure, printed trace break, board cracks, and heat damage.

Lead failure

Normally, a well-made solder joint will hold a wire or component lead tightly into its connection on a PC board. However, if that wire or connection is suddenly placed under a lot of stress, the solder joint can fail partially or completely as shown in Fig. 3-22. Stress can be applied with sudden, sharp movements such as dropping or striking the computer.

Lead failure is not always an obvious problem unless the lead or wire is away from its PC land entirely. If the conductor is still making contact with the PC board, its electrical connection may be broken or intermittent. You can test an intermittent connection by exposing the PC board, then *gently* rapping on the board or suspect conductor. By tapping different areas of the board, it may be possible to focus on an intermittent connection in the area which is most sensitive to the tapping. You can also test suspected intermittent connections by gently wiggling wires or component

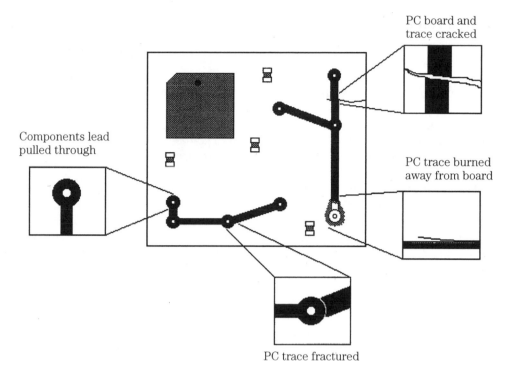

PC board and
trace cracked

Components lead
pulled through

PC trace burned
away from board

PC trace fractured

3-22 Four typical PC board problems.

leads. The component or conductor most sensitive to the touch will probably be the one that is intermittent.

Another case of lead failure can occur on double-sided or multilayer PC boards during desoldering. Various layers are connected together by plated holes. Through-hole component leads are typically soldered into plated through-holes. If you pull out a conductor without removing all of the solder, you can rip out part or all of the hole's plating along with the conductor. When this happens, the electrical integrity at that point of the PC board is broken.

For double-sided PC boards, this can often be corrected by resoldering the new component lead on both sides of the PC board. There is usually enough exposed copper on the component side to ensure a reasonable solder fillet. Unfortunately, there is no reliable way to solder a new lead to each layer of a multilayer board. As a result, a damaged through-hole on a multilayer board may be beyond repair, and the board will have to be replaced.

The best way to avoid damaging a plated through-hole is to heat a joint while removing the lead simultaneously. Grasp the lead with a pair of needlenose pliers while heating the joint. When solder is molten, gently pull out the component lead. You can then safely clean up any residual solder with conventional desoldering tools. *Never* grasp the component lead with your bare fingers. The entire lead will reach soldering temperatures almost immediately. *Always wear safety glasses when soldering or desoldering.*

Printed trace break

Another common problem that takes place in printed circuits is known as trace break. This can also be the result of a physical shock or sudden impact to the PC board. In this case, a portion of the printed trace (usually where a solder pad meets the remainder of the trace) can suffer a fine, hairline fracture that results in an open or intermittent circuit. What makes this particular problem especially difficult is that a trace break can be almost impossible to see upon visual inspection. You must often wiggle each solder pad until you find the fractured connection. Large, heavy components, such as transformers or relays, are often prime candidates for trace breaks, so start your search there.

Do *not* attempt to create a bridge of solder across the break, or jumper directly across the fracture. Solder does not adhere well to the chemical coatings often used with PC boards, so such quick fixes rarely last long. In order to correct a printed trace break, you should desolder and remove the broken portion of the trace, then solder a jumper wire between two associated component leads. Do not solder directly to the printed trace. You can also use the materials in commercial PC board repair packages such as the CIR-KIT PC repair kit from PACE, Inc. (Fig. 3-23).

Board cracks

Under extreme conditions, the phenolic or glass-epoxy circuit board itself may actually crack. This is not unusual for equipment that has been dropped or abused.

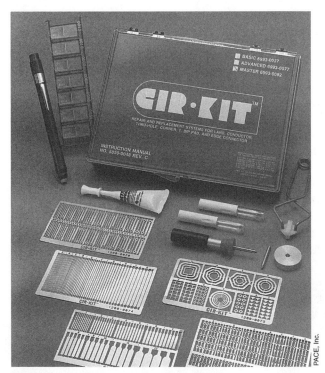

3-23 A circuit board repair kit.

When a crack occurs, the course of the crack may sever one or more printed traces. Luckily, board cracks are fairly easy to detect on sight. By following the crack, it is a simple matter to locate any severed traces on the board surface.

As with trace breaks, the best, most reliable method of repairing broken traces is to solder a wire jumper between two associated solder pads or component leads. *Never* try to make a solder bridge across a break. Solder does not adhere well to the chemicals used on many PC board traces, so such fixes will not last long. If the physical crack is severe, you may want to work a bit of good-quality epoxy adhesive into the crack to help reinforce the board. Multilayer PC boards cannot be repaired practically.

Heat damage

Printed copper traces are bonded firmly to the phenolic or glass epoxy board underneath. When extreme heat is applied to the copper traces, however, it is possible to separate the copper trace from the board. This type of damage usually occurs during soldering or desoldering when concentrated heat is applied with a soldering iron. The only real remedy for this type of damage is to carefully cut off that portion of the separated trace to prevent the loose copper from accidentally shorting out other components, and solder a wire jumper from the component lead to an adjacent solder pad or component lead.

4
CHAPTER

Solid-State
Memory Devices

Memory (Fig. 4-1) is a cornerstone of the modern PC. It is memory that holds the program code and data that are processed by the CPU, and it is this intimate relationship between memory and the CPU that forms the basis of computer performance. With larger and faster CPUs constantly being introduced, more complex software is developed to take advantage of the processing power. In turn, the more complex software demands larger amounts of memory. With the explosive growth of Windows (and more recently Windows 95), the demands made on memory performance are more acute than ever. These demands have resulted in a proliferation of memory types that go far beyond the simple, traditional dynamic RAM (DRAM). Cache (static RAM, SRAM), page-mode memory, EDO memory, video memory, flash BIOS, and other exotic memory types now compete for the attention of PC technicians. These new forms of memory also present some new problems. This chapter will provide you an understanding of memory types, configurations, installation concerns, and troubleshooting options.

Essential Memory Concepts

The first step in any discussion of memory is to understand basically how memory works. If you already have a good grasp of memory basics, feel free to skip this part of the chapter.

Memory organization

All memory is basically an *array* organized as rows and columns as shown in Fig. 4-2. Each row is known as an *address*—there may be 1 million or more addresses on a single memory IC. The columns represent data bits. A typical high-density memory IC has 1 bit, but may have 2 or 4 bits depending on the overall amount of memory required.

4-1 A 16-Mb memory IC die.

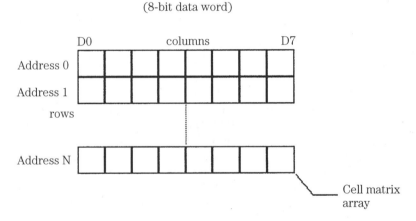

4-2 A typical storage cell array.

As you probably see in Fig. 4-2, the intersection of each column and row is an individual memory bit (known as a *cell*). This is important because the number of components in a cell—and the way those components are fabricated onto the memory IC—will have a profound impact on memory performance. For example, a classic DRAM cell is a single MOS transistor, while SRAM cells often pack several transistors and other components onto the IC die. Although you do not have to be an expert on IC design, you should realize that the *internal fabrication* of a memory IC has more to do with its performance than the way it is soldered into your computer.

Memory signals

A memory IC communicates with the "outside world" through three sets of signals: address lines, data lines, and control lines. Figure 4-3 illustrates these signal types. *Address lines* define which row of the memory array will be active. In actual prac-

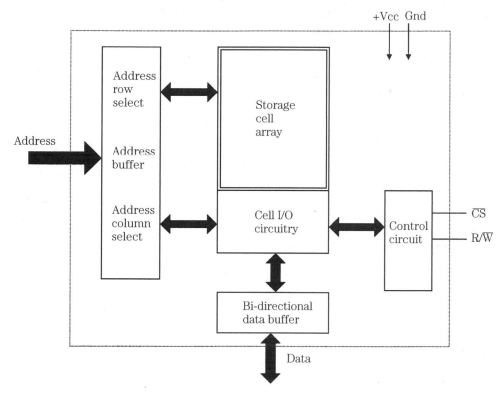

4-3 Block diagram of a simple RAM IC.

tice, the address is specified as a binary number, and conversion circuitry inside the memory IC translates the binary number into a specific row signal. *Data lines* pass binary values back and forth to the defined address.

Control lines are used to operate the memory IC. A read/write (R/W) line defines whether data are being read from the specified address or written to it. A chip enable (CE) signal makes a memory IC active or inactive (this ability to "disconnect" from a circuit is what allows a myriad of memory ICs to all share common address and data signals in the computer). Some memory types require additional signals such as row address-select (RAS) and column address-select (CAS) for refresh operations. More exotic memory types may require additional control signals.

Understanding Package Styles and Structures

Ultimately, the memory die is mounted in a package just like any other IC. The completed memory packages can then be soldered to your motherboard, or attached to plug-in structures such as SIMMs and memory cards. There are four typical memory packages that you should be familiar with:

Dual in-line package (DIP). This is the classic IC package used for through-hole mounting (prior to surface-mount technology). The advantage of DIP ICs is their compatibility with IC sockets, which allows ICs to be inserted or removed as required. Unfortunately, the long metal pins can bend and break if the IC is inserted or removed incorrectly. Also, the overall size of the package demands extra space. DIP ICs can be found in older PCs (286 and earlier systems) and older VGA/SVGA video boards. DIPs are still used on motherboards to provide cache RAM.

Single in-line package (SIP). This type of IC package is rarely used today. There are simply not enough pins. However, they did make a short appearance with memory devices in late-model 286 and early 386 systems which flirted with proprietary memory expansions. I remember NEC using such devices in a 2-MB add-on for their 386SX/20—and you needed to add that module before you added even more memory in the form of proprietary SIMMs. SIPs can be troublesome because they are difficult to find replacements for, so expect replacement memory modules using them to cost a premium.

Small-outline J-lead (SOJ). This is the contemporary package style for surface-mount circuits. The leads protrude from the package like a DIP, but are bent around just under the package in the form of a **J**. There are sockets for SOJ packages which are often employed for replaceable memory ICs like the BIOS ROM, but most RAM devices are soldered directly to the motherboard as system memory (or a video board as video RAM). SIMMs often make use of SOJ memory components.

Thin, small-outline package (TSOP). Like the SOJ, a TSOP is also a surface-mount package style. However, its small, thin body makes TSOP memory ideal for narrow spaces. Expect to find such devices serving as memory in notebook/subnotebook systems, or PCMCIA cards (a.k.a. PC Cards).

Add-on memory devices

Memory has always pushed the envelope of IC design. This trend has given us tremendous amounts of memory in very small packages, but it also has kept memory relatively expensive. Manufacturers responded by providing a minimum amount of memory with the system, then selling more memory as an add-on option. This keeps the cost of a basic machine down and increases profit through add-on sales. As a technician, you should understand the three basic types of add-on memory.

Proprietary add-on modules   Once the Intel i286 opened the door for more than 1 MB of memory, PC makers scrambled to fill the void. However, the rush to more memory resulted in a proliferation of nonstandard (and incompatible) memory modules. Each new motherboard came with a new add-on memory scheme, and this invariably led to a great deal of confusion among PC users and makers alike. You will likely find proprietary memory modules in 286 and early 386 systems.

Single in-line memory modules and dual in-line memory modules (SIMMs and DIMMs) By the time 386 systems took hold in the PC industry, proprietary memory modules had been largely abandoned in favor of the *memory module* (Fig. 4-4). A SIMM is light, small, and contains a relatively large block of memory, but perhaps the greatest advantage of a SIMM is *standardization.* Using a standard pin layout, a SIMM from one PC can be installed in any other PC. The 30-pin SIMM (Table 4-1) provides 8 data bits, and generally holds up to 4 MB. The 30-pin SIMM proved its worth in 386 and early 486 systems, but fell short when providing more memory to later-model PCs. The 72-pin SIMM (Table 4-2) supplanted the 30-pin version by providing 32 data bits, and may hold up to 32 MB (or more).

You may also find such structures referred to as DIMMs (or dual in-line memory modules). DIMMs appear virtually identical to SIMMs, but where each electrical contact on the SIMM is tied together between the front and back, the DIMM keeps front and back contacts separate—effectively doubling the number of contacts available on the device. For example, if you look at a 72-pin SIMM, you will see 72 electrical contacts on both sides of the device (144 contacts total)—but these are tied together, so there are only 72 signals (even with 144 contacts).

On the other hand, a DIMM keeps the front and back contacts electrically separate, and usually adds some additional pins to keep SIMMs and DIMMs from accidentally being mixed. Typical DIMMs provide 168 pins (84 pins on each side). DIMMs are appearing in high-end 64-bit data bus PCs (such as Pentiums and

 Dual in-line package (DIP)

 Single in-line package (SIP)

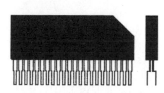 Zig-zag in-line package (ZIP)

 Single in-line memory module (SIMM)

4-4 A comparison of memory packages.

Table 4-1. Pinout for a 30-pin SIMM

Pin	Description	Pin	Description
1	+5 Vdc	2	CAS
3	Data Bit 0	4	Address Bit 0
5	Address Bit 1	6	Data Bit 1
7	Address Bit 2	8	Address Bit 3
9	Ground	10	Data Bit 2
11	Address Bit 4	12	Address Bit 5
13	Data Bit 3	14	Address Bit 6
15	Address Bit 7	16	Data Bit 4
17	Address Bit 8	18	Address Bit 9
19	Address Bit 10	20	Data Bit 5
21	Write Enable	22	Ground
23	Data Bit 6	24	No connection
25	Data Bit 7	26	Parity Bit Out
27	RAS	28	CAS Parity
29	Parity Bit In	30	+5 Vdc

PowerPC RISC workstations). As PCs move from 64 to 128 bits over the next few years, DIMMs will likely replace SIMMs as the preferred memory expansion device.

Finally, you may see SIMMs and DIMMs referred to as composite or noncomposite modules. These terms are used infrequently to describe the technology level of the memory module. For example, a *composite* module uses older, lower-density memory, so more ICs are required to achieve the required storage capacity. Conversely, a *noncomposite* module uses newer memory technology, so fewer ICs are needed to reach the same storage capacity. In other words, if you encounter a high-density SIMM with only a few ICs on it, chances are that the SIMM is noncomposite.

Megabytes and memory layout

Now is a good time to introduce the idea of bytes and megabytes. Very simply, a *byte* is 8 bits (binary 1s and 0s), and a *megabyte* is one million of those bytes (1,048,576 bytes to be exact—but manufacturers often round down to the nearest million or so). The idea of megabytes (MB) is important when measuring memory in your PC. For example, if a SIMM is laid out as 1M by 8 bits, it has 1 MB. If the SIMM is laid out as 4M by 8 bits, it has 4 MB. Unfortunately, memory has not been laid out as 8 bits since the IBM XT.

More practical memory layouts involve 32-bit memory (for 486 and OverDrive processors), or 64-bit memory (for Pentium processors). When memory is wider, it is still measured in megabytes. For example, a 1M by 32-bit (4 bytes) SIMM would be 4 MB, while a 4M by 32-bit SIMM would be 16 MB. So when you go shopping for an 8-MB 72-pin SIMM, chances are you're getting a 2M by 32-bit memory module.

Memory Organization

The memory in your computer represents the result of evolution over several computer generations. Memory operation and handling is taken care of by your system's microprocessor, so as CPUs improved, memory-handling capabilities have improved as well. Today's microprocessors such as the Intel Pentium or Pentium Pro

Table 4-2. Pinout for a 72-pin SIMM

Pin	Description	Pin	Description
1	Ground	2	Data Bit 0
3	Data Bit 16	4	Data Bit 1
5	Data Bit 17	6	Data Bit 2
7	Data Bit 18	8	Data Bit 3
9	Data Bit 19	10	+5 Vdc
11	CAS Parity	12	Address Bit 0
13	Address Bit 1	14	Address Bit 2
15	Address Bit 3	16	Address Bit 4
17	Address Bit 5	18	Address Bit 6
19	Reserved	20	Data Bit 4
21	Data Bit 20	22	Data Bit 5
23	Data Bit 21	24	Data Bit 6
25	Data Bit 22	26	Data Bit 7
27	Data Bit 23	28	Address Bit 7
29	Block Select 0	30	+5 Vdc
31	Address Bit 8	32	Address Bit 9
33	RAS 3	34	RAS 2
35	Parity Bit 2	36	Parity Bit 0
37	Parity Bit 1	38	Parity Bit 3
39	Ground	40	CAS 0
41	CAS 2	42	CAS 3
43	CAS 1	44	RAS 0
45	RAS 1	46	Block Select 1
47	Write Enable	48	Reserved
49	Data Bit 8	50	Data Bit 24
51	Data Bit 9	52	Data Bit 25
53	Data Bit 10	54	Data Bit 26
55	Data Bit 11	56	Data Bit 27
57	Data Bit 12	58	Data Bit 28
59	+5 Vdc	60	Data Bit 29
61	Data Bit 13	62	Data Bit 30
63	Data Bit 14	64	Data Bit 31
65	Data Bit 15	66	Block Select 2
67	Presence Detect 0	68	Presence Detect 1
69	Presence Detect 2	70	Presence Detect 3
71	Block Select 3	72	Ground

are capable of addressing more than 4 GB of system memory—well beyond the levels of contemporary software applications. Unfortunately, the early PCs were not nearly so powerful. Older PCs could only address 1 MB of memory due to limitations of the 8088 microprocessor.

Since backward compatibility is so important to computer users, the drawbacks and limitations of older systems had to be carried forward into newer computers instead of being eliminated. Newer systems overcome their inherent limitations by adding different "types" of memory, along with the hardware and software to access the memory. This part of the chapter describes the three classic types of computer memory: conventional, extended, and expanded memory. This chapter also describes high memory concepts. Note that these memory types have nothing to do with the actual ICs in your system, but the way in which software *uses* the memory.

Conventional memory

Conventional memory is the traditional 640 kB assigned to the DOS memory area. The original PCs used microprocessors that could only address 1 MB of memory (called *real-mode memory* or *base memory*). Out of that 1 MB, portions of the memory must be set aside for basic system functions. BIOS code, video memory, interrupt vectors, and BIOS data are only some of the areas that require reserved memory. The remaining 640 kB become available to load and run your application, which can be any combination of executable code and data. The original PC only provided 512 kB for the DOS program area, but computer designers quickly learned that another 128 kB could be added to the DOS area while still retaining enough memory for overhead functions, so 512 kB became 640 kB.

Every IBM-compatible PC still provides a 640-kB base memory range, and most application programs continue to fit within that limit to ensure backward compatibility to older systems. However, the drawbacks to the 8088 CPU were soon apparent. More memory had to added to the computer for its evolution to continue. However, memory had to be added in a way that did not interfere with the conventional memory area.

Extended memory

The 80286 introduced in IBM's PC/AT was envisioned to overcome the 640-kB barrier by incorporating a *protected mode* of addressing. The 80286 can address up to 16 MB of memory in protected mode, while its successors (the 80386 and later) can handle 4 GB of protected-mode memory. Today, virtually all computer systems provide several megabytes of *extended memory*. Besides an advanced microprocessor, another key element for extended memory is *software*. Memory management software must be loaded in advance for the computer to access its extended memory. Microsoft's DOS 5.0 provides an extended memory manager utility, but there are other off-the-shelf utilities as well.

Unfortunately, DOS itself cannot make use of extended memory. You may fill the extended memory with data, but the executable code making up the program remains limited to the original 640 kB of base memory. Some programs written with DOS *extenders* can overcome the 640-kB limit, but the additional code needed for the extenders can make such programs a bit clunky. A DOS extender is basically a software module containing its own memory management code which is compiled into the final application program.

The DOS extender loads a program in real-mode memory. After the program is loaded, it switches program control to the protected-mode memory. When the program in protected mode needs to execute a DOS (real-mode) function, the DOS extender converts protected-mode addresses into real-mode addresses, copies any necessary program data from protected-mode to real-mode locations, switches the CPU to real-mode addressing, and carries out the function. The DOS extender then copies any results (if necessary) back to protected-mode addresses, switches the system to protected mode once again, and the program continues to run. This back-and-forth conversion overhead results in less-than-optimum performance compared to strictly real-mode programs.

With multiple megabytes of extended memory typically available, it is possible (but unlikely) that any one program will utilize all of the extended memory. Multiple programs that use extended memory must *not* attempt to utilize the same memory locations. If conflicts occur, a catastrophic system crash is almost inevitable. To prevent conflicts in extended memory, memory manager software can make use of three major industry standards: the *Extended Memory Specification* (XMS), the *Virtual Control Program Interface* (VCPI), or the *DOS Protected-Mode Interface* (DPMI). This chapter will not detail these standards, but you should know where they are used.

Expanded memory

Expanded memory is another popular technique used to overcome the traditional 640-kB limit of real-mode addressing. Expanded memory differs from extended memory in the way memory is used. Instead of trying to address physical memory locations outside of the conventional memory range as extended memory does, expanded memory blocks are switched into the base memory range where the CPU can access it in real mode. The original expanded memory specification (called the Lotus-Intel-Microsoft, LIM, or EMS specification) used 16-kB banks of memory which were mapped into a 64-kB range of real-mode memory existing just above the video memory range. Thus, four "blocks" of expanded memory could be dealt with simultaneously in the real mode.

Early implementations of expanded memory utilized special expansion boards that switched blocks of memory, but later CPUs that support memory mapping allowed expanded memory managers (EMMs or LIMs) to supply software-only solutions for 80386- and 80486-based machines. EMS/LIM 4.0 is the latest version of the expanded memory standard which handles up to 32 MB of memory. An expanded memory manager such as the DOS utility EMM386.EXE allows the extended memory sitting in your computer to emulate expanded memory. For most practical purposes, expanded memory is more useful than extended memory because its ability to map directly to the real mode allows support for program multitasking.

To use expanded memory, programs must be written specifically to take advantage of the function calls and subroutines needed to switch memory blocks. Functions are completely specified in the LIM/EMS 4.0 standard.

High DOS memory

The upper 384-kB of real-mode memory is not available to DOS because it is dedicated to handling memory requirements of the physical computer system. This is called the *high DOS memory range.* However, even the most advanced PCs do not use the entire 384 kB, so there is often a substantial amount of unused memory existing in your system's real-mode range. Late-model CPUs like the 80386 and 80486 can remap extended memory into the range unused by your system. Since this "found" memory space is not contiguous with your 640-kB DOS space, DOS application programs cannot use the space, but small independent drivers and TSRs (terminal and stay residents) *can* be loaded and run from this area. The advantage to using high DOS memory is that more of the 640-kB DOS range remains available for your application program. Memory management programs (such as the utilities found with DOS 5.0) are needed to locate and remap these memory "blocks."

High memory

There is a peculiar anomaly that occurs with CPUs supporting extended memory—they can access one *segment* (about 64 kB) of extended memory beyond the real-mode area. This capability arises because of the address line layout on late-model CPUs. As a result, the real-mode operation can access roughly 64 kB above the 1-MB limit. Like high DOS memory, this "found" 64 kB is not contiguous with the normal 640-kB DOS memory range, so DOS cannot use this high memory to load a DOS application, but device drivers and TSRs can be placed in high memory. DOS 5.0 is intentionally designed so that its 40 to 50 kB of code can be easily moved into this high memory area. With DOS loaded into high memory, an extra 40 to 50 kB or so will be available within the 640-kB DOS range.

Memory Considerations

Memory has become far more important than a place to store bits for the microprocessor. It has proliferated and specialized to the point where it is difficult to keep track of all the memory options and architectures that are available. This part of the chapter reviews established memory types, and explains some of the current memory architectures.

Memory speed and wait states

The PC industry is constantly struggling with the balance between price and performance. Higher prices usually bring higher performance, but low cost makes the PC appealing to more people. In terms of memory, cost-cutting typically involves using cheaper (slower) memory devices. Unfortunately, slow memory cannot deliver data to the CPU quickly enough, so the CPU must be made to wait until memory can catch up. All memory is rated in terms of speed—specifically *access time.* Access time is the delay between the time data in memory are successfully addressed to the point at which the data have been successfully delivered. For PC memory, access time is measured in nanoseconds (ns), and current memory offers access times of 50 to 60 ns; 70-ns memory is extremely common.

Often the question arises, "Can I use faster memory than the manufacturer recommends?" The answer to this question is almost always "yes," but there is rarely ever a performance benefit. As you will see in the following sections, memory and architectures are typically tailored for specific performance. Using memory that is faster should not hurt, but it costs more and will not produce a noticeable performance improvement. The only time such a tactic would be advised is when your current system is almost obsolete and you would want the new memory to be usable on a new, faster motherboard if you choose to upgrade the motherboard later on.

A *wait state* orders the CPU to pause for one clock cycle in order to give memory additional time to operate. Typical PCs use one wait state, though very old systems may require two. The latest PC designs with high-end memory or aggressive caching may be able to operate with no (zero) wait states. As you might imagine, a wait state is basically a waste of time, so more wait states result in lower system performance. Zero wait states allow optimum system performance. Table 4-3 illustrates the general relationship between CPUs, wait states, and memory speed. It is interesting to note that some of the fastest systems allow the most wait states. This flexibility lets the system support old, slow memory, but the resulting system performance would be so poor that there would be little point in using the system in the first place.

There are three classic means of selecting wait states. First, the number of wait states may be fixed (common in old XT systems). Wait states may be selected with one or more jumpers on the motherboard (typical of 286 and early 386 systems).

Table 4-3. CPUs, Wait States, and Memory Speed

CPU	Wait states	Memory access, ns
8088	1	200
8086	0	150
80286	1	150
80286	1	120
80286	0	85
80386SX	0-2	100
80386SX/DX	0-2	85
80386SX	0-2	80
80386DX	0-5	80
80386SX	0-2	70
80486DX	0-5	80
80486DX	0-5	70
80486SLC2	0-2	70
80486SLC3	0-2	70
80486SX	0-2	70
80486DX4	0-2	70
80486DX2	0-2	70
Pentium	0-5	60
Pentium	0-2	50

Current systems such as 486 and Pentium computers place the wait state control in the CMOS setup routine. You may have to look in an "advanced settings" area to find the entry. When optimizing a computer, you should be sure to set the minimum number of wait states.

Note: Setting too few wait states can cause the PC to behave erratically.

The meaning of "refresh"

The electrical signals placed in each DRAM storage cell must be replenished (or *refreshed*) periodically every few milliseconds. Without refresh, DRAM data will be lost. In principle, refresh requires that each storage cell be read and rewritten to the memory array. This is typically accomplished by reading and rewriting an entire row of the array at one time. Each row of bits is sequentially read into a sense/refresh amplifier (part of the DRAM IC), which basically recharges the appropriate storage capacitors, then rewrites each row bit to the array. In actual operation, a row of bits is automatically refreshed whenever an array row is selected. Thus, the entire memory array can be refreshed by reading each row in the array every few milliseconds.

The key to refresh is in the *way* DRAM is addressed. Unlike other memory ICs that supply all address signals to the IC simultaneously, a DRAM is addressed in a two-step sequence. The overall address is separated into a row (low) address and a column (high) address. Row address bits are placed on the DRAM address bus first, and the Row Address Select (RAS) line is pulsed logic 0 to multiplex the bits into the IC's address decoding circuitry. The low portion of the address activates an entire array row and causes each bit in the row to be sensed and refreshed. Logic 0s remain logic 0s, and logic 1s are recharged to their full value.

Column address bits are then placed on the DRAM address bus, and the Column Address Select (CAS) is pulsed to logic 0. The column portion of the address selects the appropriate bits within the chosen row. If a read operation is taking place, the selected bits pass through the data buffer to the data bus. During a write operation, the read/write line must be logic 0, and valid data must be available to the IC before CAS is strobed. New data bits are then placed in their corresponding locations in the memory array.

Even if the IC is not being accessed for reading or writing, the memory must *still* be refreshed to ensure data integrity. Fortunately, refresh can be accomplished by interrupting the microprocessor to run a refresh routine which simply steps through every row address in sequence (column addresses need not be selected for simple refresh). This row-only (or RAS only) refresh technique speeds the refresh process. Although refreshing DRAM every few milliseconds may seem like a constant aggravation, the computer can execute quite a few instructions before being interrupted for refresh. Refresh operations are generally handled by the chipset on your motherboard. Often, memory problems (especially "parity errors") which cannot be resolved by replacing a SIMM can be traced to a refresh fault on the motherboard.

Memory types

In order for a computer to work, the CPU must take program instructions and exchange data directly with memory. As a consequence, memory must keep pace with the CPU (or make the CPU wait for it to catch up). Now that processors are so incredibly fast (and getting faster), traditional memory architectures are being replaced by specialized memory devices that have been tailored to serve specific functions in the PC. As you upgrade and repair various systems, you will undoubtedly encounter new memory designations.

Dynamic random access memory (DRAM)   This remains the most recognized and common form of computer memory. DRAM achieves a good mix of speed and density while being relatively simple and inexpensive to produce—only a single transistor and capacitor is needed to hold a bit. Unfortunately, DRAM contents must be refreshed every few milliseconds, or the contents of each bit location will decay.

Static random access memory (SRAM)   The SRAM is also a classic memory design; it is even older than DRAM. SRAM does not require regular refresh operations and can be made to operate at access speeds that are much faster than DRAM. However, SRAM uses six transistors or more to hold a single bit. This reduces the density of SRAM and increases power demands (which is why SRAM was never adopted for general PC use in the first place). Still, the speed of SRAM has earned it a place as the PC's L2 (or external) cache.

Video random access memory (VRAM)   DRAM has been the traditional choice for video memory, but the ever-increasing demand for fast video information (i.e., high-resolution SVGA displays) requires a more efficient means of transferring data to and from video memory. Originally developed by Samsung Electronics, video RAM achieves speed improvements by using a "dual data bus" scheme. Ordinary RAM uses a single data bus—data enters or leaves the RAM through a single set of signals. Video RAM provides an "input" data bus and an "output" data bus. This allows data to be read from video RAM at the same time new information is being written to it. You should realize that the advantages of VRAM will only be realized on high-end video systems such as $1024 \times 768 \times 256$ (or higher) where you can get up to 40 percent more performance than a DRAM video adapter. Below that, you will see no perceivable improvement with a VRAM video adapter.

Fast-page-mode DRAM (FPMDRAM)   This is a popular twist on conventional DRAM. Typical DRAM access is accomplished in a fashion similar to reading from a book. A memory "page" is accessed first, and then the contents of that page can be located. The problem is that every access requires the DRAM to relocate the page. Fast-page-mode operation overcomes this delay by allowing the CPU to access multiple pieces of data on the same page without having to relocate the page every time—as long as the subsequent read or write cycle is on the previously located page, the FPDRAM can access the specific location on that page directly.

Enhanced DRAM (EDRAM)   This is another, lesser-known variation of the classic DRAM developed by Ramtron International and United Memories. First demonstrated in August 1994, the EDRAM eliminates an external cache by placing a small amount of SRAM (cache) into each EDRAM device. In essence, the cache is distributed within the system RAM, and as more memory is added to the PC, more cache is effectively added as well.

The internal construction of an EDRAM allows it to act like page-mode memory; if a subsequent read requests data that are in the EDRAM's cache (known as a *hit*), the data are made available in about 15 ns—roughly equal to the speed of a good external cache. If the subsequent read requests data that are not in the cache (called a *miss*), the data are accessed from the DRAM portion of memory in about 35 ns, which is much faster than ordinary DRAM.

Extended data out RAM (EDO RAM) EDO RAM is a relatively well-established variation to DRAM which extends the time which output data are valid—thus the word "extended." This is accomplished by modifying the DRAM's output buffer, which prolongs the time where read data are valid. The data will remain valid until a motherboard signal is received to release it. This eases timing constraints on the memory and allows a 15 to 30 percent improvement in memory performance with little real increase in cost. Because a new external signal is needed to operate EDO RAM, the motherboard must use a chipset designed to accommodate EDO. Intel's Triton chipset was one of the first to support EDO, though many chipsets (and most current motherboards) now support EDO. You should realize that EDO RAM can be used in non-EDO motherboards, but there will be no performance improvement.

Synchronous (or synchronized) DRAM (SDRAM) Typical memory can only transfer data during certain portions of a clock cycle. The SDRAM modifies memory operation so that outputs can be valid at *any* point in the clock cycle. By itself, this is not really significant, but SDRAM also provides a "pipeline burst" mode which allows a second access to begin before the current access is complete. This "continuous" memory access offers effective access speeds as fast as 10 ns, and can transfer data at up to 100 MB/s.

Cached DRAM (CDRAM) Like EDRAM, the CDRAM from Mitsubishi incorporates cache and DRAM on the same IC. This eliminates the need for an external (or L2) cache, and has the extra benefit of adding cache whenever RAM is added to the system. The difference is that CDRAM uses a "set-associative" cache approach which can be 15 to 20 percent more efficient than the EDRAM cache scheme. On the other hand, EDRAM offers better overall performance.

Rambus DRAM (RDRAM) Most of the memory alternatives so far have been variations of the same basic architecture. Rambus Inc. (joint developers of EDRAM) has created a new memory architecture called the Rambus Channel. A CPU or specialized IC is used as the master device, and the RDRAMs are used as slave devices. Data are then sent back and forth across the Rambus channel in 256-byte blocks. With a dual 250-MHz clock, the Rambus Channel can transfer data based on the timing of both clocks. This results in data transfer rates approaching 500 MB/s (roughly 2 ns access time).

The problem with RDRAM is that a Rambus Channel would require an extensive redesign to the current PC memory architecture—a move that most PC makers strenuously resist. As a result, you are most likely to see RDRAM in high-end, specialized computing systems. Still, as memory struggles to match the microprocessor, PC makers may yet embrace the Rambus approach for commercial systems.

Windows RAM (WRAM)   Samsung Electronics has recently introduced WRAM as a new video-specific memory device. WRAM uses multiple bit arrays connected with an extensive internal bus and high-speed registers that can transfer data almost continuously. Other specialized registers support attributes such as foreground color, background color, write-block control bits, and true-byte masking. Samsung claims data transfer rates of up to 640 MB/s—about 50 percent faster than VRAM—yet WRAM devices are cheaper than their VRAM counterparts. It is likely that WRAM will receive some serious consideration in the next few years.

Memory techniques

Rather than incur the added expense of specialized memory devices, PC makers often use inexpensive, well-established memory types in unique architectures designed to make the most of low-end memory. There are three popular architectures that you will probably encounter: paged memory, interleaved memory, and memory caching.

Paged memory   This architecture basically divides system RAM into small groups (or "pages") from 512 bytes to several kilobytes long. Memory management circuitry on the motherboard allows subsequent memory accesses on the same page to be accomplished with zero wait states. If the subsequent access takes place outside of the current page, one or more wait states may be added while the new page is found. This is identical in principle to FPM DRAM explained above. You will find page-mode architectures implemented on high-end 286, PS/2 (model 70 and 80), and many 386 systems.

Interleaved memory   This is a technique which provides better performance than paged memory. Simply put, interleaved memory combines two banks of memory into one. The first portion is even, while the second portion is odd—so memory is alternated between these two areas. This allows a memory access in the second portion to begin before the memory access in the first portion has finished. In effect, interleaving can double memory performance.

The problem with interleaving is that you must provide twice the amount of memory as matched pairs. Most PCs that employ interleaving will allow you to add memory one bank at a time, but interleaving will be disabled and system performance will suffer.

Memory caching   This is perhaps the most recognized form of memory enhancement architecture. Cache is a small amount (anywhere from 8 kB to 512 kB) of very fast SRAM which forms an interface between the CPU and ordinary DRAM. The SRAM typically operates on the order of 10 to 15 ns, which is fast enough to keep pace with a CPU using zero wait states. A *cache controller* IC on the motherboard keeps track of frequently accessed memory locations (as well as predicted memory locations), and copies those contents into cache. When a CPU reads from memory, it checks the cache first. If the needed contents are present in cache (called a *cache hit*), the data are read at zero wait states. If the needed contents are not present in the cache (known as a *cache miss*), the data must be read directly from DRAM at a penalty of one or more wait states. A well-designed caching system can achieve a hit ratio of 95 percent or more—in other words, memory can run *without* wait states 95 percent of the time.

There are two levels of cache in the contemporary PC. CPUs from the 80486 onward have a small internal cache, known as *L1 cache,* while external cache (SRAM installed as DIPs on the motherboard) is referred to as *L2 cache.* The 80386 CPUs have no internal cache (though IBM's 386SLC offers 8 kB of L1 cache). Most 80486 CPUs provide an 8-kB internal cache. Pentium processors are fitted with two 8-kB internal caches—one for data and one for instructions.

Shadow memory   ROM devices (whether the BIOS ROM on your motherboard or a ROM IC on an expansion board) are frustratingly slow, with access times often exceeding several hundred nanoseconds. ROM access then requires a large number of wait states which slow down the system's performance. This problem is compounded because the routines stored in BIOS (especially the video BIOS ROM on the video board) are some of the most frequently accessed memory in your computer.

Beginning with the 80386-class computers, some designs employed a memory technique called *shadowing.* ROM contents are loaded into an area of fast RAM during system initialization, then the computer maps the fast RAM into memory locations used by the ROM devices. Whenever ROM routines must be accessed during run time, information is taken from the "shadow ROM" instead of the actual ROM IC. The ROM performance can be improved by at least 300 percent.

Shadow memory is also useful for ROM devices that do not use the full available data bus width. For example, a 16-bit computer system may hold an expansion board containing an 8-bit ROM IC. The system would have to access the ROM not once but *twice* to extract a single 16-bit word. If the computer is a 32-bit machine, that 8-bit ROM would have to be addressed four times to make a complete 32-bit word. You can imagine the hideous system delays that can be encountered. Loading the ROM to shadow memory in advance virtually eliminates such delays. Shadowing can usually be turned on or off through the system's setup routines.

The Issue of Parity

As you might imagine, it is vital that data and program instructions remain error-free. Even one incorrect bit due to electrical noise or a component failure can crash the PC, corrupt drive information, cause video problems, or result in a myriad of other faults. PC designers approached the issue of memory integrity by employing a technique known as *parity* (the same technique used to check serial data).

The parity principle

The basic idea behind parity is simple—each byte written to memory is checked, and a ninth bit is added to the byte as a checking (or "parity") bit. When a memory address is later read by the CPU, memory-checking circuitry on the motherboard will calculate the *expected* parity bit, and compare it to the bit actually read from memory. In this fashion, the PC can continuously diagnose system memory by checking the integrity of its data. If the read parity bit matches the expected parity bit, the data (and indirectly the RAM) are assumed to be valid, and the CPU can go on its way. If the read and expected parity bits do not match, the system registers an error and halts. Every byte is given a parity bit, so for a 32-bit PC, there will be 4 parity bits for every address. For a 64-bit PC, there are 8 parity bits, and so on.

Even versus odd

There are two types of parity—even and odd. With *even parity,* the parity bit is set to 0 if there are an even number of 1s already in the corresponding byte (keeping the number of 1s even). If there is not an even number of 1s in the byte, the even parity bit will be 1 (making the number of 1s even). With *odd parity,* the parity bit is set to 0 if there is an odd number of 1s already in the corresponding byte (keeping the number of 1s odd). If there is not an odd number of 1s in the byte, the odd parity bit will be 1 (making the number of 1s odd).

Although even and odd parity work opposite of one another, both schemes serve exactly the same purpose and have the same probability of catching a bad bit. The memory device itself does not care at all about what type of parity is being used—it just needs to have the parity bits available. The use of parity (and the choice of even or odd) is left up to the motherboard's memory control circuit.

The problems with parity

While parity has proven to be a simple and cost-effective means of continuously checking memory, there are two significant limitations. First, though parity can detect an error, it cannot correct the error because there is no way to tell which bit has gone bad. This is why a system simply halts when a parity error is detected. Second, parity is unable to detect multibit errors. For example, if a 1 accidentally becomes a 0 and a 0 accidentally becomes a 1 within the same byte, parity conditions will still be satisfied. Fortunately, the probability of a multibit error in the same byte is extremely remote.

Circumventing parity

Over the last few years, parity has come under fire from PC makers and memory manufacturers alike. Opponents claim that the rate of parity errors due to hardware (RAM) faults is very small, and that the expense of providing parity bits in a memory-hungry marketplace just isn't justified any more. There is some truth to this argument considering that the parity technique is over 15 years old and has serious limitations.

As a consequence, a few motherboard makers have begun removing parity support from their low-end motherboards, and others are providing motherboards that will function with or without parity (usually set in CMOS or with a motherboard jumper). Similarly, some memory makers are now providing nonparity and "fake" parity memory as cheaper alternatives to conventional parity memory.

Nonparity memory simply foregoes the ninth bit. For example, a nonparity SIMM would be designated x8 or x32 (i.e., 4 Mx8 or 4 Mx32). If the SIMM supports parity, it will be designated x9 or x36 (i.e., 4 Mx9 or 4 Mx36). *Fake parity* is a bit more devious; the ninth bit is replaced by a simple (and very inexpensive) parity generator chip which "looks" like a normal DRAM IC. When a read cycle occurs, the parity chip on the SIMM provides the proper parity bit to the motherboard *all the time*. In effect, memory is lying to the motherboard.

While there is a cost savings, your memory is left with no means of error checking. It's a little like driving a car without a speedometer—you could go for miles without a problem, but sooner or later you'll cross a speed trap. In actual practice, you can go indefinitely without parity, but when an error *does* occur, having parity in place can save you immeasurable frustration. Unless the lowest cost is your absolute highest priority, it is recommended that you spend the extra few dollars for parity RAM.

Abuse and detection of fake memory

Another potential problem with fake parity memory is fraud. There have already been reported instances where memory was purchased as "parity" at full price—only to find that the parity ICs were actually parity generators. This was determined by dissecting the IC packages and finding that the IC die in the parity position did not match the IC dies in the other bit positions. The buyer doesn't know because parity generators are packaged to look just like DRAM ICs, and there is no other obvious way to tell just by looking at the SIMM or other memory device. System diagnostic software also cannot detect the presence of parity memory versus fake memory.

There are really only two ways to protect yourself from fake memory fraud. First, industry experts indicate that many fake parity ICs (the parity generators) are marked with designations such as BP, VT, GSM, or MPEC. If you find that one out of every nine ICs on your SIMM carries such a designation (or any other designation not matching the first eight), you may have a fraud situation. Of course, the first step in all justice is a "benefit of the doubt," so contact the organization you purchased the memory from—they may simply have sent the wrong SIMMs.

Second, you can check the IC dies themselves. Unfortunately, this requires you to carefully dissect several IC packages on the SIMM and compare the IC dies—resulting in the destruction of the memory device(s). If the ninth die looks radically different (usually much simpler) than the other eight, you likely have fake parity. A nondestructive way to check the SIMM is to use a SIMM checker (if you have access to one) with a testing routine specially written to test parity memory. If the SIMM works but the parity IC test fails (i.e., the tester cannot write to the parity memory), chances are you have fake parity.

If you determine that you have been sold fake parity memory in place of real parity memory and you cannot get any satisfaction from the seller, you are encouraged to contact the Attorney General in the seller's state and convey your information to them. After all, if you're being cheated, chances are a lot of other people are too—and they probably don't even know it.

Alternative error correction

Although this book supports the use of parity, it recognizes its old age. In the world of personal computing, parity is an ancient technique. Frankly, it could easily be replaced by more sophisticated techniques such as *error correction code* (ECC) or *ECC-on-SIMM* (EOS). ECC (which is already being employed in high-end PCs and file servers) uses a mathematical process in conjunction with the motherboard's memory controller and appends a number of ECC bits to the data bits. When data are read back from memory, the ECC memory controller checks the ECC data read back as well. ECC has two important advantages over parity. It can actually *correct* single-bit errors on the fly without the user ever knowing there's been a problem. In addition, ECC can successfully detect 2-bit, 3-bit, and 4-bit errors, which makes it an incredibly powerful memory management tool. If a rare multibit error is detected, ECC is unable to correct it, but it will be reported and the system will halt.

It takes 7 or 8 bits at each address to successfully implement ECC. For a 32-bit system, you will need to use ×39 or ×40 SIMMs (i.e., 8 Mx39 or 8 Mx40). These are relatively new designations, so you should at least recognize them as ECC SIMMs if you encounter them. As an alternative, some 64-bit systems use two 36-bit SIMMs for a total of 72 bits—64 bits for data and 8 bits (which would otherwise be for parity) for ECC information.

EOS is a relatively new (and rather expensive) technology which places ECC functions on the memory module itself, but provides ECC results as parity—so while the memory module runs ECC, the motherboard continues to see parity. This is an interesting experiment, but it is unlikely that EOS will gain significant market share. Systems that use parity can be fitted with parity memory much less expensively than EOS memory.

Memory Installation and Options

Installing memory is not nearly as easy as it used to be. Certainly, today's memory modules just plug right in, but deciding which memory to buy, how much (or how little) to buy, and how to use existing memory in new systems, presents technicians with a bewildering variety of choices. This part of the chapter illustrates the important ideas behind choosing and using memory.

Getting the right amount

"How much memory do I need?" This is a question which has plagued the PC industry ever since the 80286 CPU broke the 1-MB memory barrier. With more memory, additional programs and data can be run by the CPU at any given time—which indirectly helps to improve the productivity of the particular PC. The problem is cost. Typical DRAM is running around $15/MB (U.S.)—compared with about $0.50/MB (U.S.) for hard drive space. The goal of good system configuration is to install enough memory to support the PC's routine tasks. Installing too much memory means that you've spent money for PC resources that just remain idle. Installing too little memory results in programs that will not run (typical under DOS), or poor system performance because of extensive swap file use (typical under Windows).

So how much memory *is* enough? The fact of the matter is that "enough" is an ever-changing figure. DOS systems of the early 1980s (8088/8086) worked just fine with 1 MB. By the mid-1980s (80286), DOS systems with 2 MB were adequate. Into the late 1980s (80386), Windows 3.0 and 3.1 needed 4 MB. As the 1990s got under way (80486), Windows systems with 8 MB were common (even DOS applications were using 4 to 6 MB).

Today, with Pentium systems and Windows 95, 16MB is considered to be a minimum requirement, and 32 MB systems are readily available. For today, this is the benchmark that you should use for general-purpose home and office systems. But by the end of the decade, 64-MB systems will probably be the norm. And this is not to say that 32-MB systems are the pinnacle of performance. Today's file servers and industrial-strength design packages are employing 64 to 128 MB of RAM—sometimes more.

Filling banks

Another point of confusion is the idea of a bank. Most memory devices are installed in sets (or banks). The amount of memory in the bank can vary depending on how much you wish to add, but there must always be enough data bits in the bank to fill each bit position. Table 4-4 illustrates a relationship between data bits and banks for the range of typical CPUs.

For example, the 8086 is a 16-bit microprocessor (2 bytes). This means that 2 extra bits are required for parity, giving a total of 18 bits. Thus, one bank is 18 bits wide. You may fill the bank by adding eighteen 1-bit DIPs, or two 30-pin SIMMs. As another example, an 80486DX is a 32-bit CPU, so 36 bits are needed to fill a bank (32 bits plus 4 parity bits). If you use 30-pin SIMMs, you will need four to fill a bank. If you use 72-pin SIMMs, only one is needed. Note that the size of the memory in megabytes does not really matter—as long as the *entire* bank is filled.

Bank requirements

There is more to filling a memory bank than just installing the right number of bits. Memory amount, memory matching, and bank order are three additional considerations. First, you must use the proper memory amount that will bring you to the expected volume of total memory. Suppose a Pentium system has 8 MB already installed in Bank 0, and you need to put another 8 MB into the system in Bank 1. Table 4-4 shows that two 72-pin SIMMs are needed to fill a bank, but each SIMM

Table 4-4. CPUs versus Memory Bank Size

CPU	Data width (with parity), bits	×MB by 1 DIPs	30-pin SIMMs	72-pin SIMMs
8088	9	9	1	—
8086	18	18	2	—
80286	18	—	2	1 (2 banks)
80386SX, SL, SLC	18	—	2	1 (2 banks)
80386DX	36	—	4	1
80486SLC, SLC2	18	—	2	1 (2 banks)
80486DX, SX, DX2, DX4	36	—	4	1
Pentium	64	—	8	2

need only be 1M. Remember from the discussion of megabytes that a 1M × 36-bit (with parity) device is 4 MB. Since two such SIMMs are needed to fill a bank, the total would be 8 MB. When added to the 8 MB already in the system, the total would be 16 MB.

How about another example? Suppose the same 8 MB is already installed in your Pentium system, and you want to add 16 MB to Bank 1 rather than 8 MB (bringing the total system memory to 24 MB). In that case, you could use two 2M 72-pin SIMMs where 2M × 36 is 8 MB (with parity) per SIMM. Two 8-MB SIMMs yield 16 MB, bringing the system total to (16 MB + 8 MB) or 24 MB.

Now for a curve. Suppose you want to outfit that Pentium as a network server with 128 MB of RAM. Remember that there's already 8 MB in Bank 0, which means there's only Bank 1 available. Since the largest commercially available SIMMs are 8M × 36 (32 MB with parity), you can only add up to 64 MB to Bank 1 (for a system total of 72 MB. To get around this, you should *remove* the existing 1M × 36 SIMMs in Bank 0, and fill both Bank 0 and Bank 1 with 8M × 36 SIMMs which would put 64 MB in Bank 0, and 64 MB in Bank 1, yielding 128 MB in total.

Another bank requirement demands *memory matching,* using SIMMs of the same size and speed within a bank. For example, when adding multiple SIMMs to a bank, each SIMM must be rated for the same access speed, and share the same memory configuration (i.e., 2M × 36).

Finally, you must follow the *bank order.* For example, fill Bank 0 first, then Bank 1, then Bank 2, and so on. Otherwise, memory will not be contiguous within the PC, and CMOS will not recognize the additional RAM.

Recycling Older Memory Devices

Given the relatively high cost of PC memory, it is only natural that users and technicians alike would choose to reuse memory as much as possible when systems are upgraded or replaced. It is a simple matter to reuse memory—just as you would reuse hard drives or video boards. But there are some special issues to consider before you make plans to transfer memory from one system to another.

Memory speed

The goal of memory is to keep pace with the microprocessor using a minimum of wait states. It is *possible* to place a 100 ns SIMM in a Pentium system, but the wait states required to allow this awful mismatch would negate any benefits from the advanced microprocessor. As a consequence, it is most effective to use memory that is fast enough to handle the CPU in the system that will be *receiving* the memory. Table 4-3 shows typical memory speeds for various microprocessors. It is possible to use memory if the speed is *faster* than the minimum requirement, but all the memory in the bank should be the same speed. Ordinarily, there is no reason to buy memory that is faster than necessary—no additional benefit is realized by the system. The only time it might be advisable to invest in faster memory is if you know in advance that the memory will eventually be transferred to another system.

Memory type

You should also be sure to use the same type of memory (i.e., EDO, FPM, SDRAM, and so on). For example, if your motherboard is designed to use EDO RAM, and you have EDO RAM already installed, you should be sure to install more EDO RAM. Using other types of RAM may cause the system to malfunction.

SIMM stackers

Although your memory type should be able to fit into the new computer, if it won't, there are ways to make it fit. One of the most popular memory adapters is the SIMM stacker. These devices are actually known by a variety of trade names, but all allow you to convert four 30-pin SIMMs into a 72-pin SIMM frame. However, there are two drawbacks with SIMM stackers.

Cramped quarters SIMM adapter products take up serious amounts of space. Remember that the adapter snaps into the SIMM socket, and SIMMs attach to the adapter. As a result, the filled SIMM adapter looks a bit like a tree with branches. This is rarely a problem when SIMM sockets are placed side to side, but with several banks close together, multiple SIMM sockets may interfere with one another.

Timing penalty Timing is everything for memory, and with signals traveling on the order of nanoseconds, the very length of a printed signal run can adversely impact system performance. Generally speaking, you can expect access times to be increased by 10 ns or so when using a SIMM adapter. This is not a problem when the memory is measurably faster than needed. But if your memory speed is on the border, a SIMM adapter may necessitate an additional wait state.

Mixing "composite" and "noncomposite" SIMMs

Most ordinary 30-pin SIMMs use nine ICs (eight for data and one for parity). From time to time, you may encounter SIMMs with just a few ICs (usually three). The composite SIMM (with nine ICs) is older, using less-dense memory. The noncomposite SIMM (with three or so ICs) generally uses newer memory devices. In theory, it should be possible to mix composite and noncomposite SIMMs in the same bank or in the same system. However, there have been system problems reported when this happens. As a rule, you can try mixing these two generations of memory, but if you encounter memory problems with the system later on, remove either memory type and see if the problem goes away.

Remounting and rebuilding memory

Memory "recycling" has taken another more unexpected turn—some small companies are actually taking older memory devices and remounting them on SIMMs and other memory structures. In this way, you can use DIPs that are remounted on a SIMM. For example, a company called Autotime in Portland, Oregon, will remove memory devices from one SIMM and install them on a SIMM that you need (i.e., remove the ICs from four 1-MB 30-pin SIMMs and install and test them on one 4-MB 72-pin SIMM).

Memory Troubleshooting

Unfortunately, even the best memory devices fail from time to time. An accidental static discharge during installation, incorrect installation, a poor system configuration, operating system problems, and even outright failures due to old age can cause memory problems. This part of the chapter looks at some of the troubles that plague memory devices and offers advice on how to deal with them.

Memory test equipment

If you are working in a repair-shop environment or plan to be testing a substantial number of memory devices, you should consider acquiring some specialized test equipment. A memory tester, such as the SIMCHECK from Innoventions, Inc. (Fig. 4-5), is a modular microprocessor-based system that can perform a thorough, comprehensive test of various SIMMs and indicate the specific IC that has failed (if any). The system can be configured to work with specific SIMMs by installing an appropriate adaptor module like the one shown in Fig. 4-6. Intelligent testers work automatically and show the progress and results of their examinations on a multiline LCD. Guesswork is totally eliminated from memory testing.

Single ICs such as DIPs and SIPs can be tested using a single-chip plug-in module. The static RAM checker illustrated in Fig. 4-7 is another test bed for checking high-performance static RAM components in a DIP package. Both Innoventions test devices work together to provide a full-featured test system. Specialized tools can be an added expense—but no more so than an oscilloscope or other piece of useful test equipment. The return on your investment is less time wasted in the repair, and fewer parts to replace.

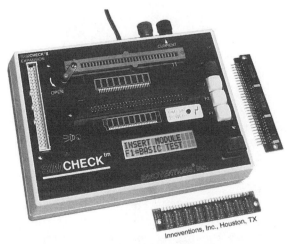

Innoventions, Inc., Houston, TX

4-5 An Innoventions SIMCHECK memory module tester.

4-6 A SIMCHECK adapter for PS/2 modules.

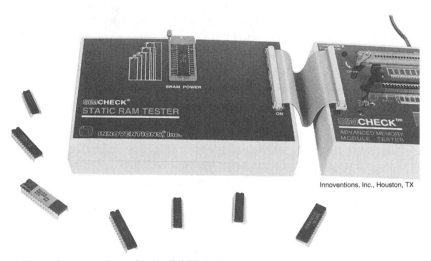

4-7 An Innoventions Static RAM tester.

Repairing SIMM sockets

If there is one weak link in the architecture of a SIMM, it is the socket which connects it to the motherboard. Ideally, the SIMM should sit comfortably in the SIMM socket, then gently snap back—held in place by two clips on either side of the socket. In actual practice, you really have to push that SIMM to get it into place. Taking it out again is just as tricky. As a result, it is not uncommon for a SIMM socket to break and render your extra memory unusable.

The best ("textbook") solution is to remove the SIMM socket and install a new one. Clearly there are some problems with this tactic. First, removing the old socket will require you to remove the motherboard, desolder the broken socket, then solder in a new socket (which you can buy from a full-feature electronics store such as DigiKey). In the hands of a skilled technician with the right tools, this is not so hard. But the PC runs of a computer motherboard are extremely delicate, and the slightest amount of excess heat can easily destroy the sensitive, multilayer connections.

Fortunately, there are some tricks that might help you. If either of the SIMM clips have bent or broken, you can usually make use of a medium-weight rubber band that is about 1 in shorter than the SIMM. Wrap the rubber band around the SIMM and socket, and the rubber band should do a fair job holding the SIMM in place. If any part of the socket should break, it can be repaired (or at least reinforced) with a good-quality epoxy. If you choose to use epoxy, be sure to work in a ventilated area and allow plenty of time for the epoxy to dry.

Contact corrosion

Here's a tip to tuck away for future reference. Corrosion can occur on SIMM contacts if the SIMM contact metal is not the same as the socket. This will eventually cause contact (and memory) problems. As a rule, check that the metal on the socket contact is the same as the SIMM contacts (usually tin or gold). You may be able get around the problem in the short term by cleaning corrosion off the contacts manually using a cotton swab and good electronics-grade contact cleaner. In the meantime, if you discover that your memory and connectors have dissimilar metals, you may be able to get the memory seller to exchange the SIMMs.

Parity errors

As you learned earlier in this chapter, parity is an important part of a computer's self checking capability. Errors in memory will cause the system to halt rather than continue blindly along with a potentially catastrophic error. But it is not just faulty memory that causes parity errors. Parity can also be influenced by your system's configuration. Here are the major causes of parity problems:

- One or more memory bits is intermittent or has failed entirely.
- Poor connections between the SIMM and socket.
- Too few wait states entered in BIOS (memory is too slow for the CPU).
- An intermittent failure or other fault has occurred in the power supply.
- A bug, computer virus, or other rogue software is operating.
- A fault has occurred in the memory controller IC or BIOS.

When you are faced with a parity error after an upgrade, you should suspect a problem with wait states, so check that first. If the wait states are correct, systematically remove each SIMM, clean the contacts, and reseat each SIMM. If the errors continue, try removing one bank of SIMMs at a time (chances are that the memory is bad). You may have to relocate memory so that Bank 0 remains filled. When the error disappears, the memory you removed is likely defective.

When parity errors occur spontaneously (with no apparent cause), you should clean and reinstall each SIMM *first* to eliminate the possibility of bad contacts. Next, check the power supply outputs. Low or noisy outputs may allow random bit errors. You may have to upgrade the supply if it is overloaded. Try booting the system "clean" from a write-protected floppy disk to eliminate the possibility of buggy software or computer viruses. If the problem persists, suspect a memory defect.

Installation symptoms

Symptom 1: New memory is installed, but the system refuses to recognize the new memory   New memory installation has always presented some unique problems, since different generations of PC deal with new memory differently. The oldest PCs require you to set jumpers or DIP switches in order to recognize new blocks of memory. The vintage 286 and 386 systems (i.e., a PS/2) use a setup diskette to tell CMOS about the PC's configuration (including new memory). More recent 386 and 486 systems incorporate an "installed memory" setting into a CMOS setup utility in BIOS. Late-model 486 and Pentium systems actually "autodetect" installed memory each time the system is booted (so it need not be entered in the CMOS setup).

Also check that an correct bank has been filled properly. The PC may not recognize any additional memory unless an entire bank has been filled, and the bank is next in order (i.e., Bank 0, then Bank 1, and so on). You may wish to check the PC's user manual for any unique rules or limitations in the particular motherboard.

Troubleshooting classic AT memory

Like the XT, IBM's PC/AT was the leader of the 80286 generation. Since there was only one model (at the time), ATs use some specific error messages to pinpoint memory (RAM or ROM) problems on the motherboard, as well as in its standard memory expansion devices. The 200 series error codes represent system memory errors (Table 4-5). ATs present memory failures in the format: AAXXXX YYYY 20x. The 10-digit code can be broken down to indicate the specific system bank and IC

Table 4-5. 200-Series Error Codes

201	Memory error (physical location will likely be displayed)
202	Memory address line 0–15 error
203	Memory address line 16–23 error; line 16–31 error (MCA)
204	Memory remapped to compensate for error (PS/2)
205	Error in first 128K (PS/2 ISA) of RAM
207	BIOS ROM failure
210	System board memory parity error
211	Error in first 64K of RAM (MCA)
212	Watchdog timer error
213	DMA bus arbitration time-out
215	Memory address error; 64K on daughter/SIP 2 failed (70)
216	Memory address error; 64K on daughter/SIP 1 failed (70)
221	ROM to RAM copy (shadowing) failed (MCA)
225	Wrong speed memory on system board (MCA)
230	Memory on motherboard and adapter board overlaps
231	Noncontiguous adapter memory installed
235	Stuck data line on memory module
241	Memory module 2 failed
251	Memory module 3 failed

number, although the particular bit failure is not indicated. The first two digits (AA) represent the defective *bank,* while the last four digits (YYYY) show the defective *IC number.* It is then a matter of finding and replacing the faulty DIP IC. Table 4-6 shows a set of error codes for early AT-class computers. For example, suppose an IBM PC/AT displayed the error message 05xxxxxx 0001 201 (we don't care about the x's). That message would place the error in IC 0 of Bank 1 on the AT's system memory.

Other classic memory errors

Symptom 1: You see the number 164 **displayed on the monitor**   This is a memory size error—the amount of memory found during the POST does not match the amount of memory listed in the AT's CMOS setup. Run the AT CMOS system setup routine on the setup diskette. Make sure that the listed memory amount matches the actual memory amount. If memory has been added or removed from the system, you will have to adjust the figure in the CMOS setup to reflect that change. If CMOS setup parameters do not remain in the system after power is removed, try replacing the battery or CMOS/RTC IC.

Symptom 2: You see an INCORRECT MEMORY SIZE **message displayed on the monitor**   This message can be displayed if the CMOS system setup is incorrect or if there is an actual memory failure that is not caught with a numerical 200-series code. Check your CMOS system setup as described in Symptom 1 and correct the setup if necessary. If the error persists, there is probably a failure in some portion of RAM.

Without a numerical code, it can be difficult to find the exact problem location, so adopt a divide-and-conquer strategy. Remove all expansion memory from the system, alter the CMOS setup to reflect base memory (system board) only, and retest the system. If the problem disappears, the fault is in some portion of expansion memory. If the problem still persists, you know the trouble is likely in your base (system board) memory. Take a known-good RAM IC and systematically swap RAM ICs until you locate the defective device. If you have access to a memory tester, the process will be much faster.

If you successfully isolate the problem to a memory expansion board, you can adopt the same strategy for the board(s). Return one board at a time to the system (and update the CMOS setup to keep track of available memory). When the error message reappears, you will have found the defective board. Use a known-good RAM IC and begin a systematic swapping process until you have found the defective IC.

Symptom 3: You see a ROM ERROR **message displayed on your monitor** To guarantee the integrity of system ROM, a checksum error test is performed as part of the POST. If this error occurs, one or more ROM locations may be faulty. Your only alternative here is to replace the system BIOS ROM(s) and retest the system.

Troubleshooting contemporary memory errors

Since the introduction of 286-class computers, the competition among motherboard manufacturers, as well as the rapid advances in memory technology, has resulted in a tremendous amount of diversity in the design and layout of memory systems.

Table 4-6. Classic AT Error Codes

AAXXXXYYYY 20x: Memory Failure

AA	Board	Bank
00 01 02 03	Motherboard	0
04 05 06 07	Motherboard	1
08 09	128-kB memory expansion	n/a
10 11 12 13	1st 512-kB memory adapter	0
14 15 16 17	1st 512-kB memory adapter	1
18 19 1A 1B	2nd 512-kB memory adapter	0
1C 1D 1E 1F	2nd 512-kB memory adapter	1
20 21 22 23	3rd 512-kB memory adapter	0
24 25 26 27	3rd 512-kB memory adapter	1
28 29 2A 2B	4th 512-kB memory adapter	0
2C 2D 2E 2F	4th 512-kB memory adapter	1
30 31 32 33	5th 512-kB memory adapter	0
34 35 36 37	5th 512-kB memory adapter	1

YYYY	Failed IC	YYYY	Failed IC
0000	Parity IC	0100	8
0001	0	0200	9
0002	1	0400	10
0004	2	0800	11
0008	3	1000	12
0010	4	2000	13
0020	5	4000	14
0040	6	8000	15
0080	7		

Although the basic concepts of memory operation remain unchanged, every one of the hundreds of computer models manufactured today use slightly different memory arrangements. Today's PCs also hold much more RAM than XT and early AT systems.

As a consequence of this trend, specific numerical (bank and bit) error codes have long-since been rendered impractical in newer systems where megabytes can be stored in just a few ICs. The 386, 486, and today's Pentium-based computers use a series of generic error codes. The *address* of a fault is always presented, but there is no attempt made to correlate the fault's address to a physical IC. Fortunately, today's memory systems are so small and modular that trial-and-error isolation can often be performed rapidly. Let's look at some typical errors.

Symptom 1: You see an XXXX OPTIONAL ROM BAD CHECKSUM = YYYY **error message on your monitor**   Part of the POST sequence checks for the presence of any other ROMs in the system. When another ROM is located, a checksum test is performed to check its integrity. This error message indicates that the external ROM (such as an SCSI adapter or video BIOS) has checked bad, or its address conflicts with another device in the system. In either case, initialization cannot continue.

If you have just installed a new peripheral device when this error occurs, try changing the device's ROM address jumpers to resolve the conflict. If the problem remains, remove the peripheral board; the fault should disappear. Try the board on another PC. If the problem continues on another PC, the adapter (or its ROM) may be defective. If this error has occurred spontaneously, remove one peripheral board at a time and retest the system until you isolate the faulty board, then replace the faulty board (or just replace its ROM if possible).

Symptom 2: You may see any one of the following general RAM errors:

```
Memory address line failure at XXXX, read YYYY, expecting
ZZZZ

Memory data line failure at XXXX, read YYYY, expecting
ZZZZ

Memory high address failure at XXXX, read YYYY, expecting
ZZZZ

Memory logic failure at XXXX, read YYYY, expecting ZZZZ

Memory odd/even logic failure at XXXX, read YYYY,
expecting ZZZZ

Memory parity failure at XXXX, read YYYY, expecting ZZZZ

Memory read/write failure at XXXX, read YYYY, expecting
ZZZZ
```

Each of the errors shown above is a general RAM error message indicating a problem in base or extended or expanded RAM. The code XXXX is the failure segment address—an offset address may be included. The word YYYY is what was read back from the address, and ZZZZ is the word that was expected. The difference between these read and expected words is what precipitated the error. In general, these errors indicate that at least one base RAM IC (if you have RAM soldered to the motherboard) or at least one SIMM has failed. A trial-and-error approach is usually the least-expensive route in finding the problem. First, reseat each SIMM and retest the system to be sure that each SIMM is inserted and secured properly. Rotate a known-good SIMM through each occupied SIMM socket in sequence. If the error disappears when the known-good SIMM is in a slot, the old SIMM that had been displaced is probably faulty. You can go on to use specialized SIMM troubleshooting equipment to identify the defective IC, but such equipment is rather expensive unless you intend to repair a large volume of SIMMs to the IC level.

If the problem remains unchanged even though every SIMM has been checked, the error is probably in the motherboard RAM or RAM support circuitry. Run a thorough system diagnostic if possible, and check for failures in other areas of the motherboard that affect memory (such as the interrupt controller, cache controller, DMA controller, or memory management chips). If the problem prohibits a software diagnostic, use a POST board and try identifying any hexadecimal error code. If a support IC is identified, you can replace the defective IC or replace the motherboard outright. If RAM continues to be the problem, try replacing the motherboard RAM (or replace the entire motherboard) and retest the system.

Symptom 3: You see a CACHE MEMORY FAILURE - DISABLING CACHE **error displayed on your monitor**   The cache system has failed. The tag RAM, cache logic, or cache memory on your motherboard is defective. Your best course is to replace the cache RAM IC(s). If the problem persists, try replacing the cache logic or tag RAM (or replace the entire motherboard). You will probably need a schematic diagram or a detailed block diagram of your system in order to locate the cache memory IC(s).

Symptom 4: You see a DECREASING   AVAILABLE   MEMORY **message displayed on your monitor**   This is basically a confirmation message that indicates a failure has been detected in extended or expanded memory, and that all memory after the failure has been disabled to allow the system to continue operating (although at a substantially reduced level). Your first step should be to reseat each SIMM and ensure that they are properly inserted and secured. Next, take a known-good SIMM and step through each occupied SIMM slot until the problem disappears. The SIMM that had been removed is the faulty SIMM. Keep in mind that you may have to alter the system's CMOS setup parameters as you move memory around the machine (an incorrect setup can cause problems during system initialization).

5
CHAPTER

Floppy Disk Drives

The ability to interchange programs and data between various computers is a fundamental requirement of almost every computer system. It was this kind of file exchange compatibility that helped rocket IBM PCs into everyday use and spurred the growth of the personal computer industry in the 1980s. A standardized recording medium and file structure also breathed life into the fledgling software industry by allowing software developers to create and distribute programs and data to a mass market of users of compatible computers. The mechanism that allowed this phenomenal compatibility is the *floppy disk drive* (Fig. 5-1).

A floppy disk drive (also called a floppy drive or FDD) is one of the least expensive and most reliable forms of mass storage ever used in computer systems. Virtually every one of the millions of personal computers sold every year

NEC Technologies, Inc.

5-1 Underside view of an NEC floppy drive.

incorporates at least one floppy drive. Most notebook and laptop computers also offer a single floppy drive. Not only are floppy drives useful for maintaining file compatibility between systems, but the advantage of a removable medium (the floppy disk itself) makes floppy drives an almost intuitive backup system. Although floppy drives have evolved through a number of iterations from 8 in (20.32 cm) to 5.25 in (13.34 cm) to 3.5 in (8.89 cm) their basic components and operating principles have changed very little. This book looks at 5.25-in (13.34-cm) and 3.5-in (8.89-cm) drives.

The Disks

Before you jump right into a detailed discussion of drive construction and operation, it is important that you have an understanding of the medium and become familiar with magnetic recording principles. One of the intriguing aspects of floppy drives is that the drive mechanism itself does not permanently retain any information. It is the medium that is placed inside the drive which actually contains useful information. In the case of floppy drives, the medium consists of a small, thin plastic disk (usually 3-mil Mylar) which is coated on both sides with a thin layer of sensitive magnetic material.

5.25-in (13.34-cm) disks

The 5.25-in (13.34 cm) diskette is shown in Fig. 5-2. The outer shell (actually 13.97 cm) is a tough, flexible plastic that is ultrasonically welded together during manufacture. Within the shell are two layers of nonwoven cloth. The circular disk itself fits within the two cloth layers. Cloth reduces any friction that might be generated as the disk rotates, and helps to remove any debris from the medium's surfaces. The large hole in the disk center is the spindle hub where the drive spindle clamps the disk in place. Since the disk is relatively free to move within its shell, it can usually float to assume the best clamping position. Since the hub is prone to damage from clamping wear, many disks place protective hub rings to reinforce the disk medium. A rectangular notch cut from the right side of the jacket is the write-

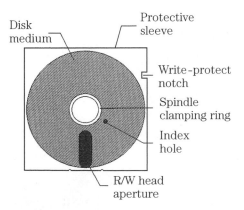

5-2 View of a 5.25-in diskette.

protect notch. When this notch is exposed, the disk can be written to. If the notch is covered, writing is prohibited. Any simple adhesive label can be used to cover the write-protect notch.

A small hole near the center hub is the index hole which aligns with a small hole cut into the circular diskette itself. Old, hard-sectored floppy drives used the index hole to note precise radial disk position. Today, however, the index hole serves little practical purpose since disks are *soft-sectored.* The large, oblong hole at the bottom of a disk is the head aperture—the place where a drive's R/W heads come into contact with the disk's medium. It is vitally important that you do *not* touch the head aperture. Dust, dirt, fingerprints, sweat and bodily oils, or any other foreign matter that reaches the medium can damage it—often permanently. This is the compelling reason why all 5.25-in disks should be kept in their paper disk sleeves when not in use.

3.5-in (8.89-cm) disks

By itself, a thin, flexible disk of medium is extremely vulnerable to damage from rough handling, dust, spills, and scratches. As a result, it is important to protect the medium from damage at all times. Protection is accomplished by mounting the medium in a hard plastic shell as shown in Fig. 5-3. The design was originally introduced by the Sony Corporation. Perhaps the most striking aspect of a 3.5-in disk is the hard shell itself, which is scratch-resistant and very difficult to bend. A spring-loaded metal shroud called a *head access cover* protects the exposed medium when the disk is removed from a drive. When a disk is inserted properly, a loading mechanism in the drive pulls the metal cover aside so that magnetic heads can contact the disk.

There are other attributes of an 3.5-in disk that you should be aware of. To ensure that the disk is inserted properly, one corner of the disk shell is cut out. The disk medium is also attached to a solid metal drive hub that is accessible only from the disk's underside. If the disk is inserted into a drive upside down, the disk simply will not be accepted. When inserted properly, the drive's spindle interlocks with the metal drive hub. Hub formation ensures that the medium will not slip against the spindle motor. A write-protect hole which is covered with a plastic slider is available on the disk. When the slider is moved to cover its hole, disk write operations are permitted. When the slider is moved to expose its hole, disk write operations are inhibited (the disk can only be read). Finally, the drive must be able to differentiate between nominal- (double-) density and high-density disks. An additional hole is punched in the disk body to indicate a high-density disk. If the hole is missing, the disk is a double-density type.

Magnetic Storage Concepts

Magnetic storage media have been attractive to computer designers for many years—long before the personal computer had established itself in homes and offices. This popularity is primarily due to the fact that magnetic media are nonvolatile. Once information is stored, no electrical energy is needed to maintain the information. While electrical energy is used to read and write magnetic data, magnetic fields do not change on their own, so data remain intact until other forces act upon it. In most systems, such

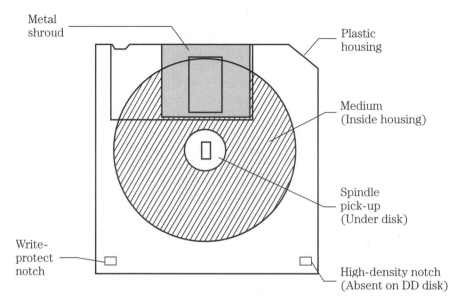

Metal shroud

Plastic housing

Medium (Inside housing)

Spindle pick-up (Under disk)

Write-protect notch

High-density notch (Absent on DD disk)

5-3 View of a 3.5-in diskette.

force is provided by other magnetic fields that are generated by electrical means. It is this smooth, straightforward transition from electricity to magnetism and back again that has made magnetic storage such a natural choice. This part of the chapter shows you the basic concepts of magnetic media used in floppy drives.

Media

As you have already seen, a medium is the physical material which actually holds recorded information. For floppy drives, the medium is a small Mylar disk coated on both sides with a precisely formulated magnetic material often referred to as the *oxide layer*. Every disk manufacturer uses its own particular formula for magnetic coatings, but most coatings are based on a naturally magnetic element (such as iron, nickel, or cobalt) that has been alloyed with nonmagnetic materials or rare earths.

The fascinating aspect of these magnetic layers is that each and every particle acts as a microscopic magnet. Each magnetic particle can be aligned in one orientation or another under the influence of an external magnetic field. If you have ever magnetized a screwdriver's steel shaft by running a permanent magnet along its length, you have already seen this magnetizing process in action. For a floppy disk, microscopic points along the disk's surfaces are magnetized in one alignment or another by the precise forces applied with read/write (R/W) heads. The shifting of alignment polarities would indicate a logic 1, while no change in polarity would indicate a logic 0. You will see much more about data recording and organization later in this chapter.

In analog recording, the magnetic field generated by R/W heads varies in direct proportion to the signal being recorded. Such linear variations in field strength cause varying amounts of magnetic particles to align as the medium moves. On the other hand, digital recordings such as floppy disks save binary 1s and 0s by applying an overwhelming amount of field strength. Very strong magnetic fields *saturate* the medium—that is, so much field strength is applied that any increase in field strength will *not* cause a better alignment of magnetic particles at that point on the medium. The advantage to operating in saturation is that 1s and 0s are remarkably resistant to the degrading effects of noise that can sometimes appear in analog magnetic recordings.

Although the orientation of magnetic particles on a disk's medium can be reversed by using an external magnetic field, particles tend to resist the reversal of polarity. *Coercivity* is the strength with which magnetic particles resist change. Higher-coercivity material has a greater resistance to change, so a stronger external field will be needed to cause changes. High coercivity is generally considered to be desirable (up to a point) because signals stand out much better against background noise and signals will resist natural degradation because of age, temperature, and random magnetic influences. As you might expect, a highly coercive medium requires a more powerful field to record new information.

Another advantage of increased coercivity is greater information density for the medium. The greater strength of each particle of the medium allows more bits to be packed into less area. The move from 5.25-in to 3.5-in floppy disks was possible largely due to a superior (more coercive) magnetic layer. This coercivity principle also holds true for hard drives which you shall see in the next chapter. In order to pack more information onto ever-smaller platters, the medium must be more coercive.

Coercivity is a common magnetic measurement with units in *oersteds* (Oe) (pronounced "or-steds"). The coercivity of a typical floppy disk can range anywhere from 300 to 750 Oe. Hard drive and magnetooptical (MO) drive media usually offer coercivities of 6000 Oe or higher.

The central premise of magnetic storage is that it is static—once recorded, information is retained without any electrical energy. Such stored information is presumed to last forever, but in actual practice, magnetic information begins to degrade as soon as it is recorded. A good magnetic medium will reliably remember (or retain) the alignment of its particles over a long period of time. The ability of a medium to retain its magnetic information is known as *retentivity*. Even the finest, best-formulated floppy disks degrade eventually (although it could take many years before an actual data error materializes).

Ultimately, the ideal answer to medium degradation is to refresh (or write over) the data and sector ID information. Data are rewritten normally each time a file is saved, but sector IDs are only written once when the disk is formatted. If a sector ID should fail, you will see the dreaded "Sector Not Found" disk error and any data stored in the sector cannot be accessed. This failure mode also occurs in hard drives. There is little that can be done to ensure the integrity of floppy disks other than maintaining one or more backups on freshly formatted disks. However, some commercial software is available for restoring disks (especially hard drives).

Magnetic recording principles

Now that you have seen some basic magnetic concepts, you can begin to apply those concepts to floppy disks as they are used in actual practice. The next few sections of this chapter show you some of the principles behind magnetic recording and the ways in which data are organized on a disk. The first step in understanding

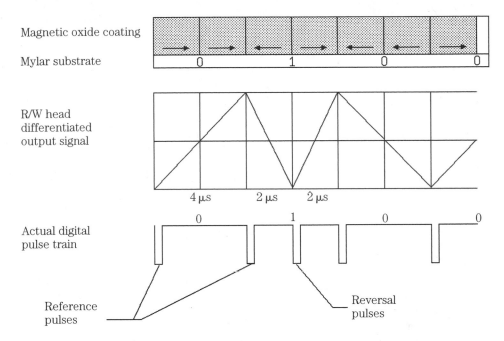

Magnetic oxide coating

Mylar substrate

R/W head
differentiated
output signal

Actual digital
pulse train

Reference
pulses

Reversal
pulses

5-4 Flux transitions in floppy disks using MFM.

digital recording is to see how binary data are stored on a disk. Binary 1s and 0s are *not* represented by discrete polarities of magnetic field orientations as you may have thought. Instead, binary digits are represented by the presence or absence of flux *transitions* as illustrated in Fig. 5-4. By detecting the *change* from one polarity to another instead of simply detecting a discrete polarity itself, maximum sensitivity can be achieved with very simple circuitry.

In its simplest form, a logic 1 is indicated by the presence of a flux reversal within a fixed time frame, while a logic 0 is indicated by the absence of a flux reversal. Most floppy drive systems insert artificial flux reversals between consecutive 0s to prevent reversals from occurring at great intervals. You can see some example magnetic states recorded on the media of Fig. 5-4. Notice that the *direction* of reversal does not matter at all—it is the reversal *event* that defines a 1 or 0. For example, the first 0 uses left-to-right orientation, while the second 0 uses a right-to-left orientation, but *both* can represent 0s. The second trace in Fig. 5-4 represents an amplified output signal from a typical R/W head. Notice that the analog signal peaks wherever there is a flux transition—long slopes indicate a 0 and short slopes indicate a 1. When such peaks are encountered, peak detection circuits in the floppy drive cause marking pulses in the ultimate data signal. Each bit is usually encoded in about 4 μs.

Often, the most confusing aspect to flux transitions is the artificial reversals. Why reverse the polarities for consecutive 0s? Artificial reversals are added to guarantee synchronization in the floppy disk circuitry. Remember that data read or written to a floppy disk is serial, and without any clock signal, such serial data are *asynchronous* of the drive's circuitry. Regular flux reversals (even if added artificially) create reference pulses that help to synchronize the drive and data without use of clocks or other timing signals. This approach is loosely referred to as the *modified frequency modulation* (or MFM) recording technique.

The ability of floppy disks to store information depends upon being able to write new magnetic field polarities on top of old or existing orientations. A drive must also be able to sense the existing polarities on a disk during read operations. The mechanism responsible for translating electrical signals into magnetic signals (and vice versa) is the R/W head. In principle, a head is little more than a coil of very fine wire wrapped around a soft, highly permeable core material as illustrated in Fig. 5-5.

When the head is energized with current flow from a driver IC, a path of magnetic flux is established in the head core. The direction (or orientation) of flux depends on the direction of energizing current. To reverse a head's magnetic orientation, the direction of energizing current must be reversed. The small head size and low current levels needed to energize a head allow very high frequency flux reversals. As magnetic flux is generated in a head, the resulting, tightly focused magnetic field aligns the floppy disk's particles at that point. In general practice, the current signal magnetizes an almost microscopic area on the medium. R/W heads actually contact the medium while a disk is inserted into a drive.

During a read operation, the heads are left unenergized while the disk spins. Just as varying current produces magnetism in a head, the reverse is also true—varying magnetic influences cause currents to be developed in the head(s). As the spinning medium moves across a R/W head, a current is produced in the head coil. The direction of induced current depends on the polarity of each flux orientation. Induced current is proportional to the flux density (how closely each flux transition is placed) and the velocity of the medium across each head. In other words, signal strength depends on the rate of change of flux versus time.

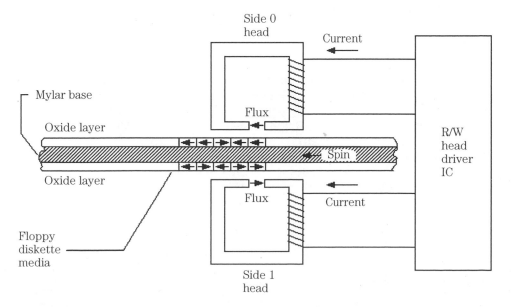

5-5 Floppy drive recording principles.

Data and disk organization

The next points to cover in floppy disk technology are where the data are actually located, and how those data are organized. You cannot place data just anywhere on the disk—the drive would have no idea where to look for the data later on, or if the data were valid. In order for a disk to be of use, information must be sorted and organized into known, standard locations. Standardized organization ensures that a disk written by one drive will be readable by another drive in a different machine. Table 5-1 compares the major parameters of several floppy drive types.

It is important to note that a floppy disk is a two-dimensional entity possessing both height and width (depth is irrelevant here). This two-dimensional characteristic allows disk information to be recorded in concentric circles that create a random access type of medium. *Random access* means that it is possible to move around the disk almost instantly to obtain a desired piece of information. This is a much faster and more convenient approach than sequential recording such as magnetic tape.

Floppy disk organization is not terribly complicated, but there are several important concepts that you must be familiar with. Figure 5-6 illustrates a typical 3.5-in floppy disk. The disk itself is rotated in one direction (usually clockwise) under R/W heads which are perpendicular (at right angles) to the disk's plane. The path of the disk beneath a head describes a circle. As a head steps in and out along a disk's radius, each step describes a circle with a different circumference—rather like lanes on a roadway.

Each of these concentric "lanes" is known as a *track*. A typical 3.5-in disk offers 160 tracks—80 tracks on each side of the medium. Tracks have a finite width which is defined largely by the drive size, head size, and medium. When a R/W head jumps from track to track, it must jump precisely the correct distance to position itself in the middle of another track. If positioning is not correct, the head may encounter data signals from two adjacent tracks. Faulty positioning almost invariably results in disk errors. Also notice that the circumference of each track drops as the head moves toward the disk's center. With less space and a constant rate of spin, data are

Table 5-1. Comparison of Floppy Drive Specifications

| Parameter | Newest ——————————→ Oldest | | | |
| | 3.5-in drives | | 5.25-in drives | |
	HD	DD	HD	DD
Drive spindle speed, RPM	300/360	300	360	300
Megabytes/drive	1.4	.720	1.2	.360
Encoding format	MFM	MFM	MFM/FM	MFM/FM
Tracks/inch, TPI	135	135	96	96
Bits/inch, BPI	17,434	8,717	9,870	5,922
Tracks/side	80	80	80	40
Sectors/track	18	9	15	9
Bytes/sector	512	512	512	512
Data transfer rate, kbits/s	500	500	500 (MFM)	250 (MFM)
			250 (FM)	125 (FM)

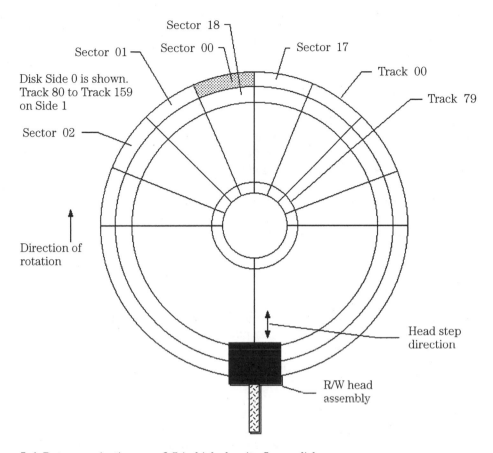

Sector 18

Sector 01 Sector 00 Sector 17

Disk Side 0 is shown.
Track 80 to Track 159
on Side 1

Track 00

Track 79

Sector 02

Direction of
rotation

Head step
direction

R/W head
assembly

5-6 Data organization on a 3.5-in high-density floppy disk.

densest on the innermost tracks (79 or 159 depending on the disk side) and least dense on the outermost tracks (0 or 80).

Every track is broken down into smaller units called *sectors*. There are 18 sectors on every track of a 3.5-in disk. Sectors serve two purposes. First, a sector stores 512 bytes of data. With 18 sectors per track and 160 tracks per disk, a disk holds 2880 sectors (18 × 160). At 512 bytes per sector, a formatted disk can handle about (2880 × 512) or 1,474,560 bytes of data. In actual practice, this amount is often slightly less to allow for boot sector and file allocation information. Sectors are grouped into sets called *clusters* (or *allocation units*). A cluster can range from 512 to 8096 bytes.

Second, and perhaps more important, a sector provides housekeeping (or over-head) data that identify the sector, the track, and error-checking results from cyclical redundancy check (CRC) calculations. The location of each sector and housekeeping information is set down during the *format* process. Once formatted, only the sector data and CRC results are updated when a disk is written. Sector ID and synchronization data are never rewritten unless the disk is reformatted. This extra information means that each sector actually holds more than 512 bytes, but you only have access to the 512 data bytes in a sector during normal disk R/W operations. If sector ID data are accidentally overwritten or corrupted, the user data in the afflicted sector becomes unreadable.

It is very important that the computer keep track of available space on a disk. When writing to a disk, the computer must check the disk first to determine the places where data are already stored so it can write to sectors that are unused. If reading from a disk, the computer must check to determine the sectors that contain pieces of the desired file—files usually take many sectors, and the sectors used to hold a file are not necessarily contiguous. In order to track the used and free sectors on a disk, a map of each sector is maintained on the disk. This map is called the *file allocation table* (FAT). As files are added and erased, the FAT is updated to reflect the contents of each sector. The FAT is typically held on track 00. As you might see, a working FAT is critical to the proper operation of a disk. If the FAT is accidentally overwritten or corrupted, the entire disk can become useless. Without a viable FAT, the computer has no other way to determine what files are available or where they are spread throughout the disk.

Media problems

Magnetic media have come a long way in the last decade or so. Today's high-quality magnetic materials, combined with the benefits of precise, high-volume production equipment, produce disks that are exceptionally reliable over normal long-term use in a floppy disk drive. However, floppy disks are removable items. The care they receive in physical handling and the storage environment where they are kept will greatly impact a disk's lifespan.

The most troubling and insidious problem plaguing floppy disk medium is the accidental influence of magnetic fields. Any magnetized item in close proximity to a floppy disk poses a potential threat. Permanent magnets such as refrigerator magnets or magnetic paper clips are prime sources of stray fields. Electromagnetic sources like telephone ringers, monitor or TV degaussing coils, and all types of motors will corrupt data if the medium is close enough. The best policy is to keep all floppy disks in a dedicated container placed well away from stray magnetic fields.

Disks and magnetic medium are also subject to a wide variety of physical damage. Substrates and medium are manufactured to very tight tolerances, so anything at all that alters the precise surface features of a floppy disk can cause problems. The introduction of hair, dirt, or dust through the disk's head access aperture, wild temperature variations, fingerprints on the medium, or any substantial impact or flexing of the medium can cause temporary loss of contact between medium and head. When loss of contact occurs, data are lost and a number of disk errors can occur. Head wear and the accumulation of worn oxides also affect head contact. Once again, storing disks in a dedicated container located well out of harm's way is often the best means of protection.

Drive Construction

Now that you have learned about the floppy disk and its medium, it is time to study the drive mechanism in detail. A floppy disk drive is a rather remarkable piece of mechanical engineering. It must accept disks of varying quality from a variety of manufacturers, align and spin the disk at a very precise rate (300 or 360 RPM accurate to within 1 or 2 percent). A drive must also be able to position a set of loaded (clamped) R/W heads precisely to any track on the disk within a few mils (thousandths of an inch), and reach the desired destination track in under a few milliseconds. Above all, the drive must function reliably over a long period of time with a minimum of maintenance. A solid understanding of floppy drive components will make your troubleshooting process much easier. Figure 5-7 shows an exploded diagram for a Teac 3.5-in floppy disk drive.

At the core of a floppy drive is a *frame assembly* (#15). It is the single main structure for mounting the drive's mechanisms and electronics. Frames are typically made from die-cast aluminum to provide a strong, rigid foundation for the drive. The *front bezel* (#18) attaches to the frame to provide a clean, cosmetic appearance and to offer a fixed slot for disk insertion or removal. For 3.5-in drives, bezels often include a small colored lens, a disk ejection button hole, and a flap to cover the disk slot when the drive is empty. A *spindle motor assembly* (#17) uses an outer-rotor dc motor fabricated onto a small PC board. The motor's shaft is inserted into that large hole in the frame. A disk's metal drive hub automatically interlocks to the spindle. For 5.25-in disks, the center hole is clamped between two halves of a spindle assembly. The halves clamp the disk when the drive lever is locked down. The *disk activity LED* (#20) illuminates through the bezel's colored lens whenever spindle motor activity is in progress.

Just behind the spindle motor is the drive's *electronics package* (#16). The electronics PC board contains the circuitry needed to operate the drive's motors, R/W heads, and sensors. A standardized interface is used to connect the drive to a floppy drive controller. The *R/W head assembly* (#7) (also sometimes called a *head carriage assembly*), holds a set of two R/W heads. Head 0 is the lower head (underside of the disk), and head 1 is on top. In order to move the head carriage assembly in and out along a disk, a *head stepping motor* (#12) is added to ensure head movements are even between tracks or parts of a disk. A threaded rod at the motor end is what actually moves the heads. A *mechanical damper* (#5) helps to smooth the disk's travel into or out of the 3.5-in drive.

When a disk is inserted through the bezel, the disk is restrained by a diskette *holder assembly* (#2). To eject the disk, you would press the *ejector button* (#19), which pushes a *slider mechanism* (#3). When the ejector button is fully depressed, the disk will disengage from the spindle and pop out of the drive. For 5.25-in drives, the disk is released whenever the drive door is opened. Your particular drive may contain other miscellaneous components. Finally, the entire upper portion of a drive can be covered by a metal shield (#1).

Read/write heads

R/W heads are at the crux of all magnetic disk systems. When a disk is inserted between a set of heads, the head assembly clamps down to bring the heads and medium into contact. Disk medium is coated with a very light lubricant to reduce friction. Figure 5-8 shows a close-up view of a head assembly. Notice how the assembly is supported on both sides to maintain stability. The right side of the

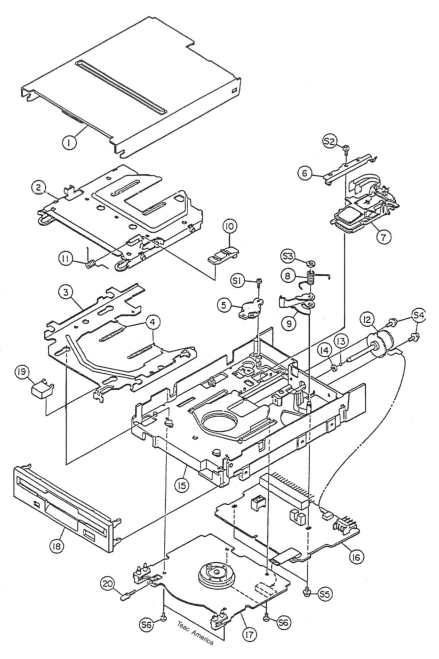

5-7 Exploded diagram of a Teac floppy drive.

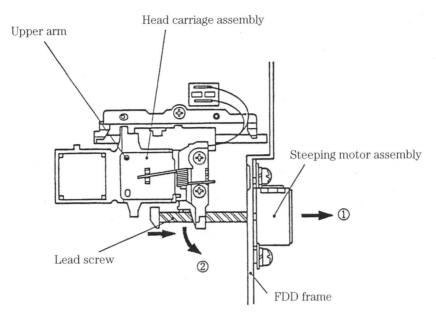

5-8 Close-up view of a R/W head assembly.

assembly is supported by a sliding *guide shaft,* while the left side is firmly at-tached to a bracket that runs along the *lead screw* of a stepping motor. Because of the electrical coil wiring in the heads, each head has its own small FPC (flexible plastic cable) that is attached to a connector on the drive's electronics PC board.

In actual practice, a R/W head is more than simply a single coil of wire around a tiny core. Most heads are actually composed of three cores: two R/W cores and an erase core. You can visualize this configuration in the layout and schematic of Figure 5-9. The erase head is powered whenever the drive is writing in order to clear any existing flux transitions before the R/W cores lay down new information. If a read op-eration is taking place, the erase core is left unpowered.

Head stepping motor

The R/W heads are positioned from track to track using a stepping motor attached to a precision lead screw. A *stepping motor* is a unique form of ac induction mo-tor which moves in small, very precise angular steps. Each step is signaled by cir-cuitry on the drive's PC board. As the stepping motor turns, the lead screw turns. This will push or pull the head carriage some linear distance across the disk radius. The exact amount of linear motion depends on the number of steps needed to complete a motor revolution, and the number of threads on the lead screw (known as *screw pitch*).

Spindle motor

A floppy drive must spin its disk at a constant rate during read or write operations. This is the task of the *spindle motor.* Older desktop floppy drives used a bulky con-stant-speed motor attached to the spindle assembly with a rubber belt. Today's

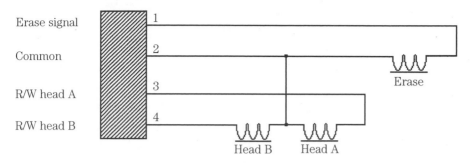

5-9 Schematic of a typical floppy drive R/W head.

small, low-profile drives use an integrated brushless dc motor where the rotor serves as a flywheel and spindle, and the stator windings are actually fabricated onto the motor PC board (Fig. 5-10). When spindle rotation is required, an IC on the motor PC board cycles the board's stator windings on and off at a rate which accelerates the spindle to a desired speed (300 or 360 RPM) and maintains that constant speed. Spindle rotation is regulated with feedback obtained from a sensor at the spindle.

Drive electronics

Proper drive operation depends on the intimate cooperation between magnetic media, electromechanical devices, and dedicated electronics. Floppy drive electronics is responsible for two major tasks: controlling the drive's physical operations and managing the flow of data in or out of the drive. These tasks are not nearly as simple as they sound, but the sleek, low-profile drives in today's computer systems are a far cry from the clunky, full-height drives found in early systems. Older drives needed a large number of ICs spanning several boards that had to be fitted to the chassis. The drive in your computer, however, is probably implemented with only a few highly integrated ICs that are neatly surface-mounted on two small, opposing PC boards. This part of the chapter discusses the drive's operating circuits. A complete block diagram for a Teac 3.5-in floppy drive is illustrated in Fig. 5-11. The figure is shown with a floppy disk inserted.

Sensors

As you look over Fig. 5-11, notice that there are four very important sensors required to govern drive operations: the file-protect (or *write-protect*) sensor, the *disk sensor,* the *index sensor,* and the *track 00 sensor.* A 3.5-in drive also incorporates a fifth sensor to check for *high-density media.* Sensors are used to check conditions in our physical world so that drive electronics will not cause system errors or drive damage. Take a moment to familiarize yourself with these sensors before you start troubleshooting. As a rule, sensors are either mechanical switches that react to the physical presence of a disk, or optoisolators that detect the presence of light. Keep in mind that different drive manufacturers may use sensor types interchangeably depending on the task at hand.

File-protect (write-protect) sensors are used to detect the position of a disk's file-protect tab. For 3.5-in disks, the write-protect notch must be *covered* to allow both

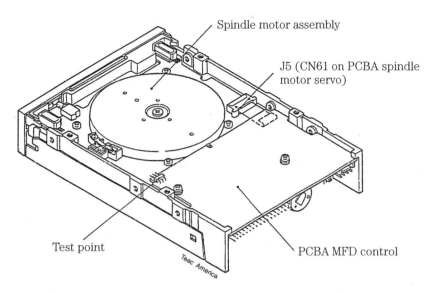

Spindle motor assembly

J5 (CN61 on PCBA spindle
motor servo)

Test point

PCBA MFD control

Teac America

5-10 View of a floppy drive spindle motor assembly.

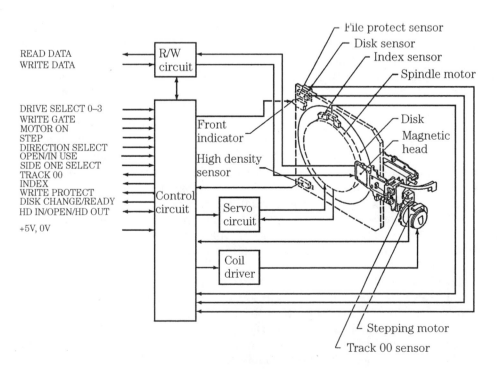

READ DATA
WRITE DATA

R/W
circuit

DRIVE SELECT 0–3
WRITE GATE
MOTOR ON
STEP
DIRECTION SELECT
OPEN/IN USE
SIDE ONE SELECT
TRACK 00
INDEX
WRITE PROTECT
DISK CHANGE/READY
HD IN/OPEN/HD OUT

+5V, 0V

Control
circuit

Front
indicator

High density
sensor

Servo
circuit

Coil
driver

File protect sensor
Disk sensor
Index sensor
Spindle motor

Disk
Magnetic
head

Stepping motor
Track 00 sensor

5-11 Electronic layout of a floppy drive.

read and write operations. If the notch is open, the disk can only be read. Mechanical contact switches are commonly used as write-protect sensors since it is a simple matter for the write protect notch to actuate a small switch when the disk is first inserted. If the notch is open, the switch will not be actuated. For 5.25-in disks, write protect is handled a bit differently. The write-protect notch cut into the jacket side must be uncovered to allow both reading and writing. Covering the notch prohibits writing. A 5.25-in drive typically uses an optoisolator to check the notch condition.

Before the drive is allowed to operate at all, a disk must be inserted properly and interlocked with the spindle. A disk-in-place sensor detects the presence or absence of a disk. Like the write-protect sensor, disk sensors are often mechanical switches that are activated by disk contact. If drive access is attempted without a disk in place, the sensor causes the drive's logic to induce a DOS "Disk Not Ready" error code. It is not unusual to find an optoisolator acting as a disk-in-place sensor.

The electronics of a 3.5-in drive must be able to differentiate whether the disk contains normal- (double-) density or high-density medium. A high-density sensor looks for the hole that is found near the top of all high-density disk bodies. A mechanical switch is typically used to detect the high-density hole, but a separate LED/detector pair may also be used. When the hole is absent (a double-density disk), the switch is activated upon disk insertion. If the hole is present (a high-density disk), the switch is not actuated. All switch conditions are translated into logic signals used by the drive electronics.

Before disk data can be read or written, the system must read the disk's "boot" information located in the FAT. While programs and data can be broken up and scattered all over a disk, however, the FAT must *always* be at a known location so that the drive knows where to look for it. The FAT is always located on track 00—the first track of disk side 0. A track 00 sensor provides a logic signal when the heads are positioned over track 00. Each time a read or write is ordered, the head assembly is stepped to track 00. Although a drive "remembers" how many steps should be needed to position the heads precisely over track 00, an optoisolator or switch senses the head carriage assembly position. At track 00, the head carriage should interrupt the optoisolator or actuate the switch. If the drive supposedly steps to track 00 and there is no sensor signal to confirm the position (or the signal occurs *before* the drive has finished stepping), the drive assumes that a head positioning error has occurred. Head step counts and sensor outputs virtually always agree unless the sensor has failed or the drive has been physically damaged.

Spindle speed is a critically important drive parameter. Once the disk has reached its running velocity (300 or 360 RPM), the drive *must* maintain that velocity for the duration of the disk access process. Unfortunately, simply telling the spindle motor to move is no guarantee that the motor is turning. A sensor is required to measure the motor's speed. This is the index sensor. Signals from an index sensor are fed back to the drive electronics which adjusts spindle speed in order to maintain a constant rotation. Most drives use optoisolators as index sensors which detect the motion of small slots cut in a template or the spindle rotor itself. When a disk is spinning, the output from an index sensor is a fast logic pulse sent along to the drive electronics. Keep in mind that some index sensors are magnetic. A magnetic sensor typically operates by detecting the proximity of small slots in a template or the spindle rotor, but the pulse output is essentially identical to that of the optoisolator.

Circuits

The drive electronics package contains four primary circuits that you should be familiar with: the *servo circuit,* the *coil driver circuit,* the *read/write circuit,* and the *control circuit.* Drive electronics also handles the physical interface connecting the drive to the drive controller board. Operation of these circuits is critical to the drive.

The coil driver circuit is solely responsible for operating the head carriage stepping motor. A driver circuit accepts logic signals from the control circuit and converts those logic pulses into the voltage and current levels needed to work a stepping motor. The coil driver is typically a single surface-mount IC, although some older drive designs might use discrete transistors.

A servo circuit performs two functions in a floppy disk drive. First, a servo drives the spindle motor. The circuit (usually located on the spindle motor PC board) accepts logic signals from the control circuit and generates the precise sequence of outputs needed to work the spindle motor's windings. The servo circuit also accepts pulse signals from the index sensor, then uses those pulses to regulate spindle motor speed. Servo circuits are usually implemented as a single IC, and a small series of discrete components. Figure 5-12 illustrates an assembly for a servo motor board.

The control circuit is the heart of the entire floppy drive. Control circuits are responsible for translating logic signals from the drive's physical interface into logic signals that operate the R/W, servo and coil driver circuits. A control circuit also accepts the logic signals returned from each of the five drive sensors and reports their conditions to the physical interface. Control circuits are usually implemented as a single surface-mount IC in an 80- to 100-pin quad flat pack (QFP).

A read/write (R/W) circuit interacts directly with the drive's R/W heads. During a read operation, the R/W circuit accepts and amplifies analog magnetic signals from the heads, then differentiates the analog signals to create a waveform such as in Fig. 5-4. After some external analog filtering with discrete components,

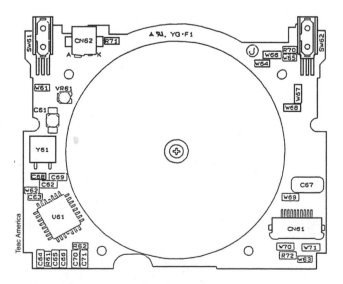

5-12 A spindle motor PC board assembly.

the filtered analog signal is returned to the R/W circuit where the signal is converted into a logic waveform representing the read data. Write operations are a bit more straightforward. Data are channeled directly from the physical interface into a write driver which translates logic signals into high-energy pulses used to cause flux transitions on the medium. The high-energy pulses are sent directly to the R/W heads. Some drives may provide a separate R/W circuit, but many drives now implement R/W circuits as a part of the control circuit ASIC. The main logic board for a floppy drive is shown in Fig. 5-13.

Physical interface

As you might expect, a floppy drive is only one part of your computer. The drive must receive control and data signals from the computer, and deliver status and data signals back to the computer as required. The series of connections between a floppy disk PC board and the floppy disk controller is known as the *physical interface*. The advantage to using a standard interface is that various drives and ICs made by different manufacturers can be "mixed and matched" by computer designers. A floppy drive working in one computer will operate properly in another computer regardless of the manufacturer as long as the same physical interface scheme is being used.

For most PC drives, a physical interface includes two cables: a power cable and a signal cable. Both cable pinouts are illustrated in Fig. 5-14. The classical *power connector* is a 4-pin mate-and-lock connector, although many low-profile drives used in "small-computers" (i.e., laptops or notebooks) may use much smaller connector designs. Floppy drives require two voltage levels: +5.0 Vdc for logic, and +12 Vdc for motors. The return (ground) for each supply is also provided at the connector. The *signal connector* is typically a 34-pin insulation displacement connector (IDC) cable. Notice that all odd-numbered pins are ground lines, while the even-numbered pins carry active signals. Logic signals are all TTL-level signals.

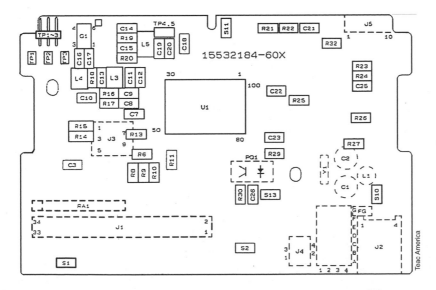

5-13 A floppy drive main logic PC board.

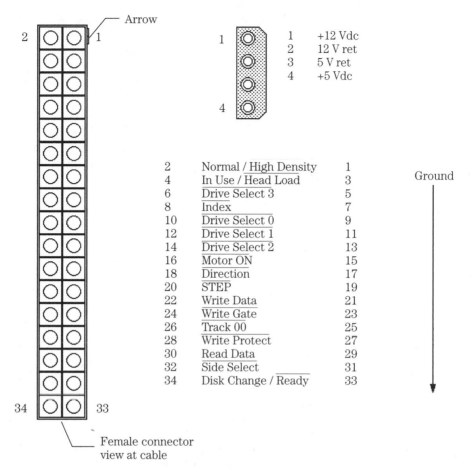

The diagram shows the pinout with labels: Arrow, and the power connector pins:

Pin	Signal
1	+12 Vdc
2	12 V ret
3	5 V ret
4	+5 Vdc

Signal list:

Pin	Signal	Pin	
2	Normal / High Density	1	Ground
4	In Use / Head Load	3	
6	Drive Select 3	5	
8	Index	7	
10	Drive Select 0	9	
12	Drive Select 1	11	
14	Drive Select 2	13	
16	Motor ON	15	
18	Direction	17	
20	STEP	19	
22	Write Data	21	
24	Write Gate	23	
26	Track 00	25	
28	Write Protect	27	
30	Read Data	29	
32	Side Select	31	
34	Disk Change / Ready	33	

Female connector view at cable

5-14 Pinout diagram for a classical floppy interface.

In a system with more than one drive, the particular destination drive must be selected before any read or write is attempted. A drive is selected using the appropriate Drive Select pinouts (Drive Select 0 to 3) on pins 10, 12, 14, and 6, respectively. For notebook or subnotebook systems where only one floppy drive is used, only Drive Select 0 is used—the remaining select inputs may simply be disconnected. The spindle motor servo circuit is controlled through the Motor ON signal (pin 16). When pin 16 is logic 0, the spindle motor should *spinup* (or come to an operating speed). The medium must be spinning at the proper rate before reading or writing can take place.

To move the R/W heads, the host computer must specify the number of steps a head carriage assembly must move, and the direction in which steps must occur. A Direction Select signal (pin 18) tells the coil driver circuit whether the heads should be moved inward (toward the spindle) or outward (away from the spindle). The Step signal (pin 20) provides the pulse sequence that actually steps the head motor in the desired direction. The combination of Step and Direction Select controls can position the R/W heads over the disk very precisely. The Side Select control pin (pin

32) determines whether head 0 or head 1 is active for reading or writing—only one side of the disk can be manipulated at a time.

There are two signals needed to write data to a disk. The Write Gate signal (pin 24) is logic 0 when writing is to occur, and logic 1 when writing is inhibited (or reading). After the Write Gate is asserted, data can be written to the disk over the Write Data line (pin 22). When reading, the data that are extracted from the disk are delivered from the Read Data line (pin 30).

Each of the drive's sensor conditions are sent over the physical interface. The track 00 signal (pin 26) is logic 0 whenever the head carriage assembly is positioned over track 00. The Write Protect line (pin 28) is logic 0 whenever the disk's write protect notch is in place. Writing is inhibited whenever the Write Protect signal is asserted. The index signal (pin 8) supplies a chain of pulses from the index sensor. Medium type is indicated by the Normal/High-Density sensor (pin 2). The status of the disk-in-place sensor is indicated over the Disk Change Ready line (pin 34).

A floppy disk system

Now that you have learned about the medium, drive, and electronics package in some detail, you should see how the floppy drive fits into the overall scheme of a small computer. The transfer of meaningful information into or out of a floppy drive is an intricate and involved process, requiring the interaction of a CPU, system controller, and core memory. The overall coordination of the drive is handled by a sophisticated floppy drive controller IC typically located on a board plugged into the computer's expansion slot. A floppy drive system is illustrated in Fig. 5-15. There are

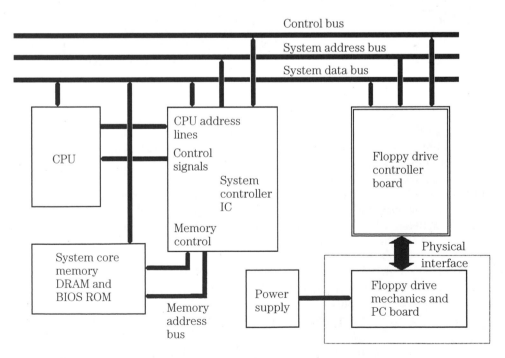

5-15 Block diagram of a floppy drive system.

three major areas here: the motherboard, the floppy drive controller board, and the drive itself. The floppy drive controller translates serial data and discrete control signals at the physical interface into data and control signals suitable for the computer's main buses, and vice versa.

As with almost every computer ever made, the CPU is the key to system operation, but it is interesting to note that the CPU does not interact with the floppy drive directly. Instead, the CPU directs the system controller IC to address the floppy controller IC and begin the data transfer to or from the drive. Any instructions or subroutines needed to operate the floppy drive are taken by the CPU from the BIOS ROM in core memory. The floppy controller instructs the drive to step to track 00 and read the FAT. This initial step learns the location of all assigned and free clusters. If the disk had been changed before access was requested, the new FAT data would have to be determined anyway. The drive's R/W heads then step to the appropriate location to begin reading or writing.

Data being written to a floppy drive are taken from core memory (DRAM) one byte at a time by the floppy controller using direct memory access (DMA) techniques, translated into serial form, then sent one bit at a time over the Write Data line of the physical interface. Control signals are sent along the interface simultaneously to handle the drive's motors, sensors, and so on. If data are being copied from another drive, that drive must be read first into a section of core memory, then that portion of memory is written to the desired drive. After data arrives at the floppy drive control circuit, bits are converted into drive signals which are written to the disk as magnetic flux transitions.

When data must be read from a floppy drive, the process is very similar. The CPU orders the system controller to address the floppy drive controller IC, then sends data instructions that cause the floppy drive to load a program or data file. Any data or subroutines needed to operate the floppy drive are contained in BIOS ROM. The floppy controller board instructs the drive to step to track 00 and read the FAT to determine the disk sector and track where the desired file begins. If the desired file is not found in the FAT, an error code is sent back to the CPU, which responds with a DOS error code. Once the sector and track file location is found, the heads are stepped to that location.

The R/W heads produce signals based on the disk's flux variations. Heads will step from sector to sector and track to track as necessary to acquire all parts of the file. Circuitry in the drive converts those analog head signals into binary 1s and 0s. Data are sent in serial form across the physical interface to the floppy drive controller board where serial data are translated into parallel form, actual data are separated from error-checking information, and the resulting parallel data are moved into core memory through the system controller across the computer's main buses.

In actual practice, the process of signaling, data transfer, and control is much more complex than just described, but the intention here is to give you an idea of the major points that are involved. The concepts of floppy system operation will be invaluable to you during the testing and troubleshooting sections that follow.

Drive Testing and Alignment

Floppy disk drives (Fig. 5-16) are electromechanical devices. Their motors, lead screws, sliders, levers, and linkages are all subject to eventual wear and tear. As a

5-16 A 5.25-in floppy drive.

result, a drive can develop problems that are due to mechanical defects instead of electronic problems. Fortunately, few mechanical problems are fatal to a drive. With the proper tools, you can test a troublesome drive and often correct problems simply through careful cleaning and alignment.

Tools and equipment

Drive alignment is not a new concept. Technicians have tested and aligned floppy drives for years using oscilloscopes and test disks containing precise, specially recorded data patterns. You may already be familiar with the classical "cat's eye" or "index burst" alignment patterns seen on oscilloscopes. This kind of manual alignment required you to find the right test point on your particular drive's PC board, locate the proper adjustment in the drive assembly, and interpret complex (sometimes rather confusing) oscilloscope displays. In many cases, manual alignment required a substantial investment in an oscilloscope, test disk, and stand-alone drive exerciser equipment to run a drive outside of the computer.

Although manual drive alignment techniques are still used today, they are being largely replaced by automatic alignment techniques. Software developers have created interactive control programs to operate with their specially recorded data disks. These software toolkits provide all the features necessary to operate a suspect drive through a wide variety of tests while displaying the results numerically or graphically right on a computer monitor (Fig. 5-17). As you make adjustments, you can see real-time results displayed on the monitor. Software-based testing eliminates the need for an oscilloscope and ancillary test equipment. You also do not need to know the specific signal test points for every possible drive. The most popular toolkit available for technicians is DriveProbe by Accurite Technologies Incorporated.

Drive cleaning

Floppy drive R/W heads are not terribly complex devices, but they *do* require precision positioning. Heads must contact the disk medium in order to read or write information reliably. As the disk spins, particles from the disk's magnetic coating wear off and form a deposit on the heads. Accumulations of everyday contaminants such as dust and cigarette smoke also contribute to deposits on the heads. Head deposits present several serious problems. First, deposits act as a wedge, forcing heads away from the disk surface resulting in lost data and R/W errors, and generally unreliable and intermittent operation. Deposits tend to be more abrasive than the head itself, so dirty heads can generally reduce a disk's working life. Finally, dirty heads can cause erroneous readings during testing and alignment. Since alignment disks are specially recorded in a very precise fashion, faulty readings will yield erroneous information that can actually cause you to maladjust the drive. As a general procedure, clean the drive thoroughly *before* you test or align it.

R/W heads can also be cleaned manually or automatically. The *manual method* is just as the name implies. Use a high-quality head cleaner on a soft, lint-free, antistatic swab, and scrub both head surfaces by hand. Wet the swab but do not soak it. You may need to repeat the cleaning with fresh swabs to ensure that all residual deposits are removed. Be certain that all computer power is *off* before manual cleaning, and allow a few minutes for the cleaner to dry completely before restoring power. If you do not have head-cleaning chemicals on hand, you can use fresh ethyl or isopropyl alcohol. The advantage to manual cleaning is thoroughness—heads can be cleaned very well with no chance of damage due to friction.

Most software diagnostic packages provide a cleaning disk and software option that allows you to clean the disk automatically. With computer power on and the software toolkit loaded and running, insert the cleaning disk and choose the "cleaning option" from your software menu. Software will then spin the drive for some period of time—10 to 30s should be adequate, but do not exceed 60s of continuous cleaning. Choose high-quality cleaning disks that are impregnated with a lubricant. Avoid "bargain" off-the-shelf cleaning disks that force you to wet the

```
AUTOMATIC Drive Test                              'Esc'- For Previous Menu
```

Test	Track	Head 0 Data		Head 1 Data		Test Limits	Results	
Speed	NA	300 RPM / 199.7 mS				300 ± 6 RPM	Pass	NA
Eccentricity	44	100 uI		NA		0 ± 300 uI	Pass	NA
Radial	0	96%	50 uI	100%	0 uI	60 – 100 %	Pass	Pass
Radial	40	93%	–100 uI	90%	–150 uI	60 – 100 %	Pass	Pass
Radial	79	96%	50 uI	90%	–150 uI	60 – 100 %	Pass	Pass
Azimuth	76	6 Min		4 Min		0 ± 30 Min	Pass	Pass
Index	0	414 uS		407 uS		400 ± 600 uS	Pass	Pass
Index	79	397 uS		380 uS		400 ± 600 uS	Pass	Pass
Hysteresis	40	100 uI		NA		0 ± 250 uI	Pass	NA

```
   uI = Micro-inches        uS = Microsecond        mS = Millisecond
   Min = Minutes            NA = Not Applicable      NT = Not Tested
```

Note: Radial is expressed as LOBE RATIO and OFFSET from track center line.
Auto Test Completed   'Esc' For Previous Menu

5-17 Automatic floppy drive test suite.

disk. Wetted cleaning disks are often harsh, and prolonged use can actually damage the heads from excessive friction. Once the drive is clean, it can be tested and aligned. There are eight major tests to gauge the performance of a floppy drive: clamping, spindle speed, track 00, radial alignment, azimuth alignment, head step, hysteresis, and head width. Not all tests have adjustments that can correct the corresponding fault.

Clamping

As you may have already seen, a floppy disk is formatted into individual tracks laid down in concentric circles along the medium. Since each track is ideally a perfect circle, it is critical that the disk rotate evenly in a drive. If the disk is not on center for any reason, it will not spin evenly. If a disk is not clamped evenly, the eccentricity introduced into the spin may be enough to allow heads to read or write data to adjoining tracks. A *clamping test* should be performed *first* after the drive is cleaned because high eccentricity can adversely affect disk tests. Clamping problems are more pronounced on 5.25-in drives where the soft Mylar hub ring is vulnerable to damage from the clamping mechanism.

Start your software toolkit from your computer's hard drive, then insert the alignment disk containing test patterns into the questionable drive. Select a clamping or eccentricity test and allow the test to run a bit. You will probably see a display similar to the one shown in Fig. 5-18. Typical software toolkits can measure eccentricity in terms of microinches from true center. If clamping is off by more than a few hundred microinches, the spindle mechanism should be replaced. You can also simply replace the floppy drive. Try reinserting and retesting the disk several times to confirm your results. Repeated failures confirm a faulty spindle system.

DISKETTE ECCENTRICITY test   **'Esc'— For Previous Menu**

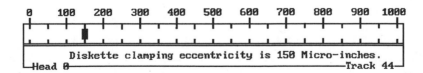

Drive 1 Selected as [3 1/2" 1.4Mb 300 RPM]   Location: Track 44   Head 0

5-18 Screen display of a floppy drive eccentricity test. (*Accurite Technologies, Inc., San Jose, CA*)

Spindle speed

The medium must be rotated at a fixed rate in order for data to be read or written properly. A drive that is too fast or too slow may be able to read files that it has written at that wrong speed without error, but the disk may not be readable in other drives operating at a normal speed. Files recorded at a normal speed also may not be readable in drives that are too fast or too slow. Such transfer problems between drives are classic signs of speed trouble (usually signaled as general disk R/W errors). Drive speeds should be accurate to within ±1.5 percent, so a drive running at 300 RPM should be accurate to ±4.5 RPM (295.5 to 304.5 RPM), and a drive running at 360 RPM should be accurate to within ±5.4 RPM (354.6 RPM to 365.4 RPM).

After cleaning the R/W heads and testing disk eccentricity, select the *spindle speed* test from your software menu. The display will probably appear much like the one in Fig. 5-19. Today's floppy drives rarely drift out of alignment because rotational speed is regulated by feedback from the spindle's index sensor. The servo circuit is constantly adjusting motor torque to achieve optimal spindle speed. If a self-compensating drive is out of tolerance, excess motor wear, mechanical obstructions, or index sensor failure is indicated. Check and replace the index sensor, or the entire spindle motor assembly as shown in Fig. 5-20. You can also replace the entire floppy drive outright.

Track 00 test

The first track on any floppy disk is the outermost track of side 0, which is track 00. Track 00 is important because it contains file allocation information vital for finding disk files. The particular files saved on a disk can be broken up and spread out all over the disk, but the FAT data must always be in a known location. If the drive cannot find track 00 reliably, the system may not be able to boot from the floppy drive or even use diskettes. Floppy drives utilize a sensor such as an optoisolator to physically determine when the R/W heads are over the outermost track.

Select the *track 00 test* from your software menu and allow the test to run. A track 00 test measures the difference between the actual location of track 00 versus the point at which the track 00 sensor indicates that track 00 is reached. The difference should be less than ±1.5 mils (thousandths of an inch). A larger error may cause the drive to encounter problems reading or writing to the disk. The easiest and quickest fix is to alter the track 00 sensor position. This adjustment usually involves loosening the sensor and moving it until the monitor display indicates an acceptable reading. Remember that you only need to move the sensor a small fraction, so a patient, steady hand is required. The track 00 sensor is almost always located along the head carriage lead screw. Mark the original position of the sensor with indelible ink so that you can return it to its original position if you get in trouble. Figure 5-21 illustrates one solution to adjusting the track 00 sensor.

Radial alignment

The alignment of a drive's R/W heads in relation to the disk is critical to reliable drive operation because alignment directly affects contact between heads and medium. If head contact is not precise, data read or written to the disk may be vulnerable. The *radial alignment test* measures the head's actual position versus the

MOTOR SPEED Test   'Esc'- For Previous Menu

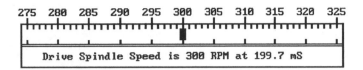

```
  275   280   285   290   295   300   305   310   315   320   325
  |лллл|лллл|лллл|лллл|лллл|лллл|лллл|лллл|лллл|лллл|лллл|
  |     |     |     |     |     ■     |     |     |     |     |
  _____
  |     Drive Spindle Speed is 300 RPM at 199.7 mS          |
```

Drive 1 Selected as [3 1/2" 1.4Mb 300 RPM]   Location: Track 0   Head 0

5-19 Screen display of a floppy drive speed test. (*Accurite Technologies, Inc., San Jose, CA*)

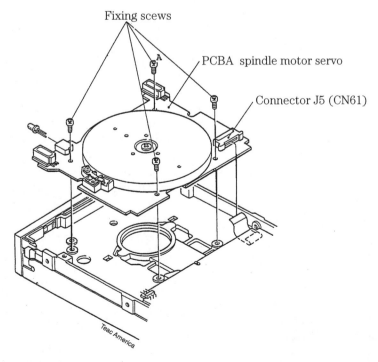

5-20 Replacing a floppy drive spindle motor assembly.

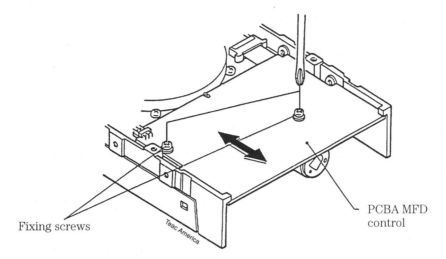

Fixing screws

Teac America

PCBA MFD
control

5-21 Adjusting the track 00 sensor.

precise center of the outer, middle, and inner tracks (as established by ANSI standards). Ideally, R/W heads should be centered perfectly when positioned over any
track, but any differences are measured in microinches. A radial alignment error
more than several hundred microinches may suggest a head alignment error.

Select the radial alignment test from your software toolkit and allow the test to
run. A typical radial alignment test display is illustrated in Fig. 5-22. If you must
perform an adjustment, you can start by loosening the slotted screws that secure
the stepping motor shown in Fig. 5-23, and gently rotate the motor to alter lead
screw position. As you make adjustments with the test in progress, watch the display for the middle track. When error is minimized on the inner track, secure the
stepping motor carefully to keep the assembly from shifting position. Use extreme
caution when adjusting radial head position—you only need to move the head a
fraction, so a very steady hand is needed. You should also recheck the track 00 sensor to make sure the sensor position is acceptable. If you are unable to effect radial
head alignment, the drive should be replaced.

Azimuth alignment

Not only must the heads be centered perfectly along a disk's radius, but the heads
must also be perfectly perpendicular to the disk plane. If the head azimuth is off
by more than a few minutes (1/60th of a degree), data integrity can be compromis-
ed and disk interchangeability between drives—especially high-density drives—
may become unreliable. When the heads are perfectly perpendicular to the disk (at
90 degrees), the azimuth should be 0 minutes.

Select the *azimuth test* from your software toolkit and allow the test to run.
Figure 5-24 shows an azimuth alignment test display. An azimuth alignment test
measures the rotation (or *twist*) of R/W heads in terms of + or − minutes. A clockwise twist is expressed as a plus (+) number, while a counterclockwise twist is expressed as a negative (−) number. Heads should be perpendicular to within about

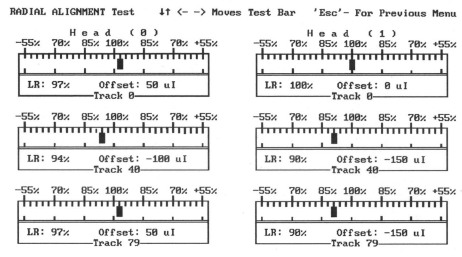

RADIAL ALIGNMENT Test   ↓↑ <- -> Moves Test Bar   'Esc'- For Previous Menu

Head (0)

-55% 70% 85% 100% 85% 70% +55%

LR: 97%   Offset: 50 uI
—Track 0—

-55% 70% 85% 100% 85% 70% +55%

LR: 94%   Offset: -100 uI
—Track 40—

-55% 70% 85% 100% 85% 70% +55%

LR: 97%   Offset: 50 uI
—Track 79—

Head (1)

-55% 70% 85% 100% 85% 70% +55%

LR: 100%   Offset: 0 uI
—Track 0—

-55% 70% 85% 100% 85% 70% +55%

LR: 90%   Offset: -150 uI
—Track 40—

-55% 70% 85% 100% 85% 70% +55%

LR: 90%   Offset: -150 uI
—Track 79—

Drive 1 Selected as [3 1/2" 1.4Mb 300 RPM]   Location: Track 79   Head 0

5-22 Screen display of a radial alignment test. (*Accurite Technologies, Inc., San Jose, CA*)

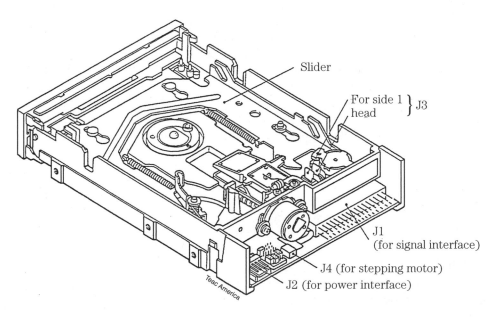

Slider

For side 1 } J3
head

J1
(for signal interface)

J4 (for stepping motor)

J2 (for power interface)

Teac America

5-23 Adjusting radial head alignment.

±10 minutes. It is important to note that most floppy drives do not allow azimuth adjustments easily. Unless you want to experiment with the adjustment, it is often easiest to replace a severely misaligned drive.

Head step

The head step (or *index step*) test measures the amount of time between a step pulse from the coil driver circuits and a set of timing mark data recorded on the test disk. In manual oscilloscope adjustments, this would be seen as the "index burst." Average index time is typically 200 μs for 5.25-in (13.34-cm) drives, and 400 μs for 3.5-in (8.89-cm) drives. In automatic testing with your software toolkit, you will see time measurements for both heads on the inner and outer tracks as shown in Fig. 5-25. The actual range of acceptable time depends on your particular drive, but variations of ±100 μs or more is not unusual.

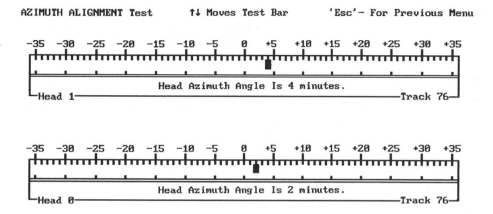

5-24 Screen display of an azimuth alignment test. (*Accurite Technologies, Inc., San Jose, CA*)

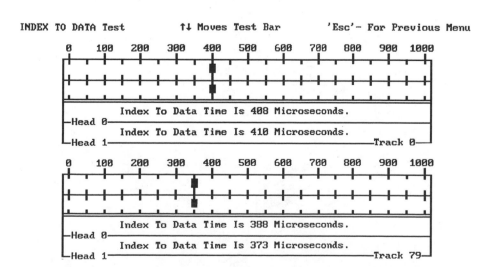

5-25 Screen display for an index-to-data test. (*Accurite Technologies, Inc., San Jose, CA*)

If the head step timing is off too far, you can adjust timing by moving the index sensor as shown in Fig. 5-26. As with all other drive adjustments, you need only move the sensor a small fraction, so be extremely careful about moving the sensor. A steady hand is very important here. Make sure to secure the sensor when you are done with your timing adjustments.

Hysteresis

It is natural for wear and debris in the mechanical head-positioning system to result in some "play"—that is, the head will not wind up in the *exact* same position moving from outside in as moving from the inside out. Excessive play, however, will make it difficult to find the correct track reliably. Testing is accomplished by starting the heads at a known track, stepping the heads out to track 00, then stepping back to the starting track. Head position is then measured and recorded. The heads are then stepped in to the innermost track, then back to the starting track. Head position is measured and recorded again. Under ideal conditions, the head carriage should wind up in precisely the same place (zero hysteresis), but natural play almost guarantees some minor difference. You can see a typical hysteresis test measurement display in Fig. 5-27. If excessive hysteresis is encountered, the drive should be replaced, since it is difficult to determine exactly where the excess play is caused in the drive.

Head width

Another test of a drive's R/W heads is the measurement of their effective width. Effective head widths are 12 or 13 mils for 5.25-in (13.34-cm) double-density drives, 5 or 6 mils for 5.25-in high-density drives, and 4 or 5 mils for all 3.5-in (8.89-cm)

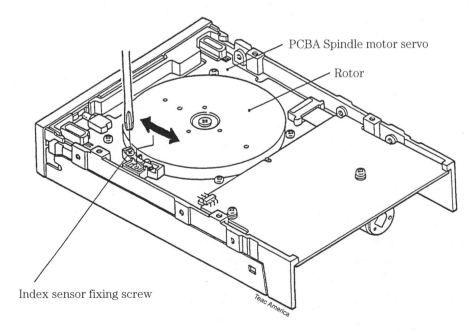

PCBA Spindle motor servo

Rotor

Index sensor fixing screw

Teac America

5-26 Adjusting index burst timing.

POSITIONER HYSTERESIS Test   'Esc'- For Previous Menu

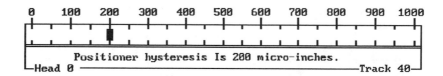

Drive 1 Selected as [3 1/2" 1.4Mb 300 RPM]   Location: Track 1 Head 0

5-27 Screen display of positioner hysteresis test. (*Accurite Technologies, Inc., San Jose, CA*)

drives. As you run the *head width test* with your software toolkit, you will see effective width displayed on the monitor as shown in Fig. 5-28. As R/W heads wear down, their effective width increases. If the effective width is too low, the heads may be contaminated with oxide buildup. When small head widths are detected, try cleaning the drive again to remove any remaining contaminates. If the width reading remains too small (or measures too large), the heads or head carriage may be damaged. You can replace the R/W head assembly as in Fig. 5-29, but often the best course is simply to replace the drive outright.

Troubleshooting Floppy Disk Systems

Beyond the process of testing and alignment, you may often have to deal with more serious or catastrophic drive failures. This section of the chapter is concerned with drive problems that cannot be corrected with cleaning or mechanical adjustments. To perform some of the following tests, you should have a known-good diskette that has been properly formatted. The disk may contain files, but be certain that any such files are backed up properly on a hard drive or another floppy disk. If you can't afford to lose the files on a disk, don't use the disk. For the following procedures, you should refer to the floppy drive diagrams in Figs. 5-11 and 5-15. If you intend to overhaul a drive periodically, you will need a battery of spare parts. Table 5-2 shows a list of regular spare parts for a Teac floppy drive, an approximate replacement interval, and the average time needed to replace each part.

Symptom 1: The floppy drive is completely dead The disk does not even initialize when inserted. Begin troubleshooting by inspecting the diskette itself. When a 3.5-in disk is inserted into a drive, a mechanism should pull the disk's metal

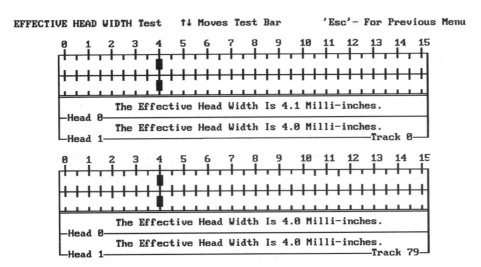

5-28 Screen display of a head width test. (*Accurite Technologies, Inc., San Jose, CA*)

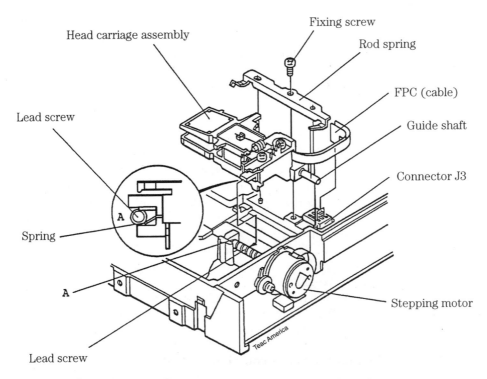

5-29 Replacing a R/W assembly.

Table 5-2. Recommended Floppy Drive Spare Parts

Part	Approximate interval	Time
Spindle motor	20,000 motor-on hours or 3×10^6 seeks	45 min
Stepping motor assembly	3×10^6 seeks	30 min
Drive electronics board	As required	30 min
Plastic front bezel	As required	2 min
Plastic eject button	As required	3 min
Eject damper	50,000 ejects	5 min

shroud away and briefly rotate the spindle motor to ensure positive engagement. Make sure that the disk is properly inserted into the floppy drive assembly. If the diskette does not enter and seat just right within the drive, disk access will be impossible. Try several different diskettes to ensure that test diskette is not defective. It may be necessary to partially disassemble the computer to access the drive and allow you to see the overall assembly. Free or adjust any jammed assemblies or linkages to correct disk insertion. If you cannot get diskettes to insert properly, change the floppy drive.

If the diskette inserts properly but fails to initialize, carefully inspect the drive's physical interface cabling. Loose connectors or faulty cable wiring can easily disable a floppy drive. Use your multimeter to measure dc voltages at the power connector. Place your meter's ground lead on pin 2 and measure +12 Vdc at pin 1. Ground your meter on pin 3 and measure +5 Vdc at pin 4. If either of both of these voltages is low or missing, troubleshoot your computer power supply.

Before disk activity can begin, the drive must sense a disk in the drive. Locate the disk-in-place sensor and use your multimeter to measure voltage across the sensor. When a disk is out of the drive, you should read a logic 1 voltage across the sensor output. When a disk is in place, you should read a logic 0 voltage across the sensor (this convention may be reversed in some drive designs). If the sensor does not register the presence of a disk, replace the sensor. If the sensor does seem to register the presence of a disk, use your logic probe to check the Disk Change/Ready signal (pin 34) of the physical interface. If the interface signal does not agree with the sensor signal, replace the control circuit IC on the drive PC board. You can also replace the entire drive control PC board, or replace the entire drive outright.At this point, the trouble is probably in the floppy drive PC board or the floppy drive controller board. Try replacing the floppy drive PC board assembly. This is not the least expensive avenue in terms of materials, but it is fast and simple. If a new floppy drive PC board corrects the problem, re-assemble the computer and return it to service. You could retain the old floppy drive board for parts. If a new drive PC board does not correct the problem (or is not available), replace the entire drive. You could retain the old floppy drive for parts. If a new floppy drive assembly fails to correct the problem, replace the floppy controller board. You will have to disassemble your computer to expose the motherboard and expansion boards.

Symptom 2: The floppy drive rotates a disk, but will not seek to the desired track This type of symptom generally suggests that the head-positioning stepping motor is inhibited or defective, but all other floppy drive functions are working properly. Begin by disassembling your computer and removing the floppy drive. Carefully inspect the head-positioning assembly to be certain that there are no broken parts or obstructions that could jam the R/W heads. You may wish to examine the mechanical system with a disk inserted to be certain that the trouble is not a disk alignment problem which may be interfering with head movement. Gently remove any obstructions that you may find. Be careful not to accidentally misalign any linkages or mechanical components in the process of clearing an obstruction.

Remove any diskette from the drive and reconnect the drive's signal and power cables. Apply power to the computer and measure drive voltages with your multimeter. Ground your multimeter on pin 2 of the power connector and measure +12 Vdc at pin 1. Move the meter ground to pin 3 and measure +5 Vdc on pin 4. If either voltage is low or absent, troubleshoot your computer power supply.

Once confident that the drive's mechanics are intact and appropriate power is available, you must determine whether the trouble is in your floppy drive PC board or floppy drive controller IC on the motherboard. Use your logic probe to measure the Step signal in the physical interface (pin 20). When drive access is requested, you should find a pulse signal as the floppy controller attempts to position the R/W heads. If Step pulses are missing, the floppy drive controller board is probably defective and should be replaced.

If Step pulses are present at the interface, check the pulses into the coil driver circuit. An absence of pulses into the coil driver circuit indicates a faulty control circuit IC. If pulses reach the coil driver, measure pulses to the stepping motor. If no pulses leave the coil driver, replace the coil driver IC. When pulses are correct to the stepping motor but no motion is taking place, replace the defective stepping motor. If you do not have the tools or inclination to replace surface-mount ICs, you can replace the drive PC board. You can also replace the entire drive outright.

Symptom 3: The floppy drive heads seek properly, but the spindle does not turn This symptom suggests that the spindle motor is inhibited or defective, but all other functions are working properly. Remove all power from the computer. Disassemble the system enough to remove the floppy drive. Carefully inspect the spindle motor, drive belt (if used), and spindle assembly. Make certain that there are no broken parts or obstructions that could jam the spindle. If there is a belt between the motor and spindle, make sure the belt is reasonably tight—it should not slip. You should also examine the floppy drive with a diskette inserted to be certain that the disk's insertion or alignment is not causing the problem. You can double-check your observations using several different diskettes. Gently remove any obstruction(s) that you may find. Be careful not to cause any accidental damage in the process of clearing an obstruction. Do *not* add any lubricating agents to the assembly, but gently vacuum or wipe away any significant accumulations of dust or dirt.

Remove any diskette from the drive and reconnect the floppy drive's signal and power cables. Restore power to the computer and measure drive voltages with your multimeter. Ground your multimeter on pin 2 and measure +12 Vdc on pin 1. Move the meter ground to pin 3 and measure +5 Vdc on pin 4. If either voltage is low or absent, troubleshoot your computer power supply.

Once you are confident that the floppy drive is mechanically sound and appropriate power is available, you must determine whether the trouble is in the floppy drive PC board or the floppy drive controller board. Use your logic probe to measure the Motor On signal in the physical interface (pin 16). When drive access is requested, the Motor On signal should become true (in most cases an active low). If the Motor On signal is missing, the floppy drive controller board is probably defective and should be replaced.

If the Motor On signal is present at the interface, check the signal driving the servo circuit. A missing Motor On signal at the servo circuit suggests a faulty control circuit IC. If the signal reaches the servo circuit, the servo IC is probably defective. You can replace the servo IC, but your best course is usually to replace the spindle motor/PC board assembly as a unit. If you are unable to replace the spindle motor PC board, you can replace the floppy drive outright.

Symptom 4: The floppy drive will not read from or write to the diskette. All other operations appear normal   This type of problem can manifest itself in several ways, but your computer's operating system will usually inform you when a disk read or write error has occurred. Begin by trying a known-good, properly formatted diskette in the drive. A faulty diskette can generate some very perplexing R/W problems. If a known-good diskette does not resolve the problem, try cleaning the R/W heads as described in the previous section. Do *not* run the drive with a head-cleaning disk inserted for more than 30 s at a time, or you risk damaging the heads with excessive friction.

When a fresh diskette and clean R/W heads do not correct the problem, you must determine whether the trouble exists in the floppy drive assembly or the floppy controller IC. When you cannot read data from the floppy drive, use your logic probe to measure the Read Data signal (pin 30). When the disk is idle, the Read Data line should read as a constant logic 1 or logic 0. During a read cycle, you should measure a pulse signal as data move from the drive to the floppy controller board. If no pulse signal appears on the Read Data line during a read cycle, use your oscilloscope to measure analog signals from the R/W heads. If there are no signals from the R/W heads, replace the head or head carriage assembly as in Fig. 5-30. When signals are available from the R/W heads, the control circuit IC is probably defective and should be replaced. If you are unable to replace the IC, you can replace the drive's control PC board. You can also replace the entire drive outright. If a pulse signal does exist during a read cycle, the floppy disk controller board is probably defective and should be replaced.

When you cannot write data to the floppy drive, use your logic probe to measure the Write Gate and Write Data lines (pins 24 and 22, respectively). During a write cycle, the Write Gate should be logic 0 and you should read a pulse signal as data flow from the floppy controller IC to the drive. If the Write Gate remains logic 1 or there is no pulse on the Write Data line, replace the defective floppy controller board. When the two Write signals appear as expected, check the analog signal to the R/W heads with your oscilloscope. If you do not find analog write

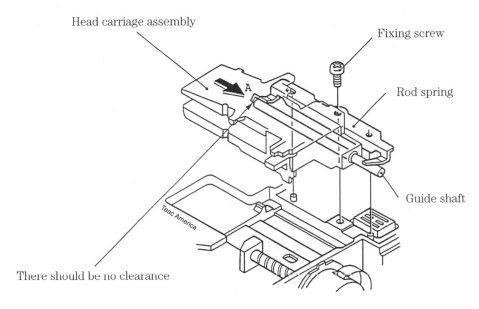

Head carriage assembly

Fixing screw

Rod spring

A

Guide shaft

Teac America

There should be no clearance

5-30 View of a R/W head assembly.

signals, replace the defective control circuit IC. If analog signals are present to the heads, try replacing the heads or the entire head carriage assembly. You can also replace the entire drive outright.

Symptom 5: The drive is able to write to a write-protected disk   Before concluding that there is a drive problem, remove and examine the disk itself to ensure that it is actually write-protected. If the disk is not write-protected, write-protect it appropriately and try the disk again. If the disk is already protected, use your multimeter to check the drive's write-protect sensor. For an unprotected disk, the sensor output should be a logic 1, while a protected disk should generate a logic 0 (some drives may reverse this convention). If there is no change in logic level across the sensor for a protected or unprotected disk, try a new write-protect sensor.

If the sensor itself appears to function properly, check the Write Protect signal at the physical interface (pin 28). A write-protected disk should cause a logic 0 on the Write Protect line. If the signal remains logic 1 regardless of whether the disk is write-protected or not, the control circuit IC in the drive is probably defective. If you are unable to replace the IC, change the drive PC board or replace the entire floppy drive outright.

Symptom 6: The drive can only recognize either high-density or double-density medium, but not both   This problem usually appears in 3.5-in drives during the disk format process when the drive must check the medium type. In most cases, the normal/high-density sensor is jammed or defective. Remove the disk and use your multimeter to measure across the sensor. You should be able to actuate the sensor by hand (either by pressing a switch or interrupting a light path) and watch the output display change accordingly on your multimeter. If the sensor does not respond, it is probably defective and should be replaced.

If the sensor itself responds as expected, check the normal/high-density signal at the physical interface (pin 2). A double-density disk should cause a logic 1 output, while a high-density disk should cause a logic 0 signal. If the signal at the physical interface does not respond to changes in the density sensor, the control circuit IC on the drive PC board is probably defective. If you are unable to replace the control circuit IC, you can replace the drive PC board or the entire floppy drive outright.

Symptom 7: Double-density (720-kB) 3.5-in disks are not working properly when formatted as high-density (1.44-MB) disks This is a common problem when double-density diskettes are pressed into service as high-density disks. In actual practice, double-density disks use a lower-grade medium than high-density disks. This makes double-density disks unreliable when used in high-density mode. Some good-quality diskettes will tolerate this misuse better than other lower-quality diskettes. As a general rule, do *not* use double-density diskettes as high-density disks.

Symptom 8: DOS reports an error such as CANNOT READ FROM DRIVE A: **even though a diskette is fully inserted in the drive, and the drive LED indicates that access is being attempted** Start by trying a known-good diskette in the drive (a faulty diskette can cause some perplexing R/W problems). If the diskette is working properly, take a few minutes to clean the drive. Oxides and debris on the R/W heads can interfere with head contact. Do *not* run the drive with a head-cleaning disk inserted for more than 30 s at a time, or you risk damaging the heads with excessive friction.

Next, remove the floppy drive and check the assembly for visible damage or obstructions. Insert a diskette and see that the disk is clamped properly. Clear any obstructions which may be preventing the disk from seating properly. Also inspect the 34-pin signal cable for obvious damage, and see that it is connected properly at both the drive and the drive controller. Try a new signal cable. If problems persist, the drive itself is probably defective. Try replacing the floppy drive. In most cases, this should correct the problem. If not, replace the floppy drive controller.

Symptom 9: When a new diskette is inserted in the drive, a directory from a previous diskette appears You may have to reset the system in order to get the new diskette to be recognized. This is the classic "phantom directory" problem, and is usually due to a drive or cable fault. Check the 34-pin signal cable first. In most cases, the cable is damaged or is not inserted properly at either end. Try a new signal cable. If this is a new drive installation, check the floppy drive jumpers. Some floppy drives allow the Disk Change signal to be enabled or disabled. Make sure that the Disk Change signal is enabled. If problems persist, the floppy drive itself is probably defective, so try replacing the floppy drive. In the unlikely event that problems remain, try replacing the drive controller board (phantom directory problems are rare in the drive controller itself).

Note: If you suspect a phantom directory, *do not* initiate any writing to the diskette—its FAT table and directories could be overwritten rendering the disk's contents inaccessible without careful data recovery procedures.

Symptom 10: Your 3.5-in high-density floppy disk cannot format high-density diskettes (but can read and write to them just fine)   This is a problem that plagues older computers (i286 and i386 systems) where after-market high-density drives were added. The problem is a lack of BIOS support for high-density formatting—the system is just too old. In such a case, you have a choice. First, you can upgrade your motherboard BIOS to a version that directly supports 3.5-in high-density diskettes. You could also use the DRIVER.SYS utility—a DOS driver which allows an existing 3.5-in to be "redefined" as a new logical drive providing high-density support. A typical DRIVER.SYS command line would appear in CONFIG.SYS such as

```
device = c:\dos\driver.sys /D:1
```

Symptom 11: You cannot upgrade an XT-class PC with a 3.5-in floppy disk   XT systems support up to four double-density 5.25-in floppy disk drives. It will not support 3.5-in floppy diskettes at all. To install 3.5-in floppy disks, you should check your DOS version (you need to have DOS 3.3 or later installed). Next, you'll need to install an 8-bit floppy drive controller board (remember to disable any existing floppy controller in the system first). The floppy controller will have its own on-board BIOS to support floppy disk operations. Finally, take a look at the XT configuration switches and see that any entries for your floppy drives are set correctly. If you're using a stand-alone floppy controller, you may need to set the motherboard jumpers to "no floppy drives."

Symptom 12: You are unable to "swap" floppy drives so that A: becomes B:, and B: becomes A: This often happens on older systems when users want to make their 3.5-in after-market B: drive into their A: drive, and relegate their aging 5.25-in drive to B: instead. First, check your signal cable. For floppy cables with a wire twist, the endmost connector is A:, and the connector prior to the twist is B:. Reverse the connectors at each floppy drive to reverse their identities. If the cable has *no* twist (this is rare), reset the jumper ID on each drive so that your desired A: drive is set to DS0 (Drive Select 0), and your desired B: drive is jumpered to DS1. If you accomplish this exchange, but one drive is not recognized, try a new floppy signal cable. Also remember to check your CMOS settings—you'll need to reverse the floppy drive entries for your A: and B: drives, then reboot the system.

Symptom 13: When using a combination floppy drive (called a "combo drive"), one of the drives does not work, while the other works fine   This problem is often caused by a drive fault. First, be sure to check the power connector—make sure that both +5 V and +12 V are adequately provided to the drive through the 4-pin "mate-n-lock" connector. If the drive is receiving the proper power, the drive itself has almost certainly failed—try a new drive.

Symptom 14: There are no jumpers available on the floppy disk, so it is impossible to change settings This is not a problem as much as it is an inconvenience. Typically, you can expect "unjumpered" floppy disks to be set to the following specifications: Drive Select 1, Disk Change (pin 34) enabled, and Frame Ground enabled. This configuration supports dual-drive systems with twisted floppy cables.

Symptom 15: The floppy drive activity LED stays on as soon as the computer is powered up This is a classic signaling problem which occurs after changing or upgrading a drive system. In virtually all cases, one end of the drive cable has been inserted backward. Make sure that pin 1 on the 34-pin cable is aligned properly with the connector on both the drive and controller. If problems remain, the drive controller may have failed. This is rare, but try a new drive controller.

6
CHAPTER

Hard Disk Drives

There are a handful of drawbacks that limit the usefulness and reliability of floppy disks. Even the finest floppy system is slow to save and recall data, consumes a substantial amount of power relative to other areas of a computer, and is prone to medium failure and incompatibility problems between various disks. Floppy drives are also limited in their storage capacity. Massive operating systems and multi-megabyte application programs simply need more than a single 1.2-or 1.44-MB disk for storage. Switching between multiple disks is a cumbersome and unreliable solution. The demands for a massive, permanent storage device gave rise to the *hard disk drive* (also called a hard drive or HDD) in the early 1980s (Fig. 6-1). Ultimately, the ability to store large quantities of data has only helped to fuel further computer development. Today, huge hard drives are standard equipment in desktop

6-1 A Maxtor 7000 series hard drive.

computers and available in every notebook and subnotebook computer now in production. This chapter presents the technology and principles of hard disk drives and provides you with some solutions for drive testing and troubleshooting.

Drive Concepts

The first step in understanding hard drives is to learn the basic concepts involved. Many of the terms covered for floppy drives in Chap. 5 also apply to hard drives, but the additional performance requirements and operating demands placed on hard drives have resulted in an array of important new ideas. In principle, a hard disk drive (Fig. 6-2) is very similar to a floppy drive. A magnetic recording medium is applied to a substrate material which is then spun at a high rate of speed. Magnetic read/write (R/W) heads in close proximity to the medium can step rapidly across the spinning medium to detect or create flux transitions as required. When you look closely, however, you can see that there are some major physical differences between floppy and hard drives.

Platters and media

Where floppy disks use magnetic material applied over a thin, flexible substrate of Mylar or some other plastic, hard drives use rugged, solid substrates called *platters*. You can clearly view the platters of a hard drive in Fig. 6-3. A platter is traditionally made of aluminum because aluminum is a light material, it is easy to machine to desired tolerances, and holds its shape under the high centrifugal forces that occur at high rotation rates. But today, most platters are made from materials like glass or ceramic composite. These materials have *very* low thermal expansion rates (so there are fewer medium problems) and can withstand higher centrifugal forces than aluminum. Since a major advantage of a hard drive is speed, platters are rotated at about 5200 RPM to as much as 7200 RPM (older drives ran at 3600 RPM). A hard

6-2 A Quantum ProDrive SCSI hard drive.

6-3 A Maxtor 1.24GB hard drive.

drive generally uses two or more platters, though extremely small drive assemblies may use only one platter.

Hard drives must be capable of tremendous recording densities—well over 10,000 bits per inch (BPI). To achieve such substantial recording densities, platter medium is far superior to the oxide medium used for floppy disks. First, the medium must possess a high coercivity so that each flux transition is well defined and easily discernible from every other flux transition. Coercivity of hard drive medium typically exceeds 1400 Oe. Second, the medium must be *extremely* flat across the entire platter surface to within just a few microinches. Hard drive R/W heads do not actually contact their platters, but ride within a few microinches over the platter surfaces. A surface defect of only a few microinches can collide with a head and destroy it. Such a *head crash* is often a catastrophic defect that requires hard drive replacement. Floppy drive heads *do* contact the medium, so minor surface defects are not a major concern. You will see more about head flight and surface defects later in this chapter.

Hard-drive medium today is a "thin film" which has long since replaced magnetic oxides. Thin-film medium is a microscopic layer of pure metal (or a metal compound) which is bonded to the substrate surface through an interim layer. The medium is then coated with a protective layer to help survive head crashing. Figure 6-4 illustrates the cross section of a typical hard-drive platter. Thin-film medium also tends to be very flat, so R/W heads can be run very close to the platter surfaces.

Air flow and head flight

R/W heads in a hard disk drive must travel extremely close to the surface of each platter, but can *never* actually contact the medium while the drive is running. The heads could be mechanically fixed, but fixed-altitude flight does not allow for shock or natural vibration that is always present in a drive assembly. Instead, R/W heads are made to float within microinches of a platter surface by suspending the heads on a layer of moving air. Figures 6-5 and 6-6 illustrate the typical air flow in a hard drive. Disk (platter) rotation creates a slight cushion that elevates the

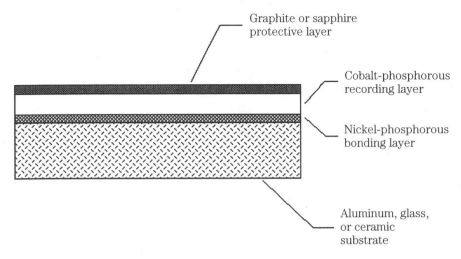

6-4 Cross-sectional view of a typical hard-drive platter.

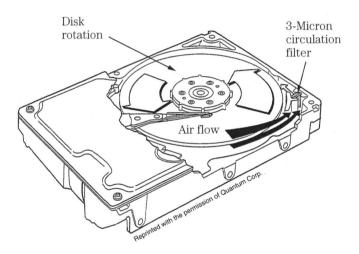

6-5 Air flow in a small hard drive.

heads. You may also notice that some air is channeled through a fine filter that helps to remove any particles from the drive's enclosure.

It is important to note that all hard drives seal their platter assemblies into an air-tight chamber. The reason for such a seal is to prevent contamination from dust, dirt, spills, or strands of hair. Contamination that lands on a platter's surface can easily result in a head crash. A head crash can damage the head, the medium, or both— and any physical damage can result in an unusable drive.

Consider the comparison shown in Fig. 6-7. During normal operation, a hard drive's R/W head flies above the medium at a distance of only about 10 microns (many technical professionals relate that specification to a jumbo jet flying 30 feet above the ground at 600 miles per hour). It follows then that any variation in surface flatness due to platter defects or contaminates can have catastrophic effects on head height. Even an average particle of smoke is 10 times wider than the flying height.

With such proportions, you can understand why it is critically important that the platter compartment remain sealed at all times. The platter compartment can only be opened in a cleanroom environment. A cleanroom is a small, enclosed room where the air is filtered to remove any contaminants larger than 3 mm. Hard-drive assemblers wear gloves and cleanroom suits that cover all but their faces—even masks cover their mouths and noses to prevent breath vapor from contaminating the platters.

Areal density

It is desirable to pack as much information as possible in the medium of hard-drive platters. The *areal density* of a medium describes this maximum amount of

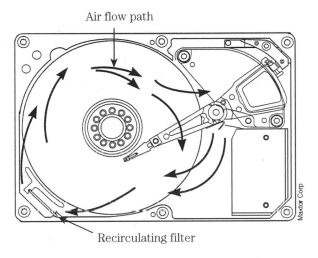

6-6 Alternate air flow in a hard drive.

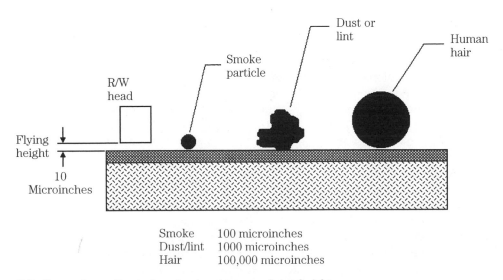

6-7 Comparison of typical contaminants versus flying height.

capacity in terms of megabytes per square inch (MB/in^2). Today's hard drives use media supporting 400 to 800 MB/in2. As you might imagine, physically smaller platters must hold media with a higher areal density to offer storage capacities similar to larger drives.

There are several major factors that affect areal density. First, the actual size of magnetic particles in the medium places an upper barrier on areal density—smaller particles allow higher areal densities. Larger coercivity of the medium and smaller R/W heads with tighter magnetization fields allow higher areal densities. Finally, head height—the altitude of a R/W head over the platter surface—controls density. The closer a R/W head passes to its medium, the higher areal densities can be. As heads fly further away, magnetic fields spread out, resulting in lower densities. Surface smoothness is then a major limiting factor in areal density, since smoother surfaces allow R/W heads to fly closer to the medium.

Latency

As fast as a hard drive is, it cannot work instantaneously. There is a finite delay between the moment that a read or write command is initiated over the drive's physical interface, and the moment that desired information is available (or placed). This delay is known as *latency*. More specifically, latency refers to the time it takes for needed bytes to pass under a R/W head. If the head has not quite reached the desired location yet, latency can be quite short. If the head has just missed the desired location, the head must wait almost a full rotation before the needed bits are available again, so latency can be rather long. In general, a disk drive is specified with *average latency*, which (statistically) is the time for the spindle to make half of a full rotation. For a disk rotating at 3600 RPM (or 60 rotations per second), a full rotation is completed in 16.7 ms. Average latency would then be (16.7/2) or 8.3 ms. Disks spinning at 5200 RPM offer an average latency of 5.8 ms, and so on. As a rule, the faster a disk spins, the lower latency will be. Ultimately, disk speed is limited by centrifugal forces acting on the platters.

Tracks, sectors, and cylinders

As with floppy drives, you cannot simply place data anywhere on a hard-drive platter—the drive would have no idea where to look for data, or if the data are even valid. The information on each platter must be sorted and organized into a series of known, standard locations. Each platter side can be considered as a two-dimensional field possessing height and width. With this sort of geometry, data are recorded in sets of concentric circles running from the disk spindle to the platter edge. A drive can move its R/W heads over the spinning medium to locate needed data or programs in a matter of milliseconds. Every concentric circle on a platter is known as a *track*. A current platter generally contains 2048 to 7752 tracks. Figure 6-8 shows data organization on a simple platter assembly. Note that only one side of the three platters is shown.

While each surface of a platter is a two-dimensional area, the number of platter surfaces involved in a hard drive (4, 6, 8, or more) bring a third dimension into play. Since each track is located directly over the same tracks on subsequent platters, each track in a platter assembly can be visualized as a cylinder that passes through

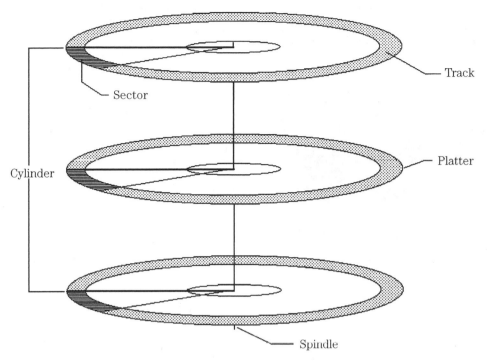

Track

Sector

Cylinder

Platter

Spindle

6-8 Data organization on a typical hard drive.

every platter. The number of cylinders is equal to the number of tracks on one side of a platter. Consider the multiple platters for the drive in Fig. 6-9.

Once a R/W head finishes reading one track, the head must be stepped to another (usually adjacent) track. This stepping process, no matter how rapid, does require some finite amount of time. When the head tries to step directly from the end of one track to the beginning of another, the head will arrive too late to catch the new track's index pulse(s), so the drive will have to wait almost an entire rotation to synchronize with the track index pulse. By offsetting the start points of each track as in Fig. 6-10, head travel time can be compensated for. This *cylinder skewing* technique is intended to improve hard-drive performance by reducing the disk time lost during normal head steps. A head should be able to identify and read the desired information from a track within one disk rotation.

Tracks are broken down even further into small segments called *sectors.* As with DOS floppy disks, a sector holds 512 bytes of data, along with error-checking and housekeeping data that identify the sector, track, and results calculated by cyclical redundancy checking (CRC). The location and ID information for each sector are developed when the drive is low-level formatted at the factory. After formatting, only sector data and CRC bytes are updated during writing. If sector ID information is accidentally overwritten or corrupted, the data recorded in the afflicted sector become unreadable.

Figure 6-11 shows the layout for a typical sector on a Maxtor SCSI drive. As you can see, there is much more than just 512 bytes of data. The start of every sector is marked with a pulse. The pulse signaling the first sector of a track is called the

6-9 A Quantum ProDrive LPS hard drive.

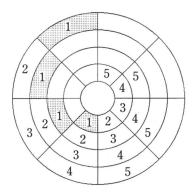

6-10 An example of sector/
cylinder skew.

index pulse. There are two portions to every sector: an address area and data area. The *address area* is used to identify the sector. This is critically important because the drive must be able to identify precisely which cylinder, head, and sector is about to be read or written. This location information is recorded in the "address field," and is followed by 2 bytes of CRC data. When a drive identifies a location, it generates a CRC code which it compares to the CRC code recorded on the disk. If the two CRC codes match, the address is assumed to be valid, and disk operation can continue. Otherwise, an error has occurred and the entire sector is considered invalid. This failure usually precipitates a catastrophic DOS error message.

After a number of bytes are encountered for drive timing and synchronization, up to 512 bytes can be read or written to the "data field." The data are processed to derive 11 bytes of error-checking code (ECC) using Reed Solomon encoding. If data are being read, the derived ECC is compared to the recorded ECC. When the codes match, data are assumed to be valid and drive operation continues. Otherwise, a data read error is assumed. During writing, the old ECC data are replaced with the new ECC data derived for the current data. It is interesting to note that only the data and ECC fields of a sector are written after formatting. All other sector data remain untouched until the drive is reformatted. If a retentivity problem should eventually allow one or more bits to become corrupt in the address area, the sector will fail.

Sector sparing

Not all sectors on a hard drive are usable. When a drive is formatted, bad sectors must be removed from normal use. The sparing process works to ensure that each track has access to the appropriate number of working sectors. When sparing is performed in-line (as a drive is being formatted), faulty sectors cause all subsequent sectors to be shifted up one sector. In-line sparing is not widely used. Field defect sparing (after the format process is complete) assigns (remaps) faulty sectors to other working sectors located in spare disk tracks that are reserved for that purpose. For example, most EIDE hard drives use field defect sparing. It reserves a full 16 tracks for spare sectors. Faulty sectors are typically marked for reallocation when the disk is formatted.

The only place where faulty sectors are *absolutely* not permitted is on track 00. Track 00 is used to hold a hard drive's partition and FAT information. If a drive cannot read or write to track 00, the entire drive is rendered unusable. If a sector in track 00 should fail during operation, reformatting the drive to lock out the bad sector will not necessarily recover the drive's operation. Track 00 failures usually necessitate reformatting the drive from scratch or replacing it entirely.

Landing zone

The R/W heads of a hard drive fly within microinches of their respective platter surfaces—held aloft with air currents produced by the spinning platters. When the drive is turned off, however, the platters slow to a halt. During this *spindown* period, air flow falls rapidly, and heads can literally crash into their platter surfaces. Whenever a head touches a platter surface, data can be irretrievably destroyed. Even during normal operation, a sudden shock or bump can cause one or more

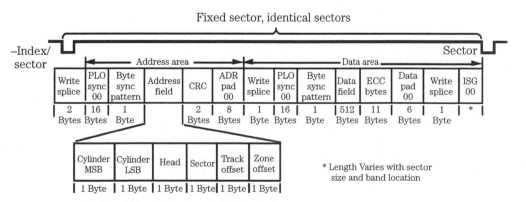

6-11 Sector layout of a typical hard drive.

heads to skid across their surfaces. Although a drive can usually be reformatted after a head crash, data and programs would have to be reloaded from scratch.

In order to avoid head crash during normal spindown, a cylinder is reserved (either the innermost or outermost cylinder) as a *landing zone*. No data are stored on the landing zone, so any surface problems caused by head landings are harmless. Virtually all hard drives today will automatically move the head assembly over the landing zone before spindown, then gently lock the heads into place until power is restored. Locking helps to ensure that random shocks and vibrations do not shake the heads onto adjacent data-carrying tracks and cause damage while power is off.

Interleave

The *interleave* of a hard drive refers to the order in which sectors are numbered on a platter. Interleave was a critical factor in older desktop computer systems where the core logic (i.e., CPU and memory) was relatively slow compared to drive performance. It was necessary to create artificial delays in the drive to allow core logic to catch up. Delays were accomplished by physically separating the sectors (numbering contiguous sectors out of order). This ordering forced the drive to read a sector, then skip one or more sectors to reach the next subsequent sector. The drive would have to make several rotations before all sectors on a track could be read.

The ratio of a sector's length versus the distance between two subsequent sectors is known as the *interleave factor*. For example, if a drive reads a sector and skips a sector to reach the next sequential sector, interleave factor would be 1:3, and so on. The greater the interleave, the more rotations that would be needed to read all the sectors on a track, and the slower the drive would be. To achieve highest disk performance, interleave should be eliminated.

Since core logic today is so much faster than even the fastest hard drive, the issue of interleave is largely irrelevant. Drives no longer interleave their sectors, so all sectors are in sequential order around the track, and the interleave factor is 1:1—all data on a track can be read in one disk rotation (minus latency). An interleave factor of 1:1 yields optimal drive performance.

Write precompensation

As you have already seen, a hard drive spins its platter(s) at a constant rate. This is known as *constant angular velocity* (or CAV). While constant rotation requires only a very simple motor circuit, extra demands are placed on the medium. Tracks closer to the spindle are physically shorter than tracks toward the platter's outer edge. Shorter tracks result in shorter sectors. For inner sectors to hold the same amount of data as outer sectors, data must be packed more densely on the inner sectors—each magnetic flux reversal is actually smaller. Unfortunately, smaller flux reversals produce weaker magnetic fields in the R/W heads during reading.

If the inner sectors are written with a stronger magnetic field, flux transitions stored in the medium will be stronger. When the inner sectors are then read, a clearer, more well-defined signal will result. The use of increased writing current to compensate for diminished disk response is known as *write precompensation*. The track where write precompensation is expected to begin is specified in the drive's parameter table in CMOS system setup. Write precompensation filled an important role in early drives that used older, oxide-based medium. Today's thin-film medium and very small drive geometries result in low signal differences across the platter area, so write precompensation (although still specified) is rarely meaningful any more.

Drive parameters and translation

A host computer must know the key parameters of its installed hard drive before the drive can be used. There are six parameters that a system must know: the number of cylinders, heads, and sectors, as well as the track where write precompensation begins, what track the landing zone is on, and the drive's formatted capacity. These parameters are stored in the computer's CMOS setup memory. If a new drive is installed, the CMOS setup can easily be updated to show the changes. Table 6-1 illustrates an example of drive parameters.

You can tell a lot about a drive by reviewing its parameters. Consider the Western Digital AC34000 shown in Table 6-1. With 16 heads and 63 sectors per track, the capacity works out as (7752 $\times$ 16 $\times$ 63 $\times$ 512) or about 4001 MB (or 4.0 GB). There are two interesting things to note about the drives of Table 6-1. First, the Write Precompensation and Landing Zone entries are essentially unused. In most cases, the landing zone is now an automated feature of the particular drive. The second issue to consider is that these numbers are *logical,* and *not* physical. Just imagine that with two heads per platter, you'd need 8 platters to support 16 heads—not too likely in today's small form-factor drives. Also, in actual practice, the number of sectors per track can differ (the outer tracks provide more sectors, and the inner tracks may offer fewer sectors). This is known as *zoned recording.* What this means is that the drive parameters you are entering into CMOS are *translation parameters.* The drive itself actually converts (or translates) those parameters into actual physical drive locations.

IDE translation limits

Unfortunately, there is a serious problem with drive parameters under conventional IDE standards—the drive size is limited to 528 MB. To understand the limitations of drive size, you must understand how IDE drives are addressed. The classic addressing scheme is known as *cylinder head sector* (or CHS) addressing. Simply stated, you place the cylinder number, head number, and sector number you need to get to into the drive controller registers, then call the Int 13 routine in BIOS, which runs

Table 6-1. An example of Drive Parameters

Parameter	Western Digital AC34000	Seagate ST3853A	Maxtor 83840A
Cylinders	7752	826	7441
Heads	16	32	16
Sectors per track	63	63	63
Write precompensation	n/a	n/a	0
Landing zone	auto	auto	0
Capacity, MB	4001	852.5	3840

the drive to the desired location for reading or writing. This is basically why you need to enter drive parameters in CMOS.

This works well in theory, but there is a problem. The limiting values for cylinders, heads, and sectors are *not* the same in BIOS and the WD1003 architecture. Table 6-2 illustrates these values, and you can see their impact on drive size. BIOS specifies a maximum of 1024 cylinders, 255 heads, and 63 sectors per track. If you multiply these together, then multiply 512 bytes/sector, you get 8,422,686,720 bytes (or 8.4 GB) of theoretical capacity. For the WD1003 controller, you should be able to have 65,536 cylinders, 16 heads, and 255 sectors per track. When this is multiplied by 512 bytes/sector, you get a whopping 1.36899×10^{11} bytes (or 136.9 GB) of theoretical capacity. So where's the problem?

The problem is that you can only use the *lowest common number* for each approach, so the maximum number of cylinders you can use is 1024, the maximum number of heads is 16, and the maximum number of sectors is 63. When you multiply these out, then multiply times 512 bytes/sector, you only get 528 MB. The real tragedy here is that if BIOS designers and WD1003 designers had sat down and come up with the *same* numbers, we could easily have had IDE drives with capacities up to 136.9 GB, and this entire issue would be moot for another 10 years. But instead, we can only use up to 528 MB. The net result is that we cannot use more than 528 MB of drive capacity unless our drive controller system has a means of overcoming traditional BIOS limitations.

Breaking the barrier with EIDE

As IDE drives continued to grow into 1991 and 1992, their limitations were becoming painfully apparent. IDE drives were limited in data transfer speed, and other devices (such as CD-ROM drives) could not take advantage of the IDE interface. Early in 1992, the Enhanced IDE (or EIDE) drives began to appear. EIDE allowed more advanced features and faster data transfer speeds. Virtually all hard drives over 1 GB are EIDE drives. The important element to remember about EIDE is that it uses the *same* 40-pin physical interface used by IDE drives. The signals are identical. In order to take advantage of the enhancements EIDE drives offer, new drive controllers were developed with on-board BIOS which could supplement existing BIOS Int 13 calls. Today, all drive controllers are compatible with EIDE standards.

Of course, there have been big IDE/EIDE drives around for a few years now (or you may use an EIDE drive on an IDE interface), and like most parts of the PC, there are ways to work around this limitation. Since BIOS is essentially software, the easiest and most economical way to overcome the 528-MB barrier is to "augment" the BIOS Int 13 routine by introducing a device driver when the PC is initialized. Int 13

Table 6-2. CHS Values versus Drive Size

	BIOS	**WD1003**	**Resulting limit**
Cylinders	1024	65,536	1024
Heads	255	16	16
Sectors	63	255	63
Max capacity	8.4 GB	136.9 GB	528 MB

enhancements allow the support of drive sizes up to 8.4 GB. The Drive Rocket and Disk Manager by Ontrack are two of the most popular drivers available. They allow the PC to access the entire space of large IDE drives—not just 528 MB. If you install a large hard drive but cannot update the controller hardware to support it, Ontrack software may be your only real option.

Large hard drives work with such drivers, and Disk Manager (or one of its cousins) is frequently bundled with large IDE and the new EIDE-compatible hard drives. However, there are some compelling reasons why drivers are not desirable. First, drivers take memory space—typically precious space within the first 640 KB of RAM. Few systems have space remaining in the upper memory area for a disk driver. Second, disk drivers do not accommodate Windows very well, so using large hard drives under Windows 3.1 and 3.11 has traditionally been a problem. Third, the disk driver may conflict with other device drivers and TSRs that may be on your PC.

Ultimately, the *preferred* method of large drive support for EIDE is to update the motherboard BIOS itself with one that contains the Int 13 enhancements. AMI and Micro Firmware are early entrants into the EIDE-compatible BIOS arena, and other BIOS makers are sure to follow. While upgrading a BIOS is a bit more involved than adding a driver, the rewards (more free memory and better OS compatibility) are almost always worth it. As an effective alternative to the trials of a motherboard BIOS upgrade, you can choose an EIDE adapter with on-board BIOS extensions for Int 13.

Note: Keep in mind that IDE drives are backward-compatible with EIDE controllers, and (using Ontrack software) EIDE drives can be made compatible with IDE controllers.

Using logical block addressing

Another great source of confusion in the migration to EIDE is its need for *logical block addressing* (or LBA). When installing an EIDE drive, set the CMOS drive mode in CMOS Setup to LBA. Where CHS addressing requires the specification of a discrete cylinder, head, and sector, an LBA address simply requires the specification of a sector (i.e., "go to sector 324534"). The LBA algorithm (implemented in BIOS) will translate the sector to the appropriate CHS equivalent. FAT-based operating systems such as DOS (and Windows, since Windows works on the DOS file system) *require* the use of LBA addressing for EIDE support. As a consequence, you *will* need to update your motherboard BIOS, or use an EIDE controller with on-board BIOS. On the other hand, non-FAT operating systems (such as OS/2 and Novell Netware) do *not* require LBA addressing. When you actually have an EIDE controller in hand, you may note that the controller provides a jumper allowing you to enable or disable LBA addressing. If you are using DOS (or Windows), keep this jumper *enabled.*

An important consideration in choosing CHS or LBA addressing is the format of your hard drive(s). If you choose to invoke LBA addressing, you will need to reformat your hard drive(s). You must also remember that once a hard drive is formatted for LBA, the drive will *only* be recognized by PCs that support LBA. As a result, if you take an LBA-formatted drive and install it into a PC whose BIOS does not support LBA, the drive will simply not be recognized, and you will have to reformat the drive again.

Note: In all cases, remember to perform a complete backup of your hard drive(s) before implementing EIDE on your system.

Data transfer rates

You can't really discuss hard drives and EIDE today without considering the implications of *data transfer* and transfer rates. In practice, there are two measures of data transfer: the rate at which data are taken from the platters, and the rate at which data are passed between the drive and controller. The *internal* data transfer between the platters and drive buffer is typically the slower rate. Older drives could run around 5 MB/s, but newer EIDE drives will transfer internal data up to about 13 MB/s. The *external* data transfer between the drive and controller is often the faster rate. Older drives provided between 5 and 8 MB/s, but new EIDE drives can operate up to 16 MB/s. The modern standards of IDE/EIDE external data transfer are listed as PIO (or Programmed I/O) and DMA (Direct Memory Access) modes. The PIO mode specifies how fast data are transferred to and from the drive as shown in Table 6-3.

You may notice that the EIDE-specific modes (PIO-3 and PIO-4) use the IORDY hardware flow control line. This means that the drive can use the IORDY line to slow down the interface when necessary. Interfaces without proper IORDY support may cause data corruption in the fast PIO modes (so you'd be stuck with the slower modes). When choosing an EIDE drive and controller, always be sure to check that the IORDY line is being used.

DMA data transfers mean that the data are transferred *directly* between the drive and memory without using the CPU as an intermediary (as is the case with PIO). In true multitasking operating systems like OS/2, Windows NT, or Linux, DMA leaves the CPU free to do something useful during disk transfers. In a DOS or Windows environment, the CPU will have to wait for the transfer to finish anyway, so in these cases DMA isn't terribly useful.

There are two distinct types of DMA: ordinary DMA and bus-mastering DMA. Ordinary DMA uses the DMA controller on the system's motherboard to perform the complex task of arbitration, grabbing the system bus, and transferring the data. With bus-mastering DMA, all this is done by logic on the drive controller card itself (this adds considerably to the complexity and the price of a bus-mastering interface). Unfortunately, the DMA controller on traditional ISA bus systems is slow, and out of the question for use with a modern hard disk. VLB (Video Local bus) cards cannot be used as DMA targets at all, and can only do bus-mastering DMA. Only EISA and PCI-based interfaces make non-bus-mastering DMA viable; EISA type "B" DMA will transfer 4 MB/s, and PCI type "F" DMA will transfer between 6 and 8 MB/s. Today, the proper software support for DMA is still rare (as well as the interfaces supporting it). Still, the DMA data transfer modes are listed in Table 6-4.

Block mode transfers

Traditionally, an interrupt (IRQ) is generated each time a read or write command is passed to the drive. This causes a certain amount of overhead work for the host system and CPU. If it were possible to transfer multiple sectors of data between the drive and host without generating an IRQ, data transfer could be accomplished much more efficiently. Block mode transfers allow up to 128 sectors of data to be transferred at a single time and can improve transfers as much as 30 percent. However,

Table 6-3. Data Transfer Speeds versus PIO Modes

PIO mode	Cycle time, ns	Transfer rate, MB/s	Notes
0	600	3.3	These are the old IDE modes
1	383	5.2	
2	240	8.3	
3	180 IORDY	11.1	These are the newer EIDE modes
4	120 IORDY	16.6	

Table 6-4. Data Transfer Speeds versus DMA Modes

DMA mode		Cycle time, ns	Transfer rate, MB/s	Notes
Single word	0	960	2.1	Also in ATA
	1	480	4.2	
	2	240	8.3	
Multiword	0	480	4.2	Also in ATA
	1	150	13.3	
	2	120	16.6	

block mode transfers are not terribly effective on single-tasking operating systems like DOS. Any improvement over a few percent usually indicates bad buffer cache management on the part of the drive. Finally, the block size that is optimal for drive throughput isn't always the best for system performance. For example, the DOS FAT file system tends to favor a block size equal to the cluster size.

Drive caching

Ideally, a mass-storage device should respond instantaneously—data should be available the moment they are requested. Unfortunately, the instant access and transfer of data are impossible with even today's magnetic (and optical) storage technologies. The inescapable laws of physics govern the limitations of mechanical systems such as spindles and head stepping, and mechanical delays will always be present (to some extent) in drive systems. The problem now facing computer designers is that mechanical drive systems—as fast and precise as they are—still lag far behind the computer circuitry handling the information. In the world of personal computers, a millisecond is a very long time. For DOS-based systems, you often must wait for disk access to be completed before DOS allows another operation to begin. Such delays can be quite irritating when the drive is accessing huge programs and data files typical of current software packages. Drives use a technique called *drive caching* to increase the apparent speed of drive systems.

Caching basically allocates a small amount of solid-state memory which acts as an interim storage area (or *buffer*) located right on the drive. A cache is typically loaded with information that is *anticipated* to be required by the system. When a disk read is initiated, the cache is checked for desired information. If the desired information is actually in the cache (a cache *hit*), that information is transferred from the cache buffer to the core logic at electronic rates—no disk access occurs, and very fast data transfer is achieved. If the desired information is not in the cache (a cache *miss*), the data are taken from the hard disk at normal drive speeds with no improvement in performance. A variety of complex software algorithms are used to predict what disk information to load and save in a cache. Figure 6-12 illustrates the caching algorithm used by Quantum Corporation for some of their ProDrive hard drives.

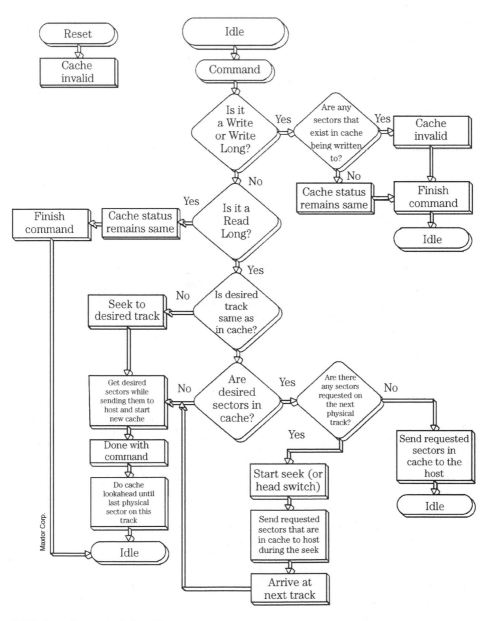

6-12 A cache control algorithm.

Although the majority of caches are intended to buffer read operations, some caches also buffer write operations. A write cache accepts the data to be saved from core logic, then returns system control while the drive works separately to save the information. Keep in mind that a cache does not accelerate the drive itself. A cache merely helps to move your system along so that you need not wait for drive delays. In terms of general implementation, a cache can be located on the hard drive itself, or on the drive controller board. For most computers using system-level hard drive interfaces (EIDE or SCSI), any cache is usually located on the drive itself.

Drive Construction

Now that you have a background in major hard-drive concepts and operations (Fig. 6-13), it is time to take a drive apart and show you how all the key pieces fit together. While it is somewhat rare that you should ever need to disassemble a hard drive, the understanding of each part and its placement will help you to appreciate drive testing and the various hard-drive failure modes. An exploded diagram for a Quantum hard drive is illustrated in Fig. 6-14. There are six areas that this book concentrates on: the frame, platters, R/W heads, head actuators, spindle motor, and electronics package. Let's look at each area instead.

Frame

The mechanical *frame* (1) is important to the successful operation of a hard drive. The frame (or chassis) affects a drive's structural, thermal, and electrical integrity. A frame must be rigid, and provide a steady platform for mounting the working components. Larger drives typically use a chassis of cast aluminum, but the small drive in your notebook or pen computer may use a plastic frame. The particular

6-13 A Quantum ProDrive ELS hard drive.

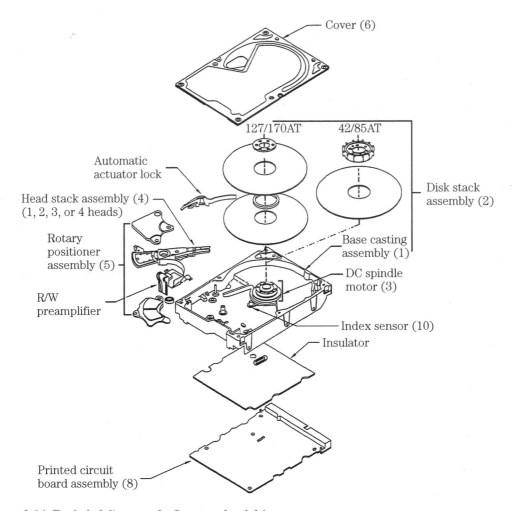

Cover (6)

127/170AT   42/85AT

Automatic
actuator lock

Head stack assembly (4)
(1, 2, 3, or 4 heads)

Rotary
positioner
assembly (5)

R/W
preamplifier

Disk stack
assembly (2)

Base casting
assembly (1)

DC spindle
motor (3)

Index sensor (10)

Insulator

Printed circuit
board assembly (8)

6-14 Exploded diagram of a Quantum hard drive.

frame material really depends on the *form factor* (dimensions) of your drive. Table 6-5 compares the form factors of several drive generations.

Platters

As you probably read earlier in this chapter, *platters* (2) are relatively heavy-duty disks of aluminum, glass, or ceramic composite material. Platters are coated on both sides with a layer of magnetic material (the actual medium) and covered with a protective layer. Finished and polished platters are then stacked and coupled to the *spindle motor* (3). Note that some drives may only use one platter. Before the platter stack is fixed to the chassis, the *R/W head assembly* (4) is fitted in between each disk. There is usually one head per platter side, so a drive with two platters should have three or four heads. During drive operation, the platter stack spins at 5200 RPM or higher.

Read/Write heads

As with floppy drives, read/write (R/W) heads form the interface between a drive's electronic circuitry and magnetic medium. During writing, a head translates electronic signals into magnetic flux transitions that saturate points on the medium where those transitions take place. A read operation works roughly in reverse. Flux transitions along the disk induce electrical signals in the head which are amplified, filtered, and translated into corresponding logic signals. It is up to the drive's electronics to determine whether a head is reading or writing.

Early hard drive R/W heads generally resembled floppy drive heads—soft iron cores with a core of 8 to 34 turns of fine copper wire. Such heads were physically large and relatively heavy, which limited the number of tracks available on a platter surface and presented more inertia to be overcome by the head-positioning system. Virtually all current hard-drive designs have abandoned classical "wound coil" heads in favor of thin-film R/W heads. Thin-film heads are fabricated in much the same way as ICs or platter medium using photochemical processes. The result is a very flat, sensitive, small, and durable R/W head, but even thin-film heads use an air gap and 8 to 34 turns of copper wire. Small size and light weight allow for smaller track widths (often more than 3000 tracks per platter side today) and faster head travel time. The inherent flatness of thin-film heads helps to reduce flying height to only 5 µm or so.

In assemblies, the heads themselves are attached to long metal arms that are moved by the head actuator motor(s) as shown in Fig. 6-15. R/W preamp ICs are typically mounted on a small PC board that is attached to the head/actuator assembly. The entire subassembly is sealed in the platter compartment and is generally inaccessible unless

Table 6-5. Comparison of Form Factor
to Actual Drive Dimensions

Form factor nomenclature		Approximate dimensions		
		Height	Width	Depth
5.25-in full-height*	mm	82.60	145.54	202.69
	in	3.25	5.73	7.98
5.25-in half-height*	mm	41.28	145.54	202.68
	in	1.63	5.73	7.98
3.5-in half-height†	mm	41.28	101.60	146.05
	in	1.63	4.00	5.75
3.5-in low-profile†	mm	25.40	101.60	146.05
	in	1.00	4.00	5.75
2.5-in low-profile	mm	19.05	70.10	101.85
	in	0.75	2.76	4.01
1.8-in low-profile	mm	15.00	51.00	77.00
	in	0.59	2.00	3.03
1.3-in low-profile	mm	10.50	36.50	50.8
	in	0.41	1.44	2.00

*Used in desktop systems *only*.

†Used in desktops and some older laptops.

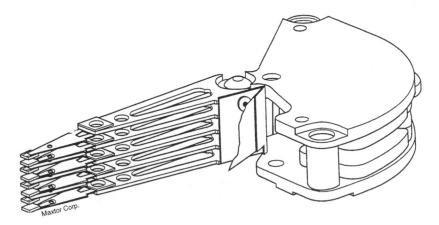

Maxtor Corp.

6-15 A conventional head/actuator assembly.

opened in a cleanroom environment. The compartment is sealed with a *metal lid/ gasket assembly* (6).

Head actuators

Unlike floppy motors that step their R/W heads in and out, hard drives *swing* the heads along a slight arc to achieve radial travel from edge to spindle. Many hard drives use *voice coil motors* (also called *rotary coil motors* or *servos*) to actuate head movement. Voice coil motors (5) work using the same principle as analog meter movements, that is, a permanent magnet is enclosed within two opposing coils. As current flows through the coils, a magnetic field is produced which opposes the permanent magnet. Head arms are attached to the rotating magnet, so the force of opposition causes a deflection that is directly proportional to the amount of driving current. Greater current signals result in greater opposition and greater deflection. Cylinders are selected by incrementing the servo signal and maintaining the signal at the desired level. Voice coil motors are very small and light assemblies that are well suited to fast access times and small hard-drive assemblies.

The greatest challenge to head movement is to keep the heads centered on the desired track. Otherwise, aerodynamic disturbances, thermal effects in the platters, and variations in voice coil driver signals can cause head-positioning error. Head position must be constantly checked and adjusted in real time to ensure that desired tracks are followed exactly. The process of track following is called *servoing* the heads. Information is required to compare the head's expected position to its actual position. Any resulting difference can then be corrected by adjusting the voice coil signal. Servo information is located somewhere on the platters using a variety of techniques.

Dedicated servo information is recorded on a reserved platter side. For example, a two-platter drive using dedicated servo tracking may use three sides for data but use a fourth surface exclusively for track-locating information. Since all heads are positioned along the same track (a cylinder), a single surface can provide data that are needed to correct all heads simultaneously. *Embedded servo* information, however, is encoded as short bursts of data placed between every sector. All surfaces then can hold data *and* provide tracking information. The servo system uses the phase shift of pulses between adjacent tracks to determine whether heads are centered on the desired track or drifting to one side or another. This book is not concerned with the particular tracking techniques—only that tracking information must be provided to keep the heads in proper alignment.

Spindle motor

One of the major factors that contribute to hard drive performance is the speed at which the medium passes under the R/W heads. Medium is passed under the R/W heads by spinning the platter(s) at a high rate of speed (at least 3600 RPM). The *spindle motor* is responsible for spinning the platter(s). A spindle motor is typically a brushless, low-profile dc motor (similar in principle to the spindle motors used in floppy disk drives).

An *index sensor* (10) provides a feedback pulse signal that detects the spindle as it rotates. The drive's *control electronics* (8) uses the index signal to regulate spindle speed as precisely as possible. Today's drives typically use magnetic sensors that detect iron tabs on the spindle shaft, or optoisolators that monitor holes or tabs rotating along the spindle. The spindle motor and index sensor are also sealed in the platter compartment.Older hard drives used a rubber or cork pad to slow the spindle to a stop after drive power is removed, but newer drives use a technique called *dynamic braking*. When power is applied to a spindle motor, a magnetic field is developed in the motor coils. When power is removed, the magnetic energy stored in the coils is released as a reverse voltage pulse. Dynamic braking channels the energy of that reverse voltage to stop the drive faster and more reliably than physical braking.

Drive electronics

Hard drives are controlled by a suite of remarkably sophisticated circuitry. The drive's *control electronics* (8) mounted below the chassis contains all of the circuitry necessary to communicate control and data signals with the particular physical interface, maneuver the R/W heads, read or write as required, and spin the platter(s). Each of these functions must be accomplished to high levels of precision. In spite of the demands and complexity involved in drive electronics, the entire circuit can be fabricated on a single PC board similar to the one shown in Fig. 6-16.

Figure 6-17 illustrates a generic block diagram for a typical hard-drive electronics system. Notice that the spindle motor, voice coil motor, index sensor, and R/W preamplifier circuitry is sealed in with the drive's platter assembly. The electronics PC board typically contains a voice coil (servo) driver circuit, a spindle motor driver circuit, and R/W processing circuitry—all of which is overseen by a drive controller IC (usually a dedicated microprocessor). An interface controller circuit is added to coordinate the flow of data between the drive and core logic. The interface controller that is used depends on the physical interface supported by the drive (i.e., EIDE or SCSI).

A practical hard disk is illustrated in the block diagram of Fig. 6-18. As you look over the Quantum Corporation's ProDrive, you may recognize many of the key elements shown in Fig. 6-17. You should understand the purpose of each part. The

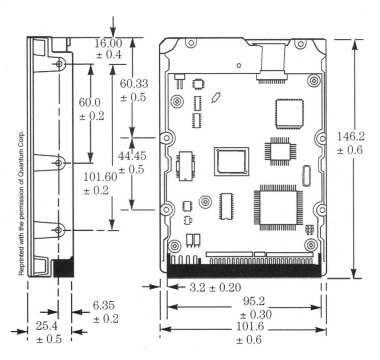

6-16 Drive electronics mounted in a frame.

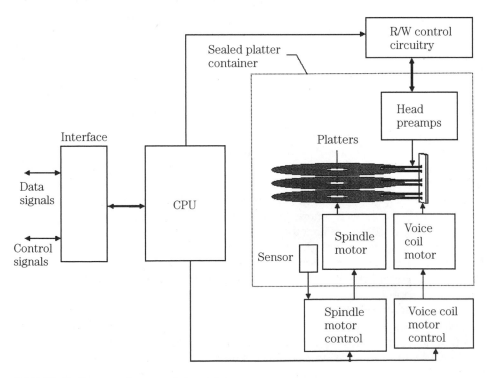

6-17 Block diagram of a generic hard drive.

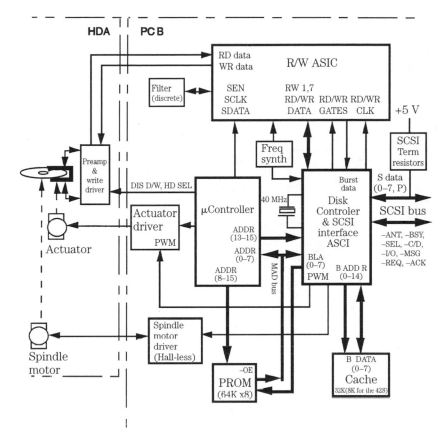

6-18 Diagram of a practical high-performance hard drive.

heart of this drive is a microcontroller (μC). A μC is basically a customized version of a microprocessor that can process program instructions as well as provide a selection of specialized control signals that are not available from ordinary microprocessors. A μC can be considered an application-specific IC (ASIC). The program that operates this drive is stored in a small, programmable read-only memory (PROM). The μC provides enable signals to the voice coil driver IC, R/W preamplifier IC, R/W ASIC, and disk controller/interface ASIC. A controller/interface ASIC works in conjunction with the μC by managing data and control signals on the physical interface. For the drive shown, the ASIC is designed to support an SCSI interface, but variations of this model can use interface ASICs that support EIDE interfaces (you will see physical interfaces in the next part of this chapter).

The primary activity of the controller/interface ASIC is to coordinate the flow of data into or out of the drive. Figure 6-19 shows a detailed view of the disk controller and SCSI interface ASIC. The controller determines read or write operations, handles clock synchronization, and organizes data flow to the R/W ASIC. The controller also manages the local cache memory (you learned about disk caching earlier). Commands received over the physical interface are passed on to the μC for processing and response. The frequency synthesizer helps to synchronize the controller and

6-19 Detailed block diagram of a hard-drive controller/interface IC.

R/W ASIC. Finally, the disk controller ASIC is responsible for selecting the head position and controlling the spindle and motor driver.

The R/W ASIC shown in Fig. 6-20 is another major IC on the drive's PC board. A R/W ASIC accepts data from the controller IC and translates data into serial signals that are sent to the write driver for writing. The R/W ASIC also receives signals amplified by the read preamp, and translates serial signals into parallel digital information available to the controller ASIC. A discrete filter affects the way in which analog signals are handled. R/W heads are connected directly to the read preamplifier/write driver IC which is little more than a bidirectional amplifier IC.

The actuator driver accepts a logic enable signal from the μC and a proportional logic signal from the controller ASIC. The actuator driver then produces an analog output current that positions the R/W heads by driving a voice coil motor. The spindle motor driver is turned on and off by a logic enable signal from the controller ASIC. Once the spindle motor driver is enabled, it will self-regulate its speed using feedback from an index sensor. All components within the dotted area marked "HDA" are located within the sealed platter compartment, while other components in the area marked "PCB" are located on the drive PC board. Most of the drive's intelligence is contained in the μC, controller ASIC, and R/W ASIC.

Drive Interfaces

Hard drives were not included in the earliest PC designs. Instead, hard drives developed as an add-on device that could be included in new computers for sale or added after market. As a result, there was no natural bus-level interface that allowed a stand-alone drive to work with a CPU's control, address, and data buses. Hard drives needed a host controller card which could plug into the computer's buses. Then, there was the problem of connecting the drive to its controller card. This connection between a drive and its controller card (or controller IC on the motherboard) is the *physical interface.* Although there are limitless variations of connectors and signals, four physical interface standards and their variations have developed since the early 1980s: ST506/412, ESDI, IDE/EIDE, and SCSI.

ST506/412

The ST506/412 standard dates back to 1980 and is largely regarded to be the ancestor of all modern hard-drive interfaces. The serial interface works at 5 Mb/s using MFM encoding just like floppy drives. Later versions of ST506 use RLL encoding instead of MFM at 17 sectors per track (512 bytes/sector). ST506 drives performed head stepping with stepping motors. ST506 drives are "dumb" (device-level) devices. Like floppy drives, ST506 drives must be told explicitly *what* to do and *when* to do it. This necessitated a complex and demanding controller board residing on a plug-in expansion board. The host computer addressed the controller board through the main computer buses and sent instructions to the controller's on-board registers.

   Note: ST506/412 hard drives and interfaces are completely obsolete today, and you will not encounter such a configuration unless working on a late-model XT

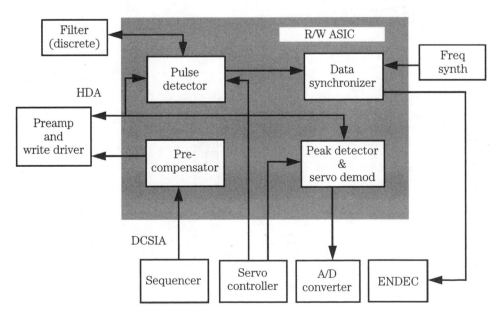

6-20 Detail of a read/write ASIC.

clone or an early-model i286 system. In virtually all cases, such configurations are universally upgraded to IDE/EIDE systems because replacement parts are almost nonexistent.

The physical interface for an ST506 drive consists of three cables: a 4-pin *power* cable, a 34-pin *control* cable, and a 20-pin *data* cable. The control cable is responsible for carrying explicit operating signals to the drive such as drive select, cylinder select, and head select. The data cable supports differential read and write lines. Figure 6-21 shows the cable pinouts for an ST506 interface. Both digital cables are flat or twisted-pair ribbon cable.

The 34-pin control cable uses 17 differential signals. Differential connections are well suited for resisting the influence of noise and for carrying signals over long distances. You may notice that almost all signals are active-high. There are three Head Select inputs (pins 14, 18, and 4, respectively) that select one of up to eight R/W heads for reading or writing. The Write Gate input (pin 6) is logic 1 during write operations and logic 0 during read operations. A Seek Complete output (pin 8) tells the controller when the heads have been moved the desired step distance. Track 000 (pin 10) is an output informing the controller when the heads move from track 001 to 000. A Write Fault (pin 12) output tells the controller if an error has occurred during the write operation. There are a number of write faults, including

- Write current in a head without the Write Gate signal true.
- No write current in the head with Write Gate true and the drive selected.
- Write Gate true when heads are off the desired track.
- DC power to the drive is outside acceptable limits.

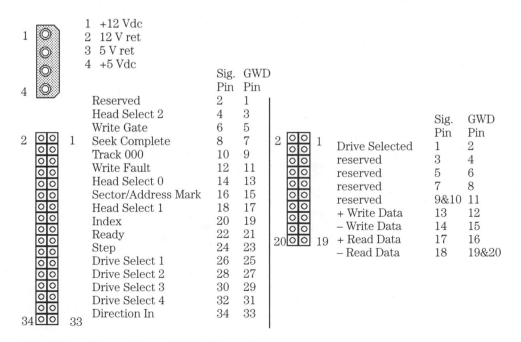

6-21 Pinout diagram for an ST506/412 interface.

The Sector/Address Mark Found signal (pin 16) sends an output pulse to the controller when the head is positioned correctly. An Index output (pin 20) provides a brief pulse whenever a track's index data mark has just passed under the R/W heads. An index pulse appears every 16.6 ms for a disk spinning at 3600 RPM (once per revolution). The Ready output (pin 22) tells the controller when drive speed and dc power are acceptable and the Track 000 signal is true. At this time the drive is considered ready for operation. A pulse on the Step input (pin 24) causes the head stepping motor to move one track position. The direction in which the heads actually step will depend on the Direction In input condition (pin 34). Finally, there are four Drive Select inputs (pins 26, 28, 30, and 32) used to identify which drive must be accessed.

Although the data cable carries 20 conductors, there are really only three meaningful signals. Four Reserved lines (pins 3, 5, 9, and 10) are not used at all. The Drive Selected output (pin 1) acknowledges to the controller when its drive address matches the drive address specified on the control cable's Drive Select lines. Differential Write Data lines (pins 13 and 14) transmit serial data to the drive from the controller. Differential Read Data signals (pins 17 and 18) send serial data read from the disk to the controller.

ESDI

The Enhanced Small Device Interface (ESDI) came into being early in 1983 in an effort to replace the already-obsolete ST506, and its variant the ST412. ESDI drives make extensive use of RLL encoding with 34 sectors per track and a direct 1:1 interleave factor. The ESDI scheme employs data separator/encoder circuitry on the drive itself, whereas ST506 drives place the circuitry on the controller card. With data separator/encoder circuitry already on the drive, an ESDI drive need only send straight binary over its data lines. This approach gives ESDI the potential for serial data rates up to 24 Mb/s. Another improvement to ESDI is the use of *buffered seeks,* which allow the drive (not the controller) to manage head step movement. The ESDI drive need only receive a single step command, which could refer to single or multiple track steps, from its controller.

Note: ESDI hard drives and interfaces are completely obsolete today, and you will not encounter an ESDI configuration unless working on an old i286 or early-model i386 system. Even then, ESDI drive configurations were typically used in server or "high-performance" PC applications. In virtually all cases, the configuration is universally upgraded to IDE/EIDE systems because replacement parts are almost nonexistent.

The pinouts for ESDI cables are illustrated in Fig. 6-22. As you look over the pinout labels, you may notice that virtually all of the signals are active-low logic (denoted by the bar over their names). Physically, the cable layout is very similar to the ST506 approach. The 34-pin *control cable* uses differential signaling and many of the same signals used for ST506. ESDI is also a "dumb" interface where most of the drive's intelligence is located on the controller card. The drive must be told explicitly what to do and when to do it.

There are four Head Select lines (pins 2, 4, 14, and 18) that select one of up to 16 R/W heads on the drive for reading or writing. The Write Gate signal (pin 6)

		1	+12 Vdc	
1		2	12 V ret	
		3	5 V ret	
		4	+5 Vdc	
4				

			Sig. Pin	GWN Pin
2 ... 1	HS3	Head Select 3	2	1
	HS2	Head Select 2	4	3
	WG	Write Gate	6	5
	CSD	Config./Status	8	7
	XACK	Xfer Ack.	10	9
	ATN	Attention	12	11
	HS0	Head Select 0	14	13
	SCT	Sector/Address	16	15
	HS1	Head Select 1	18	17
	INDEX	Index Signal	20	19
	DRDY	Drive Ready	22	21
	XREQ	Transfer Req.	24	23
	DS0	Drive Select 0	26	25
	DS1	Drive Select 1	28	27
	DS2	Drive Select 2	30	29
34 ... 33	RG	Read Gate	32	31
	CMD	Command Data	34	33

			Sig. Pin	GWN Pin
2 ... 1	DSLTD	Drive Sel.	1	
	SCT	Select/Address	2	
	CCMPL	Cmd. Comp.	3	
	AME	Address Mark	4	5
	WCLK	+ Write Clock	7	6
	WCLK	– Write Clock	8	9
	RCLK	+ Read/Ref. Clk.	10	
	RCLK	– Read/Ref. Clk.	11	
20 ... 19	WNRZ	+ Write Data	13	12
	WNRZ	– Write Data	14	
	RNRZ	+ Read Data	17	15
	RNRZ	– Read Data	18	16
	INDEX	Index	20	19

6-22 Pinout diagram for an ESDI interface.

enables the selected head for writing. A Config/Status Data line (pin 8) responds to the controller's request for information by sending 16 or more serial condition bits back to the controller. A Transfer Request input (pin 24) indicates that the host system wants to begin a data transfer, while the Transfer Acknowledge output (pin 10) sends a handshaking signal to the controller when a data transfer is permitted to begin. The Attention output (pin 12) is sent by the drive when the controller must read drive status—usually due to a fault.

The Sector/Address Mark Found line (pin 16) outputs a pulse to the controller whenever a sector's address data passes under a head. An Index signal (pin 20) produces a pulse every 16.6 ms corresponding to a track's index mark data. The Drive Ready line (pin 22) outputs a signal to the controller when the drive is at operating speed and is ready to accept commands. A Read Gate signal (pin 32) enables the selected R/W head for a read operation. Commands and data can be sent from controller to drive using the 16-bit serial line called Command Data (pin 34). Finally, three Drive Select lines (pins 26, 28, and 30, respectively) form a binary value corresponding to the drive number which the computer wishes to access.

The 20-pin *data cable* uses a mix of differential and single-ended signals. A Drive Selected output (pin 1) tells the controller that the selected drive is responding to commands. The Sector/Address Mark Found (pin 2) is essentially the same signal used in the 34-pin cable, but is available at all times. When the ESDI drive has finished its last function, it outputs a Command Complete signal (pin 3) to tell the host that a new command can be accepted. An Address Mark Enable signal (AME, pin 4) causes the drive to search for the next address mark. The AME can also be used to enable writing address marks and sync data fields to the disk during the format process. The +Write Clock and −Write Clock (pins 7 and 8) are used for synchronizing write data. The +Read/Reference Clock and −Read/Reference Clock (pins 10 and 11) are used for synchronizing read data and for determining the drive's appropriate data transfer rate.

Write data are carried to the drive over the +Write Data and −Write Data lines (pins 13 and 14), and read data are carried to the controller by the +Read Data and −Read Data lines (pins 17 and 18). Finally, an Index signal (pin 20) generates a pulse signal each time the platters rotate. This index signal serves the same purpose as the index signal in the 34-pin cable, but it is available at all times.

IDE/EIDE

The *Integrated Drive Electronics* (IDE) interface was developed in 1988 in response to an industry push to create a standard software interface for SCSI peripherals. The industry consortium, known as the *Common Access Method Committee* (or CAMC) attempted to originate an *AT Attachment* (ATA) interface which could be incorporated into low-cost AT-compatible motherboards. The CAM committee completed its specification, which was later approved by ANSI. The term *ATA interface* generally refers to the controller interface, while IDE refers to the drive. Today, IDE can refer to either the drive or controller.

As you saw earlier in this chapter, there are three major limitations to IDE which have been noticeable over the last few years. First, it does not provide very fast data transfer—about as fast as ESDI. Second, drive capacities are limited to about 528 MB, and an IDE interface only supports two drives (almost always hard drives). *Enhanced IDE* (EIDE) was developed in 1992 as another step in IDE evolution which addresses these limitations. EIDE interfaces support up to four devices (hard drives as well as CD-ROM drives and tape drives which have traditionally relied on proprietary interfaces). EIDE increases the 528-MB capacity limit to 8.4 GB. The data transfer rate for EIDE approaches 17 MB/s as opposed to IDEs 8 MB/s. The physical interface used for EIDE works with the same 40-pin approach now used with the IDE/ATA architecture. To enjoy the benefits of EIDE, you will need an EIDE drive and drive controller. However, EIDE is backwardly compatible with current IDE drives.

Unlike ST506/412 and ESDI drive architectures, IDE/EIDE drives are typically *intelligent*—that is, almost all functions relegated to a controller board in older drives are now integrated onto the drive itself. Data are transferred through a single cable attached to a simple *paddle board* (a simple controller board which is often little more than a buffer) attached to the system's expansion bus. Exterior circuitry is so limited that multiple IDE/EIDE ports can easily be added to new motherboards. While IDE/EIDE lacks the flexibility and expandability of SCSI, IDE/EIDE systems are relatively inexpensive to implement. Thus it is often the choice for simple, inexpensive, midrange PCs that are not expected to expand much. The use of an EIDE interface has extended beyond just hard drives to include such devices as CD-ROMs and tape drives.

The physical interface for a standard IDE drive consists of two cables: a 4-pin power cable and a 40-pin data/control cable (IBM uses either a 44-pin or 72-pin cable). The *power cable* is a standard, keyed mate-n-lock connector which provides

+5 Vdc, +12 Vdc, and ground to the drive. The *signal cable* is responsible for carrying data and control signals between the drive and paddle board. Where other drive designs rely on terminating resistors to establish reliable signal characteristics, IDE drives do not use discrete terminating resistors. While there will be several jumpers on the drive, a set of drive select jumpers allow the drive to be set as Drive 0 or Drive 1.

The signal cable for an IDE/EIDE drive is typically a 40-pin insulation displacement connector (IDC) cable as shown in Fig. 6-23. IDE/EIDE interfaces uses both the even- and odd-numbered wires as signal-carrying lines. Also note that most of the signal labels have dashes beside their names. The dash indicates that the particular signal is *active-low*—that is, the signal is *true* in the logic 0 state instead of being true in the logic 1 state. All signal lines on the IDE/EIDE interface are fully TTL-compatible.

Data points and registers in the hard drive are addressed using the Drive Address Bus lines DA0 to DA2 (pins 35, 33, and 36, respectively) in conjunction with the −Chip Select Drive inputs −CS1FX and −CS3FX (pins 37 and 38). When a true signal is sent along the −Drive I/O Read (−DIOR, pin 25) line, the drive executes a read cycle, while a true on the −Drive I/O Write (−DIOW, pin 23) line initiates a write cycle. The IDE interface provides TTL-level input and output signals. Where older interfaces were serial, the IDE interface provides 16 bidirectional data lines (DD0 to DD15, pins 3 to 18) to carry data bits into or out of the drive. Once a data

1	+12 Vdc
2	12 V ret
3	5 V ret
4	+5 Vdc

Pin	Signal	Pin	Signal
2	Ground	1	Reset
4	DD8	3	DD7
6	DD9	5	DD6
8	DD10	7	DD5
10	DD11	9	DD4
12	DD12	11	DD3
14	DD13	13	DD2
16	DD14	15	DD1
18	DD15	17	DD0
20	key pin	19	Ground
22	Ground	21	DMARQ
24	Ground	23	DIOW
26	Ground	25	DIOR
28	reserved	27	IORDY
30	Ground	29	DMACK
32	IOCS16	31	INTQ
34	PD1AG	33	DA1
36	DA2	35	DA0
38	CS3FX	37	CS1FX
40	Ground	39	DASP

6-23 Pinout diagram for an IDE/EIDE interface.

transfer is completed, a −DMA Acknowledge (−DMACK, pin 29) signal is provided to the drive from the hard disk controller IC. Finally, a true signal on the drive's Reset line (pin 1) will restore the drive to its original condition at power on. A reset is sent when the computer is first powered on or rebooted.

The IDE/EIDE physical interface also provides a number of outputs back to the motherboard. A Direct Memory Access Request (DMARQ, pin 21) is used to initiate the transfer of data to or from the drive. The direction of data transfer is dependent on the condition of the −DIOR and −DIOW inputs. A −DMACK signal is generated in response when the DMARQ line is asserted (made true). −IORDY (pin 27) is an −I/O Channel Ready signal that keeps a system's attention if the drive is not quite ready to respond to a data transfer request. A drive Interrupt Request (INTRQ, pin 31) is asserted by a drive when there is a drive interrupt pending (i.e., the drive is about to transfer information to or from the motherboard). The −Drive Active line (DASP, pin 39) becomes logic 0 when there is any hard-drive activity occurring. A −Passed Diagnostic (PDIAG, pin 34) line provides the results of any diagnostic command or reset action. When PDIAG is logic 0, the system knows that the drive is ready to use. Finally, the 16-bit −I/O Control line (IOCS16, pin 32) tells the motherboard that the drive is ready to send or receive data. Notice that there are several return (ground) lines (pins 2, 19, 22, 24, 26, 30, and 40), and a key pin (20) which is removed from the male connector.

An older XT variation of the IDE signal cable is outlined in Fig. 6-24. The first thing you should notice about this setup is that there are much fewer signal lines. Even though the same 40-pin cable is used, all of the even- numbered pins are ground lines. There are only eight data signals (D0 to D7). The signals on each odd-numbered pin are rearranged somewhat, but are identical to those listed for the full AT implementation. The only real exception is the Address Enable (AEN, pin 21) signal, which is asserted during a DMA cycle to disable the processing of I/O port addresses.You may encounter problems when running two IDE/EIDE drives together. Older IDE drives did not adhere to the CAMC ATA IDE specification. When older drives are run together (especially drives from different manufacturers), they may not respond to their master/slave relationship properly, and conflicts will result. In many cases, such problems will disable both drives. When planning a dual-IDE installation, try to use newer drives from the same manufacturer.

IDE/EIDE low-level formatting

The question of whether or not to low-level (LL) format an IDE/EIDE drive continues to be a thorn in the side of all technicians. Drive manufacturers claim that LL formatting may destroy the drive's servo information recorded at the factory. Diagnostic manufacturers claim that their products are smart enough to recognize critical areas of an IDE/EIDE drive and perform a safe LL format. Even today, there is no single consensus on IDE/EIDE LL formatting. But there are some guidelines that you can follow.

First, you *cannot* LL format an IDE/EIDE drive using the BIOS formatter at C800h the same way you do with ST506/412 or ESDI drives. Although the heart of an IDE controller is an extension of the basic Western Digital ST506/412 controller architecture, ATA specifications allow for additional commands that are needed to

1	+12 Vdc	
2	12 V ret	
3	5 V ret	
4	+5 Vdc	

Pin	Name	Pin	Name
1	Reset	2	Ground
3	DD7	4	Ground
5	DD6	6	Ground
7	DD5	8	Ground
9	DD4	10	Ground
11	DD3	12	Ground
13	DD2	14	Ground
15	DD1	16	Ground
17	DD0	18	Ground
19	Ground	20	Key (slot only)
21	Address Enable (AEN)	22	Ground
23	–I/O Write Data (–DIOW)	24	Ground
25	–I/O Read Data (–DIOR)	26	Ground
27	–DMA Acknowledge (–DMACK)	28	Ground
29	DMA Request (DRQ)	30	Ground
31	Interrupt Request (INTRQ)	32	Ground
33	DA1	34	Ground
35	DA0	36	Ground
37	–Host Chip Sel 0 (–CS1FX)	38	Ground
39	unused	40	Ground

6-24 Pinout diagram for an IDE/XT interface.

step over servo tracks. However, the fact remains that IDE/EIDE drives *can* be LL formatted—after all, the manufacturers do it. Ultimately, you will need to obtain a LL formatter routine directly from the drive manufacturer. Seagate, Western Digital, Maxtor, and other drive makers offer LL format and spare sector defect management software for their respective drives. In some cases, the LL formatter routine is included on a setup diskette included with many new drives. In the case of Conner drives, you will need a piece of hardware that connects directly to the drive's diagnostic port. TCE makes a Conner hardware formatter. You may also be able to obtain a LL formatter from the manufacturer's technical support department, from their BBS, or from their CompuServe forum.

Note: Even under the best of circumstances, and using the proper software tools, LL formatting should be reserved as a measure of *last resort*—when no other disk management software will correct a problem. Also remember that LL formatting is completely destructive to drive data.

BIOS support of IDE

Unlike SCSI controllers which use an expansion ROM to provide supplemental BIOS, the firmware needed to provide IDE support is written into the main system BIOS. While systems manufactured in the last few years (after 1990) are fully compatible with ATA IDE drives, adding an IDE drive to an older PC often resulted in problems. After the broad introduction of IDE, it was discovered that IDE drive operations placed different timing demands on the PC which frequently caused disk errors such as data corruption and failure to boot. BIOS makers quickly found a solution to this timing problem which was incorporated into BIOS that appeared after early 1990. If you encounter a PC with pre-1990 BIOS or if the current IDE drive is exhibiting problems, you should consider upgrading it before adding an IDE drive (you may also replace the controller with one incorporating an on-board BIOS).

File Systems

When you purchase an IDE/EIDE or SCSI hard drive, it is already LL formatted—that is, the cylinder, track, and sector information is already written onto the drive. From there, you can partition the drive with FDISK, then format the drive with FORMAT. The process of FDISK and FORMAT prepare the drive for a particular file system. We won't talk much about file systems in this edition, but you should understand the basic FAT system, and know some implications of FAT 16 and FAT 32.

FAT basics

Microsoft DOS, Windows 3.1x, and Windows 95 use an FAT to organize files on the drive. Sectors are organized into groups called *clusters*, and each cluster is assigned a number. Early drives used a 12-bit number (known as FAT 12), but drives today use a 16-bit number (called FAT 16). The newest releases of Windows 95 assign a 32-bit number to each cluster (called FAT 32). By assigning each cluster its own number, it is possible to store files in any available (unused) clusters throughout the drive without worrying about the file's size. As files are erased, those clusters become available for reuse. Overall, the FAT system has proven to be a versatile and reliable file-management system.

The problem with the FAT system is that you can only have as many clusters as can be specified by the number of bits available. For a 12-bit FAT, you can only have 4096 clusters. If the drive is 120 MB, each cluster must then be about (120 MB/4096) or 29 kB—16 kB in actual practice. If the drive were 500 MB, each cluster must be about (540 MB/4096) or 130 kB—128 kB in actual practice. Since only *one* file can be assigned to any given cluster, the entire space for that cluster is assigned (even if the file is very small). So if you were to store a 16-kB file in a 128-kB cluster, you'd waste (128 kB−16 kB)=112 kB! This wasted space is known as *slack space*. Of course, the FAT 12 system was long since abandoned while drives were still about 32 MB, but you get the idea that very large drives can waste a serious amount of space when using a FAT system.

FAT 16

DOS (including DOS 7.0 of Windows 95) uses the FAT 16 file system to store data. The FAT 16 system uses 16-bit-cluster address numbers which allow up to 65,536 clusters. Under FAT 16, a cluster can be as big as 32 kB, which translates into a maximum partition size of 2.1 GB. While a 16-bit cluster number is much more efficient than a 12-bit cluster number, every file *must* take up at least one cluster—even if the file size is much smaller than the cluster. For very large drives which we have today, the correspondingly large clusters can result in a significant amount of slack space. If the drive is larger than 2.1 GB, you must create subsequent partitions to utilize the additional space. For example, if you have a 3.1-GB drive, you can create one 2.1-GB partition, then create a second 1.0-GB partition. One way to reduce slack space is to create a larger number of smaller logical partitions. Table 6-6 illustrates the relationship between partition size and cluster size.

FAT 32

Obviously, the limitations of FAT 16 are presenting a problem as hard drives reach 5 GB and beyond. Microsoft has responded by developing a 32-bit FAT system to implement in a service release of Windows 95 (called OSR 2)—also implementing DOS 7.1. The upper 4 bits are reserved, so the system will access 2^{28} clusters (over 256 million clusters). This allows individual partitions of 8 GB with clusters only 4 kB in size. The maximum size of any given partition is 2 TB (yes, terrabytes—thousands of gigabytes). FAT 32 also eliminates the fixed size for a root directory, so you can have as many files and directories in the root as you want.

On the surface, this probably sounds like a great deal, but there are some serious problems that you'll need to consider before updating to FAT 32. First, DOS applications (without being rewritten) can only access files up to 2 GB, and Win32 applications can work with files up to 4 GB. By itself, that's not so bad, but FAT 32 partitions are only accessible through the OSR 2–enhanced Windows 95 and DOS 7.1. No other operating system can read the partitions (including Windows NT). Also, any disk utilities written for FAT 16 won't work for FAT 32 (and can seriously damage your data).

Even though the OSR 2 release ships with FAT 32 versions of FDISK, FORMAT, SCANDISK, and DEFRAG, the version of DriveSpace 3 will *not* support FAT 32. So if you're using drive compression, you're out of luck. Further, there are APIs (application programming interfaces) that simply won't support FAT 32, so some programs may refuse to work. And MS-DOS device drivers (such as those needed to support SCSI devices) will have to be updated for FAT 32. In other words, you'll lose your SCSI drives until suitable drivers become available. Finally, the OSR 2 version of Windows 95 appears to decrease FAT 32 drive performance. Hard numbers are not yet available, but initial figures suggest a performance penalty of as much as 10 percent below FAT 16 drives. In short, FAT 32 is an idea whose time has come, but it will take more work from Microsoft before FAT 32 takes over our drives.

**Table 6-6. Partition Size
versus Cluster Size**

Partition size	Cluster size
2 GB	32 kB
<1 GB	16 kB
<512 MB	8 kB
<256 MB	4 kB
<128 MB	2 kB

Drive Testing and Troubleshooting

Hard disk drives present some perplexing challenges for computer technicians and everyday users alike. The problem with hard drives is that they are inaccessible devices. Unless you have the cleanroom environment to open the sealed drive platters, it is pointless to even consider replacing failed drive mechanics. And even if you *could* open a drive safely, the advances in hard-drive technology have been so fast and furious that no spare parts market has ever developed. Drive manufacturers themselves rarely bother to repair faulty drives or invest in specialized drive-testing equipment. Clearly, the course for hard-drive repair is to replace faulty drives with new (usually better) devices.

Fortunately, not all hard-drive problems are necessarily fatal. True, you may lose some programs and data (backup your hard drive frequently), but many drive problems are recoverable without resorting to drive replacement. Instead of focusing on repairing a hard drive's electronics or mechanics, today's repair tactics focus on repairing a drive's *data*. By reconstructing or relocating faulty drive information, it is possible to recover from a wide variety of drive problems. Before you dig into the symptoms and solutions, you should take a moment to gather your software tools. You can purchase third-party tools, but operating systems such as MS-DOS provide a number of handy diagnostic utilities that can at least get you started.

You will need a floppy disk formatted and configured with system files so that you can boot the computer to DOS from the floppy drive. Refer to your DOS manual for creating a bootable (system) floppy disk. In addition to DOS system files, your bootable disk should also contain six utilities: CHKDSK.EXE, FDISK.EXE, FORMAT.COM, RECOVER.EXE, SYS.COM, and UNFORMAT.COM (note that all six files are available in DOS 5.0 and higher). You may also add other utilities to the floppy—such as DEFRAG—but these six are most important for our purposes. It is *highly* recommended that you prepare several of these bootable disks *before* you encounter drive problems. You may not be able to access the necessary files to create a bootable disk after a problem arises, but you can make the disk on another compatible machine if necessary.

The CHKDSK.EXE program checks the directory and FAT, and reports current disk and memory status on your monitor. Any *logical* errors will be reported and bad sectors will be marked, but CHKDSK.EXE will not locate *physical* disk errors. FDISK.EXE allows you to create logical partitions on the drive prior to formatting. The FORMAT.COM file formats the drive to accept DOS files within the drive partition area specified by FDISK.EXE. Use extreme caution when using FORMAT utilities. Formatting a disk can destroy the original data contained there. The drive should be repartitioned (if appropriate) and reformatted *only* if data are unrecoverable and the drive cannot be made operable by any other means. Once the drive is reformatted, use SYS.COM to copy system files to the hard drive so it will become bootable. The RECOVER.EXE program can be used to recover readable text or data files from a defective drive (no .EXE or .COM files can be recovered). The UNFORMAT.COM program can be used to restore a drive that had been corrupted or inadvertently formatted. As with all DOS utilities, refer to your DOS reference manual for specific information on using each function.

Symptoms and solutions

Now that you have some tools available, you can take a look at some problems and software solutions. The important concept here is that a hard-drive *problem* does not necessarily mean a hard drive *failure.* The failure of a sector or track does not automatically indicate physical head or platter damage—that is why software tools have been so successful. Even if one or more sectors *are* physically damaged, there are millions of sectors on a hard drive. A few bad sectors do not render a drive faulty. One of the only times a drive is truly irreparable is when physical medium damage occurs on track 00, but software tools help you to identify the scope of the problem.

Note: Drive troubleshooting has the potential of destroying any data on the drive(s). Before attempting to troubleshoot hard disk drive problems, be sure to back up as much of the drive as possible. If there is no backup available, do not repartition or reformat the drive unless *absolutely* necessary, and all other possible alternatives have been exhausted.

Symptom 1: The hard drive is completely dead   The drive does not spin up, the drive light doesn't illuminate during power-up, or you see an error message indicating that the drive is not found or ready. In most cases, you should suspect a power problem first. Make sure the 4-pin power connector is inserted properly and completely. If the drive is being powered by a Y-connector, make sure any interim connections are secure. Use a voltmeter and measure the +5-V (pin 4) and +12-V (pin 1) levels. If either voltage (especially the +12-V supply) is unusually low or absent, replace the power supply. Also check your signal cable. See that the drive's signal interface cable is connected securely at both the drive and controller ends. For IDE/EIDE drives, this is the 40-pin ribbon cable. If the cable is visibly worn or damaged, try a new cable.

The PC cannot use a hard drive that it can't recognize, so enter the CMOS Setup routine and see that all of the parameters entered for the drive are correct. Heads, cylinders, sectors per track, landing zone, and write precompensation must all correct—otherwise, POST will not recognize the drive. If you have an "autodetect" option available, try that also. Remember to save your changes in CMOS and reboot the system.

If problems continue, the hard drive itself may be defective. Try a known-good hard drive. If a known-good drive works as expected, your original drive is probably defective and should be replaced. If a known-good hard drive fails to operate, replace the drive controller board.

Symptom 2: You see drive activity, but the computer will not boot from the hard drive   In most cases, there is a drive failure, boot sector failure, or DOS/Windows file corruption. Check the signal cable first. Make sure that the drive's signal interface cable is connected securely at both the drive and controller. If the cable is visibly worn or damaged, try a new one. You should check the CMOS Setup next—see that all of the parameters entered for the drive are correct. Heads, cylinders, sectors per track, landing zone, and write precompensation must all correct, otherwise POST will not recognize the drive. If there is an option to autodetect the drive, try that as well.

The boot sector may also be defective. Boot from a floppy disk and try accessing the hard drive. If the hard drive is accessible, chances are that the boot files are missing or corrupt. Try a utility such as DrivePro's Drive Boot Fixer or DISKFIX with PC Tools. You might also try running FDISK/MBR, which will rebuild the drive's master boot record. **Careful:** The FDISK/MBR command may render the files on your drive inaccessible.

Finally, you may have a problem with your drive system hardware. If you cannot access the hard drive, run a diagnostic such as Windsor Technologies' PC Technician. Test the drive and drive controller. If the controller responds but the drive does not, try repartitioning and reformatting the hard drive. If the drive still doesn't respond, replace the hard drive outright. If the controller doesn't respond, replace the hard-drive controller.

Symptom 3: One or more subdirectories appear lost or damaged   Both the root directory of a drive and its FAT contain references to subdirectories. If data in either the root directory or file allocation table are corrupt, one or more subdirectories may be inaccessible by the drive. Try repairing the drive's directory structure. Use DISKFIX (with PC Tools) or SCANDISK (with DOS 6.2 or later) to check the disk's directory structure for problems.

Symptom 4: There are errors during drive reads or writes   Magnetic information does not last forever, and sector ID information can gradually degrade to a point where you encounter file errors. Start by checking for file structure problems on the drive. Use a utility such as DISKFIX or SCANDISK to examine the drive and search for bad sectors. If a failed sector contains part of an .EXE or .COM file, that file is now corrupt and should be restored from a backup. If you cannot isolate file problems, you may need to consider a LL format. This is an ideal solution because LL formatting rewrites sector ID information, but the sophistication of today's drives makes LL formatting almost impossible. If the drive manufacturer provides a "drive preparation" utility, you should back up the drive, run the utility, FDISK, FORMAT, and restore the drive.

Symptom 5: The hard drive was formatted accidentally   A high-level format does not actually destroy data, but rather it clears the file names and locations kept in the root directory and FAT. This prevents DOS from finding those files. You will need to recover those files. Use a utility such as UNFORMAT (with PC Tools), which can reconstruct root directory and FAT data contained in a MIRROR file. This is not always a perfect process and you may not be able to recover all files.

Note: In order for MIRROR data to be useful, do *not* save new files before running UNFORMAT.

Symptom 6: A file has been deleted accidentally   Mistyping or forgetting to add a drive specification can accidentally erase files from places you did not intend to erase. You can often recover those files if you act quickly. Use a utility such as UNDELETE (with PC Tools and DOS) to restore the deleted file. This is not always a perfect process, and you may not be able to recover every file.

Note: In order for UNDELETE to be useful, do *not* save new files before running UNDELETE.

Symptom 7: The hard drive's root directory is damaged   A faulty root directory can cripple the entire disk, rendering all subdirectories inaccessible. You may be able to recover the root directory structure. Use a utility like DISKFIX (with PC Tools) to reconstruct the damaged FATs and directories. If you have been running MIRROR, DISKFIX should be able to perform a very reliable recovery. You may also try other recovery utilities such as DrivePro or ScanDisk. However, if you cannot recover the root directory reliably, you will need to reformat the drive, then restore its contents from a backup.

Symptom 8: Hard drive performance appears to be slowing down over time   In virtually all cases, diminishing drive performance can be caused by file fragmentation. To a far lesser extent, you may be faced with a computer virus. Start the PC with a clean boot disk and make sure there are no TSRs or drivers being loaded. After a clean boot, run your antivirus checker and make sure that there are no memory-resident or file-based viruses.

If the system checks clean for computer viruses, you should next check for file fragmentation. Start your defragmentation utility (such as COMPRESS with PC Tools or DEFRAG with DOS), and check to see the percentage of file fragmentation. If there is more than 10 percent fragmentation, you should consider running the defragmentation utility after preparing Windows. Before defragmenting a drive, reboot the system normally, start Windows, access the Virtual Memory controls for your version of Windows, and shut down virtual memory. Then leave Windows and boot the system clean again. Restart your defragmentation utility and proceed to defragment the disk. This process may take several minutes depending on the size of your drive. Once defragmentation is complete, reboot the system normally, start Windows, access the Virtual Memory controls for your version of Windows, and re-create a permanent swap file to support virtual memory. You should now notice a performance improvement.

Symptom 9: You can access the hard drive correctly, but the drive light stays on continuously   A continuous LED indication is not *necessarily* a problem as long as the drive seems to be operating properly. Check the drive and drive controller for drive "light jumpers"—examine the drive itself for any jumper that might select "latched" mode vs. "activity" mode. If there are no such jumpers on the drive, check the drive controller or motherboard. Set the jumper to "activity" mode to see the drive light during access only. Next, consider the possibility of drive light *error messages.* Some drive types (especially SCSI drives) use the drive activity light to signal drive and controller errors. Check the drive and controller documents and see if there is any error indicated by the light remaining on.

Symptom 10: You cannot access the hard drive, and the drive light stays on continuously   This usually indicates a reversed signal cable and is most common when upgrading or replacing a drive system. In virtually all cases, one end of the signal cable is reversed. Make sure that both ends of the cable are installed properly (remember that the red or blue stripe on one side of the cable represents pin 1). If problems persist, replace the drive controller. It is rare for a fault in the drive controller to cause this type of problem, but if trouble persists, try a known-good drive controller board.

Symptom 11: You see a `No fixed disk present` **error message displayed on the monitor**   This kind of problem can occur during installation or at any point in the PC's working life. Check the power connector first, and make sure the 4-pin power connector is inserted properly and completely. If the drive is being powered by a Y connector, make sure any interim connections are secure. Use a voltmeter and measure the +5-V (pin 4) and +12-V (pin 1) levels. If either voltage (especially the +12-V supply) is unusually low or absent, replace the power supply. Next, check the signal connector. Make sure the drive's signal cable is connected securely at both the drive and controller. If the cable is visibly worn or damaged, try a new one.

If problems persist, check the CMOS Setup — enter the CMOS Setup routine and see that all of the parameters entered for the drive are correct. Heads, cylinders, sectors per track, landing zone, and write precompensation must all correct — otherwise, POST will not recognize the drive. You might also try autodetecting the drive and checking for hardware conflicts. Make sure that there are no other expansion devices in the system using the same IRQs or I/O addresses used by your drive controller. If so, change the resources used by the conflicting device. If your drive system uses a SCSI interface, make sure that the SCSI cable is terminated properly.

If problems continue, try a known-good hard drive. If a known-good drive works as expected, your original drive is probably defective. If problems persist with a known-good hard drive, replace the drive controller board.

Symptom 12: Your drive spins up, but the system fails to recognize the drive   Your computer may flag this as a `HARD DISK ERROR` or `HARD DISK CONTROLLER FAILURE` during system initialization. Start by checking the signal connector. Make sure that the interface signal cable is inserted properly and completely at the drive and controller. Try a new signal cable. Next, check any drive jumpers and see that a primary (master) drive is configured as primary, and a secondary (slave) drive is configured as secondary. For SCSI drives, see that each drive has a unique ID setting, and check that the SCSI bus is terminated properly.

Enter the CMOS Setup routine and see that all of the parameters entered for the drive are correct. Heads, cylinders, sectors per track, landing zone, and write precompensation must all correct—otherwise, POST will not recognize the drive. Try using the autodetect feature if it is available. If the CMOS is configured properly, you should suspect a problem with the partition. Boot from a floppy disk and run FDISK to check the partitions on your hard drive. Make sure that there is at least one DOS partition. If the drive is to be your boot drive, the primary partition must be active and bootable. Repartition and reformat the drive if necessary.

If problems persist, try a known-good hard drive. If a known-good drive works as expected, your original drive is probably defective. If a known-good hard drive fails to work as expected, replace the drive controller. If problems persist with a known-good floppy drive, replace the drive controller board.

Symptom 13: Your IDE drive spins up when power is applied, then rapidly spins down again   The drive is defective, or it is not communicating properly with its host system. Check the power connector first. Make sure the 4-pin power connector is inserted properly and completely into the drive. Always check the signal connector next, and see that the interface signal cable is inserted properly and completely at the drive and controller. Try a new signal cable.

Inspect the drive jumpers—the primary (master) drive should be configured as primary, and a secondary (slave) drive should be configured as secondary. For SCSI drives, see that each drive has a unique ID setting, and check that the SCSI bus is terminated properly. If problems persist, try a known-good hard drive. If a known-good drive works as expected, your original drive is probably defective.

Symptom 14: You see a `Sector not found` **error message displayed on the monitor**   This problem usually occurs after the drive has been in operation for quite some time and is typically the result of a medium failure. Fortunately, a bad sector will only affect one file. Try recovering the file. Use a utility such as SpinRite (from Gibson Research) or other data recovery utility and attempt to recover the damaged file. Note that you may be unsuccessful and have to restore the file from a backup later. Check the medium itself. Use a disk utility such as ScanDisk to evaluate the drive, then locate and map out any bad sectors that are located on the drive.

If problems persist, perform a LL format (if possible). Lost sectors often occur as drives age and sector ID information degrades. LL formatting restores the sector IDs, but LL formatting is performed at the factory for IDE/EIDE and SCSI drives. If there is a LL formatting utility for your particular drive (available right from the drive manufacturer), and ScanDisk reveals a large number of bad sectors, you may consider backing up the drive completely, running the LL utility, repartitioning, re-formatting, then restoring the drive. Finally, if ScanDisk maps out bad sectors, you may need to restore those files from a backup.

Symptom 15: You see a `1780 ERROR` **or** `1781 ERROR` **displayed on the monitor**   The classical 1780 error code indicates a `HARD DISK 0 FAILURE`, while the 1781 error code marks a `HARD DISK 1 FAILURE`. Start the PC with a clean boot disk and make sure there are no TSRs or drivers being loaded. If you haven't done so already, run your antivirus checker and make sure that there are no memory-resident or file-based viruses. Next, if you can access the hard drive once your system is booted, chances are that the boot files are missing or corrupt. Try a utility such as DrivePro's Drive Boot Fixer or DISKFIX with PC Tools. Otherwise, you will need to repartition and reformat the disk, then restore disk files from a backup.

Check the hardware next. If you cannot access the hard drive, run a diagnostic such as Windsor Technologies' PC Technician. Test the drive and drive controller. If the controller responds but the drive does not, try repartitioning and reformatting the hard drive. If the drive still doesn't respond, replace the hard drive outright. If the controller doesn't respond, replace the hard-drive controller.

Symptom 16: You see a `1790 ERROR` **or** `1791 ERROR` **displayed on the monitor**   The classical 1790 error code indicates a `HARD DISK 0 ERROR`, while the 1791 error code marks a HARD DISK 1 ERROR. Check the signal connector first. Make sure that the interface signal cable is inserted properly and completely at the drive and controller. Try a new signal cable. There may also be a problem with the drive's partition. Boot from a floppy disk and run FDISK to check the partitions on your hard drive. Make sure that there is at least one DOS partition. If the drive is to be your boot drive, the primary partition must be active and bootable. Repartition and reformat the drive if necessary.

If problems persist, replace the hard drive. If a known-good drive works as expected, your original drive is probably defective. If problems persist with a known-good floppy drive, replace the drive controller board.

Symptom 17: You see a 1701 ERROR **displayed on the monitor** The 1701 error code indicates a hard drive POST error—the drive did not pass its POST test. Check the power connector first, and make sure the 4-pin power connector is inserted properly and completely. If the drive is being powered by a Y-connector, make sure any interim connections are secure. Use a voltmeter and measure the +5-V (pin 4) and +12-V (pin 1) levels. If either voltage (especially the +12-V supply) is unusually low or absent, replace the power supply.

Enter the CMOS Setup routine and see that all of the parameters entered for the drive are correct. Heads, cylinders, sectors per track, landing zone, and write precompensation must all correct—otherwise, POST will not recognize the drive. Try "autodetecting" the drive.

If problems persist, perform a LL format (if possible). ST506/412 and ESDI drives may require LL formatting, but LL formatting is performed at the factory for IDE/EIDE and SCSI drives. If there is a LL formatting utility for your particular drive (available right from the drive manufacturer), you may consider backing up the drive completely, running the LL utility, repartitioning, reformatting, then restoring the drive.

Symptom 18: The system reports random data, seek, or format errors Random errors rarely indicate a permanent problem, but identifying the problem source can be a time-consuming task. Check the power connector first. Make sure the 4-pin power connector is inserted properly and completely. If the drive is being powered by a Y-connector, make sure any interim connections are secure. Use a voltmeter and measure the +5-V (pin 4) and +12-V (pin 1) levels. If either voltage (especially the +12-V supply) is unusually low, replace the power supply.

Check the signal connector next. Make sure that the interface signal cable is inserted properly and completely at the drive and controller. Try a new signal cable. Also try rerouting the signal cable away from the power supply or "noisy" expansion devices. Check the drive orientation. If problems occur after remounting the drive in a different orientation, you may need to repartition and reformat the drive, or return it to its original orientation. Try relocating the drive controller away from cables and "noisy" expansion devices. If your system has a "turbo" mode, your ISA drive controller may have trouble operating while the system is in turbo mode. Take the system out of turbo mode. If the problem disappears, try a new drive controller. The medium may also be defective. Use a utility such as ScanDisk to check for and map out any bad sectors. Once bad sectors are mapped out, you may need to restore some files from your backup. Try the hard drive and controller in another system. If the drive and controller work in another system, there is probably excessive noise or grounding problems in the original system. Reinstall the drive and controller in the original system and remove all extra expansion boards. If the problem goes away, replace one board at a time and retest the system until the problem returns. The last board you inserted when the problem returned is probably the culprit. If the problem persists, there may be a ground problem on the motherboard. Try replacing the motherboard as an absolute last effort.

Symptom 19: You see a BAD OR MISSING COMMAND **interpreter error message** This is a typical error that appears when a drive is formatted in one DOS version but loaded with another. Compatibility problems occur when you mix DOS versions. Start by booting the PC with a clean boot disk, and make sure there are no TSRs or drivers being loaded. If you haven't done so already, run your antivirus checker and make sure that there are no memory-resident or file-based viruses. Finally, make sure that the drive is partitioned and formatted with the version of DOS you intend to use. Also be sure to use FORMAT with the /S switch, or SYS C: in order to transfer system files to the drive.

Symptom 20: You see an ERROR READING DRIVE C: **error message** Read errors in a hard drive typically indicate problems with the disk medium, but may also indicate viruses or signaling problems. Check the signal connector first. Make sure that the interface signal cable is inserted properly and completely at the drive and controller. Try a new signal cable. Next, start the PC with a clean boot disk and make sure there are no TSRs or drivers being loaded. If you haven't done so already, run your antivirus checker and make sure that there are no memory-resident or file-based viruses.

Consider the drive's orientation. If problems occur after remounting the drive in a different orientation, you may need to repartition and reformat the drive, or return it to its original orientation. Also check the medium—use a utility such as ScanDisk to check for and map out any bad sectors. Once bad sectors are mapped out, you may need to restore some files from your backup. Try a known-good hard drive. If a known-good drive works as expected, your original drive is probably defective.

Symptom 21: You see a TRACK 0 NOT FOUND **error message** A fault on track 00 can disable the entire drive since track 00 contains the drive's FAT. This can be a serious error which may require you to replace the drive. Before going too far with this type of problem, check the signal connector and see that the interface signal cable is inserted properly and completely at the drive and controller. Try a new signal cable.

Boot from a floppy disk and run FDISK to check the partitions on your hard drive. Make sure that there is at least one DOS partition. If the drive is to be your boot drive, the primary partition must be active and bootable. Repartition and reformat the drive if necessary. Try a known-good hard drive. If a known-good drive works as expected, your original drive is probably defective.

Symptom 22: Software diagnostics indicate an average access time that is longer than specified for the drive   The average access time is the average amount of time needed for a drive to reach the track and sector where a needed file begins. Before you do anything else, check the drive specifications and verify the timing specifications for your particular drive. Start your defragmentation utility (such as COMPRESS with PC Tools or DEFRAG with DOS), and check to see the percentage of file fragmentation. If there is more than 10 percent fragmentation, you should consider running the defragmentation utility after preparing Windows (see Symptom 8).

Also keep in mind that different software packages measure access time differently. Make sure that the diagnostic subtracts system overhead processing from the access time calculation. Try one or two other diagnostics to confirm the measurement. Before you panic and replace a drive, try testing several similar drives for comparison. If only the suspect drive measures incorrectly, you may not *need* to replace the drive itself just yet, but you should at least maintain frequent backups in case the drive is near failure.

Symptom 23: Software diagnostics indicate a slower data transfer rate than specified   This is often due to less-than-ideal data transfer rates rather than an actual hardware failure. Enter the CMOS Setup routine and verify that any enhanced data transfer modes are enabled (such as PIO Mode 3). This can increase data transfer rate substantially. Also check the drive specifications and verify the timing specifications for your particular drive.

Check for fragmentation next. Start your defragmentation utility (such as COMPRESS with PC Tools or DEFRAG with DOS), and check to see the percentage of file fragmentation. If there is more than 10 percent fragmentation, you should consider running the defragmentation utility after preparing Windows (see Symptom 8). Also keep in mind that different software packages measure access time differently. Make sure that the diagnostic subtracts system overhead processing from the access time calculation. Try one or two other diagnostics to confirm the measurement.

If the drive is an IDE/EIDE type, make sure that the original user did not perform a LL format. This may remove head and cylinder skewing optimization and result in a degradation of data transfer. This error cannot be corrected by end-user software. Finally, if the drive is a SCSI type, make sure the SCSI bus is terminated properly—poor termination can cause data errors and result in retransmissions that degrade overall data transfer rates.

Symptom 24: Your LL format operation is taking too long, or it hangs up the system   Note: This procedure does *not* apply to IDE/EIDE or SCSI drives. You probably see a large number of format errors such as code 20 or 80. You may also see UNSUCCESSFUL FORMAT error messages. Check the LL format DEBUG string, and make sure that your specific DEBUG command is correct for the ST506/412 or ESDI drive being used. A list of typical DEBUG strings is shown in Table 6-7.

If the ST506/412 or ESDI drive is installed on an i286 or later system, make sure that the drive parameters entered for the drive in CMOS are correct. When working on an XT (without CMOS), check that the drive controller board is set correctly for the drive. Also check the signal connector, and see that the interface signal cables are inserted properly and completely at the drive and controller. Try some new signal cables. Finally, check the turbo mode—your ISA drive controller may have trouble operating while the system is in turbo mode. Take the system out of turbo mode. If the problem disappears, try a new drive controller.

Symptom 25: You are unable to access the LL format utility from the DEBUG address **Note:** This procedure does *not* apply to IDE/EIDE or SCSI drives. First, check the LL format DEBUG string, and make sure that your DEBUG command is correct for the ST506/412 or ESDI drive being used. A list of typical DEBUG strings is shown in Table 6-7. Examine the CMOS Setup next—some systems will not LL format a drive while its parameters are entered in the CMOS setup, so enter your CMOS setup menu and remove the drive type entries (remember to record them first). If that fails to clear the problem, return to the CMOS setup again and restore the drive parameters. Make sure the drive controller's on-board BIOS is fully enabled. Otherwise, the DEBUG command may not be interpreted properly. Also make sure that the controller's base address matches with the DEBUG command.

Symptom 26: The LL format process regularly hangs up on a specific head, cylinder, or sector **Note:** This procedure does *not* apply to IDE/EIDE or SCSI drives. Check the hard error list. Not all portions of an ST506/412 or ESDI drive are usable. These are called *hard errors* and the LL format procedure must recognize and avoid these hard errors. Some LL format procedures require you to enter these hard errors manually. If you forget to enter a hard error (or enter the wrong location), the format process will stop when the hard error is encountered. Try LL formatting the drive again, but make sure to enter the proper hard error locations. Also check the CMOS Setup and make sure that the drive parameters entered for the drive in CMOS are correct. When working on an XT (without CMOS), check that the drive controller board is set correctly for the drive.

Symptom 27: The FDISK procedure hangs up or fails to create or save partition record for the drive(s) You may also see an error message such as RUNTIME ERROR. This type of problem often indicates a problem with track 00 on the drive. Before you do anything else, check the signal connector and make sure

Table 6-7. Typical DEBUG Command Strings

G=C800:5
G=CC00:5
G=C800:CCC
G=C800:6
G=D800:5
G=DC00:5

that the interface signal cables are inserted properly and completely at the drive and controller. Try some new signal cables.

Enter the CMOS Setup routine and see that all of the parameters entered for the drive are correct. Heads, cylinders, sectors per track, landing zone, and write pre-compensation must all be appropriate. Check with the drive maker and see if there is an alternate "translation geometry" that you can enter instead. If the BIOS supports autodetection, try autodetecting the drive.

Check your version of FDISK. The version of FDISK you are using must be the same as the DOS version on your boot diskette. Older versions may not work. Next, run FDISK and see if there are any partitions already on the drive. If so, you may need to erase any existing partitions, then create your new partition from scratch. *Remember that erasing a partition will destroy any data already on the drive.* Use a utility such as DrivePro (from MicroHouse) or ScanDisk to check the medium for physical defects, especially at track 00. If there is physical damage in the boot sector, you should replace the drive.

Finally, check for emergency drive utilities. Some drive makers provide LL preparation utilities which can rewrite track 00. For example, Western Digital provides the WD_CLEAR.EXE utility. If problems still persist, replace the defective hard drive.

Symptom 28: You see a HARD DISK CONTROLLER FAILURE **or a large number of defects in last logical partition** This is typically a CMOS Setup or drive controller problem. Enter the CMOS Setup routine and see that all of the parameters entered for the drive are correct. If the geometry specifies a larger drive, the system will attempt to format areas of the drive that don't exist, resulting in a large number of errors. If CMOS is configured correctly, there may be a problem with the hard-drive controller. Try a new hard-drive controller. If a new drive controller does not correct the problem, the drive itself is probably defective and should be replaced.

Symptom 29: The high-level (DOS) format process takes too long In almost all cases, long formats are the result of older DOS versions. Check your DOS version. MS-DOS version 4.x tries to recover hard errors, which can consume quite a bit of extra time. You will probably see a number of "Attempting to recover allocation units" messages. Your best course is to upgrade the MS-DOS version to 6.22 (or MS-DOS 7.0 with Windows 95). Later versions of DOS abandon hard error retries.

Symptom 30: The IDE drive (<528 MB) does not partition or format to full capacity When relatively small hard drives do not realize their full capacity, the CMOS Setup is usually at fault. The drive parameters entered into CMOS must specify the *full* capacity of the drive, using a geometry setup that is acceptable. If you use parameters that specify a smaller drive, any extra capacity will be ignored. If there are over 1024 cylinders, you must use an alternate "translation geometry" to realize the full drive potential. The drive maker can provide you with the right translation geometry. Also check your DOS version—older versions of DOS use a partition limit of 32 MB. Upgrade your older version of DOS to 6.22 (or MS-DOS 7.0 with Windows 95).

Symptom 31: The EIDE drive (.528 MB) does not partition or format to full capacity   This type of problem may also be due to a CMOS Setup error, but is almost always due to poor system configuration. Check the CMOS Setup for drive geometry—the drive parameters entered into CMOS must specify the *full* capacity of the drive. If you use parameters that specify a smaller drive, any extra capacity will be ignored. If there are over 1024 cylinders, you must use an alternate "translation geometry" to realize the full drive potential. The drive maker can provide you with the right translation geometry. Also check the CMOS Setup for Logical Block Addressing (LBA). EIDE drives need LBA to access over 528 MB. Make sure that there is an entry such as "LBA Mode" in CMOS. Otherwise, you may need to upgrade your motherboard BIOS to have full drive capacity.

Check the drive controller. If you cannot upgrade an older motherboard BIOS, install an EIDE drive controller with its own controller BIOS. This will supplement the motherboard BIOS. Finally, check the drive management software. If neither the motherboard nor controller BIOS will support LBA mode, you will need to install drive management software such as EZ-Drive or Drive Manager from Ontrack.

Symptom 32: You see DISK BOOT FAILURE, NONSYSTEM DISL, **or** NO ROM BASIC—SYSTEM HALTED **error messages**   There are several possible reasons for these errors. Start by checking the signal connector. Make sure that the interface signal cables are inserted properly and completely at the drive and controller. Try some new signal cables. Boot the PC with a clean boot disk and make sure there are no TSRs or drivers being loaded which interfere with drive operation. If you haven't done so already, run your antivirus checker and make sure that there are no memory-resident or file-based viruses.

Next, enter the CMOS Setup routine and see that all of the parameters entered for the drive are correct. Heads, cylinders, sectors per track, landing zone, and write pre-compensation must all be entered. Boot from a floppy disk and run FDISK to check the partitions on your hard drive. Make sure that there is at least one DOS partition. If the drive is to be your boot drive, the primary partition must be active and bootable.

It is also possible that the hard drive itself is defective. Try a known-good hard drive. If a known-good drive works as expected, your original drive is probably defective. If problems persist with a known-good floppy drive, replace the drive controller.

Symptom 33: The hard drive in a PC is suffering frequent breakdowns (i.e., between 6 to 12 months)   When drives tend to fail within a few months, there are some factors to consider. Check the PC power first. If the ac power supplying your PC is "dirty" (i.e., lots of spikes and surges), power anomalies can often make it through the power supply and damage other components. Remove any high-load devices such as air conditioners, motors, or coffee makers from the same ac circuit used by the PC, or try the PC on a known-good ac circuit. You might also consider a good-quality UPS (uninterruptible power supply) to power your PC.

Drive utilization may be another factor. If the drive is being worked hard by applications and swap files, consider upgrading RAM or adding cache to reduce dependency on the drive. Keep the drive defragmented. Periodically run a utility like

DEFRAG to reorganize the files. This reduces the amount of "drive thrashing" that occurs when loading and saving files.

Finally, check the environment. Constant low-level vibrations, such as those in an industrial environment, can kill a hard drive. Smoke (even cigarette smoke), high humidity, very low humidity, and caustic vapors can ruin drives. Make sure the system is used in a stable office-type environment.

Symptom 34: A hard drive controller is replaced, but during initialization, the system displays error messages such as HARD DISK FAILURE **or** NOT A RECOGNIZED DRIVE TYPE The PC may also lock up. Some drive controllers may be incompatible in some systems. Check with the controller manufacturer and see if there have been any reports of incompatibilities with your PC. If so, try a different drive controller board.

Symptom 35: A new hard drive is installed, but it will not boot, or a message appears such as HDD CONTROLLER FAILURE The new drive has probably not been installed or prepared properly. Check the power connector first. Make sure the 4-pin power connector is inserted properly and completely. If the drive is being powered by a Y-connector, make sure any interim connections are secure. Use a voltmeter and measure the +5-V (pin 4) and +12-V (pin 1) levels. If either voltage (especially the +12-V supply) is unusually low or absent, replace the power supply.

Next, make sure the drive's signal interface cable is connected securely at both the drive and controller. If the cable is visibly worn or damaged, try a new one. Enter the CMOS Setup routine and see that all of the parameters entered for the drive are correct. Heads, cylinders, sectors per track, landing zone, and write precompensation must all correct—otherwise, POST will not recognize the drive. Finally, the drive may not be prepared properly. Run FDISK from a bootable diskette to partition the drive, then run FORMAT to initialize the drive. Then run SYS C: to make the drive bootable.

Symptom 36: You install Disk Manager to a hard drive, then install DOS, but DOS formats the drive back to 528 MB After Disk Manager is installed, you must create a "rescue disk" to use in conjunction with your DOS installation. There are two means of accomplishing this. First,

- Create a clean DOS-bootable disk.
- Copy 2 files from the original Disk Manager disk to your bootable disk: XBIOS.OVL and DMDRVR.BIN.
- Create a CONFIG.SYS file on this bootable disk with these 3 lines:

```
DEVICE=DMDRVR.BIN
FILES=35
BUFFERS=35
```

- Remove the bootable diskette and reboot the system.
- When you see "Press space bar to boot from diskette, do so—the system will halt.

- Insert the rescue disk in drive A:, and press any key to resume the boot process.
- At the A: prompt, remove your rescue disk, insert the DOS installation disk, then type SETUP.
- You will now install DOS files without overwriting the Disk Manager files.

or

- Create a clean DOS-bootable disk.
- Insert the original Disk Manager diskette in the A: drive and type

```
DMCFIG/D=A:
```

- You will prompted to inert a bootable floppy in drive A:.

- You will need to remove and insert the bootable disk a few times as Drive Manager files are copied.
- Remove the floppy and reboot the system.
- When you see "Press space bar to boot from diskette," do so—the system will halt.
- Insert the rescue disk in drive A:, and press any key to resume the boot process.
- At the A: prompt, remove your rescue disk, insert the DOS installation disk, then type SETUP.
- You will now install DOS files without overwriting the Disk Manager files.

Symptom 37: ScanDisk reports some bad sectors, but cannot map them out during a surface analysis You may need a surface analysis utility for your particular drive which is provided by the drive maker. For example, Western Digital provides the WDATIDE.EXE utility for its Caviar series of drives. It will mark all "grown" defects, and compensate for lost capacity by utilizing spare tracks.

Note: These types of surface analysis utilities are typically destructive. Make sure to have a complete backup of the drive before proceeding. Also, the utility may take a very long time to run depending on your drive's capacity.

Symptom 38: The drive will work as a primary drive, but not as a secondary (or vice versa) In most cases, the drive is simply jumpered incorrectly, but there may also be timing problems. Check the drive jumpers first. Make sure that the drive is jumpered properly as a primary (single drive), primary (dual drive), or secondary drive. The drive signal timing may also be off. Some IDE/EIDE drives do not work as primary or secondary drives with certain other drives in the system. Reverse the primary/secondary relationship. If the problem persists, try the drives separately. If the drives work individually, there is probably a timing problem, so try a different drive as the primary or secondary.

Symptom 39: You cannot get 32-bit access to work under Windows 3.1x You are probably not using the correct hard-drive driver. Check your EIDE BIOS. If your motherboard (or drive controller) BIOS supports LBA, obtaining a driver should be easy. The drive maker either provides a 32-bit driver on a diskette accompanying the drive, or a driver can be downloaded from the drive maker's BBS or Internet Web site. If the motherboard (or drive controller) does not support LBA directly, you can install Ontrack's Disk Manager (6.03 or later) and run DMCFIG to install the 32-bit driver software.

Symptom 40: Drive diagnostics reveal a great deal of wasted space on the drive   You probably have a large drive partitioned as a single large logical volume. Check the cluster size (Table 6-6 shows a comparison of partition size vs. cluster size). If you deal with large numbers of small files, it may be more efficient to create multiple smaller partitions utilizing smaller clusters.

Symptom 41: You install a Y-adapter which fails to work   Some Y-adapters are incorrectly wired and can cause severe damage to any device attached to it. Examine the power connector first. Make certain that both of the female connectors are lined up with the two chamfered (rounded) corners facing up and both of the squared corners facing down. The four wires attached to the female connectors should now be in the following order from left to right: *yellow* (12 V), *black* (ground), *black* (ground), *red* (5 V). If this order is reversed on one of the connectors, then your Y power adapter is faulty and should not be used.

Symptom 42: During the POST, you hear a drive begin to spin up and produce a sharp noise   This problem has been encountered with some combinations of drives, motherboards, and motherboard BIOS. This type of problem can easily result in data loss (and medium damage). Check the motherboard BIOS version first, then contact the PC system manufacturer and see if a BIOS upgrade is necessary. Try a BIOS upgrade. Otherwise, replace the drive controller. Often a new drive controller may resolve the problem if the motherboard BIOS cannot be replaced.

Symptom 43: Opening a folder under Windows 95 seems to take a long time   When you open a folder in Microsoft Explorer on a drive using the FAT 32 file system, it may seem to take an unusually long time before the window is accessible, or the "working in the background" pointer may appear for prolonged periods. This is a typical sign of FAT 32 problems under Windows 95, and is usually because the total space used by all directory entries in the particular folder exceeds 32 kB. Until Microsoft provides a fix for their service release, you should simply move some files in the overloaded folder to a different folder.

Disk Manager troubleshooting

It is often too expensive or too inconvenient to upgrade a motherboard BIOS or drive controller in order to accommodate a large (EIDE) hard drive. Ontrack's Disk Manager software provides a software driver that partitions and formats the drive, then supports full access even when there is no direct hardware support in the PC. Late versions of Disk Manager are also compatible with Windows 3.1x and Windows 95. As with most driver software, however, there are some circumstances where trouble can occur.

Symptom 1: You are having difficulty installing Ontrack's Disk Manager software from the B: drive   Ontrack software must be installed from the A: drive. If your A: drive is the wrong size for your Ontrack distribution diskette, copy the diskette to a floppy disk sized properly for drive A:, then try reinstalling Disk Manager.

Symptom 2: Windows 95 does not appear to function properly with Disk Manager   This is usually due to an older version of Disk Manager. You need Disk Manager 6.0 or higher to function properly with Windows 95. You can download the DMPATCH.EXE utility from Ontrack or Western Digital to update your DDO (Dynamic Drive Overlay) to version 6.03d.

Symptom 3: Windows 95 reports that it is in the DOS compatibility mode—even though Disk Manager 6.0x (or later) is in use   A real-mode driver is running and preventing 32-bit access. Check your CMOS Setup first. CMOS setting for your hard drive should use a number equal to or less than 1024 for cylinders. The drive's documentation may offer an alternate "translation geometry" that can be entered in CMOS. The 32-bit real-mode disk driver may be causing a problem. Your 32-bit disk driver must be disabled before installing Windows 95. Open SYSTEM.INI and disable the following line in the [386Enh] area

```
;32BitDiskAccess=On
```

or

```
32BitDiskAccess=Off
```

Finally, you need Disk Manager 6.0 or higher to function properly with Windows 95. You can download the DMPATCH.EXE utility from Ontrack or Western Digital to update your DDO to version 6.03d.

Symptom 4: There is trouble using the drive manufacturer's disk driver for 32-bit access under Windows 95   Windows 95 has built-in support for EIDE devices and does not need the 32-bit drivers that you may have used with Windows 3.1x. Open your SYSTEM.INI file and remove (or disable) any references to 32-bit disk access or manufacturer-specific disk drivers.

Symptom 5: Disk Manager refuses to work properly with Windows 95 and disk compression   You probably have an older version of Disk Manager. You need Disk Manager 6.0 or higher to function properly with Windows 95. You can download the DMPATCH.EXE utility from Ontrack or Western Digital to update your DDO to version 6.03d. Compression software may also be a problem. If you are using a compression utility other than DriveSpace, check with the compression utility manufacturer to see if there are any compatibility issues with Disk Manager and Windows 95.

Symptom 6: When loading, Disk Manager does not identify the hard disk correctly   This usually occurs because drive ID queries are intercepted incorrectly. When using Disk Manager, try disabling the BIOS on your hard-drive controller. If problems persist, try formatting the drive using a different drive controller.

Symptom 7: You are having trouble removing Disk Manager   This calls for a complete repartitioning of the drive. Be sure to have a complete drive backup before proceeding. Boot from a clean floppy disk (make sure the disk has FDISK and FORMAT). Run FDISK to repartition the drive—this overwrites the boot information—then reformat the drive with FORMAT. Restore the contents of your backup to the drive.

Symptom 8: Disk Manager appears to be conflicting with other programs   Disk Manager first loads into conventional memory where it consumes 6 kB. It then moves to take 4 kB of upper memory—leaving behind a 62-byte "footprint" at the top of conventional memory. This can sometimes conflict with other programs or drivers. You can change how Disk Manager loads into memory. Try staying in conventional memory. When you see the boot message which tells you to press the space bar to boot from a floppy, press the S key instead, and then answer "Y" to the next question. This will cause Disk Manager to stay in conventional memory rather than moving to high memory and may resolve the conflicts you are experiencing. If this resolves the problem, there is a special version of Disk Manager (LOADLOW.ZIP) which will load into conventional memory automatically. You can download the file from Ontrack.

Symptom 9: When installing DOS on a drive with Disk Manager, the drive wound up with only 504 MB of accessible space   You must load Disk Manager *before* booting from a floppy. Start the boot process from your hard drive. When you see a message such as "Press spacebar to boot from diskette," press the spacebar, insert your DOS boot disk, then press any key. This way, the DDO will have loaded before booting your DOS setup disk.

Symptom 10: You see a message such as DDO INTEGRITY ERROR **and the hard drive cannot be accessed**   The sector containing the DDO has probably been corrupted. Start the PC with a clean boot disk and make sure there are no TSRs or drivers being loaded. If you haven't done so already, run your antivirus checker and make sure that there are no memory-resident or file-based viruses. Trouble with the power supply can also cause DDO corruption. Use a voltmeter to check the +12-V and +5-V signals powering the drive. If either voltage appears unusually low (or high), the supply may be defective. You may install a diagnostic board such as PC Power Check (from Data Depot) to check for spikes or surges that may be passing through the supply.

If trouble persists, try reinstalling Disk Manager. This effectively repartitions your drive, so be ready to restore your files from a backup. If you cannot reinstall Disk Manager (or the error message returns shortly thereafter), try a new hard drive.

Symptom 11: You only get 16-bit file access under Windows for Workgroups using a secondary drive with Disk Manager   When Disk Manager is installed on the primary drive, the DDO is loaded during the boot process, from the "non data area" of the drive. As a result, there is no device=dmdrvr.bin line in the CONFIG.SYS file. However, if Disk Manager is used *only* on the secondary drive (and the primary drive was prepared with conventional DOS only), the `device=` line *will* be entered in CONFIG.SYS, and the DDO is loaded differently. When Disk Manager is loaded to a secondary drive in this fashion, only 16-bit file access is available. The solution is to install Disk Manager to the primary drive. Back up all the data on your primary drive and install Disk Manager. This would cause the DDO to be loaded during the boot process and allow 32-bit file access on both the primary and secondary drives.

Symptom 12: When booting from a Disk Manager "rescue disk," the hard drive letters are assigned differently   This is because DOS assigns drive letters *before* the DDO is invoked. Start booting from the hard drive to install the DDO, *then* boot from the floppy. When you see a message such as `PRESS SPACEBAR TO BOOT FROM DISKETTE,` press the spacebar, insert your DOS boot disk, then press any key. The DDO will have loaded before booting your DOS setup disk.

Symptom 13: Data on the Disk Manager drive is corrupted after installing another drive-related utility   Chances are that if software uses DOS and Interrupt 13 calls to access the hard drive, the software should interact correctly with Disk Manager, and corruption should not occur. When the utility bypasses DOS and Interrupt 13, however, data corruption *can* result. Check with the utility maker and see if there have been any reports of compatibility problems with Disk Manager.

Symptom 14: Disk Manager cannot autoidentify a hard drive   Instead, a list of drives will appear. This is often because of caching drive controllers interfering with Disk Manager. There are two options for dealing with this problem: you could select the proper drive from the list and continue as usual, or temporarily disable the controller's cache.

EZ-Drive troubleshooting

EZ-Drive is a software enhancement product very similar to Disk Manager. EZ-Drive provides "large drive" support for older BIOS. This eliminates the need to update your motherboard BIOS or drive controller. It also works around problems with BIOS versions that hang up when working with drives larger than 2.1 GB. EZ-Drive can be found on the diskette bundled with many new hard drives.

Symptom 1: EZ-Drive is interfering with local-bus IDE controllers   Some local-bus IDE chipsets and drivers do not work properly with EZ-Drive. The following list outlines the major known issues:

- **Appian ADI2.** This is fully compatible with EZ-Drive. The companion HVLIDE.SYS driver is also fully compatible with EZ-Drive.
- **ADI2C143.SYS.** This driver is fully compatible with EZ-Drive. Install EZ-Drive to your hard disk first, then install one of the drivers into your CONFIG.SYS file.
- **CMD640x.** This is fully compatible with EZ-Drive. The companion CMD640X.SYS driver is also fully compatible with EZ-Drive. Install EZ-Drive to your hard disk first, then install the driver into your CONFIG.SYS file.

- **PC Tech RZ1000.** This system is not supported, and ZEOS/Phoenix BIOS does not need EZ-Drive because it natively supports large (EIDE) drives. If EZ-Drive sets up a large drive, it will take over from the BIOS, and the drive will be *slower* than BIOS support would provide alone.
- **Opti 611A and 621A.** These are not supported by any product or hardware. The OPTIVIC.SYS (dated 5-11-94) driver is incompatible with large drives both with and without EZ-Drive.

Symptom 2: The keyboard or mouse does not function normally after exiting Windows on a drive using EZ-Drive This is almost always due to a mouse driver attached to a keyboard. Change your keyboard driver. A mouse driver installation may change a line in SYSTEM.INI to something like

```
Keyboard=C:\MOUSE\mousevkd.386
```

To correct the problem, change that line in the SYSTEM.INI file back to

```
Keyboard=*vkd
```

You will need to restart Windows for your changes to take effect.

Symptom 3: QEMM 7.5 will not load in stealth mode in a system with EZ-Drive You will need to add a switch to the QEMM command line. Add the following switch to the QEMM command line in CONFIG.SYS

```
XSTI=76
```

Symptom 4: Windows crashes with EZ-Drive installed on the drive There is a known issue with Award BIOS version 4.50G. Update your version of EZ-Drive. Download EZPCH502.EXE from MicroHouse BBS at (303) 443-9957. This is a self-extracting file that will update the EZ-Drive MBR.

Symptom 5: You are having trouble removing EZ-Drive In order to remove EZ-Drive, the Master Boot Record (MBR) will have to be rewritten. *You should have a complete system backup before proceeding.* Check the CMOS Setup and disable any MBR virus protection features in the BIOS. Save your changes (if any) and reboot the system. Boot the system "clean." Start the PC with a "clean" boot disk and make sure there are no TSRs or drivers being loaded. Make sure your boot diskette contains the correct version of FDISK. Run the command FDISK /MBR to rewrite the drive's master boot record and eliminate EZ-Drive.

Note: If the hard drive was set up as a Custom Drive Type, access to the data on the drive will be lost. Restore the drive's contents from your backup.

Symptom 6: You see a NO IDE DRIVE INSTALLED **message from EZ-Drive** Normally, EZ-Drive should be able to identify a drive even with no geometry figures in CMOS. Occasionally, it will fail to identify the drive, and an error message will be generated. Enter the proper geometry figures (heads, sectors, cylinders, and so on) for your hard disk in CMOS Setup. As an alternative, set the CMOS drive type to "autodetect."

Symptom 7: You have trouble removing EZ-Drive from a system with an LBA option in BIOS In most cases, you have upgraded the drive controller or motherboard BIOS and no longer need EZ-Drive support. Be sure to have a complete backup of the drive before proceeding. If you are using EZ-Drive 5.00 or later, you can try the following procedure:

- Insert the EZ-Drive distribution diskette and run EZ.
- Choose the "Change Installed Features" option.
- Enable the Windows NT Compatibility Mode for EZ-Drive 5.00.

For EZ-Drive 5.02, you can use the procedure below:

- Disable floppy boot protection for EZ 5.02 or later.
- Choose the "Save Changes" option and exit EZ-Drive.
- Reboot the system and enter your CMOS Setup.
- Set your CMOS drive geometry to "autodetect."
- Enable the LBA mode.
- Save your changes and exit the CMOS Setup.
- Reboot the system from a bootable floppy diskette (bypassing EZ-Drive).
- If all drives/directories are still accessible, run the command FDISK/MBR to remove EZ-Drive's MBR.
- If all drives/directories are not accessible, the BIOS LBA translation is different from the translation EZ-Drive used. In that case, boot directly from a floppy, run FDISK /MBR, repartition, and format the drive using FDISK and FORMAT, then restore your data.

Symptom 8: You are continuously receiving the message HOLD DOWN THE CTRL KEY In virtually all reported cases of this symptom, the problem is caused by an infection of the Ripper virus. You could try using an antivirus checker, but chances are that even clearing the virus will damage the master boot sector. If you have EZ-Drive 5.00 or later, try the following procedure:

- Boot directly from a bootable floppy diskette, then insert the EZ-Drive distribution diskette.
- Type EZ/MBR and press <Enter>.
- Run EZ.
- Choose the "Change Installed Features" option.
- Enable Windows NT Compatibility Mode for 5.00

For EZ-Drive 5.02, you can use the procedure below:

- Disable floppy boot protection for EZ 5.02 and later.
- Choose the "Save Changes" option.
- Run your virus scan software.

Note: Any time a virus is suspected or found, any diskettes used in the system recently should also be suspected of infection. Discard all boot and antivirus disks used to detect and eliminate any virus.

Symptom 9: A system hangs after booting from a nonsystem disk The user boots a system with a nonbootable diskette in the floppy drive. Once the message "Nonsystem disk or disk error" is displayed, the user removes the floppy and reboots the system. Now the system hangs up and will not boot. All cases of this error have been linked to the Antiexe virus. If you have EZ-Drive 5.00 or later, try the following procedure:

- Boot directly from a bootable floppy diskette, then insert the EZ-Drive distribution diskette.
- Type EZ/MBR and press <Enter>.
- Run EZ.
- Choose the "Change Installed Features" option.
- Enable Windows NT Compatibility Mode for 5.00

For EZ-Drive 5.02, you can use the procedure below:

- Disable floppy boot protection for EZ 5.02 and later.
- Choose the "Save Changes" option.
- Run your virus scan software.

Note: Any time a virus is suspected or found, any diskettes used in the system recently should also be suspected of infection. Discard all boot and antivirus disks used to detect and eliminate any virus.

Symptom 10: You see the EZ-Drive error message "Unrecognized DBR"
There is trouble with the Diskette Boot Record (DBR) of a floppy disk. Suspect the floppy disk first—the DBR on the floppy diskette has been corrupted or simply is not one that is easily recognized by the operating system (such as a language-specific version of DOS). Try to re-SYS the diskette. When the problem is on an important diskette (such as DOS disk 1), answer "Yes" to proceed with a data transfer when the UNRECOGNIZED DBR error appears.

Check the hard drive boot files next. If the hard drive does not boot with a Non-system disk error message, reboot the system and hold down the <Spacebar> when prompted. Insert a bootable floppy and press any key to boot to an A: prompt. Then SYS the hard drive to transfer new bootable files. The hard drive should now be able to boot without any problems.

Symptom 11: You have trouble getting the MH32BIT.386 driver to operate in block transfer mode The MH32BIT.386 driver does not support DMA Type F—or block transfer mode—data transfers. Use a different driver, or check in with Ontrack or MicroHouse resources to obtain a newer version of the driver.

Symptom 12: You have trouble getting the MH32BIT.386 driver to work with Windows 95 Although the MH32BIT.386 driver *should* interact properly with Windows 95, the driver is not needed. Open the SYSTEM.INI file and comment out any references to the MH32BIT.386 driver.

Symptom 13: You cannot get EZ-Drive to run on PS/1, PS/2, and microchannel systems EZ-Drive does not run on all versions of PS/1 and PS/2 computers. It also will not run on microchannel systems. If you cannot get EZ-Drive to load or run on such a system, you should abandon the attempt.

Symptom 14: EZ-Drive has been removed, and the hard drive is no longer accessible The drive system must support large hard drives (through motherboard BIOS or drive controller BIOS) before removing EZ-Drive. It may be necessary to upgrade the motherboard BIOS, or use an EIDE drive controller with its own on-board BIOS. Also make sure that the CMOS Setup for your hard drive uses the same parameters as EZ-Drive. If the parameters match, your drive should remain accessible.

Symptom 15: You cannot recover data after invoking the EZWIPE.EXE utility The EZWIPE.EXE utility erases the entire first cylinder of the hard drive completely, and all data will be inaccessible. If you invoke EZWIPE.EXE by accident, you will have to repartition and reformat the drive, then restore files from a backup.

Drive Rocket troubleshooting

Drive Rocket is not caching software. Rather, Drive Rocket takes advantage of an IDE drive's ability to transfer data in multiple-block "chunks," and can speed the effective throughput of data across an IDE bus. However, Drive Rocket can cause several problems with memory managers or unusual system configurations.

Symptom 1: When running Drive Rocket, the QEMM Stealth ROM feature reports DISABLING STEALTH ROM, **and then a reference to INT 76** QEMM is disabling itself when Drive Rocket grabs Interrupt 13. Update the QEMM command line. Open CONFIG.SYS and add the following switch to the QEMM command line

```
XSTI=76
```

This tells QEMM to ignore Interrupt 76.

Symptom 2: During installation, Drive Rocket produces an error indicating that it can't recognize the driver (i.e., "inconfigurable driver") Chances are that Drive Rocket is simply not compatible with your particular system. The highest probability of failure is reported on systems which *already* enhance drive speed such as Pentium systems with PCI drive controllers using LBA. Check with Ontrack to be sure you have the latest version of Drive Rocket.

Symptom 3: You have trouble removing Drive Rocket Unlike other Ontrack software, Drive Rocket does not reside in the MBR. Update your CONFIG.SYS file. You can effectively "uninstall" Drive Rocket by removing the following line from CONFIG.SYS

```
device=rocket.bin
```

Also delete the ROCKET.BIN file from the root directory.

Symptom 4: When loading, Drive Rocket does not identify the hard disk correctly This usually occurs because drive ID queries are intercepted incorrectly when using OEM versions of Drive Rocket. Replace your OEM version of Drive Rocket with a generic version.

Symptom 5: Drive Rocket cannot be loaded into upper memory
Chances are that this is a problem with the QEMM load high statement. Try a different memory manager. If you absolutely cannot live with 6 kB less conventional memory, try a different memory manager (such as EMM386.EXE).

Symptom 6: Drive Rocket reports that the system will experience a "negative" (−x%) performance increase In most cases, Drive Rocket is conflicting with another driver or device in the system. As a result, you should not use Drive Rocket on that system.

Symptom 7: You encounter a GPF when trying to work with the Control Panel in Windows You will need to tweak the Drive Rocket command line. Add the following switch to your Drive Rocket command line in the CONFIG.SYS file:

/w=1,   if Drive Rocket is on the primary drive only, or
/w=,1   if Drive Rocket is on the secondary drive only, or
/w=1,1   if Drive Rocket is on both the primary and secondary drives

7

CHAPTER

PC Cards

Desktop computers have always provided a standardized interface—the expansion bus. On the other hand, mobile computers have traditionally lacked all the most basic upgrade potential. By the late 1980s, it was clear that a standard would be needed to allow rapid and convenient upgrades for the exploding field of mobile computing. Neil Chandra of Poquet Computer (now part of Fujitsu) took a vision originally conceived to provide memory for the hand-held Poquet computer, and brought together industry leaders to forge a standard. In 1989 Chandra's brainchild, the Personal Computer Memory Card International Association (or PCMCIA), was formed as a standards body and trade association. The objective of the PCMCIA is to provide universal, nonproprietary expansion capability for mobile computer systems (Fig. 7-1). More than 475 organizations are affiliated with the PCMCIA, which also works very closely with other major standards organizations such as the Japan Electronics Industry Development Association (JEIDA), the Electronics Industries Association (EIA), the Joint Electron Device Engineering Council (JEDEC), and the International Standards Organization (ISO). This chapter explains the inner workings of a PCMCIA interface and cards that use it. You will also find a broad selection of troubleshooting procedures intended to help you overcome many of the problems attributed to the PCMCIA interface, and the difficulties it can encounter under Windows 95.

Understanding the PC Card

Ultimately, the universal expansion standard envisioned by the PCMCIA has taken the form of a "card" (called a *PC Card*), which is roughly the length and width of a credit card (Fig. 7-2). This basic shape has remained virtually unchanged since the initial release of PCMCIA standards (version 1.0) in September 1990. The original specification (reflecting the original Poquet vision) defined an interface that was intended exclusively for memory cards such as DRAM, flash EEPROM, and ROM. However, a memory-only interface did not even come close to fulfilling the promise of mobile expansion capability—there is much more to PCs than memory.

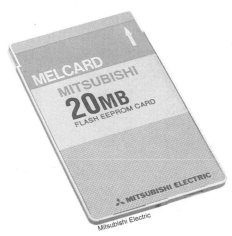

7-1 A 20-MB Mitsubishi flash
EEPROM card.

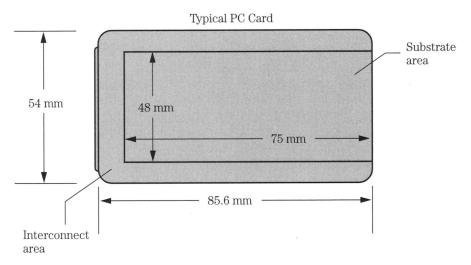

7-2 Basic PC Card dimensions.

PCMCIA release 2.0 followed a year later in September 1991. Version 2.0 took
the quantum leap that version 1.0 ignored and incorporated I/O capability and software support into the PC Card. It was this addition of I/O capability that PC Card
technology finally began to attract serious attention from mobile computer manufacturers. PC Card makers could now move past memory products and offer a wealth
of other expansion products such as LAN cards, fax/modems, and disk drives. Release 2.1 followed in July of 1993. It specifies software support and BIOS card and
socket services. The newest set of PCMCIA standards appeared in February of 1995
(loosely referred to as PCMCIA '95 or Release 3.0). Release 3.0 added support for
"multifunction" PC Cards such as modem/LAN cards, as well as support for 3.3-V operation, DMA handling, and 32-bit CardBus bus mastering.

Since February of 1995, there have been some important revisions of the PCMCIA standards, but no "new" revision levels. In May of 1995, the second printing of PCMCIA standards addressed timing problems during card power up/power down sequences. In November of 1995, the third printing of PCMCIA standards included provisions for custom card interfaces and indirect CIS addressing. The latest standards update in July of 1996 provided for a Zoomed Video (ZV) interface for fast video systems, and a Flash Translation Layer (FTL) for reprogrammability.

Making it work

Of course, integrating a PC Card into a computer is not as easy as just attaching a connector to the PC buses. A selection of system hardware and software is needed as illustrated in Fig. 7-3. This multilayered approach is typical of most PC peripherals. If you've ever installed a CD-ROM drive, this type of diagram probably looks very familiar.

At the foundation of PC Card architecture is the *hardware* layer. This represents the physical card itself, its connectors, and the circuitry needed to interface the card to the PC buses. In most cases, PC Card support can be added to a computer with one or two VLSI (very large scale integration) ICs and a bit of "glue" logic. You can see this hardware implemented for a desktop or tower PC in the Adtron Data Drive shown in Fig. 7-4.

The next layer above hardware is called the *socket services* layer. Socket services act as a supplement for system BIOS by providing the low-level routines needed to access the card hardware. It is important to note that socket services software is frequently implemented as firmware—either in the system BIOS itself (often in new BIOS versions) or on an expansion ROM included on the adapter board. Socket services are used by the computer to identify how many sockets are in the system, and whether cards are inserted or removed while system power is applied.

The *card services* layer forms the interface between the operating system and socket services. When socket services detects the presence of a card, card

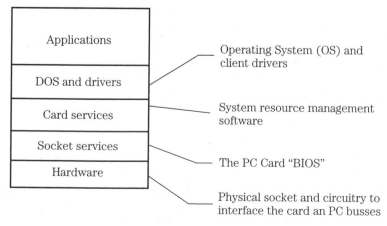

7-3 Simplified PC Card architecture.

7-4 PC Cards and an Adtron card drive.

services allocates and manages the system resources (interrupts, DMA channels, and addressing) needed by the card(s). When a card is removed, card services will free those system resources again. It is this unique ability to find, use, and then free system resources that gives PC Cards their powerful I/O capability and "plug and play"-type flexibility. Since card services software is universal across hardware platforms, it can be loaded either as a DOS device driver or may be part of the operating system, such as IBM's DOS 6.22 and OS/2 4.0.

Unfortunately, not all notebook and subnotebook systems use socket and card services. This is a major reason for PC Card compatibility problems. Some PC Cards come with software device drivers that attempt to communicate directly with the system hardware. These cards were developed prior to the release of the PCMCIA card services standard, and such cards will *only* work on certain hardware platforms. Also, not all notebooks provide PCMCIA socket services. Some vendors provide proprietary BIOS firmware that supports a specific, limited set of PC Cards. Just recently, some vendors have begun bundling compatible card and socket services with their systems. These card support device drivers are loosely termed "enablers," and are discussed in detail below.

Above card services, you see the familiar DOS and Application layers. Specialized (client) device drivers that may be needed for particular cards (such as an ATA card driver or flash file driver) are considered as part of the DOS layer.

Enablers

Many PC Cards offer an additional wrinkle before they work on your system—they need an *enabler.* While socket services interface the card to your hardware, and card services provide resource management, the PC Card is still not always fully configured. An enabler is often required to place the PC Card at a particular I/O address, memory address, or IRQ. There are three types of enabler software: generic enablers, specific enablers, and point enablers.

Perhaps the most common type of enabler is called a *generic enabler* (some vendors also refer to these as "super client drivers"). Generic enablers are capable of configuring a wide range of the most common card types such as modems and network adapters, and are usually provided with PCMCIA system software. Generic enablers typically require socket services and card services to be loaded before it can run. The problem with generic enablers is their demand on conventional memory. It is not uncommon to see a generic enabler demand 40 to 50 kB. Along with socket and card services, the memory requirements to support a PC Card can easily reach over 100 kB. This memory problem is most acute when running large native DOS applications. However, unless you're running more than one type of PC Card, you might be able to use a specific enabler.

A *specific enabler* is a program designed to configure a single type of PC Card and may be provided by the PC Card maker (or by a third-party software company). There are two compelling advantages to specific enablers. First, a specific enabler demands only a fraction of the memory used by generic enablers. If you use only one specific type of card, a specific enabler can save up to 40 kB of memory. Second, your generic enabler may not support a particular type of PC Card, so a specific enabler can be used to supplement a generic enabler using a minimum amount of additional RAM.

There *is* the potential for some problems when both a generic enabler and specific enabler are loaded—and both recognize and configure a particular type of I/O card. An oversight in the PCMCIA specification allows the first enabler to be loaded and configure the card if the card is installed when the machine is booted; if the card is inserted after the machine is booted, however, the last enabler loaded will configure the card. This can create serious problems if the two enablers have different ideas about how the card should be configured, or if the application software depends on a particular enabler to configure the card. Here are the rules for loading generic and specific enablers together:

- If you have the need for a generic enabler to configure your modem or another device which doesn't have a specific enabler, load it.
- If the only PC Card you use has a specific enabler, load the specific enabler instead of the generic one.
- If you have one or more cards which are configured by the generic enabler *and* a card which needs a specific enabler, first see if the generic enabler can handle the particular card (or a new version is available which can handle the specific card). If the generic enabler (or its updated version) can handle all the cards, don't load the specific enabler. Otherwise, load both.

There is also a third type of enabler called a *point enabler.* This is similar to a specific enabler in that it is designed to configure a single type of PC Card. Unlike generic or specific enablers, however, point enablers do *not* require socket services or card services to be loaded. Instead, they talk *directly* to the PCMCIA adapter hardware. This has both advantages and drawbacks. The most compelling advantage is memory—since socket and card services are not needed, a point enabler takes up very little memory. Unfortunately, that is where the advantages end. In order to communicate with hardware directly, a point enabler must be designed for specific hardware. As a result, a point enabler usually doesn't work on all PC Card systems. Also, the point enabler will bypass the socket and card services if they are loaded. This can be a real problem if you want to use other cards at the same time. Generally speaking, bypassing your socket and card services is not a good idea, so reserve point enablers as a last resort (and only if you use no other PC Cards in the system at the same time).

Card types

PCMCIA standards also define the physical dimensions that a PC Card is limited to. There are three types of cards: Types I, II, and III. Although the length and width of each card remains the same, the thickness of their *substrate area* can vary (as shown in Fig. 7-5) to accommodate different applications. The classic type I card is only 3.3-mm thick. While this is too thin for mechanical assemblies, it is ideal for most types of memory enhancements. Type II cards run 5.0-mm thick, which makes them ideal for larger memory enhancements and most I/O cards such as LAN adapters. Note in Fig. 7-5 that the edges and connector area (the *interconnect area*) of the card remain at 3.3 mm. The type III card is a full 10.5-mm thick, which is large enough to accommodate the components for a complete hard drive or radio communication device like a cellular modem. Like type II cards, the interconnect area remains 3.3 mm. This 3.3-mm rail height permits thinner cards to be inserted into thicker slots (but not vice versa).

CardBus

If you work with PC Cards at all, chances are that you're going to encounter CardBus architecture. The CardBus is an interface that allows PC Cards and hosts to utilize 32-bit bus mastering and 33-MHz operation. In short, the CardBus is PCMCIA's answer to the PCI interface used on modern motherboards. Of course, CardBus is not identical to PCI, but it is as close as PC Cards have been able to come.

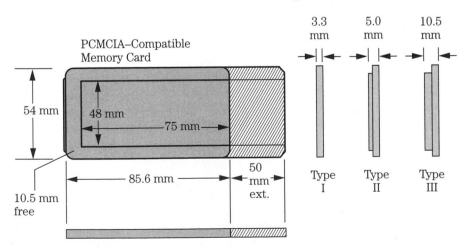

7-5 Form factors for typical PC Cards.

Inside the card

You can develop a tremendous respect for PC Cards by understanding the fragile and compact assemblies that are inside it. Consider the Maxtor MobileMax Lite shown in Fig. 7-6. The drive contains a single platter, upper and lower R/W heads, a voice coil servo motor to position the heads, a spindle motor to spin the platters, and the circuitry required to handle all drive functions and interfacing. As you might imagine, each element of the PC Card must be kept extremely thin. Still, it is sometimes difficult to believe that the assembly actually fits into a shell only 0.5-cm thick (type II). Another important consideration in PC Card design is the control and suppression of *electrostatic discharge* (ESD). Static electricity must be prevented from reaching the card's PC board where IC damage can occur. Once a card is inserted into a system, a *discharge tab* at the physical interface connector carries away any accumulation of charges to system ground. Until a card is inserted, a card protects its circuitry from damage using the Faraday cage principle—the same principle used by antistatic bags to protect their contents. The shell of most PC Cards is either constructed of a metal (such as stainless steel) or some sort of metallized plastic. Both shell halves are bonded together by a small spring. Any charge introduced to the card is quickly dispersed over the entire shell surface instead of being allowed to enter the card.

Hot insertion and removal

One of the great disadvantages to most expansion devices is that computer power must be completely off before the device can be installed or removed. Not only is this necessary to prevent accidental damage from improper insertion, but the traditional BIOS and DOS only allocate system resources when the system is first initialized. They were not designed to accommodate allocating system resources "on the fly." Even plug-and-play devices only allocate resources during initialization. PC Cards take a major step toward this type of "dynamic resource allocation" with the support of *hot swapping.* Hot swapping (or hot insertion and removal) refers to the ability to insert and remove cards while the PC power is still on without any degradation or damage to the system or card. Ideally, software applications can recognize the card's function and adjust accordingly.

While PC Cards support hot swapping, very few operating systems or application programs are currently "PC Card aware." That is, they do not recognize when cards have been inserted or removed. Therefore, users of any computer with PC Card slots should close any open application programs before inserting or removing a PC Card. Otherwise, the application may not initialize a card that has been inserted, and may lock up when a card is removed.

Understanding attribute memory

One of the greatest challenges facing PC Cards is cross-compatibility—the ability to use various card species from diverse manufacturers in the same card slot. There are quite a few card sizes and types currently in production, and many more card models will be available by the time you read this book. How does the computer "know" when you have replaced your 2-MB SRAM card with a 20-MB Flash card or a 100-MB PCMCIA hard drive? You should understand that a computer capable of

Maxtor Corp.

7-6 A Maxtor PC Card hard drive.

accepting PCMCIA cards must be able to detect and adjust to the diverse attributes of each card it may encounter, even though each card may utilize the same physical interface.

The best analogy to this is hard drives which are available in a staggering array of capacities, heads, cylinders, sectors, and so on, but all those drives can use the same physical interface. A computer interacts properly with a hard drive because you enter the drive's key parameters in the computer's CMOS setup routine. The same basic problem exists for PC Cards. However, memory cards are intended to be transient items—inserted and removed at will. Imagine the inconvenience of having to reenter a card's key parameters each time a new card is inserted. Even a single typing error can be disastrous for some cards and their contents.

The PCMCIA has supported a standard for memory card services that defines the software interface for accessing cards. The interface can either be a device driver loaded when the computer boots, or designed directly into BIOS ROM or the operating system. In order for this driver system to work, each card must be able to identify itself to the computer. The complete characteristic and ID data for a memory card is held in the *attribute memory* area of each individual card. Attribute memory contains a surprising amount of information. It must, considering the huge number of potential differences in card layout and features. Attribute memory tells the computer how much storage a card contains, the particular device type (memory, disk, I/O, and so on), the card's data format, speed capabilities, and many other variables.

The contents of attribute memory are typically setup information that falls into one of four categories of PCMCIA's Card Identification System (CIS), otherwise known as the card's "metaformat." Those four layers are: the *basic compatibility layer,* indicating how the card's storage is organized; the *data recording format layer,* specifying how blocks of card information are to be stored; the *data organization layer,* defining the card's operating system format (i.e., DOS, Microsoft's FlashFile system, PCMCIA's XIP, and so on), and any *specific standards* (or *system-specific standards*) needed to support an operating system.

The CIS data contained in attribute memory are a collection of related data blocks which are interlinked rather like a chain. Each "link" in the chain (a data block) is called a *tuple,* and can be up to 128 bytes long. The first byte of a tuple encodes the function of that tuple and its parameters. The second byte in a tuple links to the next tuple (if any) and specifies the precise number of bytes in that tuple. Since you know how long the present tuple is, you know exactly where the next tuple begins. In addition to standard tuples, individual card manufacturers are also free to add their own unique tuples to support proprietary features. It is not necessary for you to know the precise operation of each tuple, but it can help you to be familiar with their nomenclature and general purpose. One of the most important tuples is the Function ID entry called CISTPL_FUNCID. This tuple tells the host computer exactly what kind of card is installed. Table 7-1 shows typical entries for the most popular PC Card types.

Connections

The standard PC Card is connected to a PC through a 68-pin header arranged in two rows of 34 pins as shown in Fig. 7-7. If you look at the header pins closely, you will notice that several of the pins are longer than the others. These are *ground pins.* By making them longer, a card will be attached to ground first when inserted. Figure 7-8 clearly illustrates how a PC Card interfaces to its mating connector. When the card is removed, ground will still be attached after the power pins have been disconnected. Good grounding helps to ensure the card's reliability and permit "hot" insertion and removal. When you look at the assignment of

Table 7-1. Typical Function ID Entries for CISTPL_FUNCID

CISTPL_FUNCID: Function Identification Tuple	
Code	**Name**
0	Multifunction
1	Memory
2	Serial Port
3	Parallel Port
4	Fixed Disk
5	Video Adapter
6	Network Adapter
7	AIMS (auto indexing mass-storage)
8	SCSI
9	Security
A-FD	Reserved (allocated as new devices are introduced)
FE	Vendor-Specific
FF	Do Not Use

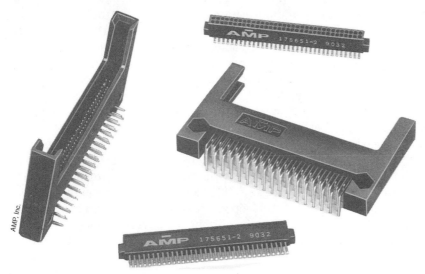

7-7 A selection of AMP PC Card connectors.

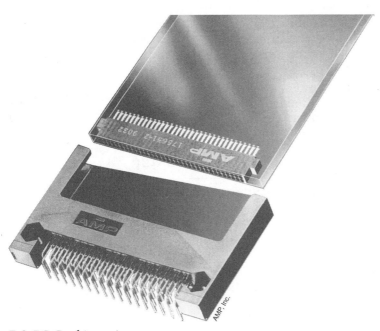

7-8 PC Card insertion.

each pin in Table 7-2, you will see that there are basically four types of signals at the PCMCIA interface: data pins, address pins, power (and ground), and control signals. It is this healthy mix of signals that makes it possible to support many of the PC Card applications that are available today. Also note that the CardBus PC Cards use the same 68-pin connector, but their signal assignments are vastly different.

PC Card Applications

Now that PC Cards are being developed according to release 2.1, they offer a series of compelling advantages for mobile computer users:

- The I/O support offered by PCMCIA specifications allows virtually any product to be incorporated into a PC Card. Modems, network adapters,

Table 7-2. Pin Assignments for PC Card and CardBus Interfaces

	16-Bit		32-bit			16-Bit		32-bit
Pin	**Memory**	**I/O+Mem**	**CardBus**	**Pin**	**Memory**	**I/O+Mem**	**CardBus**	
1	GND	GND	GND	35	GND	GND	GND
2	D3	D3	CAD0	36	CD1#	CD1#	CCD1#
3	D4	D4	CAD1	37	D11	D11	CAD2
4	D5	D5	CAD3	38	D12	D12	CAD4
5	D6	D6	CAD5	39	D13	D13	CAD6
6	D7	D7	CAD7	40	D14	D14	RSRVD
7	CE1#	CE1#	CCBE0#	41	D15	D15	CAD8
8	A10	A10	CAD9	42	CE2#	CE2#	CAD10
9	OE#	OE#	CAD11	43	VS1#	VS1#	CVS1
10	A11	A11	CAD12	44	RSRVD	IORD#	CAD13
11	A9	A9	CAD14	45	RSRVD	IOWR#	CAD15
12	A8	A8	CCBE1#	46	A17	A17	CAD16
13	A13	A13	CPAR	47	A18	A18	RSRVD
14	A14	A14	CPERR#	48	A19	A19	CBLOCK#
15	WE#	WE#	CGNT#	49	A20	A20	CSTOP#
16	READY	IREQ#	CINT#	50	A21	A21	CDEVSEL#
17	Vcc	Vcc	Vcc	51	Vcc	Vcc	Vcc
18	Vpp1	Vpp1	Vpp1	52	Vpp2	Vpp2	Vpp2
19	A16	A16	CCLK	53	A22	A22	CTRDY#
20	A15	A15	CIRDY#	54	A23	A23	CFRAME#
21	A12	A12	CCBE2#	55	A24	A24	CAD17
22	A7	A7	CAD18	56	A25	A25	CAD19
23	A6	A6	CAD20	57	VS2#	VS2#	CVS2
24	A5	A5	CAD21	58	RESET	RESET	CRST#
25	A4	A4	CAD22	59	WAIT#	WAIT#	CSERR#
26	A3	A3	CAD23	60	RSRVD	INPACK#	CREQ#
27	A2	A2	CAD24	61	REG#	REG#	CCBE3#
28	A1	A1	CAD25	62	BVD2	SPKR#	CAUDIO
29	A0	A0	CAD26	63	BVD1	STSCHG#	CSTSCHG
30	D0	D0	CAD27	64	D8	D8	CAD28
31	D1	D1	CAD29	65	D9	D9	CAD30
32	D2	D2	RSRVD	66	D10	D10	CAD31
33	WP	IOIS16#	CCLKRUN#	67	CD2#	CD2#	CCD2#
34	GND	GND	GND	68	GND	GND	GND

video capture modules, audio cards, and hard drives are just some of the
devices that PCMCIA standards now embrace.

- PC Cards can be made to operate in a *dual-voltage mode* (either 5.0 or
  3.3 V) depending on the design of the mobile PC. Low-voltage compatibility
  saves power and extends battery life.
- The programs and applications stored on PC Cards can now be executed in
  place rather than having to load the card's contents into main memory. This
  execute-in-place (or XIP) technology reduces the demand for large amounts
  of on-board RAM.
- The socket services software defined by release 2.1 describes a BIOS-level
  interface that allows applications to access the card's hardware. The device
  drivers written to operate specific PC Cards will run on any PC that supports
  socket services.
- The card services software automatically allocates system resources (i.e.,
  memory and IRQs) once a PC Card is inserted into a system (referred to
  as dynamic resource allocation). Information (called *tuple information*)
  contained in the CIS of a card describes the characteristics and abilities of
  that card. In turn, the host system can automatically configure the card for
  proper operation. This type of operation is the earliest implementation of a
  plug-and-play architecture.

PC Card problems

Like all new PC technologies, however, there are some disappointing problems with
the early implementations of PC Cards. Before you decide to buy that next "PC
Card–compatible" system, you should understand some of the factors that have
contributed to PCMCIA's poor early showing. When the PCMCIA issued release 1.0 in
1990, socket and card services did not exist. Card makers had to supply their own
specific drivers which had to be tested on each specific computer. If the host computer were updated or upgraded, the cards that worked on the older systems would
probably not work on the newer ones. This resulted in perplexing compatibility
problems.

Socket and card services were added in 1991 with PCMCIA release 2.0, but the
release also brought I/O devices into the PC Card picture. Although this made
PCMCIA much more versatile, I/O brought in a host of new problems. Although all
I/O cards are supposed to be treated as a generic device, an operating system does
not see all devices the same way. For example, an operating system does not treat
a hard drive and a modem the same way, but card makers did not take that into
account, so compatibility between systems is still an issue. Also, most operating
systems are designed to work with resources that are present when a system is
booted, so although you may be able to insert and remove cards safely, the operating system can rarely adjust the system resources properly. As a result, many cards
have to be installed before the system boots.

Today, most PCMCIA cards work in most systems and can be inserted and
removed without rebooting the computer—but there are no guarantees. The situation has gotten much better over the last year or so, but beware of older PCMCIA
systems.

Today's cards

PCMCIA cards have come a long way since the early memory cards of 1990. Virtually any device that can be implemented on an expansion card can be fabricated as a PC Card. As a technician, you should understand the range of devices that you may encounter when servicing notebook and subnotebook systems.

- **Memory cards.** Memory expansion devices continue to be popular PC Card devices—not so much for added system memory, but to run prefabricated applications directly off the card.
- **Modem cards.** PCMCIA modems are rapidly replacing proprietary modems as internal communication devices. PCMCIA modems are easily matching the speed and performance of stand-alone modems, and are even being equipped with cellular connections for true mobile operation.
- **LAN cards.** LANs are becoming more popular as businesses integrate their operations and add connections to such resources as the Internet. LAN cards allow mobile computers to play a constructive role on networks using topologies such as Ethernet, Token Ring, and 3270 Emulation.
- **Digital video cards.** The soaring popularity of multimedia applications has dramatically increased the demand for video and still-frame capture products. PCMCIA technology allows video and audio capture capability in PC Card products for high-quality multimedia "on the road."
- **Hard drive cards.** Until the advent of PCMCIA, it was virtually impossible to add a second hard drive to a portable PC. Fortunately, the use of PCMCIA combined with the stunning advances in hard-drive technology allow substantial hard-drive capacities in a type III form factor.
- **Audio cards.** Games and music composition software demand high-quality sound reproduction. PCMCIA audio cards provide SoundBlaster-compatible sound to external speakers. The trend toward mobile multimedia is integrating sound systems and speakers right into the mobile PC, but stand-alone sound cards are available.
- **SCSI adapter cards.** The Small Computer System Interface (SCSI) is a system-level interface scheme that allows a multitude of devices (i.e., CD-ROM, scanners, tape drives, and so on) to be connected to a system. A PCMCIA SCSI adapter card opens a whole new level of compatibility for a mobile computer.
- **Floppy drive cards.** The recent trend among subnotebook and palmtop computers has been to forego the floppy drive in favor of a PCMCIA slot. However, PCMCIA floppy disk adapters such as the Accurite Technologies PassportCard bring a standard floppy drive to any mobile PC that lacks an internal floppy drive.

Installing a PC Card

Like so many things in PC service, proper installation can avoid a round of troubleshooting later on. This is particularly true for PC Cards, because they are completely dependent on software for proper configuration and operation. This part of the chapter describes the general steps involved in setting up a typical PC Card. Of course, always be sure to read the manual that accompanies your card for specific instructions or caveats. Most PC Cards require access to four different pieces of software: the socket services, the card services, the "enabler," and a resource manager (usually a high-level driver).

If your system does not yet support PC Cards (of if you are restoring a failed hard drive), you will need to install the socket and card services first. This should usually be done before installing the card itself. However, keep in mind that most mobile computers come with card and socket services installed already, so you should *not* reinstall those applications since they may be optimized for your particular hardware. Power up the PC and read the driver banners. If you see mention of card and socket services, that software is probably installed already. Windows 95 has a small suite of card and socket service drivers (refer to the PCMCIA plug-and-play card wizard under your Control Panel).

Next, you will need to install the PC Card enabler (you may also see this grouped with card services software). In many cases, the diskette accompanying the PC Card will have an installation routine that will add the enabler's command line to CONFIG.SYS. Otherwise, you will have to add the enabler's command line manually by editing the CONFIG.SYS file. Once the enabler is added to CONFIG.SYS, save the file and turn off the PC. Insert the card in its card slot, then restart the PC. If the software is installed correctly so far, you should hear a beep as the card is recognized. You will hear two beeps if the card is not recognized (check the card and software installation).

Finally, you will need to install the "resource manager" (or client driver) that accompanies the particular card. For example, a PC Card fax/modem usually requires a fax/modem client driver, or a PC Card hard drive requires an ATA IDE client driver, and so on. Client drivers are often card-specific, so be sure to install the client driver that accompanies your particular card.

You can see an example of how this works by looking at the combination of software in Table 7-3. The program names are examples only (your particular software will use different names). Notice that PC Card support requires several different pieces of software—and the software varies depending on the particular cards that you need to support. For example, an ATA IDE card and a fax/modem card use the same socket services, card services, and enabler, but require two different client drivers.

Troubleshooting PC Card Problems

The PCMCIA represents an *interface*—not a particular card. As a consequence, PC Card troubleshooting is rather like solving problems with any other type of bus interface (SCSI, ISA, VL, and so on). The objective is not to repair a PC Card, but rather to isolate a functional problem to the card, the interface itself, or some portion of the system's configuration and operating system. When you determine a PC Card to be defective, your best course is to replace the card outright.

Symptom 1: The SRAM or flash card loses its memory when powered down or removed from the system   Since flash cards make use of advanced EEPROMs, you might wonder why batteries would be incorporated. Some flash cards use a small amount of SRAM to speed the transfer of data to or from the

Table 7-3. PC Card Software versus Application

Filename	ATA IDE	Flash memory	LAN	Fax/modem	SRAM memory
PCMSS.EXE (socket services)	Yes	Yes	Yes	Yes	Yes
PCMCS.EXE (card services)	Yes	No	Yes	Yes	Yes
PCMCSFUL.EXE (card enabler)	Yes	Yes	Yes	Yes	Yes
PCMSCD.EXE (comm. client)	No	No	Yes	Yes	No
PCMATA.EXE (HDD client)	Yes	No	No	No	Yes
PCMFFCS.EXE (flash client)	No	Yes	No	No	Yes

card. Batteries would be needed to back up the SRAM only. If your memory card does not appear to hold its memory, you should start your investigation by removing the memory card and testing its batteries. Make sure the card's batteries are inserted properly. Use your multimeter to check the battery voltage(s). Replace any memory card batteries which appear marginal or low. You should expect a 2- to 5-year backup life from your memory card batteries depending on the amount of card memory. More memory results in shorter battery life. All battery contacts should be clean and bright, and contacts should make firm connections with the battery terminals.

Try a known-good working card in your system. You may verify a new or known-good memory card on another computer with a compatible card slot. If another card works properly, your original memory card is probably defective and should be replaced. Under no circumstances should you actually *open* the card.

Symptom 2: You are unable to access a memory card for reading. You may not be able to write to the card either   Begin troubleshooting by checking memory card compatibility (programmed OTPROM cards and Mask ROM cards cannot be written to). If a memory card is not compatible with the interface used by your small computer, the interface may not access the card. For example, a PCMCIA-compatible 68-pin card will probably not work in a 68-pin card slot that is not 100 percent PCMCIA-compatible. Try a known-good compatible card in the suspect card slot. Also check your CONFIG.SYS or AUTOEXEC.BAT files to be sure that any required device drivers have been installed during system initialization. If you are having difficulty writing to an SRAM or flash card, take a moment and inspect the card's write-protect switch. A switch left in the "protected" position prevents new information from being written to the card. Move the switch to the "unprotected" position and try the memory card again.

If you are having difficulty writing to EEPROM or Flash EEPROM cards, check your programming voltages (Vpp1 and Vpp2). Without high-voltage pulses, new data cannot be written to such cards. Measure Vpp1 and Vpp2 with your oscilloscope with the card removed from your system [it may be necessary to ground the card detect lines (CD1 and CD2) to fool the host system into believing that a card is actually installed]. You will probably have to disassemble your small-computer's housing to gain easy access to the motherboard's card connector. If one or both programming pulses are missing during a write operation, check your power supply output(s). When high-voltage supplies are missing, troubleshoot your computer's power supply. If programming voltage(s) are present, there may be a defect in the card controller IC or board, or any discrete switching circuitry designed to produce the programming pulses. Try replacing the card controller (or motherboard).

The memory card may be inserted incorrectly. Two card-detect signals are needed from a PCMCIA-compatible card to ensure proper insertion. If the card is not inserted properly, the host system will inhibit all card activities. Remove the card and reinsert it completely. Make sure the card is straight, even, and fully inserted. Try accessing the card again.

If trouble remains, remove the card and inspect the connector on the card *and* inside the computer. Check for any contacts that may be loose, bent, or broken. It may be necessary to disassemble the mobile computer in order to inspect its connector, but a clear view with a small flashlight will tell you all you need to know. Connections in the computer that are damaged or extremely worn should be replaced with a new connector assembly. When a memory card connector is worn or damaged, the memory card should be replaced.

If your results are still inconclusive, try a known-good memory card in the system. Keep in mind that the new card must be fully compatible with the original one. Make sure that there are no valuable or irreplaceable files on the known-good card before you try it in a suspect system. If a known-good card works properly, then the old memory card is probably damaged and should be replaced. If a known-good card also does not work, the original card is probably working properly. Your final step is to disassemble your small computer and replace the memory card controller or motherboard. A defective controller can prevent all data and control signals from reaching the card.

Symptom 3: You see an error message indicating that a PCMCIA card will not install or is not recognized   Chances are that one or more device drivers in the system are interfering with the offending PCMCIA card. Load your CONFIG.SYS file into an ordinary text editor and systematically edit out any other PCMCIA drivers. Try reinitializing the system after each change. Once you locate the offending driver, try reconfiguring the driver such that it will not interfere (maybe a new driver or patch is available).

Symptom 4: Even though a desired card is installed, an error message or warning is displayed asking you to insert the card   The PCMCIA card may not be installed properly. Try removing the card, then reinsert it carefully. The card socket may not be enabled, so the application may not be able to see it. Make sure that the card socket is enabled. For most systems (such as the Canon NoteJet 486 which ships with the PCMCIA socket turned off), the solution is to get into the BIOS setup for the computer and to enable the PCMCIA socket. Check the documentation for your system to find out how to get into the BIOS setup. Sometimes this feature is located in the "advanced settings" or in the "power management" area of the BIOS settings. After you have changed the settings, save the changes and restart your system. In more advanced systems (such as the Compaq Concerto), you can turn the PCMCIA socket off and on with the computer's setup utility under Windows. After changing the settings, save the changes and restart your system.

Another possibility might be that the application program interacting with the PCMCIA slot is addressing the wrong interrupt line for insertion or removal. Check for any card socket diagnostics and determine which interrupt(s) the application is trying to use for Card Status Change. Check the device driver for the card and add an explicit command line switch to specify the desired interrupt. If an interrupt is already specified, make sure that this is the correct one.

Symptom 5: You encounter a number of card service errors or other problems when antivirus programs are used   Such errors include CARD SERVICES ALLOCATION ERROR, ERROR: CONFIGURATION FILE NOT FOUND, ERROR: COULD NOT OPEN CONFIGURATION FILE, or ERROR USING CARD SERVICES. Under some circumstances, an antivirus program can interfere with PCMCIA card services. The Norton antivirus program NAV&.SYS is known to cause this sort of problem if it is loaded *before* the card services software. There are typically three ways around this type of problem. First, rearrange the order of drivers called in your CONFIG.SYS file so that NAV&.SYS comes *after* the card services software. Second, use NAV_.SYS instead of NAV&.SYS. While NAV_.SYS requires more space than NAV&.SYS, it is better at coexisting with other memory-resident programs. Third, remove NAV&.SYS and use NAVTSR instead. If you are using antivirus programs, try remarking them out of CONFIG.SYS or AUTOEXEC.BAT.

Symptom 6: There are no pop-up displays when a PC Card is inserted or removed   Normally, when a card is installed or removed, a dialog box will appear indicating the card that has been inserted or removed. However, there are three reasons why this might happen. First, the DOS pop-up function is disabled under DOS (but still works under Windows). Check the card services software and make sure that the proper command line switches are set to enable the DOS pop-up. Second, there may be an upper memory area (UMA) conflict. Many card managers require 10 kB or more of UMA (each). If there is no free UMA, the card manager cannot read the card's attribute memory to install the card. Make sure that there is plenty of UMA space available for the card services software, and check that it loads properly. Third, the PCMCIA card may not be supported by the card services software—the two might not be fully compatible. Try a different card or update the card services software.

Symptom 7: The application locks up when a PC Card is inserted or removed Not all applications are fully PCMCIA-aware—that is, they do not recognize card insertion and removal properly. If your application crashes or locks up when a card is inserted or removed, chances are that the application is not written to handle hot insertion or removal with the card services software being used. Try inserting the card before starting the application, or close the application before removing it.

Symptom 8: The fax/modem card works fine in DOS, but refuses to work in Windows 95 In virtually all cases, the port addresses and IRQ assigned by Windows 95 do not match the assignments the card is expecting. Go to the Control Panel, double-click on Ports, and double-click on the COM Port you are assigning to your fax/modem. Then go to Advanced and check to see if the Port Address and IRQ match your fax/modem settings. If they don't, put in the proper settings and restart Windows 95.

Symptom 9: The mouse/trackball locks up or acts strangely after a fax/modem card is installed Chances are that the pointing device is sharing the same IRQ as the fax/modem card. In most cases, changing the fax/modem card IRQ assignments will correct the problem (though you may change the pointing device IRQ instead).

Symptom 10: A peripheral (i.e., sound card, scanner, or so on) no longer works now that the PC Card is installed This type of problem almost always indicates a hardware conflict. In most cases, the IRQ assigned to the PC Card is conflicting with the IRQ assigned to the malfunctioning device. Survey your system and determine the IRQs used by every device. You can change the IRQ of the PC Card, or change the IRQ of the other conflicting device. In either case, you'll need to restart the PC after you make those changes.

Symptom 11: The PCMCIA CardSoft enabler software won't install You probably have a PCMCIA enabler already installed on the system. If enabler software is already installed, it *may* support your card. If so, you can skip the new enabler software. If not, you need to remove the current enabler software, and then install the new enabler software.

Symptom 12: When installing a PC Card such as a fax/modem card, you find that the desired COM port or IRQ is not available In virtually all cases, the needed COM port or IRQ is being used by another device. Check for hardware conflicts and reset the PC Card to use different resources.

Symptom 13: You don't hear the proper number of beeps when inserting a PCMCIA card When the PC Card is inserted into a slot properly, you should hear a certain number of beeps. In most cases, this will be either one or two beeps (depending on your particular card software). If you don't hear the correct number of beeps, chances are that the card has not been inserted properly into its socket.

Symptom 14: The card's configuration refuses to accept memory addresses (if needed) Some PC Cards require certain memory resources for proper operation. If you are prohibited from assigning those addresses to the PC Card, chances are that those memory locations are being used by another device in the system. Check for resource conflicts. You can usually resolve memory conflicts by changing the address assigned to the PC Card, or the address assigned to the conflicting device.

Symptom 15: Other programs stop working or change their behavior after the card software is installed In most cases, new .DLL files installed to support the PC Card have changed shared files used by other programs. Check with the technical support for your particular PC Card maker and see if there are any problem files identified—and see if there are any updated files available. If so, you can usually download the corrected file and copy it to the /windows/system directory (or other suitable directory). If no corrected file is available, you will need to uninstall the PC Card and restore the original shared files from installation disks or tape backups.

Symptom 16: When starting a client driver under Windows 95, the message "Client registration failed" appears In most cases, the client driver is not installed or not installed properly. In principle, you'll need to remove any traces of the client driver, then reinstall the client driver from scratch. You may also have resource conflicts which prevent the client driver from loading. For example, consider problems with Nogatech's CaptureVision 95 client driver.

- Open the Control Panel, then double-click on the System icon.
- Click the Device Manager tab and select VIEW DEVICES BY TYPE.
- If you have the line OTHER DEVICES, and under it you see NOGATECH NOGAVISION, do the following:

  1. Highlight the NOGATECH NOGAVISION entry and click the Remove button. Now, remove the card from your computer.
  2. Go to the Windows\INF directory.
  3. Look for an OEMx.INF file (where x can be any digit)—don't worry if you can't find any OEMx.INF files.
  4. Rename the file(s) to OEMx.BAK (where x is the digit).
  5. Look for a NOGATECH.INF file and delete the file—don't worry if you can't find the file.
  6. Now go to the Windows\System directory.
  7. Look for any files starting with "noga." Delete any files starting with "noga."
  8. Now, reinstall the software and start CaptureVision 95 when finished with the setup.

- If you do not have the line UNKNOWN DEVICE, continue with the following:

  1. Double-click the line SOUND, VIDEO, AND GAME CONTROLLERS.
  2. You should see the line NOGATECH NOGAVISION VIDEO CAPTURE.

3. If you do not get this line, try to install the software once again.
4. If you see an exclamation mark in front of the line NOGATECH NOGAVISION VIDEO CAPTURE you have resource problems and the drivers have not been loaded.

Symptom 17: The PC Card will not configure properly. An I/O Address conflict message is displayed   There is a resource conflict between several PC Cards. For example, network and SCSI PC Cards often require the same I/O addresses. You will need to find available I/O space, then reconfigure one of the conflicting devices to use that available space.

Check for point enablers. Most PC Cards depend on card and socket services software, as well as generic enablers, for proper configuration. However, point enablers bypass card and socket services. If you can use a generic enabler instead of a point enabler, try removing the point enabler. As a rule, point enablers should not be used when there is more than one PC Card in the system.

Check for I/O resources using a program such as MSD (Microsoft Diagnostics), and note any regions of I/O space that are unused. If the cards provide several different "prefabricated" configurations, try each of those configurations—chances are that one of those configurations will work on your computer. If none of the "prefabricated" configurations will resolve the problem, you will need to manually change one of the cards to use free space available in the system. In many cases, this can be accomplished by making command line changes to the card's enabler or client driver. Once you finish making changes, you'll need to reboot the computer for your changes to take effect.

Symptom 18: My system hangs when card services loads   First, check to see that you are only loading one copy of card services software. Attempting to load a second copy can sometimes hang the system. It is also possible that the PC Card software configuration file (typically an .INI file such as PCM.INI) may be set up improperly. You may need to modify the configuration file to place the card services software in the "poll" mode (i.e., /POLL). Refer to the documentation that accompanied your software or system for more information on configuration modes.

Symptom 19: You get an "Invalid command line switch" message displayed when loading services or client drivers   You may be placing command line switches in the wrong places. Traditionally, command line switches are placed on the actual command lines in CONFIG.SYS or AUTOEXEC.BAT. For some PC Card installations, however, command line switches must be entered in the PC Card configuration file (an .INI file such as PCM.INI). In some cases, switches must be entered in the configuration file *instead* of the actual command line entry.

Symptom 20: You have a Xircom Combo card (i.e., fax/modem and LAN) and cannot get it to work with standard card manager software   This is typically because Xircom developed a non-PCMCIA compliant combo card (marked "Combo Card") prior to the ratification of the new PCMCIA standards. As a consequence, the card is supported with proprietary software. You will have to install proprietary software in order to use the Xircom Combo Cards. Only cards marked "PC Card compliant multifunction cards" are supported by standard software.

Symptom 21: You get an ABORT, RETRY, IGNORE **message when accessing an ATA PC Card**   In most cases, you are missing the client driver for your ATA PC Card (in CONFIG.SYS), or the wrong client driver is installed. You will need to install the proper client driver for your ATA PC Card, then reboot the system and watch for the drive letter assigned to the socket.

Symptom 22: You can't get any sound from the PC Card sound device, or you get an error message saying that it can't talk to card services   As with many network cards, most PC Card sound devices have their own client driver software that configures the card. If you try to use the card with standard card management software, you will need to remove the sound device from that software, then install the PC Card–specific software *after* socket and card services (other card management software) has been loaded.

Symptom 23: When you insert a Practical Peripherals PractiCard 14,400 bps modem (revision A) in a PCMCIA slot, the modem may not be initialized   This is a hardware problem with older Practical Peripherals PC Card modems. You will need to upgrade the modem to revision B or later in order to correct the problem.

Symptom 24: The SRAM card refuses to work   In many cases, this is a software problem. SRAM cards are supported by an ATA PC Card driver. In effect, the SRAM card is treated like a drive. Make sure that the proper client driver is installed for your particular SRAM card. Also make note of the drive letter assigned to the SRAM card during system initialization. Point enablers for an SRAM card can also cause problems when there are other cards in the system being supported with socket and card services or other enablers.

Symptom 25: When you first install your PC Card software, you get the error message; NO PCMCIA CONTROLLER FOUND   In virtually all cases, the software version that you are using does not support the PCMCIA controller used in your system. You will need to contact the software maker (or the system maker) and see if there is an updated version or patch available for the PC Card software. It is also possible that the system's PCMCIA controller is disabled (in CMOS), or that it is defective.

Symptom 26: When a program attempts to identify or check the status of a PC Card modem, the program may stop responding (or cause the computer to hang) if the modem has been powered off using power management features   The problem occurs when the program makes calls to the modem, but the modem had been powered off with power management features. Ideally, you should not be able to make calls to a device while it is in idle or power-down mode, but some programs allow this to happen. In turn, the program making the calls can crash and take the system with it. This is a known problem in Microsoft's OSR2 for Windows 95. For now, the only ways around the problem are to disable power save functions on the PC Card or shut down the offending program before allowing the PC Card to go idle.

Symptom 27: When you eject a PC Card network adapter from a CardBus socket without stopping the card in PC Card properties, your computer may restart   This is a software-related problem encountered under Windows 95. The PC Card network adapter is removed from the CardBus socket without properly notifying VMM (the software that controls the resources used by the PC Card). The software continues to "think" the PC Card is installed, even after the card is removed, and subsequent access causes the system to crash. The only workaround at this time is to stop the PC Card network adapter using the PC Card tool in your Control Panel (or the PC Card icon on the taskbar) before you remove the network adapter PC Card.

Symptom 28: After a multifunction PCMCIA adapter is installed, the adapter may appear as a "parent" node below a "child" node in the Windows 95 Device Manager   In almost all cases, this is due to a problem during device installation—the .INF file used to install the device has been processed incorrectly. Unfortunately, this is not a Windows 95 problem, but a manufacturer-specific .INF file problem. Contact the PC Card manufacturer and see if there is an updated .INF file or other workaround for the problem.

Symptom 29: After a second boot with a CardBus PCMCIA controller installed in your computer, the Device Manager may display a red X for one or more PCMCIA sockets on your system   Red Xs mean that the sockets are disabled. CardBus controllers are dynamically enabled during the *first* boot after installation (even though they are installed disabled). On the second boot, Windows 95 recognizes that the device is disabled and reports this to the Device Manager. Enable the PCMCIA CardBus controller:

- Open the Control Panel and double-click the System icon.
- Click the PCMCIA controller, and then click Properties.
- In the Device Usage box, click the "(Current)" check box to select it, then click OK.
- Click Close, then restart the computer when prompted.

When Windows 95 restarts, the PCMCIA Wizard runs to help you configure the PCMCIA controller. CardBus controllers must be explicitly enabled to start the PCMCIA wizard on the second boot.

Symptom 30: After installing Windows 95 OSR2, the Device Manager may display a PCIC-compatible PCMCIA controller as a conflicting resource (an exclamation point in a yellow circle)   This typically happens with CardBus PCMCIA controllers. CardBus controllers had been initialized by BIOS into the PCIC-compatible mode for backward compatibility. Unfortunately, OSR2 disables the PCIC compatibility mode in BIOS and configures the controller straight to CardBus mode. However, it neglects to remove the PCIC-compatible controller entry from your Device Manager. You will have to remove the PCIC-compatible entry from your Device Manager manually.

- In the Device Manager, click the PCIC-compatible controller to select it.
- Click Remove and then select Yes.
- Click OK to save your changes.

Symptom 31: When using a 3COM Elnk3 PCMCIA network card and a Xircom CE2ps PCMCIA network card together on a DEC HiNote Ultra CT475 computer, the Xircom card is not recognized You'll find that the Xircom card does not appear in the Device Manager or the PCMCIA tool in your Control Panel. This is a system-specific problem which can be rectified by inserting the Xircom CE2ps card first, then inserting the 3COM Elink3 card.

Symptom 32: When you use the Suspend command on certain Gateway laptop computers, battery power continues to drain This is a known problem with Gateway ColorBook 4SX25, ColorBook 4SX33, ColorBook 4DX33, Liberty, and Solo systems, and is due to a BIOS bug. When the Suspend mode is implemented, the PCMCIA slots should receive 0.0 V. Instead, the slots are receiving 2.5 V. This continues to drain the battery. Upgrade the BIOS on those systems to correct the problem.

Symptom 33: When you insert a Hayes Optima 14.4 PCMCIA modem into a PC Card socket, you hear a single (low) tone (or other indication) that the PCMCIA modem has not been recognized This is typically a modem hardware problem—versions of the Hayes Optima PCMCIA 14.4 modem before version 2.6H do NOT work with Windows 95 PC Card Socket Services. These older modems can be easily identified by their beige color (later modems are silver). In a situation like this, there is no workaround other than to upgrade the PCMCIA modem to a later version.

Symptom 34: When you use the Windows 95 Compression Agent with a removable PCMCIA hard disk, the Compression Agent may restart continuously at 10 percent finished This can occur if the drive is marked as "removable" in the Device Manager. Fortunately, there is a workaround.

- In the Control Panel, double-click the System icon.
- Click the Device Manager tab, and then double-click Disk Drives.
- Double-click the appropriate drive to display its properties.
- Click the Settings tab, and then click the Removable check box to clear it.
- Click OK to save your changes, then restart the PC when prompted.

Unfortunately, once the PCMCIA drive is no longer marked as "removable," you may no longer be able to swap drives on the fly.

Symptom 35: When you start Windows 95 with a PCMCIA hard disk inserted in the computer's PCMCIA slot, the hard disk seems to be recognized, but may not be available in Windows 95 This is a problem with Windows 95 which can occur if your computer does not have an IDE hard disk controller installed. If there is no IDE hard disk controller installed, the PCMCIA hard disk is assigned IDE port 1F0h. Since this port is normally associated with the primary hard disk controller, Windows 95 treats it differently from other IDE ports and does not assign it a drive letter. To get around this problem, remove the PCMCIA hard disk after Windows 95 starts, and then insert the disk into the PCMCIA slot again.

Symptom 36: When you insert a PCMCIA disk drive into a PCMCIA slot, your computer beeps (indicating that the PCMCIA card is recognized) but the disk drive is unavailable in Windows 95 This is often due to a hardware conflict—the PCMCIA disk controller may be configured to use I/O ports 170 to 177 and your computer may use the same ports for other purposes. Check the resource settings in Device Manager. If the PCMCIA disk controller is using ports 170 to 177, you can try reserving I/O ports 170 to 177 (forcing Windows 95 to configure the PCMCIA disk controller at another I/O address):

- In the Control Panel, double-click the System icon.
- On the Device Manager tab, click Properties.
- On the Reserve Resources tab, click the Input/Output (I/O) option button, and then click Add.
- In the Start Value box, enter 170.
- In the End Value box, enter 177.
- Click OK to save your changes.
- Restart the computer.

As an alternative, try disabling any secondary disk controller that uses I/O ports 170 to 177 in the computer's CMOS settings.

Symptom 37: When you attempt to dial under Windows 95 using an Integrated Services Digital Network (ISDN) connection, your computer may stop responding (hang) This is a hardware-specific problem that has been known to occur with Eicon PCMCIA ISDN adapters. The hardware version of the adapter does not support dialing under Windows 95 properly. Unfortunately, you will have to correct this hardware problem by updating to a new ISDN adapter.

Symptom 38: When you try to send a fax from a cellular phone using Microsoft Exchange and a Motorola Power 14.4 PCMCIA modem, your fax feature may not work This is a problem with Microsoft Exchange—the default initialization string sent to the modem from Microsoft Exchange initializes the modem for noncellular calls only (regardless of the status of the Use Cellular Protocol option in Modems properties). You will need to edit your Windows 95 Registry with REGEDIT.EXE to correct the problem.

Note: Altering Registry values can have devastating effects on your Windows 95 system. Always make a backup copy of the Registry files (SYSTEM.DAT and USER.DAT) before starting your edit.

The following registry key contains the initialization strings for installed modems (where <xxxx> is the modem ID number). To determine which ID is the correct modem, see the DriverDesc key.

```
HKEY_LOCAL_MACHINE\System\CurrentControlSet\Services\Class\
Modem\<xxxx>\Init
```

Use the following value to use the modem with a cellular phone:

```
"2"="AT&F1&D2&C1\\V1S0=0E0V1<cr>"
```

To return the initialization string to normal (land use), change the key to:

```
"2"="AT&F&D2&C1\\V1S0=0E0V1<cr>"
```

Note: You can reset these values to their default settings by removing the modem in Device Manager and then reinstalling it.

Symptom 39: When you run Windows 95 on a Dell Latitude XP Notebook computer with a port replicator, PC Card services may not be available There will probably be no listing for the PC Card socket in the Device Manager, and the PC Card icon may be missing in your Control Panel. The Dell port replicator is fitted with a SCSI adapter, but by default, both the PC Card socket and the SCSI port use the same IRQ (often IRQ 11). You will have to change the setting for the PC Card socket:

- Detach the port replicator from the computer, and then use the Add New Hardware wizard in your Control Panel to search for new hardware.
- After the PC Card socket is detected and installed, restart the computer when you are prompted to do so.
- In Control Panel, double-click the System icon, and then click the Device Manager tab.
- Double-click the PCMCIA Socket entry, double-click the PCMCIA controller, and then click the Resources tab.
- Click the Use Automatic Settings check box to clear it, click Interrupt Request, and then click Change Settings.
- In the Value box, click an available IRQ setting.
- Click OK to save your changes.
- Shut down Windows 95, and then turn your computer off and back on (cold boot).
- Reattach the port replicator unit.

Symptom 40: When you try to undock a laptop computer with a PCMCIA card installed in a Databook PCMCIA controller socket, you may receive the following error message; THE COMPUTER FAILED TO UNDOCK This is generally a problem where the PC Card adapter is interfering with the docking port adapter. The only known workaround to this problem is to remove all PC Cards from their sockets before undocking the mobile computer. Afterward, the Eject command on your Start menu should work correctly.

Symptom 41: When you insert a PCMCIA SRAM or flash memory card into a Windows 95 computer that has been configured to use protected-mode PCMCIA card drivers, there may be no drive letter in My Computer or

Windows Explorer associated with the PCMCIA card This can occur even though the card seems to be recognized properly and the appropriate driver appears to be installed. The problem is often that while the drivers may be installed, they are not installed correctly. The protected-mode drivers for SRAM and flash PC Cards must be installed differently than drivers for other cards.

To install a PCMCIA SRAM card in Windows 95, you must place one or more entries in the CONFIG.SYS file such as

```
device=c:\<windows>\system\csmapper.sys
device=c:\<windows>\system\carddrv.exe /slot=<x>
```

where <windows> is the Windows folder and <x> indicates the number of PCMCIA card slots in the computer.

To install a PCMCIA flash memory card in Windows 95, you must also place some driver entries in CONFIG.SYS such as

```
device=c:\<windows>\system\csmapper.sys
device=c:\<windows>\system\carddrv.exe /slot=<x>
device=c:\<windows>\ms-flash.sys
```

where <windows> is the Windows folder and <x> indicates the number of PCMCIA slots in the computer.

Note: Not all SRAM and flash card drivers are included with Windows 95. In many cases, you will need to use drivers provided with the particular cards.

Note: If you use only protected-mode drivers for SRAM and flash cards, you will not have access to the cards if you boot your computer to a command prompt.

Symptom 42: You are logged on without a password When you remove a plug-and-play network adapter in Device Manager and then restart your computer, the network adapter is redetected, and you are logged on to the network and validated by a Microsoft Windows NT server without entering a password. This problem also manifests itself when you remove a PCMCIA network adapter from the PCMCIA socket in your computer, restart your computer, and then reinsert the PCMCIA network adapter, you are logged on to the network and validated by a Windows NT server without entering a password. This can occur under three circumstances: you have a null Windows password, password caching is enabled, or user profiles are enabled.

To correct these problems, configure Windows 95 so that your Windows password is not null, or use the System Policy Editor to disable password caching. To configure Windows 95 so that your Windows password is not null, follow these steps:

- In the Control Panel, double-click on Passwords.
- Click Change Windows Password.
- If you want your network password to be the same as your Windows password, click the Microsoft Networking check box to select it, and then click OK. If you do not want your network password to be the same as your Windows password, verify that the Microsoft Networking check box is *not* selected, and then click OK.

- Type your new password in the New Password and Confirm New Password boxes, and then click OK.

Use the following steps to edit the registry with System Policy Editor and disable password caching in Windows 95:

- Click the Start button, and then click Run.
- Type POLEDIT in the Open box, and then click OK.
- On the File menu, click Open Registry, and then double-click Local Computer.
- Click the plus sign (+) next to Network, and then click the plus sign next to Passwords.
- Click the Disable Password Caching check box to select it, and then click OK.
- Save the changes to the Registry, exit the System Policy Editor, and then restart Windows 95.

Symptom 43: You have trouble with incompatible NDIS driver versions
When you are using a portable computer with a PCMCIA network adapter that uses NDIS 2.0 (16-bit) drivers, the computer may stop responding (hang) or reboot when you try to start it while it is not docked in its docking station *if* the docking station contains a network card that is capable of using NDIS 3.x (32-bit) network adapter drivers. This happens because Windows 95 detects the NDIS 2.0 drivers for the PCMCIA network adapter and forces the loading of NDIS 2.0 drivers for the other network adapter (which is not currently present because the computer is undocked). Because one of the network adapters is not present, an incomplete binding occurs, which can cause the computer to hang or reboot. To enable Windows 95 to start whether the computer is docked or undocked, create a multiple-boot configuration.

Note: Before you attempt to create a multiboot configuration, make sure that you have a docked state that requires an NDIS 3.x driver to be loaded and an undocked state that requires an NDIS 2.0 driver to be loaded (or vice versa).

Symptom 44: You can't set up the PCMCIA slot in an AT&T Globalyst 130 laptop   This is because the Globalyst 130 requires an unusual PCMCIA card setup compared to other Globalyst laptops. The AT&T Globalyst 130 does not have any options in the BIOS for enabling/disabling the PCMCIA socket services on the laptop. Instead, the socket must be enabled by loading the device driver, SS365SL.EXE, in the CONFIG.SYS file. This file is a socket enabler, and must be loaded for protected-mode socket services to initialize in Windows 95. Without this file, the PCMCIA socket services are disabled.

Symptom 45: When you are using a Motorola Power 14.4 cellular modem with Windows 95, you may not be able to dial the second time you try to use the modem   The initialization string used for this modem in Windows 95 enables a "dial suffix." The dial suffix (also known as "staged dialing") enables transmission of tones after the connection has been made *without* breaking the connection. This feature is often used in such applications as electronic banking. With staged dialing enabled, you must remove and reinsert the PC Card modem each time you want to dial. You can disable staged dialing by editing the MDMMOTO.INF file.

Note: Be sure to make a backup of the .INF file before beginning your edit.

- Use any text editor to open the MDMMOTO.INF file in the Windows\Inf folder (note that this is a hidden folder).
- Add the following line to the end of the [Modem16.AddReg] section of the file:

```
HKR, Settings, DialSuffix,, ""
```

- Save and then close the file.
- Remove the Motorola Power 14.4 modem using the Modems tool in Control Panel.
- Remove and reinsert the modem.

Symptom 46: A PCMCIA Token Ring network adapter refuses to work in the computer   This type of problem can occur when the following combination of conditions exists. First, the Token Ring network adapter uses an address range of A20h to A2Fh. Second, the PC has a sound board or other device in the address range of 220h to 22Fh. And third, only the 10 least-significant digits are used to resolve I/O addresses. Since the Windows 95 I/O arbitrator only pays attention to the first 10 bits of any I/O allocation, devices that have I/O allocations that conflict in a 10-bit decode are registered by the system as having an I/O address conflict. As a consequence, this is a problem with Windows 95. You can work around this problem by manually configuring both devices:

- In the Control Panel, double-click the System icon.
- On the Device Manager tab, double-click IBM TOKEN-RING CREDIT CARD ADAPTER II OR COMPATIBLES.
- Click the Resources tab and note the resources the network adapter is using. To change a resource, click the Use Automatic Settings check box to clear it, click the resource, and then click Change Setting.
- Change the Interrupt Request (IRQ) setting so that it does not conflict with the IRQ used by any other device.
- Change the first memory range to D4000 to D5FFF. Change the second memory range to E0000 to EFFFF.

Note: If these values continue to conflict with other devices, you may have to use different values.

- Click OK to save those resource changes.
- Double-click Sound, Video, and Game Controllers, and then double-click the sound card or the conflicting device.
- Make sure that the Use Automatic Settings check box is clear.
- Click OK and return to the Control Panel.
- Restart the computer.

Symptom 47: You restart the computer improperly after installing PCMCIA drivers   After you run the PCMCIA Wizard to install protected-mode socket services for a PC Card, you are instructed to shut down Windows 95 and then turn your computer off and back on. If you restart your computer by pressing <Ctrl>+<Alt>+<Del> *instead* of turning the computer off and back on, you may receive an error message stating that the PCMCIA drivers are not working correctly. The problem is that the protected-mode drivers for the PCMCIA controller may not initialize correctly when you perform a warm boot because the real-mode drivers still have control of the device. Correct the problem by performing a cold reboot of the system.

Symptom 48: In System Agent, the Last Result column for a ScanDisk task may report CHECK WAS STOPPED BECAUSE OF AN ERROR   However, the SCANDISK.LOG file does not list any errors, and you do not encounter any errors if you run ScanDisk manually. This problem may be caused by an invalid drive in ScanDisk's DrivesToCheck registry setting. The setting can become invalid if a drive that existed when the ScanDisk task was created is subsequently removed. For example, this problem can occur when you remove a PCMCIA drive, uncompress or unmount a compressed drive, or remove a laptop computer from its docking station. The way around this problem is to delete the existing ScanDisk task and schedule a new task—or run ScanDisk manually.

Symptom 49: When you start Windows 95 on a Zenith ZDS 1762 laptop computer, the computer may stop responding (hang) while Windows 95 is running the CONFIG.SYS file This problem occurs if PCENABLE.EXE (Zenith's PCMCIA driver) is loaded before MZTINIT.SYS (Zenith's Mozart sound system driver) in the CONFIG.SYS file. When this occurs, PCENABLE.EXE installs a hook for IRQ 7, which MZTINIT.SYS also tries to use. Edit the CONFIG.SYS file and move the Mozart sound driver above any PC Card drivers. Save your changes, then restart the computer.

Symptom 50: When you use the Suspend feature on a Dell Latitude XP laptop computer connected to a port replicator, your PCMCIA devices may not reactivate when you exit the Suspend mode This problem can occur with BIOS version A05 or earlier. BIOS versions A05 and earlier do not send an Advanced Power Management (APM) "resume" event to reactivate PCMCIA devices when the computer is connected to a port replicator. You may avoid this problem by *not* using the Suspend feature while the laptop is connected to a port replicator. To resolve the problem on a more permanent basis, you will need to update the laptop's BIOS version.

Symptom 51: You have trouble using similar cards simultaneously For example, if you start Windows 95 with one Xircom PCMCIA network card inserted in the computer, the card works correctly until you insert a second Xircom PCMCIA network card. When you insert the second card, the second card works correctly and the first stops working. If you remove and reinsert the first card, it works correctly and the second card stops working. This happens because both cards have the same PCMCIA ID but different checksums. The cards both appear to be the *same* card to

Windows 95, so Windows 95 switches system resources from one card to the other. Ultimately, if you *must* run two network cards at the same time, they cannot *both* be Xircom network cards.

Symptom 52: The Zenith Zplayer PCMCIA CD-ROM adapter does not function correctly using Windows 95 32-bit drivers   In virtually all cases, the 32-bit PCMCIA drivers included with Windows 95 are not compatible with the Zenith Zplayer PCMCIA adapter. You will need to disable the 32-bit PCMCIA drivers:

- In the Control Panel, double-click the System icon.
- On the Device Manager tab, double-click the PCMCIA adapter.
- Click the check box for the current configuration to clear it.
- Click OK or Close until you return to Control Panel, then restart your computer.
- To use the PCMCIA adapter with real-mode drivers, use the installation program included with the adapter.

Note: Do not run the PCMCIA Wizard to install the 32-bit PCMCIA drivers.

Symptom 53: On a computer with only one PCMCIA socket, Windows 95 cannot set up a new PCMCIA card if the original PCMCIA card is being used to access the Windows 95 source files   If you remove the PCMCIA card that is providing access to Windows 95 source files to set up a new card, Windows 95 cannot access the source files. When you are prompted to provide the source files, you cannot remove the new card and insert the original card because Windows 95 does not detect the removal and insertion of PCMCIA cards during the configuration of the new card. To get around this problem, use the Add New Hardware wizard to install the new PCMCIA card manually. This process preinstalls the necessary driver files, so that you can set up the new card without accessing Windows 95 source files.

Symptom 54: You cannot format an SRAM card using the Windows 95 graphical user interface because the Full and Quick format options are not available   In almost all cases, there is a problem with the device driver for the SRAM card. The device driver is probably returning device parameters for a 128-kB SRAM card regardless of what card is actually inserted in the PC Card slot. You will need to contact the SRAM card maker to obtain an updated driver which corrects the problem.

Symptom 55: After you dock or undock a Compaq Elite laptop computer, the computer's PCMCIA devices may stop working   Also, multiple disabled PCMCIA controllers may appear in Device Manager. This is a problem with early versions of Compaq Elite PnP BIOS. Some versions report incorrect PCMCIA resources. When this happens, Windows 95 disables the PCMCIA controller. To correct this problem on a permanent basis, you'll need to update the Compaq BIOS with a current version (5/95 or later). To remove incorrect PCMCIA devices in the meantime,

- In the Control Panel, double-click the System icon.
- On the Device Manager tab, click each PCMCIA device and then click Remove (remove all the PCMCIA devices).
- Click Computer, and then click Refresh (this will redetect the correct PCMCIA device).
- Click OK to save your changes.

Symptom 56: When you set up Windows 95, it will not install more than one PCMCIA network adapter correctly This is because the Windows 95 32-bit socket drivers are not enabled. To install the Windows 95 32-bit PCMCIA socket drivers:

- Double-click on My Computer.
- Double-click the Control Panel.
- Start the 32-bit PCMCIA wizard, and follow the instructions on the screen.

Note: Windows 95 is specifically designed to detect and install only *one* PCMCIA network card during setup.

Symptom 57: When you try to connect to a network using an IBM Token Ring PCMCIA network card on an Omnibook 600 computer, you are unable to view any resources There is a resource conflict between the Omnibook's proprietary PCMCIA controller and the IBM Token Ring PCMCIA network card. The Omnibook's proprietary PCMCIA controller supports I/O ranges up to 3FFh. The IBM Token Ring PCMCIA network card can only reside at I/O address A20h. There is no solution to this problem. The IBM Token Ring PCMCIA network card cannot be used on an Omnibook 600 computer.

Symptom 58: When you run ScanDisk, the SELECT THE DRIVE YOU WANT TO CHECK FOR ERRORS **box may show drives that do not exist, or may not show drives that do exist** In most cases, you have removed or inserted an ATA PC Card. Unfortunately, the drive list in ScanDisk is static. That list is generated when you start ScanDisk, and it is not updated while ScanDisk is running. If you add or remove drives (such as PCMCIA drives or DriveSpace-compressed drives) while ScanDisk is running, the list is not updated to reflect the changes. You must update the drive list by exiting and then restarting ScanDisk.

Symptom 59: When you insert a Xircom CE2 PCMCIA network adapter card, the card may not work and the computer may not be connected to the network When this occurs, your computer may stop responding. The network adapter may require a real-mode enabler or different client drivers to work properly. To correct this problem, load the real-mode card and socket services drivers in the CONFIG.SYS file. The actual drivers that are required vary from one system to another, but they typically look like

```
device=cs.exe
device=sscirrus.exe
```

Symptom 60: PCMCIA cards are not configuring properly on your Compaq computer   In many cases, you have an outdated or buggy BIOS in the system. You can usually correct this kind of problem by updating the BIOS version.

Symptom 61: When the system boots up, you see the error message DIVIDE OVERFLOW **before entering Windows 95. This forces you to boot Windows 95 in Safe Mode**   The drivers installed for the PCMCIA card are obsolete or otherwise incompatible with Windows 95. You will need to disable those real-mode drivers in CONFIG.SYS and AUTOEXEC.BAT, and ultimately install the current drivers for Windows 95.

Symptom 62: Your PC Card client drivers refuse to load, and an error message appears when starting Windows 95   In most cases you have real-mode PCMCIA drivers starting in CONFIG.SYS and AUTOEXEC.BAT which are causing problems for Windows 95. Try disabling those real-mode PC Card drivers in CONFIG.SYS and AUTOEXEC.BAT first. Turn off the PC and remove the PC Card. Boot to Windows 95 normally, then insert the card. You may need to run the PCMCIA wizard to install the proper card drivers. You may also need to download the latest protected-mode drivers from the PC Card maker, then install the new drivers with the Have Disk option.

Symptom 63: PCMCIA cards are not configuring properly on IBM Thinkpads   This is because you must run a specific IBM utility to update the BIOS on IBM Thinkpads *first.* Install IBM WIN95SETUP *before* installing Windows 95. This utility updates the BIOS, which has several plug-and-play fixes. This utility can be obtained from: www.pc.ibm.com or IBM's BBS. You can then install Windows 95 and proceed to reinstall your PCMCIA cards.

Symptom 64: The computer produces a single, low beep when the PCMCIA card is inserted, but the PC Card icon will show no information about the socket, and the "Stop" feature shows the error that a DEVICE CANNOT BE REMOVED   In almost all cases, the PC Card has not been assigned the proper memory exclusion, and is experiencing a memory conflict with another device in the system. Go into the Control Panel, then select the PC Card icon. Choose Global Settings and make sure that the Automatic Setting check box is checked. Then restart Windows 95. This should clear the problem.

Symptom 65: Windows 95 does not recognize the parameters of the PCMCIA Note Disk   You will have to perform a hard disk drive setup for an unformatted drive. Before proceeding, be sure to back up any vital information on the PC Card disk—it will be erased.

- Choose My Computer and select the Control Panel icon.
- Choose the System icon and select the Device Manager tab.
- Select Disk Drives, then choose the Settings tab.
- Select Int. 13 unit.

- Save your changes, and restart the system when prompted.
- When Windows 95 has fully rebooted, choose the Start, then Run.
- Type in FDISK, and choose OK.
- When you start FDISK make sure to choose DISK 2 before partitioning the drive.
- Create partition(s) as required.
- Repeat the first four steps and remove the check mark from Int. 13 unit.
- Save your changes, and restart the system when prompted.
- When Windows 95 is fully rebooted, choose My Computer.
- Click the right mouse button on the D: drive, then select Format.
- After formatting the drive, run ScanDisk.
- The PCMCIA disk should now be ready for use.

8
CHAPTER

Tape Drives

The single most pervasive problem with magnetic media such as floppy drives and hard drives is that, sooner or later, the drive is going to fail. Old age, recording medium problems, and even rogue software like computer viruses can render your valuable data useless. When a problem arises, you are going to have to restore your data (regardless of whether you replace the drive itself). Unfortunately, restoring data is not always as simple and straightforward a process as you might think. When a drive fails, it can take hours (if not days) to restore your operating system and applications and then tweak them to work together correctly. But even more frightening is the threat of files you *can't* restore, like those important documents, drawings, databases, and so on. Without a system of backups, you can find your business severely crippled or shut down entirely. Tape drives (Fig. 8-1) have long been a popular means of backup because of their capacity. Tape drives are the only mechanisms with the capacity to backup multigigabyte hard drives onto a single, relatively inexpensive data cartridge. However, tape drives are not without their unique problems. This chapter explains the construction and operation of typical tape drives and offers some maintenance and troubleshooting procedures that can help you resolve tape drive problems.

Understanding Tape Media

Magnetic tape is the oldest form of magnetic mass storage. Tape systems served as the primary mass-storage technique for older mainframes (making obsolete the punched card and punched paper tape environment of the day). Tape systems proved to be inexpensive and reliable, so much so that even the original IBM PC was outfitted with a drive port for cassette tape storage. With the development of floppy and hard drives, tape systems became obsolete as a primary storage method, but retain a valuable role as backup systems.

Although the size, shape, and standards used for tape packaging and recording have advanced, the tape itself is virtually unchanged in principle from its very first incarnation. Figure 8-2 illustrates a tape cartridge used in an Iomega tape backup system. A tape is a long, slender length of polyester substrate which is much more

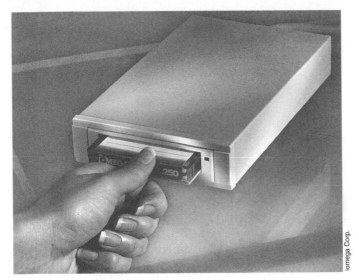

8-1 An Iomega tape drive.

Drive roller ————————
Write protect ————————

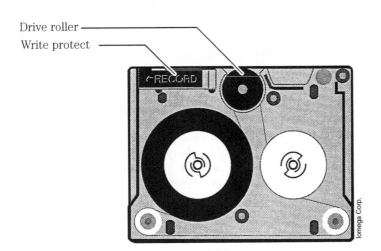

8-2 A typical minicartridge.

flexible than the Mylar substrate used in floppy disks. Polyester also sustains a bit of stretch to help the tape negotiate the high tensions and sharp turns encountered in today's tape cartridge assemblies. As with all other magnetic storage media, the substrate is coated with a layer of magnetic material which is actually magnetized to retain digital information. Many different coatings have been tried through the years, but tapes still employ coatings of conventional magnetic oxides similar to older floppy disk coatings. More exotic coatings such as metal films and pure metal particles suspended in a binder material have also been used.

Unlike floppy disks and hard-drive platters which are random-access media, tapes represent a *sequential* (or serial) type of storage medium—that is, a tape drive stores its data sequentially along the length of its medium. Where floppy and hard disks store bits along a two-dimensional plane which read/write (R/W) heads can access in a matter of milliseconds, tapes must be searched bit by bit from beginning to end in order to locate a desired file. A tape search can take minutes, which is totally impractical for use as primary storage today. There are three major types of tape drives to consider: quarter-inch cartridges, Travan tape cartridges, and helical scan cartridges.

Quarter-inch cartridge

The concept of the quarter-inch tape cartridge (QIC) is identical to the compact cassette tape; a plastic shell contains two spools that hold a length of tape. Enclosing the tape supply in a prefabricated shell eliminates the need for handling open-reel tape or threading the tape through the labyrinth of a mechanical handling system. The original QIC was introduced by 3M in the early 1970s as a recording medium for telecommunication system programming and high-volume data acquisition.

While QIC and cassette tapes may look similar, the means used to drive both tapes is radically different. Cassette tapes are driven using a capstan drive system where the tape is pulled by a take-up reel as it winds across a R/W head. A QIC (Fig. 8-3) uses a small belt that loops around and contacts both the supply and take-up spools, as well as a rubber drive wheel. The capstan in a QIC system contacts the drive wheel (but not the tape), so only the belt's contact friction is used to drive the tape. Drive forces are spread evenly over a long length of tape, so the tape can be moved faster and sustain more direction reversals than a cassette, greatly improving tape reliability and working life. Since the components needed to handle the

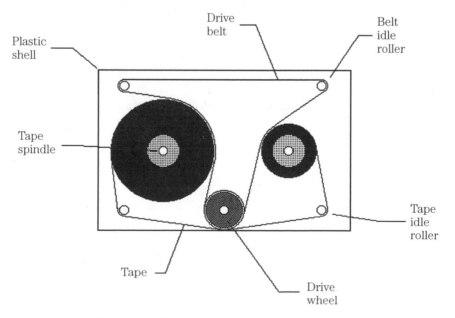

8-3 Diagram of a QIC mechanism.

tape are already contained in the QIC shell, the drive mechanism is simple because only a motor and R/W head is required.

With the introduction of personal computers and the subsequent discard of audio cassettes as mass-storage devices, QICs emerged as the premier tape mechanism, but early systems were riddled with incompatibilities. Each manufacturer had its own ideas about how QIC systems should work. A number of tape drive companies met in the early 1980s to decide on a set of standards for the new QIC devices. In 1982, this group of industrial manufacturers formed an organization called the *QIC Committee*. The QIC Committee is responsible for developing standards for all aspects of tape drive construction and application.

QIC cartridge details

A classic (or "full-size") QIC can be identified by its general dimensions. The cartridge is 6 in (15.24 cm) wide, 4 in (10.16 cm) long, and ⅝ in (1.59 cm) deep—somewhat smaller than a VHS videocassette. While dimensions have not changed significantly through the years, there have been several iterations of "standard" quarter-inch cartridges. The earliest type of QIC tape was the DC300 cartridge produced by 3M Company—named for the 300 ft (91.44 m) of tape that it contained. However, the DC300 cartridge proved limited, so the tape length was increased to 600 ft (181.88 m) and renamed as the DC600 cartridge (although the designation was later changed to DC6000). For our purposes, all current QIC drives will be using DC6000 cartridges. Storage capacities for the DC6000 cartridge vary from 60 MB at the low end, to 2.1 GB at the high end. There are many notable QIC standards for full-size cartridges as shown in Table 8-1. For ordinary end-user PCs, you probably will not encounter these QIC designations very often. The full-size cartridges are usually reserved for file servers and high-end systems with SCSI-2 interfaces.

QIC minicartridge details

The major drawback to standard QICs is their overall large size—they do not fit well into today's small drive bays, so most QIC systems are external desktop devices. To

Table 8-1. QIC Standards for Full-Size Cartridges

QIC standard	Capacity	Tracks	Data transfer rate, MB/min	Interface
QIC-11	45 MB	9	N/A	QIC-02
QIC-24	45 MB/60 MB	9	N/A	SCSI/QIC-02
QIC-120	125 MB	15	N/A	SCSI/QIC-02
QIC-150	150 MB/250 MB	18	N/A	SCSI/QIC-02
QIC-525	320 MB/525 MB	26	12	SCSI/SCSI-2
QIC-1000	1.0 GB	30	18	SCSI/SCSI-2
QIC-1350	1.35 GB	30	18	SCSI-2
QIC-2100	2.1 GB	30	18	SCSI-2
QIC-2GB	2.0 GB	42	18	SCSI-2
QIC-5GB	5.0 GB	44	18	SCSI-2
QIC-5010	13 GB	144	18	SCSI-2

address the need for smaller-sized QIC systems, the QIC Committee created the *minicartridge,* a 3.25 in (8.26 cm) × 2.5 in (6.35 cm) × ⅝ in (1.59 cm) assembly holding about 205 ft (62.48 m) of quarter-inch tape. Minicartridges use a DC2000 designation, where the last three digits in the number reflect the cartridge's capacity. For example, a DC2080 minicartridge is designated to hold 80 MB, and so on. Any time you see a tape or tape drive associated with a DC2000 designation, you know you must use a minicartridge. There are also many differing QIC designations for today's minicartridges. Table 8-2 outlines the major minicartridge standards.

QIC tape compatibility

One of the problems with tape drives has been the lack of compatibility—not all tapes work in all drives. For example, the QIC-5010 tape will not work in a QIC-80 drive, even though both are based on the same minicartridge. In actual practice, most drives are capable of reading several different classes of tape, but can write to only a few specific tape versions. Table 8-3 lists the compatibility specifications between the most popular tape standards. The issue of compatibility can have a profound impact when choosing to add or update an existing tape drive. For example, suppose you have a large number of QIC-80 backup tapes but you need to increase your backup capacity with a larger drive. You can get up to 4 GB of storage by choosing a QIC-3070 drive, but it will not read QIC-80 tapes, so your existing backups will be rendered inaccessible. You might be better off choosing a QIC-3010 2-GB drive. There is less capacity, but its backward compatibility may be well worth the trade-off.

Travan tape cartridges

By the early 1990s, tape drives had simply not kept pace with the explosive growth of hard drives. Large tape drives were available, but they cost a premium and were not always easy to interface to everyday PCs. By late 1994, 3M and several other key manufacturers had developed and introduced a new high-density tape technology called Travan. Travan technology allows much higher recording densities on a tape, and Travan tapes are now readily available with recording capacities from 400 MB to 4 GB (though many tape drive manufacturers factor in 2:1 data compression when quoting capacities such as 8 GB). Another attribute to Travan drives is that the larger drives are highly backward compatible with smaller Travan tapes and QIC tapes. Table 8-4 illustrates the relationship between the four available Travan tapes.

Helical-scan tapes

The rate at which data are transferred in tape systems has long been an issue. Transfer rates of 250 or 500 kB/s can seem extraordinarily slow when there are gigabytes worth of data to move onto a tape. Since the conventional tape systems you have seen so far move tape across stationary heads, data transfer rates are ultimately limited by the tape speed, and a tape can only be moved just so fast. Data transfer is also affected by the drive electronics, but even new encoding techniques are of limited utility. Tape drive designers realized that the head and tape can be moved *together* to increase the relative speed between the two, while allowing the tape transport mechanism itself to continue operating at a normal speed.

Table 8-2. QIC Standards for Minicartridges

QIC standard	Capacity	Tracks	Data transfer rate, MB/min	Interface
QIC-40	40 MB/60 MB	20	2–8	Floppy/proprietary
QIC-80	80 MB/120 MB	28	3–9	Floppy/proprietary
QIC-100	20 MB/40 MB	12/24	N/A	SCSI/QIC
QIC-128	86 MB/128 MB	32	N/A	SCSI/QIC
QIC-3010	255 MB	40	9	Floppy/IDE
QIC-3020	500 MB	40	9	Floppy/IDE
QIC-3030	555 MB	40	N/A	SCSI-2/QIC
QIC-3040	840 MB	42/52	N/A	SCSI-2/QIC
QIC-3050	750 MB	40	N/A	SCSI-2/QIC
QIC-3060	875 MB	38	N/A	SCSI-2/QIC
QIC-3070	4.0 GB	144	N/A	SCSI-2/QIC
QIC-3080	1.6 GB	50	N/A	SCSI-2/QIC
QIC-3110	2.0 GB	48	N/A	SCSI-2/QIC
QIC-5010	13.0 GB	144	N/A	SCSI-2/QIC

Table 8-3. QIC Tape Compatibility

The following drive...	...will *read* the following tape(s):
QIC-24	N/A
QIC-40	N/A
QIC-80	QIC-40
QIC-100	N/A
QIC-120	QIC-24
QIC-128	QIC-100
QIC-150	QIC-24 and QIC-120
QIC-525	QIC-24, QIC-120, and QIC-150
QIC-1000	QIC-120, QIC-150, and QIC-525
QIC-1350	QIC-525 and QIC-1000
QIC-2GB	QIC-120, QIC-150, QIC-525, and QIC-1000
QIC-2100	QIC-525 and QIC-1000
QIC-3010	QIC-40 and QIC-80
QIC-3030	QIC-3010
QIC-3070	QIC-3030
QIC-5GB	QIC-24, QIC-120, QIC-150, QIC-525, and QIC-1000
QIC-5010	QIC-150, QIC-525, and QIC-1000

Table 8-4. Travan Tape Specifications*

	TR-1	TR-2	TR-3	TR-4
Capacity†	400 MB	800 MB	1.6 GB	4.0 GB
Data rate, kB/s	62.5	62.5–125	125–250	567
Tracks	36	50	50	72
Interface	Floppy	Floppy	Floppy	SCSI/EIDE

*All Travan tapes are 750 ft long and .315-in wide.

†All capacities are shown uncompressed.

It was discovered that a set of R/W heads mounted on a cylindrical drum could be spun across a length of moving tape wrapped about 90 degrees around the drum's circumference as illustrated in Fig. 8-4. The drum itself would be offset (or canted) at a slight angle relative to the tape's path of travel. During normal operation, the spinning drum describes a helical path (thus the term *helical scan*) across the tape as shown in Fig. 8-5. Such a helical pattern allows more information to be written to the tape faster than conventional stationary head systems. There are currently two major helical recording systems: 4-mm digital audio tape (DAT) and 8-mm tape. DAT heads are cantered about 6 degrees, while 8-mm tape heads use a 5-degree tilt. DAT heads spin at 2000 RPM, and lay down 1869 tracks (traces) in every linear inch (2.54 cm) of tape. Each trace is only 4 mm wide.

Data can be packed very tightly on DAT tapes because each trace (or scan line) is recorded at a unique *azimuth angle.* Each head in the drum is skewed slightly from the perpendicular such that the data on adjacent traces is oriented very differently. During playback, a head responds well to signals written in the same orientation, but it responds poorly to signals written in the other orientation, so blank space between each signal is not required. Another advantage to helical scan is data integrity. By adding two more heads to the rotating drum (total of four heads), data can be read immediately after writing. Any errors that are detected can be corrected by repeating the data on subsequent traces until data are valid. Physically, helical-scan DAT is about 4 mm wide and wound into a plastic cartridge roughly the size of a credit card. A DAT usually packs 2.0 to 4.0 GB of data in up to 90 m of 1450-Oe tape.

Probably the greatest disadvantage of helical-scan tape systems is the additional mechanical complexity required to wrap the tape around a spinning drum. Whereas cassettes, QICs, and minicartridges allow only a single point of contact with a stationary R/W head, helical-scan tapes must be pulled out and away from its shell and wrapped around the rotating drum as illustrated in Fig. 8-6. Note the series of rollers and guides that are needed to position and tension the tape properly.

Eight-millimeter tape is twice as wide as DAT medium in a 3.75 in (9.53 cm) × 2.5 in (6.35 cm) × 0.5 in (1.27 cm) cassette that appears rather like a VHS cassette. In actual practice, 8-mm systems can store up to 10.0 GB (uncompressed) on a single cassette. The high cost of helical tape backup systems is well beyond the means of most hobbyists and enthusiasts (even some small companies). Still, costs are continuing to fall.

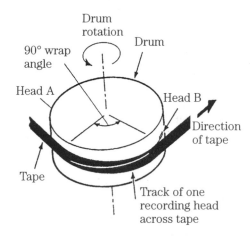

8-4 Diagram of helical scan operation. (*Hewlett-Packard Co. Computer Peripherals, Bristol Division.*)

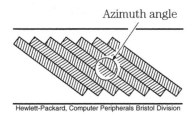

8-5 The concept of azimuth angle.

Tape Drive Construction

Now that you have an understanding of basic tape styles and drive standards, this part of the chapter will show you how tape drives are physically assembled. Figure 8-7 shows an exploded diagram for a Teac D/CAS tape drive mechanism. While the construction of most fixed-head tape drives is not incredibly complex, it is rather involved and delicate. Helical-scan tape drives, however, can offer significant technical challenges because of the added heads and tape-handling mechanisms.

Mechanical construction

At the core of the mechanical assembly is the *drive chassis* (1), also called the *transport subassembly*. This chassis forms the foundation for all other drive components including two PC boards. The chassis is built with four assemblies already in place (two loading base assemblies, a lever base assembly, and a loading arm assembly). These mechanical assemblies are responsible for loading and ejecting the tape. When you encounter difficulties with tape loading or unloading, you should suspect a problem in one or more of these mechanical areas. The chassis mechanics are also responsible for allowing tapes to be inserted on one side only (side A). If the tape is inserted with side B up, the mechanics will not allow the tape to seat in the drive. A *front bezel/door assembly* (28) and an *eject button* (29) give the drive its cosmetic appearance once the completed drive is mounted in its drive bay.

A D/CAS tape is transported through the drive using two reel motors: a *forward reel motor* (9), and a *reverse reel motor* (10). These are both dc motors which are driven by control circuitry on the *drive control PC board* (26). Ideally, these reel motors should turn at a constant rate of speed, but tape speed tends to vary as tape is unwound from one spool and wound onto another. To keep tape velocity constant, the tape contacts an *encoder roller* (15), which drives an *encoder assembly* (12). Data generated by the encoder are used to regulate reel motor speed, much the same way that an index sensor is used to regulate spindle speed in a floppy or hard drive. Tension on the encoder roller is maintained and adjusted by tweaking the *encoder spring* (13) and *pin spring* (14) with a screw.

D/CAS tape is separated into individual tracks along the tape's width. The *R/W head assembly* (22) is actually composed of five separate magnetic heads: two read heads, two write heads, and an erase head. During a write operation, the erase head erases any previous data that may have existed on the tape, the write head(s) then lay down new flux transitions, and the read head(s) immediately reread the written data to ensure their integrity. During a read operation, the erase and write heads are

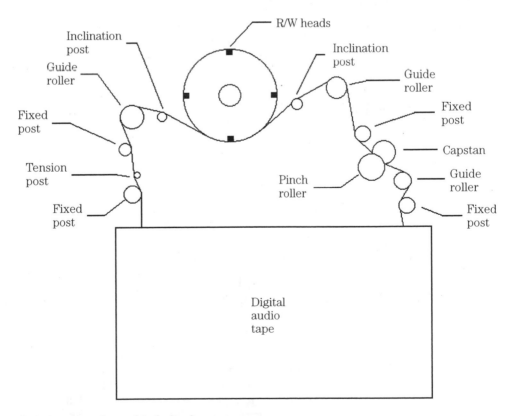

8-6 A tape path used in helical tape systems.

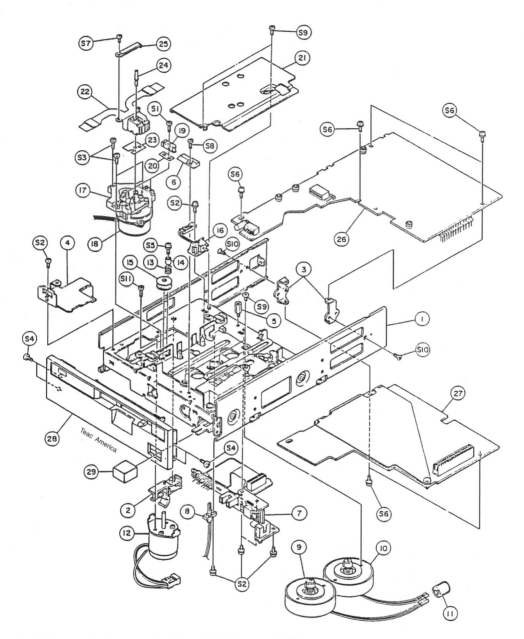

8-7 Exploded diagram of a Teac D/CAS tape drive.

idle, and only the read(s) respond. The head assembly is held in place with a *head mounting screw* (24). A *clamp* (25) holds the head's flat cable.

The head assembly is mounted to a *head seek assembly* (17) through an *electrical isolation sheet* (23). A head seek unit raises or lowers the head to the desired track as the tape moves past. A *stepping motor* (18) drives the head seek assembly using a lead screw. As the stepping motor turns in one direction, the force of rotation is translated to linear motion by the lead screw. The head moves in a fashion similar to head stepping in a floppy drive. There are also several *tape guides* (6 and 19). The remainder of mechanical parts are generally brackets and screws. Always make it a point to note the locations of all screws and brackets during disassembly.

Electronic circuitry

The electronics involved in the Teac D/CAS drive are also called out in the exploded view of Fig. 8-7. There are two PC boards: the *drive control PC board* (26) and the *drive interface PC board* (27). The drive control board contains all the circuitry necessary for operating the drive's physical devices such as the R/W head(s), the reel motors, the stepping motor, reading the encoder, and reading the other drive sensor elements. A drive interface board contains the high-level processing circuitry needed to communicate with a host computer and operate the drive control board.

There are three discrete sensors in the drive (not counting the encoder); a *cassette load sensor* (7), a *file-protect sensor* (7), an *LED hole sensor* (8), and a *sensor guide pair* (16). Notice that cassette and file sensors are both held on the same sub PC board. The cassette load sensor is an optoisolator that produces a logic 0 when a tape is absent and a logic 1 when a tape is present (similar to the disk-in-place sensor of a floppy drive). A file-protect sensor produces a logic 0 when the tape is protected (writing is inhibited), and a logic 1 when writing is allowed (similar to a floppy drive's write-protect sensor). All sensors are important parts of the drive and its ability to interact with the outside world.

Figure 8-8 presents these major electronic sections as a block diagram. The left portion of the diagram shows you how a D/CAS tape will interact with the R/W head

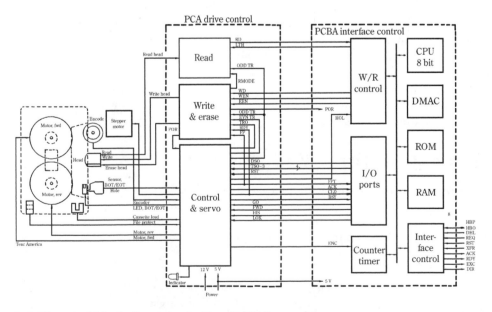

8-8 Electrical block diagram of a Teac D/CAS tape drive system.

and system sensors. When the cassette is inserted properly, it will engage into the forward and reverse reel motors. A properly inserted tape also asserts the cassette load sensor. The signal being generated by a file-protect sensor depends on whether the cassette's write-protect notch is exposed or covered. The beginning of tape (BOT) and end of tape (EOT) contain a short series of holes. An LED source is placed on one side of the tape, and a sensor is placed on the other side. When EOT and BOT holes are encountered, a pulse signal is returned to drive control circuitry. During reading or writing, a R/W head assembly is engaged to contact the tape. The encoder wheel also contacts the tape. Resulting encoder signals are used by drive control circuits to regulate tape speed by adjusting reel speed. The head is mounted to its track-seeking stepping motor, which is also operated by drive control circuits.

The tape drive control PC board handles the drive's physical operations and processes all sensor readings. Analog head signals are processed through a read circuit where they are converted into logic signals and sent along to the R/W head control circuit on the drive's interface control PC board. Write signals leave the R/W control circuit in logic form and are sent to the write/erase circuit on the drive control PC board. Logic write signals are converted to analog signals and sent to the R/W head. During writing, the write/erase circuit also actuates the erase head to clear any previous data before new data are written. The drive control board is managed by the control/servo circuit which communicates with I/O ports on the drive interface board. The control/servo circuit also lights an LED on the drive's front panel when any drive activity takes place.

The tape drive interface control PC board is a microprocessor-driven system that handles high-level drive operations. A CPU is responsible for processing system instructions provided by an on-board ROM, as well as any variables or data information held in RAM. The CPU handles the physical interface through the interface control circuit, and directs the drive's control board utilizing I/O circuits. Data flowing into or out of the drive are processed through a write/read control circuit. System synchronization is maintained by reading the counter/timer circuit being driven by the control/servo circuit. The particular layout and control structure of your particular tape drive may vary quite a bit from the Teac system illustrated here, but all major operating areas should be present to one extent or another. You may also encounter several functions integrated into a single high-density ASIC, so you should regard Fig. 8-8 as more of a conceptual guideline than an absolute rule.

Drive and Tape Maintenance

Tape drives require periodic maintenance for proper operation. In general, there are two types of maintenance that you will need to handle: drive cleaning and tape maintenance. While these hardly sound like exciting procedures, they can have profound effects on your drive's overall performance and the reliability of your backups.

Drive cleaning

As with floppy disk drives, tape drives bring magnetic media directly into contact with magnetic R/W heads. Over time and use, magnetic oxides from the tape rub off onto the head surface. Oxides (combined with dust particles and smoke contamination) accumulate and act as a wedge that forces the tape away from the head surface. Even if you never have cause to actually disassemble your tape drive, you should make it a point to perform routine cleaning. Regular cleaning improves the working life of your recording medium and can significantly reduce the occurrence of data errors—especially during file restores where problems can keep you shut down.

The objective of drive cleaning is remarkably simple: to remove any buildup of foreign material that may have accumulated on the R/W head. The most common cleaning method employs a prepackaged cleaning cartridge. The cartridge contains a length of slightly abrasive cleaning material. When cleaning tape is run through the drive, any foreign matter on the head is rubbed away. The cleaning tape can often be used for several cleanings before being discarded. Some cleaning tapes can be run dry, while others may have to be dampened with an alcohol-based cleaning solution. The advantage to a cleaning cartridge is *simplicity*—the procedure is quick, and you never have to disassemble the drive. Since QIC and Travan-type tape moves much more slowly across a R/W head than floppy medium does, you need not worry about damaging the R/W head due to friction. DAT and 8-mm (helical) heads *do* move across the tape quickly, so you must be cautious about cleaning times. You will likely have better results over the long term using dry cleaning cartridges that are impregnated with a lubricating agent to reduce friction.

You can also clean R/W heads manually, which can be convenient during a repair when the drive is already opened. Start by vacuuming away any dust, debris, or pet hair that may be in the drive. Use a small, hand-held vacuum to reach tight spots. Heads and capstans can be cleaned with a fresh, lint-free swab dipped lightly in a head-cleaning solution as shown in Fig. 8-9. If no head-cleaning solution is available, use fresh ethyl or isopropyl alcohol. Rub the head gently but firmly to remove any

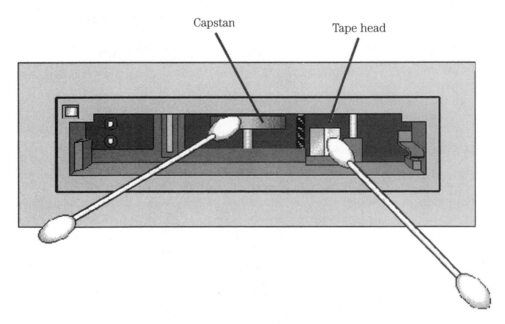

8-9 Cleaning a tape drive.

debris. You may wish to use several swabs to ensure a thorough cleaning. Allow the head to dry *completely* before running a tape.

   Note: Remember that these are only general guidelines. Refer to the user's manual or reference manual for your particular drive to find the specific cleaning recommendations, procedures, and cautions listed by the manufacturer. Every drive has slightly different cleaning and preventive maintenance procedures. Some drives may also require periodic lubrication.

Tape maintenance

Tape cartridges are one of the more rugged items in the PC world. Tape is contained in a hard plastic shell, and the R/W head aperture is usually guarded by a metal or plastic shroud. However, tapes are certainly not indestructible. They must be handled with care to ensure the integrity of their data. The following guidelines will help you get the most from your tapes:

- **Avoid fingerprints on the tape.**   Do not open the tape access door of the cartridges or touch the tape itself. One fingerprint can prevent the drive from reading the tape.
- **Set the write protect switch.**   Be sure to set the write-protect switch after backing up your data. This will reduce the possibility of accidentally overwriting critical data if you forget to label the tape.
- **Be careful of magnetic fields.**   Tapes are sensitive to magnetic fields from monitors, electromechanical telephone ringers, fans, and so on. Keep the tape away from sources of magnetic fields.
- **Be careful of toner.**   The toner used by laser printers and photocopiers is a microfine dust which may filter out of the device in small quantities. Keep your tapes away from printers and copiers to avoid contamination by toner dust.
- **Be careful of the tape environment.**   Keep the tape out of direct sunlight, keep the tape dry, and keep the tape safe from temperature extremes (sudden hot-to-cold or cold-to-hot transitions). Before using a tape, allow it to assume the current room temperature slowly.
- **Retension your tapes regularly.**   Before using a tape that has been idle for a month or more, use your backup software to retension the tape first. This removes any "tight spots" that often develop on the tape.

You've probably noticed that if you play a video tape often, the picture and sound quality on the tape will begin to degrade. This is a natural effect of wear as the medium passes repeatedly over the R/W heads. Tapes do not last forever, and after a period of use, they should be destroyed before their reliability deteriorates to a point where your data are not safe. Tape life is generally rated in terms of *passes*. But passes are difficult to track because a single backup or restore operation may involve many passes. Tape life also depends on how the tape is used. For example, a nightly backup to an 8-mm tape may use only the first half or the tape, but leave the last half of the tape almost unused. As a rule, follow the "20-use" rule: If a tape is used daily, replace the tape every month. If a tape is used weekly, replace the tape every 6 months. If a tape is only used monthly, replace it every 18 to 24 months.

Note: Regardless of how you schedule tape replacement, you should replace a tape immediately if it has been physically damaged (i.e., dropped); if it has become wet, frozen, or overheated; or if your backup application reports repeated media errors.

Freeing Caught Tapes

One of the worse times for a tape drive to fail is while a tape is actually installed. For minicartridge tape drives (like the Colorado Trakker series), this is not so serious, because the tape never leaves its cartridge—you can simply pull the tape cartridge out. But with helical-scan tape drives (such as Exabyte EXB-series drives), the implications are much more serious. As with ordinary videotapes, helical-scan tape is pulled from the cartridge and wound around a complex series of rollers and capstans. Under normal operation, the tape is released and withdrawn back into the cartridge during the ejection process. Unfortunately, if the tape drive should fail (and the tape remains wound in the drive), you cannot remove the tape without ruining it. But you may be able to rescue a helical-scan tape while preserving the maximum amount of data.

Note: This procedure is delicate and may vary somewhat from drive to drive. As a result, there is no guarantee that the tape (or the data it contains) will be undamaged. It is also possible that this procedure will void your drive's warranty. *Use this procedure as a last resort.*

The power trick

There may be very rare occasions when a helical-scan tape drive may "hang up" (rather than suffer a hard failure). This may be due to a hardware or software conflict in the computer, intermittent cabling, a bad driver (or backup software), or a signal glitch in the drive or its controller. Before attempting an invasive procedure, try powering the PC down, waiting several moments, and power the system up again. If there has been an error, cycling the power may clear it and restore drive operation. If the drive's "ready light" is lit, press the Eject or Unload button and see if the tape will eject of its own accord. If so, you have saved yourself a great deal of time and effort.

Rescuing the tape

The objective of this procedure is to preserve your tape. This is accomplished by removing the drive, opening it up, and temporarily disabling some of the drive mechanics in order to free the tape from its tape path and wind it safely back into the cartridge. Before proceeding, you will need a selection of tools including a small regular and Phillips screwdriver, adhesive tape, and a nonconductive tool such as a molded potentiometer adjustment tool. Depending on the design of your particular tape drive, you may need some Torx drivers (often T-10 and T-8 sizes), and perhaps even a torque-limiting screwdriver (3.4 to 5.0 in-lb, or 3.9 to 5.8 kg•cm).

Disconnect your power   Power down the PC and disconnect the ac cord to ensure the maximum amount of safety while working inside the computer. Remove the computer's enclosure to expose the tape drive assembly and its cabling.

Remove the drive   Your first goal is to remove the tape drive so that you can work on it without the obstructions of the PC. In most cases, your tape drive will be internal, so disconnect the power and signal cabling from the drive. You may wish to use masking tape to note the position of signal pin 1. The drive is probably held in its drive bay with four small Phillips screws, so remove them and slide the drive (with the tape still inserted) from the computer. You can then rest the drive on a comfortable work surface—preferably a static-safe surface.

Remove the drive cover   Once the drive is free, you need to remove the top cover to expose the inner workings. This is where those Torx drivers will come in handy. If the top cover is held in place by conventional screws, you only need screwdrivers of the appropriate size. Under no circumstances should you force the cover. If it is not free after removing the screws, check for additional screws or tabs that you may have to disengage.

Check the tape path   You should now have a clear view of the tape path inside the drive. You will find one of two conditions—either the tape has been unloaded from its tape path (and simply has not ejected), or the tape is still wound in its tape path. If the tape has already unloaded, you may skip the following steps by using a thin, nonconductive tool to move the *door release lever.* The release lever is typically located on the left side of the drive chassis and can be actuated by moving the lever toward the front of the machine (though this may not be the case for all drives). Keep in mind that you need *very little force* to actuate the door release lever, and it should move no more than ⅛ in (about 3 mm). This should successfully eject the tape cartridge, and you can then just replace the top cover.

Remove the "deck hanger"   In order to rescue your tape, you will need to access all of the elements of your tape path. If there is any supplemental support or guard hardware covering the tape path (sometimes referred to as a *deck hanger*), you will also need to remove that hardware before continuing. In some cases, this deck hanger may be bolted into place—in other cases, it can be removed simply by popping out several clips.

Tape the cartridge door open   Use some adhesive tape to hold the tape cartridge door open. This is only temporary and will be removed when the cartridge is free.

Remove the erase head bracket and tape guide   The tape is being held under a *tape guide.* Before you can remove the tape from its path, you must remove the tape guide, and the *erase head bracket* which is holding the tape guide in place. Once you find the erase head bracket, it is usually held in place by a single Phillips screw. Remove the screw and ease the erase head bracket straight off its post (you may wish to mark the starting position with a marker so that you can easily replace the bracket later). Once the erase head bracket is free, ease the tape guide from all three of its posts and set the guide aside. You are now ready to free the tape from its path.

Removing the tape Using your nonconductive tool (do not use your fingers or metal objects), pull the tape gently to establish some slack in the tape. Use your finger to move the *pinch roller flange* toward the left, then hold the flange in that position. *Do not* release the pinch roller until the tape is completely removed from around the pinch roller and capstan. Otherwise, the tape may be damaged. Insert the nonconductive tool into the tape loop and gently lift the tape from around the pinch roller and capstan. Once the tape is completely clear, you can release the pinch roller flange.

Next, gently remove the tape from around the guideposts and rollers. Remember to use the nonconductive tool from *inside* the loop to avoid touching the tape recording surface or head assembly. Position the nonconductive tool inside the loop. You'll see an L-shaped black part that prevents the tape from riding up over the drum. Gently move the tape up so that it passes between the L and the edges of the *head assembly.* Finally, lift the tape from around the guideposts and roller. Once again, remember to place the tool *inside* the tape loop to avoid damaging the tape.

Note: The procedure above has a high potential for damage to the tape and the heads on the tape drive. Use *extreme* caution when attempting to remove the tape using this procedure. When removing the tape from the guideposts and rollers, use a nonconductive tool, such as a molded adjustment tool. *Do not* touch the side of the tape where data are recorded (the side of the tape that comes in direct contact with the head assembly is the side where data are recorded).

Remove the cartridge and wind the tape Now that the tape is free, you need to free the cartridge without damaging the tape loose inside the drive. Use a thin, nonconductive tool to move the *door release lever.* The release lever is typically located on the left side of the drive chassis and can be actuated by moving the lever toward the front of the machine (though this may not be the case for all drives). Keep in mind that you need *very little force* to actuate the door release lever, and it should move no more than $\frac{1}{8}$ in (about 3 mm).

You should now be able to remove the cartridge, but pull the cartridge out *just enough* to see the cartridge *spindles* (you don't want to pull the cartridge all the way out and have loose tape flapping around). Place the drive on its left side with the cartridge exposed enough to see the two tape spindles. The upper spindle is the *takeup reel.* Insert a screwdriver into the takeup reel and slowly turn the reel counterclockwise to wind the loose tape into the cartridge. Keep an eye on the loose tape to be sure that it doesn't catch on anything as you wind it into the cartridge. *Do not overwind the tape!* At this point, you can remove the adhesive tape holding the cartridge door open and gently close the cartridge door (be sure that the tape is taut enough to that it will not contact the door when it is closed. You can then remove the tape cartridge.

Note: When opening the drive door, hold the door gently so that it opens slowly—this will prevent the data cartridge from ejecting suddenly and damaging the tape.

Replace the tape guide and erase head bracket Now that the tape is successfully free and removed from the drive, you must reassemble the components that you removed earlier. The first order of business should be to replace the *tape guide*, which simply fits onto the three guide posts where you removed it from. Once the tape guide is in place, replace the *erase head bracket*. If you had made a reference mark before removal, replacing the bracket should be a simple matter. Secure the bracket with its screw (remember not to overtighten the screw).

Replace the deck hanger   If you have removed any supplementary guards or shields during the disassembly procedure, you should replace them now. Be especially careful not to pinch any wiring or cables running through the drive. Make sure that nothing interferes with the tape path.

Replace the cover   Finally, you must replace the drive cover. If there are any tabs or clips holding the cover in place, engage them first, then install any screws to secure the cover. In most cases, these screws will be quite small, so be sure to avoid overtightening any of the screws.

Service the drive as necessary   At this point, the drive should be fully reassembled and ready to reinstall in the computer. However, you may take this opportunity to package the drive in its original container (or other suitable container) and send it to the manufacturer for repair.

Tape Drive Troubleshooting

The motors, sensors, and mechanisms in a typical tape drive are all prone to eventual failure. Even the natural wear that occurs in mechanical systems has an impact on drive performance and data error rates. This part of the chapter is intended to provide some general service guidelines and basic troubleshooting procedures. Bear in mind that tape drives (especially helical drives such as DAT drives) contain a substantial amount of mechanical and electromechanical components. Given the nature of mechanical parts, many of your problems will be mechanically oriented.

Symptom 1: The tape drive does not work at all   Begin your repair by checking for obvious setup and configuration errors. First, make sure that power is available to the drive (a power indicator will usually be lit on the drive). An internal tape drive is usually powered from the host computer, so be sure that the internal 4-pin power connector is correctly attached. External drives are almost always powered from a separate ac adapter or power supply, but a few proprietary drives can be powered through their interface cables. Check the output of any external ac adapter or power supply. If the ac adapter output is low or nonexistent, replace the ac adapter.

Check that the interface cable between drive and tape controller card is connected properly. Also check that your backup software is running and properly configured to your particular drive. If you are troubleshooting a new, unproven installation, inspect the tape controller board address, interrupt, and DMA settings as necessary. Configuration conflicts can lock up a software package or render a drive inoperative. Check the tape itself to be sure it is inserted properly and completely.

If power, interface cables, and software setup check properly, your trouble is likely in your drive or host controller. Ideally, your next step would be to isolate further by substitution. Try a known-good tape drive and/or controller card in your system. For most of us, however, tape drives are few and far between, so simply "plugging in" a compatible system from a friend or colleague is not nearly as likely as it would be with floppy or even hard drives.

If your tape drive is being controlled by an ordinary floppy drive controller board, turn system power off and try disconnecting your tape drive and plugging in a floppy drive. When power is restored, you may have to disable any TSRs installed (to manage the tape drive) and change the CMOS system setup such that the floppy drive will be recognized. If your test floppy drive works properly, you can be confident that the controller board works properly. The problem is then likely in your tape drive, or there is still a problem in your tape system setup. If you cannot get the test floppy drive to work, the floppy controller board may be defective, so try a new controller board. If a new controller board supports the test floppy drive, return the floppy drive to its original port, reinstall the tape drive, restore the system setup for the tape drive, and try the tape drive again.

As an alternative to hardware swapping, many drives are now shipped with a simple diagnostic routine on the installation disk. Try a diagnostic if it is available. If a diagnostic recognizes the controller but not the drive, the drive is either defective or is connected or set up incorrectly. You may see an error message such as NO TAPE DRIVE FOUND. If the diagnostic does not recognize the tape controller at all, the controller is probably defective or is configured improperly. A typical error message may be something like NO TAPE CONTROLLER FOUND.

Symptom 2: The tape does not read or write, but the tape and head seem to move properly You will probably find R/W errors indicated by your backup software. Start your repair by inspecting the tape cartridge itself. The cartridge should be inserted completely and properly into the drive and sit firmly over the reel as shown in Fig. 8-10. If the current tape is inserted properly, try loading from another tape. Old tapes may have degraded to a point where data can no longer be read or written reliably. If an alternate tape works properly, discard and replace the old tape. If problems persist, try cleaning the tape drive's R/W heads. Excessive buildups of dust or residual oxides can easily interfere with normal tape recording/playback operations. If you still encounter R/W trouble, the R/W heads or their associated circuitry has probably failed. Try replacing the tape drive.

Symptom 3: The R/W head does not step from track to track The remainder of the drive appears to work properly. This problem may also result in tape read or write errors. The head assembly must step across very small tracks laid out along the width of the tape. Depending on the vintage of tape and drive you are faced with, the tape may have 9 to 144 tracks. When the tape reaches its end, the head is positioned to another track, tape direction reverses, and reading or writing continues. There are two physical elements responsible for positioning a R/W head: a *head stepping motor* and a mechanism called the *head seek assembly*. A defect or jam in either one of these components can prevent the head from moving. You can see the stepping motor in the underside view of Fig. 8-11.

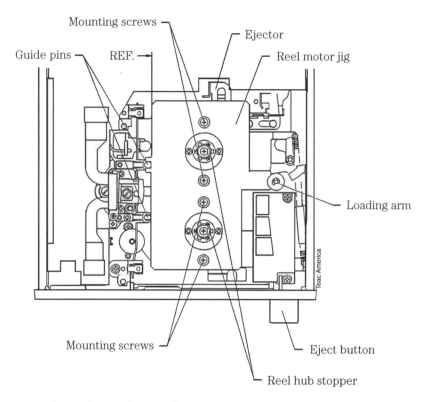

8-10 The reel area of a tape drive.

Check the LED/sensor pair that detects the EOT/BOT holes. If the LED transmitter or phototransistor receiver is defective, the drive will not know when to switch tracks. Remove the tape and place your multimeter across the receiving sensor. As you alternately pass and interrupt the light path from transmitter to receiver, you should see the logic output from the detector sensor switch from logic 1 to logic 0 (or vice versa). If the sensor does not work, replace the LED and phototransistor and try the sensor pair again. If the sensor pair still malfunctions, replace the drive's control PC board or replace the entire drive. If problems persist, the drive's control circuitry has probably failed. Try replacing the drive.

Symptom 4: The tape does not move, or its speed does not remain constant When a tape is set into motion for reading or writing, it is vitally important that tape speed remain constant. Tape speed is a function of the reel motors and the encoder which produces speed feedback signals. Begin by removing the tape and check for any accumulation of dust and debris that may be interfering with drive operation. Carefully clear away any obstruction that you may find.

If the tape does not move at all, check the dc motor signal across the reel motor(s) with your multimeter. When activated, there should be about +12 Vdc across the appropriate motor (forward or reverse motor depending on the tape's initial direction). If no excitation voltage is present, there is probably a fault in the drive's control PC board. Try replacing the drive control PC board or replace the entire drive. If drive voltage is present but the tape does not turn, replace both reel motors as in Fig. 8-12, or replace the drive.

If the reel motors turn as expected but their speed is not constant, the problem may be in the encoder. Tape is normally kept in contact with a rubber encoder roller. As a tape moves, the encoder roller turns and spins the encoder. Pulse signals from the encoder are used by the drive control PC board to regulate reel motor speed. Check the encoder roller. Tighten the encoder roller if it is loose or worn. A heavily worn encoder roller should be replaced. Make sure one roller turn results in one encoder turn—the roller must not slip on the encoder shaft. Place your logic probe on the encoder output and check for pulses as the tape moves. If there are no pulses, replace the defective encoder or replace the drive. If pulses are present, replace the drive's control PC board, or replace the entire drive.

Symptom 5: There are problems in loading or ejecting the tape Most of the mechanisms for loading or unloading a tape are incorporated directly into the drive chassis itself. Physical abuse and the accumulation of dust and debris can eventually cause problems in your tape-handling mechanisms. Before you disassemble your drive, however, check your tape very carefully. Old tapes can jam or wear out, and some tapes (such as Teac's digital cassette) can only be inserted into the drive in one orientation. Try a fresh tape and make sure that the tape is inserted properly into the drive.

If the tape continues to load or unload with resistance, expose the drive's mechanical assemblies and inspect all levers and linkages (such as in Fig. 8-13) for any signs of obstruction or damage. Gently clear away any obstructions that you may find. You may wish to use a fresh, dry cotton swab to wipe away any accumulations of debris. *Do not add any lubricant to the load/unload mechanism unless there was lubricant there to begin with*—and then, use only the same type of lubricant.

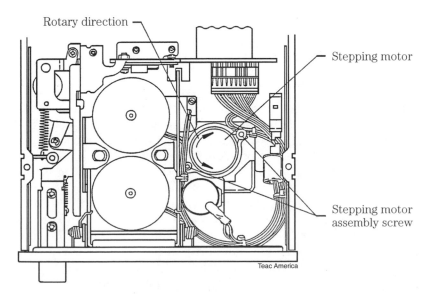

8-11 Head stepping motor illustration.

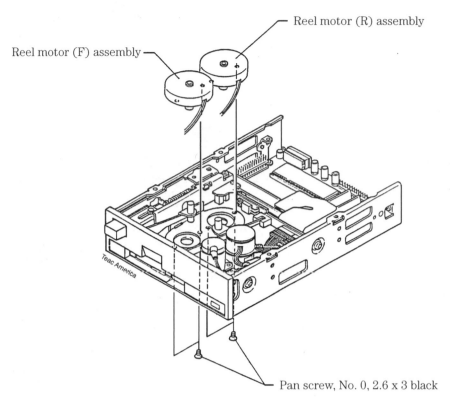

Reel motor (R) assembly

Reel motor (F) assembly

Teac America

Pan screw, No. 0, 2.6 x 3 black

8-12 Replacing the tape reel motors.

Replace any components that show signs of unusual wear. Use extreme caution when working with tape assemblies. Mechanical systems are very precisely designed, so make careful notes and assembly diagrams during disassembly. An improperly reassembled mechanical system may damage the tape or hold the tape in an improper position resulting in R/W or motor speed errors. If you cannot rectify the problem, replace the drive outright.

Symptom 6: The drive writes to write-protected tapes   When a tape is write-protected, the drive should not be able to write to that protected tape. Your first step should be to remove and inspect the tape itself. Check to make sure that the write-protect lever is in the "protect" position. If the protect lever is not in the right place, the tape is vulnerable to writing. If the tape protect lever is set properly, expose the drive mechanism and place your voltmeter across the sensor's output. Alternately, interrupt and free the optoisolator beam by hand and watch the sensor's output on your multimeter. If the output switches logic levels as you actuate the sensor manually, the trouble is probably in your drive's control PC board. Replace the drive control PC board, or replace the entire drive. If the output does not shift logic levels as expected, the sensor may be defective. Replace the write-protect sensor and repeat your test. If the sensor remains inoperative, replace the drive control PC board or replace the entire drive.

Symptom 7: The drive does not recognize the beginning or end of the tape A tape drive must know when the end or beginning of a tape has been reached. The majority of tapes use a series of small holes at each end of the tape. An optoisolator provides a pulse signal to the drive control PC board when holes pass by. Begin by removing the tape and checking for the presence of end holes. The wrong type of tape (i.e., a tape without holes) can cause problems for the drive. If the wrong type of tape is being used, retry the system using the correct type of tape.

Focus next on the BOT/EOT sensor, which is an optoisolator located across the tape path (an LED on one side and a detector on the other). Remove the tape, expose the system, and place your multimeter across the detector's output. Alternately, interrupt and free the light path by hand and watch the detector's output on your multimeter. If the output switches logic levels as expected, the trouble is probably in your drive's control PC board. Replace the drive control PC board or replace the entire drive. If the output does not shift as expected, replace the LED source and detector elements together and retest the sensor pair. If the sensor remains inoperative, replace the drive control PC board or replace the entire drive.

Symptom 8: A software program using a hardware copy-protection device on the parallel-port locks up This symptom is typical of parallel-port tape drives. The backup software attempts to communicate with the tape drive, but it winds up communicating with the copy-protection device (a.k.a. *dongle*) instead. You can either switch the tape to a free parallel port, or remove the copy-protection device.

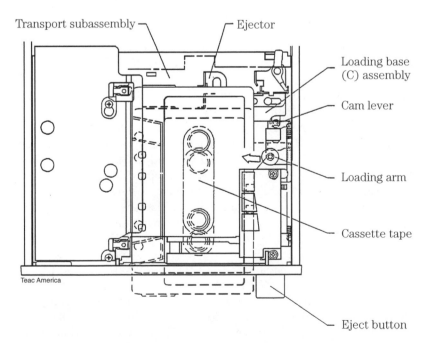

8-13 Top view of the Teac tape drive loading mechanism.

Symptom 9: The backup software indicates TOO MANY BAD SECTORS ON THE TAPE You may also see an error such as ERROR CORRECTION FAILED. This type of error generally indicates that more than 5 percent of the sectors on a tape are unreadable. In many cases, this is due to dirty R/W heads. Try cleaning the R/W head assembly. If problems continue, try a new tape cartridge. If problems persist, check the drive's power and signal cables and make sure that they are installed properly and completely.

Symptom 10: The tape backup software produces a TAPE DRIVE ERROR XX **where XX is a specific fault type** The fault type will depend on the particular drive and tape backup software you are using, so refer to the user manual for exact code meanings. The following code examples are for Colorado tape backup software:

- **0Ah**—Broken or dirty tape. Clean the R/W heads carefully, and replace the tape (if broken).
- **0Bh**—Gain error. Reformat the tape before attempting a backup.
- **1Ah** Power-on reset occurred. Check the drive's power and signal connections and try again.
- **1Bh**—Software reset occurred. Shut down any application that might be conflicting with the tape backup software.
- **04h**—Drive motor jammed. Remove the tape and make sure that there is nothing (including the tape) blocking the motor(s). Insert a new tape and try the system again.

Symptom 11: The tape drive is not found by the backup software There are several possible reasons for this problem. First, the tape backup software must be compatible with the particular tape drive *and* operating system. For example, the Micro Solutions Backpack tape drive is only supported by the BPBackup Windows 95 software program packaged with the drive itself. If you're using the Windows 95 native backup utility, you may not be able to access the drive at all. If you know the backup software is correct for your drive, the drive (or its controller board) may not be installed or configured properly.

When using a parallel-port tape drive, you may encounter such "Not detected" or "Not found" errors because of an IRQ conflict between the parallel port and other devices in the system. LPT1 typically uses IRQ7, and LPT2 often uses IRQ5. However, sound boards often use IRQ5 also. If you lose tape drive capability after installing new hardware, check the configuration of your new hardware.

"Not Found/Not Detected" errors could also indicate that the parallel port is using a nonstandard parallel-port data transfer mode. Most parallel-port backup software will automatically detect and utilize IEEE-1284 compatible Enhanced Parallel Ports (EPP). Some nonstandard EPP ports (or parallel ports configured for other types of high-speed data transfer) may cause the backup software to report problems. Try changing the port mode in CMOS Setup.

Note: Some notebook and desktop computers with multimedia sound chips integrated onto the motherboard must be reconfigured in the Windows Control Panel under Drivers—Setup. Change ESS Audio Driver, or Microsoft Windows Sound System to IRQ5 or IRQ10, then restart Windows.

Symptom 12: The tape drive works in DOS, but refuses to work in Windows 95 First make sure that the backup software you are using under Windows 95 is able to detect the tape drive. If the backup software is working properly, chances are that one or more Windows 95 drivers are interfering with the tape drive. Try starting Windows 95 in the Safe Mode and try your tape access again. If the tape drive is accessible now, you are going to have to check for driver conflicts. This often happens with parallel-port tape backups when Windows 95 drivers block parallel-port access using third-party printer drivers loaded by SYSTEM.INI. You should check the [386Enh] section of SYSTEM.INI and use semicolons to "remark out" any offending "device=" lines.

Symptom 13: The backup software generates an overlay error such as: COULD NOT OPEN FILE: QBACKUP.OVL Failures to open overlay files are often due to insufficient buffers. For example, you should usually have a BUFFERS = 30 or higher entry in your CONFIG.SYS file. Otherwise, the backup utility may not function properly. If you do edit changes to your CONFIG.SYS file, remember to save your changes before rebooting the computer.

Note: Always make it a point to have backup copies of your CONFIG.SYS and AUTOEXEC.BAT files available before making changes to them. That way, you can easily restore your original startup files if necessary without having to reedit the files.

Symptom 14: You see an error using older versions of backup software (i.e., GENERAL TAPE FAILURE: 187**)** This was a common problem with older parallel-port tape backup systems and was usually caused by timing problems in the parallel-port signals—the software was unable to utilize the parallel port at its proper timing. In virtually all cases, such problems are eliminated in new versions of backup software. Check the backup software version. Update older software as appropriate.

Symptom 15: You encounter media errors, bad block errors, system errors, or lockups These types of problems are known to occur with Travan tapes, and there are several possible problems to consider. First, try removing and reinserting the Travan data cartridge. In many cases this allows the drive mechanism to clear any errors. If problems continue, try reinitializing the data cartridge (typically handled through the backup software such as "Tools" and "Initialize"). Note that reinitializing the cartridge will render all data on it unusable. Finally, try disabling data compression, especially if you notice a high frequency of "shoeshining" (frequent reversals of tape direction), which often results in error messages.

Note: All TR-4 data cartridges are preformatted, and these TR-4 tapes cannot be reformatted unless your tape drive mechanism is designed to format TR-4 tapes. As a consequence, do *not* "bulk erase" a TR-4 cartridge using an electromagnet or similar device.

Symptom 16: During initialization under DOS or Windows, the SCSI tape driver (i.e., BPASPI.SYS) reports the error AN ASPI DRIVE WAS NOT FOUND In many cases the driver's test for enhanced parallel ports (EPP) is causing the problem, so try disabling the EPP test by adding a command line switch to the ASPI tape driver. For example,

```
device=\bpaspi\bpaspi.sys NOEPP
```

Note that your particular drive mechanism and driver may use different command line switches. Once you make the changes to CONFIG.SYS, save your changes, then turn off the tape drive and computer before rebooting the system.

Symptom 17: When using a Colorado Trakker tape drive, you cannot get the drive to save or restore files reliably   You will probably see error messages like UNABLE TO TRANSFER DATA PROPERLY. RETRY THE OPERATION, TAPE HEADER CONTAINS UNEXPECTED OR INVALID VALUES, MICROSOFT BACKUP ENCOUNTERED AN ERROR READING THIS TAPE. THIS ERROR MAY BE CAUSED BY AN UNFORMATTED OR INCORRECTLY FORMATTED TAPE. REFORMAT THE TAPE, AND THEN TRY AGAIN. In virtually all cases, the drive (or backup software) does not function with EPP- or ECP-type parallel ports. You should enter the CMOS Setup and change the parallel-port mode to "Compatibility Mode."

Note: You may not receive any error messages when you back up files, but you may then be unable to compare or restore the files. If you *can* restore the files, the data that are restored to your hard disk may be damaged.

Symptom 18: It takes much longer than you expect to perform a backup This poor backup performance may also be accompanied by poor hard disk performance while you perform other tasks in Windows 95. There are a number of problems that can cause this poor performance. First, there may be a lack of available RAM—you may have too many programs open at the same time or not have enough physical RAM installed in the computer. Try closing all programs before starting the backup process. If performance does not improve, remove all programs from the Startup folder, and from the load= and run= lines in WIN.INI, then restart Windows 95. If performance is still poor, you may need to add more physical RAM to your computer to improve performance.

One or more of your hard disks may be running in the Compatibility mode. If the Performance tab in System properties shows that one or more of the hard disks in your computer is using the MS-DOS Compatibility mode, resolving this problem should improve performance in backup. You may need a new protected-mode driver for the hard drive. Even if your hard disks are not using MS-DOS Compatibility mode, the speed of your backup may be affected by the overall performance of your hard disks. For example, if you are using an IDE hard disk, the performance of the hard disk may be affected by another device that is connected to the same IDE controller channel (such as CD-ROM drives). Try moving the slower device to a separate IDE controller, or to the second IDE channel on an EIDE dual-port controller.

If you are using disk compression on a computer with an older CPU, hard disk performance may not be as good as if you were not using disk compression. If you are using third-party disk compression software that uses a real-mode driver to access your compressed drives, you may be able to improve performance by replacing the real-mode driver with a protected-mode driver (contact the maker of your compression software).

Check the file fragmentation on your hard drive. Badly fragmented hard disks can affect the performance of backup software, as well as the performance of other tasks in Windows 95. Run DEFRAG to defragment your hard disks. Finally, backup software can often detect and avoid unusable sectors on a tape, but the process that it uses to do so can be time-consuming. If you suspect that performance problems are caused by unusable sectors on a tape, try using a new tape or a tape that you know does not contain unusable sectors.

Symptom 19: When you try to format a DT-350 tape in a Conner 250 tape drive, you may receive the following error message: Errors occurred during this operation In virtually all cases, this is a limitation of the tape drive itself. Most 250 tape drives cannot format DT-350 tapes. Try a tape that is compatible with the drive.

Symptom 20: When you try to perform a backup, restore, or compare operation in Microsoft Backup, or close Backup after performing one of these operations, you may receive the following error message: Microsoft Backup has encountered a serious error in the Memory Manager. Quit and restart Backup, and then try again There are several possible problems that can cause this behavior. First, there may be an incompatible device driver or TSR running on the system which is interfering with the backup software. Try running backup from the Windows 95 Safe Mode. You may have trouble with your swap file. Try disabling the swap file, then restoring it. The files for your backup software may be damaged or corrupted. Try removing Backup from your Windows 95 installation, then reinstall it to ensure a fresh set of files. It is also possible that you have a damaged tape drive or tape cartridge. Try a new tape cartridge. If problems persist, try a new tape drive. Finally, you may have a fault in RAM. Run a DOS diagnostic with an aggressive RAM test and see if you can identify any failed memory. Replace defective RAM as necessary. If the defective RAM is hard-soldered to your motherboard, you may have to replace the motherboard.

Symptom 21: Your QIC-3020 formatted tape not recognized by tape drive for writing This is often an issue with tape controllers. Some floppy-based tape drives require a floppy controller operating at 1 Mb/s to support writing on all compatible tapes. If the floppy controller does not support at least 1 Mb/s, the drive may not be able to write to larger tapes. Try a high-speed floppy controller board. Note that it is probably more cost-effective to use a high-performance drive controller than to reformat the larger tape for the smaller format (which can take up to 18 hours).

Symptom 22: Your backup software does not autoskip busy files This is almost always a limitation of the particular backup software. You may consider upgrading to the latest version of your backup software for best performance.

Symptom 23: You cannot connect a floppy port tape drive to a floppy controller This often happens with Compaq systems because Compaq floppy controller cables are keyed differently from ordinary floppy drive cables. Try a generic floppy drive cable that will connect the drive to the controller.

Symptom 24: You see an error message such as DMA setting specified for this device may be incorrect This is a common problem when using floppy-based drive accelerator controllers. First, make sure that the accelerator controller uses the same setting for DRQ and DACK signals. Next, try a different DMA setting. If necessary, try sharing DMA 2 with the floppy drive controller. There may be a driver or TSR conflict, so shut down any screen savers or TSRs on the system. Try disabling any "High-Speed Burst Mode" feature of the controller through Windows 95 in the Device Manager. Finally, make sure that your SYSTEM.INI file is not loading other tape drivers (or device drivers that may be conflicting with your tape drive).

Symptom 25: The tape drive makes no sound when a minicartridge is inserted In virtually all cases, the tape drive is not receiving power. Check the power to your tape drive. If problems continue, there is likely to be a problem with the drive itself. Try replacing the tape drive.

Symptom 26: You see an error message such as File not found in file set directory This is almost always a problem with the backup software itself rather than the drive. Try downloading and installing the latest version of the backup software. If there is no later version available, try the following:

- Deselect the backup software directory during a backup.
- Turn off file compression.
- Deselect the registry.

Symptom 27: You find that formatting minicartridge takes from 7 to 18 hours This is not necessarily a problem. The time it takes to format a data cartridge depends on the length of the tape and the mode of your controller. In QIC-3020 mode (using a 1-Mb/s or 2-Mb/s controller), it may take 7 to 9 h to completely format a tape. In QIC-3010 mode (using a 500-kb/s controller), it can take up to 18 h. You may need to install a drive accelerator card to use QIC-3020 preformatted cartridges. Try retensioning the cartridge.

Symptom 28: You experience low capacity, or slow read and writes to your tape drive If you connect the tape drive to a floppy controller, you may experience slower transfer rates and lower capacities than expected—transfer rates and capacities are affected by the speed of the controller. Many ordinary floppy controllers operate at 500 kb/s, while the accelerated controller cards operate at 1 or 2 Mb/s. At 500 kb/s, 680 MB of data can take up to 2.5 h to back up. A 1-Mb/s accelerator card can back up that amount of data in 1.25 h. A 2-Mb/s card takes 40 minutes. Most 386 and 486 systems will operate at 500 kb/s, while newer

486 and Pentium systems contain floppy controller cards that offer 1-Mb/s and 2-Mb/s speeds. Try cleaning the tape drive.

Note: If your minicartridge was formatted in QIC-3010 format (using a 500-kb/s controller), you will achieve only half the capacity of a minicartridge formatted in QIC-3020 format (using a 1-Mb/s or 2-Mb/s controller). This is so even if you are currently running off a high-speed controller.

There are also other issues to consider. Run CHKDSK or ScanDisk to clean up any bad files or lost clusters, then defragment the disk with DEFRAG. Make sure that you are using the latest version of your backup software. You may try removing any screen savers or TSRs that might be putting an unusual load on the computer's resources. Finally, try minimizing the backup application's window under Windows 95.

Symptom 29: You experience a parsing or logic error   This type of problem is almost always related to the backup software itself. Make sure to use the very latest version of the backup software, and make sure that the software is directly compatible with your specific tape drive and operating system.

Symptom 30: You are running out of space during DOS backups   This is almost always due to a lack of conventional memory space, and can happen quite frequently when using a DOS program under a window. Make sure that you have the minimum conventional memory available to run the DOS backup utility. You should also have some limited amount of hard drive space available for creating temporary files or buffering the file transfer. Finally, make sure that you have the minimum number of buffers required in CONFIG.SYS for the backup program (often BUFFERS=40).

Symptom 31: You experience excessive "shoe shining" during backups
In normal tape drive operations, the tape drive writes data to a single track from one end of the tape to another; it then writes data in a parallel data track back to the beginning of the tape, and so on, until the tape is full. *Shoe shining* refers to frequent back-and-forth tape motion. If you have the backup window open, minimize it. With the window open, the system has to update the screen continually, and this takes resources away from the software sending data to the tape drive. If the PC offers a "turbo mode," try disabling the turbo mode (especially when using parallel-port tape drives).

9
CHAPTER

Optical Drives

The push for ever-greater and more reliable information storage has been a relentless one. Every few years, technological breakthroughs and enhancements seem to yield stunning improvements in the way we computer users store and access information. Classical magnetic storage (floppy, hard, and tape drives) are constantly being challenged by a family of storage systems using light instead of (or in addition to) magnetic fields to read and write information to storage media. The CD-ROM drive is the most popular implementation of optical storage, but the new generation of DVD drives that are appearing promise to offer at least 10 times more storage than the traditional CD.

CD-ROM Drives

The *compact disc* (or CD) first appeared in the marketplace in early 1982. Sony and Philips developed the CD as a joint venture and envisioned it as a reliable, high-quality replacement for aging phonograph technology. With the introduction of the audio CD, designers demonstrated that huge amounts of information can be stored simply and very inexpensively on common nonmagnetic media. Unlike previous recording media, the CD recorded data in *digital* form through the use of physical "pits" and "lands" in the disc. The digital approach allowed excellent stereo sound quality but also attracted the attention of PC designers who saw CDs as a natural solution for holding all types of computer information (i.e., text, graphics, programs, video clips, audio files, and so on). This part of the chapter explains the technologies and troubleshooting techniques for CD-ROM drives (Fig. 9-1).

The argument for computer CDs (dubbed *CD-ROM* from "compact disc—read-only memory") was compelling; a CD-ROM disc can hold over 650 million characters, which is roughly analogous to over 1500 high-density floppy diskettes, or more than 200,000 pages of printed text. By including compression to reduce file sizes, this capacity can be extended significantly. Such capacities support the development and distribution of massive databases and complex programs on inexpensive plastic discs no more than 12 cm in diameter. By 1985, the first CD-ROM

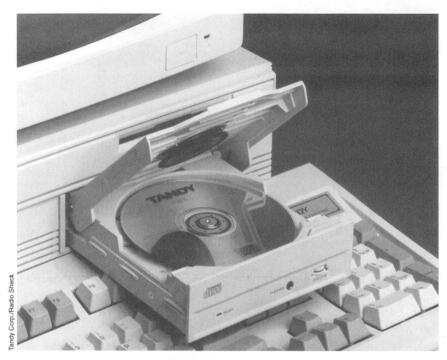

Tandy Corp./Radio Shack

9-1 A Tandy CD-ROM drive.

drives and applications had become available for the PC. By the mid-1990s, CD-ROMs are virtually standard equipment in all new PCs.

The similarities between audio CDs and CD-ROM discs are startling—in fact, most CD-ROM drives can actually play audio CDs (as long as the PC is running a program which will interpret the audio data). However, a PC needs additional information to handle programs and other computerized data. Unlike audio CDs, CD-ROM discs include a header (called a *volume table of contents* or VTOC) which describes the nature and location of all data on the disc. Multiple layers of error-correction codes and error-correcting circuitry are added to the CD-ROM drive to ensure that there are no errors introduced as programs and data are read from the disc. Your ear won't notice a few dropped bits on an audio disc, but a single bad program bit can crash your PC. The structure of data and the use of error-correction techniques are clearly defined through a set of comprehensive standards called *books*.

Understanding CD Media

CDs are mass-produced by stamping the pattern of pits and lands onto a molded polycarbonate disc. It is this stamping process (much like the stamping used to produce vinyl records) that places the data on the disc. But the disc is not yet readable. There are finish steps that must be performed to transform a clear plastic disc into viable, data-carrying medium. The clear polycarbonate disc is given a silvered (reflective) coating so that it will reflect laser light. Silvering coats all parts of the disc side (pits and lands) equally. After silvering, the disc is coated with a tough, scratch-resistant lacquer that seals the disc from the elements (especially oxygen, which will oxidize and ruin the reflective coating). Finally, a label can be silk-screened onto the finished disc before it is tested and packaged. Figure 9-2 illustrates each of these layers in a cross-sectional diagram.

CD data

CDs are not segregated into concentric tracks and sectors as magnetic media are. Instead, CDs are recorded as a single, continuous spiral track running from the spindle to the lead-out area. Figure 9-3 shows the spiral pattern recorded on a CD. The inset illustrates the relationship between the pits and lands. Each pit is about 0.12 μm (micrometers) deep and 0.6 μm wide. Pits and lands may range from 0.9 to 3.3 μm in length. There are approximately 1.6 μm between each iteration of the spiral. Given these microscopic dimensions, a CD-ROM disc offers about 16,000 tracks per inch (tpi).

During playback, CDs use a highly focused laser beam and laser detector to sense the presence or absence of pits. Figure 9-4 illustrates the reading behavior. The laser/detector pair is mounted on a carriage which follows the spiral track across the CD. A laser is directed at the underside of the CD where it penetrates more than 1 mm of clear plastic before shining on the reflective surface. When laser light strikes a land, the light is reflected toward the detector which, in turn, produces a very strong output signal. As laser light strikes a pit, the light is slightly out of focus. As a result, most of the incoming laser energy is scattered away in all directions, so very little output signal is generated by the detector. As with floppy and hard drives, it is the *transition* from pit to land (and back again) that corresponds to binary levels, *not* the presence or absence of a pit or land. The analog light signal returned by the detector must be converted to logic levels and decoded. A process known as *eight-to-fourteen modulation* (EFM) is very common with CD-ROMs.

EFM and CD storage

A complex decoding process is necessary to convert the arcane sequence of pits and lands into meaningful binary information. The technique of EFM is used with CD-ROMs. For hard disc drives, techniques such as *2,7 RLL encoding* can be used to place a large number of bits into a limited number of flux transitions. The same is true for CDs using EFM. User data, error-correction information, address information, and synchronization patterns are all contained in a bit stream represented by pits and lands.

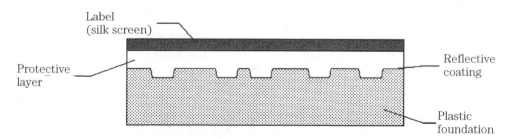

9-2 Cross-section of a CD-ROM disc.

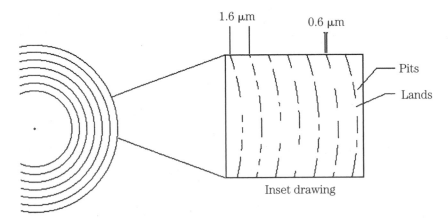

9-3 Close-up view of CD-ROM disc tracks.

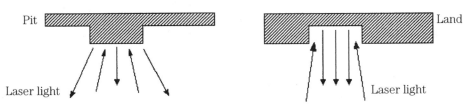

9-4 Reading pits and lands.

Magnetic media encode bits as flux transitions—not the discrete orientation of any magnetic area. The same concept holds true with CD-ROMs where binary 1s and 0s do not correspond to pits or lands. A binary 1 is represented wherever a transition (pit-to-land or land-to-pit) occurs. The length of a pit or land represents the number of binary 0s. Figure 9-5 illustrates this concept. The EFM technique equates each byte (8 bits) with a 14-bit sequence (called a *symbol*) where each binary 1 must be separated by at least two binary 0s. Table 9-1 shows part of the eight-to-fourteen conversion. Three bits are added to merge each 14-bit symbol together.

A CD-ROM *frame* is composed of 24 synchronization bits, 14 control bits, 24 of the 14-bit data symbols you saw previously, and 8 complete 14-bit error-correction (EC) symbols. Keep in mind that each symbol is separated by an additional 3 merge bits, bringing the total number of bits in the frame to 588. Thus, 24 bytes of data is represented by 588 bits on a CD-ROM expressed as a number of pits and lands. There are 98 frames in a data *block,* so each block carries (98 × 24) −2048 bytes (2352 with error correction, synchronization, and address bytes). The basic CD-ROM can deliver 153.6 kB of data (75 blocks) per second to its host controller.

Remember that the CD-ROM disc is recorded as one continuous spiral track running around the disc, so ordinary sector and track ID information that we associate with magnetic discs does not apply very well. Instead, information is divided in terms of 0 to 59 *minutes,* and 0 to 59 *seconds* recorded at the beginning of each block. A CD-ROM (like an audio CD) can hold up to 79 minutes of data. However, many CD-

ROMs tend to limit this to 60 minutes since the last 14 minutes of data are encoded in the outer 5 mm of disc space, which is the most difficult to manufacture and keep clean in everyday use. There are 270,000 blocks of data in 60 minutes. At 2048 data bytes per block, the disc's capacity is 552,950,000 bytes (553 MB). If all 79 minutes is used, 681,984,000 bytes (681 MB) will be available in 333,000 blocks. Most CD-ROMs run between 553 and 650 MB in normal production.

Caring for a compact disc

A CD is a remarkably reliable long-term storage medium (conservative expectations place the life estimates of a current CD at about 100 years). However, the longevity of a CD is affected by its storage and handling. A faulty CD can cause file and data errors that you might otherwise interpret as a defect in the drive itself. This part of the chapter looks at ways to protect and maintain the disc itself. First, some don'ts are in order:

- **Don't bend the disc.** Polycarbonate is a forgiving material, but you risk cracking or snapping (and thus ruining) the disc.
- **Don't heat the disc.** Remember, the disc is plastic. Leaving it by a heater or on the dashboard of your car will cause melting.
- **Don't scratch the disc.** Laser wavelengths have a tendency to "look past" minor scratches, but a major scratch can cause problems. Be especially careful of circular scratches (one that follows the spiral track). A circular scratch can easily wipe out entire segments of data, which would be unrecoverable.

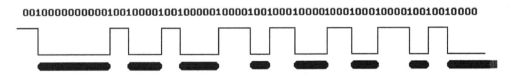

001000000000010010000100100000100001001000100001000100010000100100010000

9-5 CD-ROM data encoding.

Table 9-1. A Sample of EFM Codes

Number	Binary pattern	EFM pattern
0	00000000	01001000100000
1	00000001	10000100000000
2	00000010	10010000100000
3	00000011	10001000100000
4	00000100	01000100000000
5	00000101	00000100010000
6	00000110	00010000100000
7	00000111	00100100000000
8	00001000	01001001000000
9	00001001	10000001000000
10	00001010	10010001000000

- **Don't use chemicals on the disc.**   Chemicals containing solvents such as ammonia, benzene, acetone, carbon tetrachloride, or chlorinated cleaning solvents can damage the plastic surface.

Eventually, a buildup of excessive dust or fingerprints can interfere with the laser beam enough to cause disc errors. When this happens, the disc can be cleaned easily using a dry, soft, lint-free cloth. Hold the disc from its edges and wipe radially (from hub to edge). *Do not wipe in a circular motion.* For stubborn stains, moisten the cloth in a bit of fresh isopropyl alcohol (*do not use water*). Place the cleaned disc in a caddie or jewel case for transport and storage.

CD-ROM Standards and Characteristics

Like so many other PC peripheral devices, the early CD-ROM faced a serious problem of industry standardization. Just recording the data to a CD is not enough—the data must be recorded in a way that any CD-ROM drive can read. Standards for CD-ROM data and formats were developed by consortiums of influential PC manufacturers and interested CD-ROM publishers. Ultimately, this kind of industrywide cooperation has made the CD-ROM one of the most uniform and standardized peripherals in the PC market. There are a number of CD-ROM standards that you should understand.

High Sierra

In 1984 (before the general release of CD-ROM), the PC industry realized that there must be a standard method of reading a disc's VTOC. Otherwise, the CD-ROM market would become extremely fragmented as various (incompatible) standards vied for acceptance. PC manufacturers prospective CD publishers, and software developers met at the High Sierra Hotel in Lake Tahoe, California, to begin developing just such a uniform standard. By 1986, the CD-ROM standard file format (dubbed the *High Sierra format*) was accepted and approved. High Sierra remained the standard for several years, but has since been replaced by ISO 9660.

ISO 9660

High Sierra was certainly a workable format, but it was primarily a domestic U.S. development. When placed before the International Standards Organization (ISO), High Sierra was tweaked and refined to meet international needs. After international review, High Sierra was absorbed (with only few changes) into the ISO 9660 standard. Although many technicians refer to High Sierra and ISO 9660 interchangeably, you should understand that the two standards are *not* the same. For the purposes of this book, ISO 9660 is the current CD-ROM file format.

By adhering to ISO 9660, CD-ROM drive makers can write software drivers (and use MSCDEX under MS-DOS) to enable a PC to read the CD's VTOC. ISO 9660 also allows a CD-ROM disc to be accessed by any computer system and CD-ROM drive that follows the standard. Of course, just because a disc is recognized does not mean that it can be used. For example, an ISO 9660-compliant Mac can access a ISO 9660 MPC disc, but the files on the disc cannot be used by the Mac.

The CD-ROM standards

When Philips and Sony defined the proprietary standards that became CD audio and CD-ROM, the documents were bound in different-colored covers. By tradition, each color now represents a different level of standardization. *Red Book* (a.k.a. Compact Disc Digital Audio Standard: CEI IEC 908) defines the medium, recording and mastering process, and the player design for CD audio. When you listen to your favorite audio CD, you are enjoying the benefits of the Red Book standard. CDs conforming to Red Book standards will usually have the words "digital audio" printed below the disc logo. Today, Red Book audio may be combined with programs and other PC data on the same disc.

The *Yellow Book* standard (ISO 10149:1989) makes CD-ROM possible by defining the additional EC data needed on the disc, and detection hardware and firmware needed in the drive. When a disc conforms to the Yellow Book standard, it will usually be marked "data storage" beneath the disc logo. Mode 1 Yellow Book is the typical operating mode which supports computer data. Mode 2 Yellow Book (also known as the *XA format*) supports compressed audio data and video/picture data.

The *Orange Book* (a.k.a. Recordable Compact Disc Standard) serves to extend the basic Red and Yellow Book standards by providing specifications for recordable products such as (Part 1) *magnetooptical* (MO) and (Part 2) *write-once CDs* (CD-R). The *Green Book* standard defines an array of supplemental standards for data recording and provides an outline for a specific computer system that supports CD-I (compact disc–interactive). *Blue Book* is the standard for laser discs and their players. The *White Book* standards define CD-ROM video.

The multispin drive

The Red Book standard defines CD audio as a stream of data that flows from the player mechanism to the amplifier (or other audio manipulation circuit) at a rate of 150 kB/s. This data rate was chosen to take music off the disc for truest reproduction. When the Yellow Book was developed to address CD-ROMs, this basic data rate was carried over. Designers soon learned that data can be transferred much faster than Red Book audio information, so the *multispin* (or *multispeed*) drive was developed to work with Red Book audio at the normal 150-kB/s rate, but run faster for Yellow Book data in order to multiply the data throughput.

The first common multispin drives available were "2X" drives. By running at 2X the normal data transfer speed, data throughput can be doubled from 150 to 300 kB/s. If Red Book audio is encountered, the drive speed drops back to 150 kB/s. Increased data transfer rates make a real difference in CD-ROM performance—especially for data-intensive applications such as audio/visual clips. CD-ROM drives with 4X transfer speed (600 kB/s) can transfer data four times faster than a Red Book drive. Today, 8X drives (1200 kB/s or 1.2 MB/s) are virtually standard, and 12X to 16X drives are readily available.

The MPC

One of the most fundamental problems writing software for PCs is the tremendous variability in the possible hardware and software configurations of individual machines. The selection of CPUs, motherboard chipsets, DOS versions, available memory, graphics resolutions, drive space, and other peripherals make the idea of a "standard" PC almost meaningless. Most software developers in the PC market use a base (or minimal) PC configuration to ensure that a product will run properly in a "minimal" machine. CD-ROM multimedia products have intensified these performance issues. Microsoft assembled some of the largest PC manufacturers to create the *Multimedia Personal Computer* (or MPC) standard. By adhering to the MPC specification, software developers and consumers can anticipate the minimal capacity needed to run multimedia products. Table 9-2 outlines the various MPC standards.

Effects of CD-ROM caching

The limiting factor of a CD-ROM is its data transfer rate. At 300 kB/s or so, it takes a fairly substantial amount of time to load programs and files into memory—this causes system delays during CD-ROM access. If the PC could *predict* the data needed from a CD and load that data into RAM or virtual memory (i.e., the hard drive) during background operations, the *effective* performance of a CD-ROM drive could be enhanced dramatically. CD-ROM caching utilities provide a "look-ahead" ability that enables CD-ROMs continue transferring information in anticipation of use.

However, CD-ROM caching is a mixed blessing. The utilities required for caching must reside in conventional memory (or loaded into upper memory). In systems that are already strained by the CD-ROM drivers and other device drivers that have become so commonplace on PC platforms, adding a cache may prohibit some large DOS programs from running. Keep this in mind when evaluating CD-ROM caches for yourself or your customers.

Bootable CD-ROM (El Torito)

Traditionally, CD-ROM drives have not been bootable devices. Since the CD-ROM drive needs software drivers, the PC always had to boot *first* in order to load the drivers. This invariably required a bootable hard drive or floppy drive. When building a new system, this required you to boot from a floppy disc, install DOS and the CD-ROM drivers, and *then* pop in your Windows 95 CD for setup. In early 1995, the El Torito standard was finalized, which provides the hardware and software specifications needed to implement a bootable CD-ROM. You need three elements to implement a bootable CD-ROM:

- A bootable CD-ROM drive mechanism
- A BIOS that supports the bootable CD-ROM
- A CD with boot code and an operating system on it

CD-ROM Drive Construction

Now that you have an understanding of CD-ROM media and standards, it is time to review a CD-ROM drive in some detail. CD-ROM drives are impressive pieces of engineering. The drive must be able to accept standard-sized discs from a variety of sources (each disc may contain an assortment of unknown surface imperfections).

Table 9-2. Comparison of MPC Standards

Component	MPC level 1	MPC level 2	MPC level 3
The CPU chip and speed	386SX at 16 MHz	486SX at 25 MHz	Pentium at 75 MHz
Main system RAM, MB	2	4	8
Video adapter and resolution	VGA graphics†	1.2 million pixels/s at 40% of CPU capacity	Color space conversion and scaling capability; direct access to frame buffer for video graphics subsystem with a resolution of 352×240@30fps, or 352×288@25 fps—both at 15 bits/pixel unscaled, without cropping.
Video playback capability	N/A	N/A	MPEG 1
Audio	8-bit DAC and ADC Linear PCM sampling 22-kHz rate for DAC 11-kHz rate for ADC Microphone input Synthesizer Multivoice Multitimbral 6 melody/2 percussive 3-channel mixer Stereo output	16-bit DAC and ADC Linear PCM sampling 44.1-kHz rate for DAC 44.1-kHz rate for ADC Stereo input and output Microphone input Synthesizer Multivoice Multitimbral 3-channel mixer 6 melody/2 percussive Stereo output	16-bit DAC and ADC Linear PCM sampling 44.1-kHz rate for DAC 44.1-kHz rate for ADC Stereo input and output Microphone input MIDI playback Multivoice Multitimbral 3-channel mixer 6 melody/2 percussive Stereo output
Data input options	101 keyboard Two-button mouse	101 keyboard Two-button mouse	101 keyboard Two-button mouse
Input/output	9600-baud serial port Bidirectional parallel port Joystick port MIDI I/O port	9600-baud serial port Bidirectional parallel port Joystick port MIDI I/O port	9600-baud serial port Bidirectional parallel port Joystick port MIDI I/O port
Main storage (hard disc)	30-MB hard disc	160-MB hard disc	540-MB hard disc
Floppy disc	1.44-MB 3.5 in floppy	1.44 MB 3.5 in floppy	1.44 MB 3.5 in floppy
CD-ROM or optical audio/video storage (removable)	150-kB/s data transfer 1 s maximum seek time	Double-speed 300 kB/s data transfer 400-ms maximum seek time Multisession, CD-DA and XA capability	Quad-speed 600 kB/s data transfer 250-ms maximum seek time Multisession, CD-DA, and XA capability

†640×480 resolution with 16 colors.

The drive must then spin the disc at a *constant linear velocity* (CLV)—that is, the disc speed varies inversely with the tracking radius. As tracking approaches the disc edge, disc speed slows, and vice versa. Keep in mind that CLV is different than the *constant angular velocity* (CAV) method used by floppy and hard drives, which move the medium at a constant speed. The purpose of CLV is to ensure that CD-ROM data are read at a constant *rate*. A drive must be able to follow the spiral data path on a spinning CD-ROM accurate to within less than 1 μm along the disc's radius. The drive electronics must be able to detect and correct any unforeseen data errors in real time, operate reliably over a long working life, and be available for a low price that computer users have come to expect.

CD-ROM mechanics

You can begin to appreciate how a CD drive achieves its features by reviewing the exploded diagram of Fig. 9-6. At the center of the drive is a cast aluminum or rigid stainless steel *frame assembly*. As with other drives, the frame is the single primary structure for mounting the drive's mechanical and electronic components. The *front bezel, lid, volume control,* and *eject button* attach to the frame, providing the drive with its clean cosmetic appearance and offering a fixed reference slot for CD insertion and removal. Keep in mind that many drives use a sliding tray, so the front bezel (and the way it is attached) will not be the same for every drive.

The drive's electronics package has been split into several PC board (PCB) assemblies: (1) the *main PCB* which handles drive control and interfacing, and (2) the *headphone PCB* which simply provides an audio amplifier and jack for headphones. The bulk of the drive's actual physical work, however, is performed by a main CD

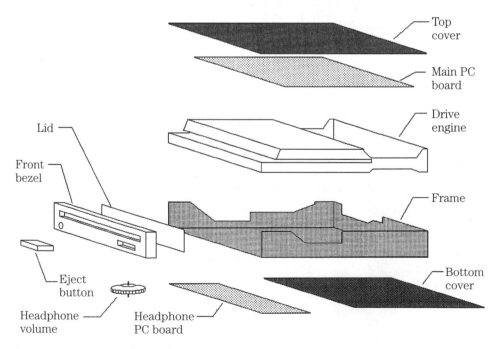

9-6 Exploded diagram of a CD-ROM drive.

subassembly called a *drive engine,* which is often manufactured by only a few companies. As a result, many of the diverse CD-ROM drives on the market actually use identical "engines" to hold/eject, spin, and read the disc. This interchangeability is part of the genius of CD-ROM drives—a single subassembly performs 80 percent of the work. Sony, Philips, and Toshiba are the major manufacturers of CD-ROM engines, but other companies such as IBM and Ikka are also producing engines.

A typical drive engine is shown in Fig. 9-7. The upper view of the engine features a series of mechanisms that accept, clamp, and eject the disc. The foundation of this engine is the *BC-7C assembly.* It acts as a subframe which everything else is mounted to. Notice that the subframe is shock-mounted with four rubber feet to cushion the engine from minor bumps and ordinary handling. Even with such mounting, a CD-ROM drive is a delicate and fragile mechanism. The *slider assembly, loading chassis assembly,* and the *cover shield* provide the mechanical action needed to accept the disc and clamp it into place over the drive spindle, as well as free the disc and eject it on demand. A number of levers and oil dampers serve to provide a slow, smooth mechanical action when motion takes place. A *motor/gear assembly* drives the load/unload mechanics.

The serious work of spinning and reading a disc is handled *under* the engine as shown in Fig. 9-8. A *spindle motor* is mounted on the subframe and connected to a *spindle motor PCB.* A *thrust retainer* helps keep the spindle motor turning smoothly. The most critical part of the CD engine is the *optical device* containing the 780-nm (nanometer) 0.6-mW gallium aluminum arsenide (GaAlAs) laser diode and detector, along with the optical focus and tracking components. The optical device slides along two guide rails and shines through an exposed hole in the subframe. This combination of device mounting and guide rails is called a *sled.*

A sled must be made to follow the spiral data track along the disc. While floppy discs (using clearly defined concentric tracks) can easily make use of a stepping motor to position the head assembly, a CD drive ideally requires a *linear motor* to act much like the voice coil motor used to position hard drive R/W heads. By altering the signal driving a sled motor and constantly measuring and adjusting the sled's position, a sled can be made to track very smoothly along a disc—free from the sudden, jerky motion of stepping motors. Some CD drives still use stepping motors with an extremely fine-pitch lead screw to position the sled. The drive's main PCB is responsible for managing these operations.

CD-ROM electronics

The electronics package used in a typical CD-ROM drive is illustrated in Fig. 9-9. The electronics package can be divided into two major areas: the *controller section* and the *drive section.* The *controller section* is dedicated to the peripheral interface—its connection to the adapter board. Much of the reason for a CD-ROM's electronic sophistication can be traced to the controller section. Notice that the controller circuitry shown in Fig. 9-9 is dedicated to handling a SCSI interface. This allows the unit's "intelligence" to be located right in the drive itself. You need only connect the drive to a system-level interface board (a SCSI adapter) and set the drive's device number to establish a working system. Most low-cost CD-ROM drives will use an IDE interface (the same interface used for hard drives).

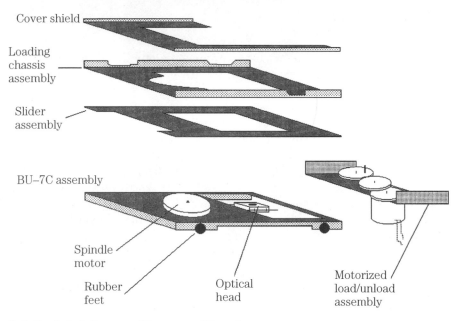

Cover shield

Loading chassis assembly

Slider assembly

BU–7C assembly

Spindle motor

Rubber feet

Optical head

Motorized load/unload assembly

9-7 Exploded diagram of the upper CD engine.

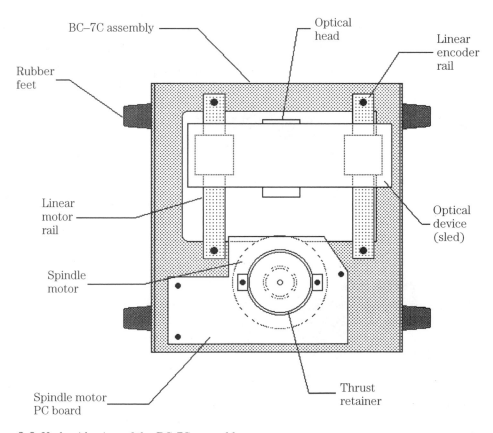

BC–7C assembly

Optical head

Linear encoder rail

Rubber feet

Linear motor rail

Optical device (sled)

Spindle motor

Spindle motor PC board

Thrust retainer

9-8 Underside view of the BC-7C assembly.

288

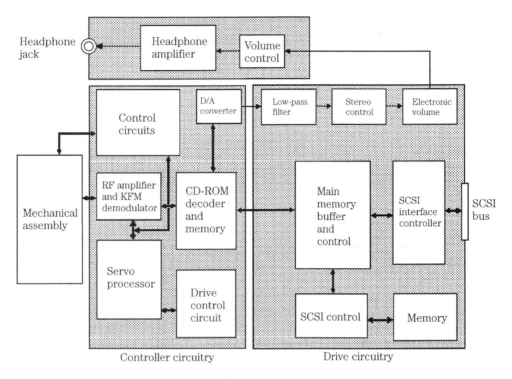

9-9 Simplified block diagram of a CD-ROM circuit.

The drive section manages the CD-ROM's physical operations (i.e., load/unload, spin the disc, move the sled, and so on), as well as data decoding (EFM) and error correction. Drive circuitry converts an analog output from the laser diode into an EFM signal which is, in turn, decoded into binary data and CIRC (Cross-Interleaved Reed-Solomon Code) information. A drive controller IC and servo processor IC are responsible for directing laser focus, tracking, sled motor control (and feedback), spindle motor control (and feedback), and loading/unloading motor control.

When it comes to CD drive electronics, you should treat the diagram of Fig. 9-9 more as a guideline than as an absolute. There are quite a few different iterations of drive electronics and interfaces. While many manufacturers use SCSI interfaces, most systems use the IDE system-level interface, and several manufacturers implement proprietary interfaces (in some cases, these are subtle, nonstandard variations of SCSI or IDE interfaces). Obtain manufacturer's service data wherever possible for specific information on your particular drive.

Understanding the Software

Hardware alone is not enough to implement a CD-ROM drive. In an ideal world, BIOS and MS-DOS would provide the software support to handle the drive, but in practice, the variations between CD-ROM designs and interfaces make it impractical to provide low-level BIOS services. Manufacturers provide a hardware-specific device driver used to communicate with the CD-ROM and interface. An MS-DOS extension (MSCDEX) provides file-handling and logical drive letter support. This part of the chapter explains the operations and features of CD-ROM device drivers and MSCDEX.

Device drivers

A low-level device driver allows programs to access the CD-ROM adapter properly at the register (hardware) level. Since most CD-ROM drives are designed differently, they require different device drivers. If you change or upgrade the CD-ROM drive at any point, the device driver must be upgraded as well. A typical device driver uses a .SYS extension and is initiated by adding its command line to the PC's CONFIG.SYS file, such as

```
DEVICE=HITACHIA.SYS /D:MSCD000 /N:1 /P:300
```

Note: The DEVICE command may be replaced by the DEVICEHIGH command if you have available space in the upper memory area (UMA).

A CD-ROM device driver will typically have three command line switches associated with it. These parameters are needed to ensure that the driver installs properly. For the example command line shown above, the /D switch is the *name* used by the driver when it is installed in the system's device table. This name must be unique, and matched by the /D switch in the MSCDEX.EXE command line (covered later). The /N switch is the number of CD-ROM drives attached to the interface card. The default is 1 (which is typical for most general-purpose systems). Finally, the /P switch is the I/O port address the CD-ROM adapter card resides at. As you might expect, the port address shoud match the port address on the physical interface. If there is no /P switch, the default is 0300h.

MSCDEX.EXE

MS-DOS was developed in a time when no one anticipated that large files would be accessible to a PC, and it is severely limited in the file sizes that it can handle. With the development of CD-ROMs, Microsoft created an extension to MS-DOS that allows software publishers to access 650-MB CDs in a standard fashion—the Microsoft CD-ROM Extensions (MSCDEX). As with most software, MSCDEX offers some vital features (and a few limitations), but it is required by a vast majority of CD-ROM products. Obtaining MSCDEX is not a problem. It is generally provided on the same disc containing the CD-ROM's low-level device driver. New versions of MSCDEX can be obtained from the Microsoft Web site (www.microsoft.com), or from the Microsoft forum on CompuServe (GO MSL-1).

In actual operation, MSCDEX is loaded in the AUTOEXEC.BAT file. It should be loaded *after* any mouse driver, and loaded *before* any MENU, SHELL, DOSSHELL, or WIN line. It should also be loaded *before* any .BAT file is started. Keep in mind that if a .BAT file loads a network, MSCDEX must be included in the batch file *after* the network driver. Further, MSCDEX must be loaded after that network driver with the /S (share) switch in order to hook into the network driver chain. If you want to use the MS-DOS drive-caching software (SmartDrive) to buffer the CD-ROM drive(s), load MSCDEX *before* SmartDrive. The MSCDEX /M (number of buffers) switch can be set to 0 when using SmartDrive. If you find that SmartDrive is interfering with MPC applications like Video for Windows, you can load SmartDrive *before* MSCDEX., and set the /M switch for at least 2. When loading MSCDEX, remember that the MSCDEX /D switch *must* match the /D label used in the low-level driver. Otherwise, MSCDEX will not load. If SETVER is loaded in the CONFIG.SYS file, be sure to use the latest version of MSCDEX.

Although the vast majority of CD-ROM bundles include installation routines that automate the installation process for the low-level driver and MSCDEX, you should understand the various command line switches (shown in Table 9-3) that make MSCDEX operate. Understanding these switches may help you to overcome setup problems.

Troubleshooting CD-ROM Drives

Though the vast majority of CD-ROM problems are due to software or setup problems, the drives themselves are delicate and unforgiving devices. Considering that their prices have plummeted over the last few months (and still continue to drop), there is little economic sense in attempting a lengthy repair. When a fault occurs in the drive or in its adapter board, your best course is typically to replace the defective drive outright.

Table 9-3. MSCDEX Command Line Switches

/D:x	Device Name	The label used by the low-level device driver when it loads. MSCDEX must match this label for the device driver and MSCDEX to work together. A typical label is MSCD000.
/M:x	Buffers Allocated	The number of 2-KB buffers allocated to the CD-ROM drives. There are typically 8 buffers (16-kB) for a single drive, and 4 buffers for each additional drive. This number can be set to 1 or 2 if conventional memory space is at a premium.
/L:x	Drive Letter	This is the optional drive letter for the CD-ROM. If this is not specified, the drive will be automatically assigned to the first available letter (usually D:). There must be a LASTDRIVE= entry in CONFIG.SYS to use a letter higher than the default letter. When choosing a letter for the LASTDRIVE entry, do not use Z—otherwise, network drives may not install after MSCDEX.
/N	Verbose Option	This switch forces MSCDEX to show memory-usage statistics on the display each time the system boots.
/S	Share Option	This switch is used with CD-ROM installations in network systems.
/K	Kanji Option	Instructs MSCDEX to use Kanji (Japanese) file types on the CD if present.
/E	Expanded Memory	Allows MSCDEX to use expanded memory for buffers. There must be an expanded memory driver running (i.e., EMM386.EXE) with enough available space to use it.

Symptom 1: The drive has trouble accepting or rejecting a CD   This problem is typical of motorized CD-ROM drives where the disc is accepted into a slot or placed in a motorized tray. Before performing any disassembly, check the assembly through the CD slot for any obvious obstructions. If there is nothing obvious, expose the assembly and check each linkage and motor drive gear very carefully. Carefully remove or free any obstruction. Be gentle when working around the load/unload assembly. Notice how it is shock mounted in four places.

Disconnect the geared dc motor assembly and try moving the load/unload mechanism by hand. If you feel any resistance or obstruction, you should track it down by eye and by feel. Replace any worn or damaged part of the mechanism, or replace the entire load/unload assembly. Also check the geared motor for any damage or obstruction. Broken or slipping gear teeth can interfere with the transfer of force from motor to mechanism. Replace any damaged gears or replace the entire geared assembly. You may also simply replace the CD-ROM drive mechanism outright.

Symptom 2: Read heads do not seek   An optical head is used to identify pits and lands along a CD-ROM, and to track the spiral data pattern as the head moves across the disc. The optical head must move very slowly and smoothly to ensure accurate tracking. Head movement is accomplished using a linear stepping motor (or *linear actuator*) to shift the optical assembly in microscopic increments—head travel appears perfectly smooth to the unaided eye. Check the drive for any damaged parts or obstructions. When the optical head fails to seek, the easiest and fastest fix is simply to replace the CD-ROM mechanism outright.

Symptom 3: The disc cannot be read   This type of problem may result in a DOS level "sector not found" or "drive not ready" error. Before you reach for your tools, however, check the CD itself to ensure that it is the right format, inserted properly, and physically clean. Cleanliness is very important to a CD. While the laser will often look past any surface defects in a disc, the presence of dust or debris on a disc surface can produce serious tracking (and read) errors. Try a different disc to confirm the problem. If a new or different disc reads properly, the trouble may indeed be in (or *on*) the original disc itself. Not only the disc must be clean, but the head optics must also be clear. Gently dust or clean the head optics as suggested by your drive's manufacturer.

If read problems persist, check the physical interface cable between the drive and its adapter board. Be sure that the cable is connected correctly and completely. Many CD drives use SCSI interfaces. If you are using multiple SCSI devices from the same controller card and other SCSI devices are operating properly, the SCSI controller board is probably intact. If other SCSI devices are also malfunctioning, try a new SCSI host controller board. At this point, either the drive's optical head or electronics are defective. Your best course here is to try replacing the drive. If problems persist on a drive with a proprietary interface, replace the adapter board.

Symptom 4: The disc does not turn   The disc must turn at a constant linear velocity which is directed and regulated by the spindle. If the disc is not spinning during access, check to be sure that the disc is seated properly, and is not jammed or obstructed. Before beginning a repair, review your drive installation and setup carefully to ensure that the drive is properly configured for operation. If the drive's BUSY LED comes on when drive access is attempted (you may also see a corresponding DOS error message), the drive spindle system is probably defective. If the computer does not recognize the CD drive (i.e., `invalid drive specification`), there may be a setup or configuration problem (either the low-level device driver or MSCDEX may not have loaded properly). If your particular drive provides you with instructions for cleaning the optical head aperture, perform that cleaning operation and try the drive again. A fouled optical head can sometimes upset spindle operation. If operation does not improve, replace the CD-ROM drive mechanism.

Symptom 5: The optical head cannot focus its laser beam   As you saw earlier in this chapter, a CD-ROM drive must focus its laser beam to microscopic precision in order to read the pits and lands of a disc properly. To compensate for the minute fluctuations in disc flatness, the optical head mounts its objective lens into a small focusing mechanism which is little more than a miniature voice coil actuator—the lens does not have to move very much at all to maintain precise focus. If focus is out or not well maintained, the laser detector may produce erroneous signals. This may result in DOS drive error messages.

If random but consistent DOS errors appear, check the disc to be sure that it is *optically* clean dust and fingerprints can result in serious access problems. Try another disc. If a new disc continues to perform badly, try cleaning the optical aperture with clean (photography-grade) air. When problems persist, the optical system is probably damaged or defective. Try replacing the CD-ROM drive mechanism outright.

Symptom 6: There is no audio being generated by the drive   Many CD-ROM drives are capable of not only reading computer data, but reading and reproducing music and sounds under computer control. Audio CDs can often be played in available CD-ROM drives through headphones or speakers. Start your investigation by testing the headphones or speakers in another sound source such as a stereo. Once you have confirmed that the speakers or headphones are working reliably, check the drive's audio volume setting, which is usually available through the front bezel. Set the volume to a good average place (perhaps midrange). Make sure that the disc you are trying to play actually contains valid Red Book audio. Check any software required to operate the CD drive's audio output to be sure that it is installed and loaded as expected. CD-ROMs will not play audio CDs without an audio driver. Also check the *line output* which would drive amplified speakers or stereo inputs. If speakers work through the line output but headphones or speakers do not work through the front bezel connector, the volume control or output audio amplifier may be defective. If the headphone output continues to fail, replace the headphone PC board or replace the entire CD-ROM drive outright.

Symptom 7: Audio is not being played by the sound card Normally, the sound card will *not* play Red Book audio from a CD—that is usually fed directly to the CD's headphone or line output. However, audio can be channeled to the sound board for playback. Most CDs offer an audio connector that allows audio signals to be fed directly to the sound board. If this "CD audio cable" is missing or defective, Red Book audio will not play through the sound board. Check or replace the cable. If the cable is intact (and audio *is* available from the CD-ROM headphone output), check the sound board's configuration for any "mixer" applet (see that any control for CD audio is turned up, and remember to save any changes). If problems persist, try replacing the sound board. If the CD audio cable is intact (and audio is *not* available from the CD-ROM headphone output), the audio amplifier circuit in the CD-ROM is probably defective. Try replacing the CD-ROM drive.

Symptom 8: You see a WRONG DOS VERSION **error message when attempting to load MSCDEX** You are running MS-DOS 4, 5, or 6 with a version of MSCDEX which does not support it. The solution is then to change to the correct version of MSCDEX. The version compatibility for MSCDEX is shown below:

- v1.01   14,913 bytes (No ISO9660 support—High Sierra support only)
- v2.00   18,307 bytes (High Sierra and ISO9660 support for DOS 3.1–3.3)
- v2.10   19,943 bytes (DOS 3.1–3.3 and 4.0–DOS 5.X support provided with SETVER)
- v2.20   25,413 bytes (same as above with Win 3.x support—changes in audio support)
- v2.21   25,431 bytes (DOS 3.1–5.0 support with enhanced control under Win 3.1)
- v2.22   25,377 bytes (DOS 3.1–6.0 & higher with Win 3.1 support)
- v2.23   25,361 bytes (DOS 3.1–6.2 and Win 3.1 support—supplied with MSDOS 6.2)

When using MS-DOS 5.x to 6.1, you will need to add the SETVER utility to CONFIG.SYS in order to use MSCDEX v2.10 or v2.20 properly (i.e., DE-VICE=C:\DOS\SETVER.EXE). SETVER is used to tell programs that they are running under a different version of DOS than DOS 5.0. This is important since MSCDEX (v2.10 and v2.20) refuses to work with DOS versions higher than 4.0. SETVER is used to fool MSCDEX into working with higher versions of DOS. In some versions of DOS 5.0 (such as Compaq DOS 5.0), you will need to add an entry to SETVER for MSCDEX (i.e., SETVER MSCDEX.EXE 4.00). This entry modifies SETVER without changing the file size or date.

Symptom 9: You cannot access the CD-ROM drive letter You may see an error message such as "Invalid drive specification." This is typically a problem with the CD-ROM drivers. The MS-DOS extension MSCDEX has probably not loaded. Switch to the DOS subdirectory and use the MEM /C function to check the loaded drivers and TSRs. If you see the low-level driver and MSCDEX displayed in the driver list, check the CD-ROM hardware. Make sure that the data cable between the drive and adapter board is inserted properly and completely. If problems persist, try replacing the adapter board. If you do *not* see the low-level driver and MSCDEX shown in the driver list, inspect your CONFIG.SYS and AUTOEXEC.BAT files. Check that the drivers are included in the startup files to begin with. Make sure that the label used in the /D switch is the same for both the low-level driver and MSCDEX. If the label is not the same, MSCDEX will not load. If you are using MS-DOS 5.0, be sure the SETVER utility is loaded. You could also try updating MSCDEX to v2.30.

Symptom 10: You see an error message when trying to load the low-level CD-ROM driver   Check that you are using the proper low-level device driver for your CD-ROM drive. If you are swapping the drive or adapter board, you probably need to load a new driver. If the driver fails to load with original hardware, the adapter board may have failed, or its jumper settings may not match those in the driver's command line switches. Check the signal cable running between the drive and adapter board. If the cable is crimped or scuffed, try replacing the cable. Next, try replacing the adapter board. If problems persist, try replacing the CD-ROM drive mechanism itself.

Symptom 11: You see an error message such as `Error: not ready reading from drive D:`   Check that a suitable disc is inserted in the drive and that the drive is closed properly. Make sure that the low-level device driver and MSCDEX are loaded correctly. If the drivers do not load, there may be a problem with the adapter board or drive mechanism itself. Also check that the data cable between the drive and adapter is connected properly and completely. If problems persist, suspect a weakness in the PC power supply (especially if the system is heavily loaded or upgraded). Try a larger supply in the system. If problems persist, replace the CD-ROM drive. If a new drive does not correct the problem, try a different interface adapter.

Symptom 12: SmartDrive is not caching the CD-ROM properly   The version of SmartDrive supplied with DOS 6.2x provides three forms of caching, although older forms of SmartDrive (such as the ones distributed with Windows 3.1 and DOS 6.0 and 6.1) will *not* adequately cache CD-ROM drives. The BUFFERS statement also does *not* help caching. So if you are looking to SmartDrive for CD-ROM cache, you should be using the version distributed with DOS 6.2x. You should also set BUFFERS=10,0 in the CONFIG.SYS file, and the SmartDrive command line should come *after* MSCDEX. When using SmartDrive, you can change the buffers setting in the MSCDEX command line (/M) to 0. This allows you to save 2 kB per buffer.

Symptom 13: The CD-ROM drivers will not install properly on a drive using compression software   This is usually because you booted from a floppy disc and attempted to install drivers without loading the compression software first. Before doing anything else, check the loading order—allow your system to boot from the hard drive *before* installing the CD-ROM drivers. This allows the compression software to assign all drive letters. As an alternative, boot from a compression-aware floppy disc. If you *must* boot the system from a floppy disc, make sure the diskette is configured to be fully compatible with the compression software being used.

Symptom 14: You see an error message indicating that the CD-ROM drive is not found   This type of problem may also appear as loading problems with the low-level driver. There are several possible reasons why the drive hardware cannot be found. Check the power connector first, and make sure the 4-pin power connector is inserted properly and completely. If the drive is being powered by a Y-connector, make sure any interim connections are secure. Use a voltmeter and measure the +5-V (pin 4) and +12-V (pin 1) levels. If either voltage (especially the +12-V supply) is unusually low or absent, replace the power supply. Check the signal connector next and see that the drive's signal interface cable is connected securely at both the drive and controller. If the cable is visibly worn or damaged, try a new one.

Inspect the drive interface adapter and make sure that the adapter's IRQ, DMA, and I/O address settings are correct. They must also match with the command line switches used with the low-level driver. If the adapter is for a CD-ROM alone, you may also try installing the adapter in a different bus slot. If your CD-ROM uses a SCSI interface, make sure that the SCSI bus is properly terminated at both ends. If problems persist, replace the drive adapter.

Symptom 15: After installing the CD-ROM driver software, the system reports significantly less available RAM   This is usually a caching issue with CD-ROM driver software, and you may need to adjust the CD-ROM driver software accordingly. This type of problem has been documented with Teac CD-ROM drives and CORELCDX.COM software. If the software offers a command line switch to change the amount of XMS allocated, reduce the number to 512 or 256. Check with tech support for your particular drive for the exact command line switch settings.

Symptom 16: In a new installation, the driver fails to load successfully for the proprietary interface card   In almost all cases, the interface card has been configured improperly. Check the drive adapter card first. Make sure that the drive adapter is configured with the correct IRQ, DMA, and I/O address settings, and check for hardware conflicts with other devices in the system. In some cases, you may simply enter the drive maker (i.e., Teac) as the interface type during driver installation. Make sure that the interface is set properly for the system, and your particular drive. Check the driver's command line next—the driver's command line switches should correctly reflect the drive adapter's configuration.

Symptom 17: The CD-ROM driver loads successfully, but you see an error message such as: CDR101 (drive not ready) **or** CDR103 (CDROM risk not HIGH SIERRA or ISO)   You are using a very old version of the low-level driver or MSCDEX. Check your driver version (it may be outdated). Contact the drive manufacturer's tech support and see that you have the very latest version of the low-level driver. For very old drives, there may also be a later "generic" driver available. Check your version of MSCDEX next. Since low-level drivers are often bundled with MSCDEX, you may also be stuck with an old version of MSCDEX. You can usually download a current version of MSCDEX from the same place you get an updated low-level driver, or download it from Microsoft at http://www.microsoft.com.

Symptom 18: You are having trouble setting up more than one CD-ROM drive You must be concerned about hardware and software issues. Check the drive adapter first—make sure that the drive adapter will support more than one CD-ROM on the same channel. If not, you will have to install another drive adapter to support the new CD-ROM drive. Low-level drivers present another problem since you will need to have one copy of a low-level driver loaded in CONFIG.SYS—one for each drive. Make sure that the command line switches for each driver match the hardware settings of the corresponding drive adapter. Finally, check your copy of MSCDEX. You need only one copy of MSCDEX in AUTOEXEC.BAT, but the /D: switch must appear twice—once for each drive ID.

Symptom 19: Your CD-ROM drive refuses to work with an IDE port It may very well be that the drive uses a nonstandard port (other than IDE). Try replacing the drive adapter board. You must connect the CD-ROM drive to a compatible drive adapter. If the drive is proprietary, it will not interface to a regular IDE port. It may be necessary to purchase a drive adapter specifically for the CD-ROM drive.

Symptom 20: You cannot get the CD-ROM drive to run properly when mounted vertically CD-ROM drives with "open" drive trays cannot be mounted vertically—disc tracking simply will not work correctly. The only CD-ROM drives that can be mounted vertically are those with caddies, but you should check with those manufacturers before proceeding with vertical mounting.

Symptom 21: The SCSI CD-ROM drive refuses to work when connected to an Adaptec SCSI interface (other drives are working fine) This is a common type of problem among SCSI adapters, and is particularly recognized with Adaptec boards because of their great popularity. In most cases, the Adaptec drivers are the wrong version or are corrupted. Try turning off Sync Negotiations on the Adaptec SCSI interface, and reboot the system. Your SCSI drivers may also be buggy or outdated. Check with Adaptec technical support (www.adaptec.com) to determine if there are later drivers that you should use instead.

Symptom 22: You see a `No drives found` **error message when the CD-ROM driver line is executed in CONFIG.SYS** In most cases, the driver command line switches do not match the hardware configuration of the drive adapter. Your low-level driver may be missing or incomplete. Open CONFIG.SYS into a word processor and see that the low-level driver has a complete and accurate command line. See that any command line switches are set correctly. Check the MSCDEX command line next. Open AUTOEXEC.BAT into a word processor and see that the MSCDEX command line is accurate and complete. Also confirm that any MSCDEX command line switches are set correctly. If you are using SmartDrive with

DOS 6.0 or later, try adding the /U switch to the end of your SmartDrive command line in AUTOEXEC.BAT. Check for hardware conflicts. Make sure that there are no other hardware devices in the system that may be conflicting with the CD-ROM drive controller. If problems persist, replace the drive controller.

Symptom 23: The LCD on your CD-ROM displays an error code   Even without knowing the particular meaning of *every* possible error message, you can be assured that most CD-based error messages can be traced to the following causes (in order of ease):

- **Bad caddy.**   The CD caddy is damaged or inserted incorrectly. The CD may also be inserted into the caddy improperly.
- **Bad mounting.**   The drive is mounted improperly, or mounting screws are shorting out the drive's electronics.
- **Bad power.**   Check the +12 and +5 V powering the CD-ROM drive. Low power may require a new or larger supply.
- **Bad drive.**   Internal diagnostics have detected a fault in the CD-ROM drive. Try replacing the drive.
- **Bad drive controller.**   Drive diagnostics have detected a fault in the drive controller. Try replacing the drive controller or SCSI adapter (whichever interface you're using).

Symptom 24: When a SCSI CD-ROM drive is connected to a SCSI adapter, the system hangs when the SCSI BIOS starts   In most cases, the CD-ROM drive supports plug and play, but the SCSI controller's BIOS does not. Disable the SCSI BIOS through a jumper on the controller (or remove the SCSI BIOS IC entirely) and use a SCSI driver in CONFIG.SYS instead. You may need to download a low-level SCSI driver from the adapter manufacturer.

Symptom 25: You see an error message such as Unable to detect ATAPI IDE CD-ROM drive, device driver not loaded You have a problem with the configuration of your IDE/EIDE controller hardware. Check the signal cable first, and make sure that the 40-pin signal cable is attached properly between the drive and controller. IDE CD-ROM drives are typically installed on a secondary 40-pin IDE port. Make sure that there is no device in the system using the same IRQ or I/O address as your secondary IDE port. Finally, make sure that any command line switches for the low-level driver in CONFIG.SYS correspond to the controller's hardware settings.

Symptom 26: The CD-ROM drive door will not open once the 40-pin IDE signal cable is connected   You should only need power to operate the drive door. If the door stops when the signal cable is attached, there are some possible problems to check. Check the power connector first, and make sure that both +5 and +12 V are available at the power connector. See that the power connector is attached securely to the back of the CD-ROM drive. Check the IDE signal cable next—the 40-pin signal cable is probably reversed at either the drive or controller. Try a different signal cable. Also make sure that the 40-pin IDE drive is plugged into a "true" IDE port—not a proprietary (non-IDE 40-pin) port. If problems persist, try a known-good CD-ROM drive.

Symptom 27: You are using an old CD-ROM and can play CD audio, but you cannot access directories or other computer data from a CD Older proprietary CD-ROM drives often used two low-level drivers—one for audio, and one for data—you probably only have one of the drivers installed. Check your low-level drivers first, and see that any necessary low-level drivers are loaded in the CONFIG.SYS file. Also see that any command line switches are set properly. Some older sound boards with integrated proprietary CD-ROM drive controllers may not work properly with the drivers required for your older CD-ROM drive. You may have to alter the proprietary controller's IRQ, DMA, or I/O settings (and update the driver's command line switches) until you find a combination where the driver and controller will work together.

Symptom 28: The front panel controls of your SCSI CD-ROM drive do not appear to work under Windows 95 Those same controls appear to work fine in DOS. Windows 95 uses SCSI commands to poll removable-medium devices every 2 s in order to see if there has been a change in status. Since SCSI commands to the CD-ROM generally have higher priority than front panel controls, the front panel controls may appear to be disabled under Windows 95. Try pressing the front panel controls repeatedly. You may be able to correct this issue by disabling the CD-ROM polling under Windows 95.

Symptom 29: You cannot change the CD-ROM drive letter under Windows 95 You need to change the drive's settings under the Device Manager.

- Open the Control Panel and select the System icon.
- Once the System Properties dialog opens, click on the Device Manager page.
- Locate the entry for the CD-ROM. Click on the + sign to expand the list of CD-ROM devices.
- Double-click on the desired CD-ROM.
- Once the CD-ROM drive's Properties dialog appears, choose the Settings page.
- Locate the current drive letter assignment box and enter the new drive designation. Multiple letters are needed only when a SCSI device is implementing LUN addressing (i.e., multidisc changers).
- Click on the OK button to save your changes.
- Click on the OK button to close the Device Manager.
- A System Settings Change window should appear. Click on the Yes button to reboot the system so that the changes can take effect, or click on the No button so that you can make more changes to other CD-ROMs before rebooting system. Changes will not become effective until the system is rebooted.

Symptom 30: You installed Windows 95 from a CD-ROM disc using DOS drivers, but when you removed the real-mode CD-ROM drivers from CONFIG.SYS, the CD-ROM no longer works You need to enable protected-mode drivers by running the Add New Hardware wizard from the Control Panel.

- Boot Windows 95 using the real-mode drivers for your CD-ROM and its interface.
- Open the Control Panel and select the Add New Hardware icon.
- Proceed to add new hardware, but do *not* let Windows 95 attempt to autodetect the new hardware. Use the diskette with protected-mode drivers for the new installation.
- When the new software is installed, Windows 95 will tell you that it must reboot before the hardware will be available—do *not* reboot yet.
- Open a word processor such as Notepad, and edit the CONFIG.SYS and AUTOEXEC.BAT files to REMark out the real-mode drivers for your CD and the reference to MSCDEX.
- Shut down Windows 95, then power down the system.
- Check to be sure that the CD-ROM interface is set to use the resources assigned by Windows 95.
- Reboot the system—your protected-mode drivers should now load normally.

Symptom 31: Your CD-ROM drive's parallel-port-to-SCSI interface worked with Windows 3.1x, but does not work under Windows 95   This problem is typical of the NEC CD-EPPSCSI01 interface, and is usually due to a problem with the driver's assessment of your parallel-port type (i.e., bidirectional, unidirectional, or enhanced parallel port). Start your CMOS setup routine first and see what mode your parallel port is set to operate in. Make sure it is set to a mode which is compatible with your parallel-port drive. Next, update your version of MSCDEX. Change the MSCDEX command line in AUTOEXEC.BAT to load from the C:\WINDOWS\CONTROL\ directory, and remove the /L:x parameter from the end of the MSCDEX command line (if present). Finally, cold boot the computer. Since typical parallel-port-to-SCSI interfaces get their power from the SCSI device, the external drive must be powered up *first*. If you're using real-mode drivers for the interface, place a switch at the end of the interface's command line that tells the driver what mode your parallel port is operating in. For example, the Trantor T358 driver (MA358.SYS) uses the following switches (yours will probably be different):

- /m02   for unidirectional mode (also known as "standard" or "output only")
- /m04   for bidirectional mode (also known as PS/2 mode)
- /m08   for enhanced mode

As an alternative, disable your real-mode drivers. Remove or REMark out any references to the interface's real-mode drivers in CONFIG.SYS, then remove or disable the MSCDEX command line in AUTOEXEC.BAT. Start Windows 95, open the Control Panel, select the System icon, then choose the Device Manager page. Find the SCSI adapter settings and expand the SCSI Controllers branch of the device tree. Select the device identification line for your parallel-port-to-SCSI interface, then click on the Properties button. Click on the Settings page. In the Adapter Settings dialog box, type in the same parameter that would have been used if you were using real-mode drivers. Click on the OK buttons to save your changes, then select Yes to reboot the system. If problems persist, check the technical support for your parallel-port-to-SCSI adapter and see if there are any known problems with your particular setup, or any updated drivers available for download.

Symptom 32: You see a message stating that the `CD-ROM can run, but results may not be as expected` This simply means that Windows 95 is using real-mode drivers. If protected-mode drivers are available for the CD-ROM drive, you should use those instead.

Symptom 33: The CD-ROM works fine in DOS or Windows 3.1x, but sound or video appears choppy under Windows 95 There are several factors that can affect CD-ROM performance under Windows 95. Windows 95 performance (and stability) is severely degraded by real-mode drivers, so start by removing or disabling any real-mode drivers. Try installing the protected-mode drivers for your CD-ROM drive instead. If protected-mode drivers are not available for your drive, you may consider upgrading the CD-ROM hardware.

Also avoid using DOS or Windows 3.1x applications under Windows 95. Real-mode applications run under Windows 95 can also cripple performance. Try exiting any DOS or Windows 3.1x applications that may be running on the Windows 95 desktop. Also exit unneeded Windows 95 applications since additional applications take a toll on processing power. Try exiting any Windows 95 applications that may be running in the background. Finally, try rebooting the system to ensure that Windows 95 has the maximum amount of resources available before running your CD-ROM application.

DVD Drives

The early appeal of CD-ROM drives were compelling; they offered huge storage compared to 100- to 200-MB hard drives of the day, and the removable medium means virtually limitless storage potential. In spite of their relatively slow speed, CD-ROM drives lived up to their potential. In today's world of 4- to 5-GB hard drives and high-performance Pentium MMX systems, the 650-MB CD-ROM is beginning to show its age—especially when faced with the challenges of real-time video and audio software. Even with file compression and MPEG techniques, the conventional CD is limited by data-intensive multimedia. The entertainment industry wants to put two hours of high-quality sound and video on a single disc, and the computer industry sees a new level of sophistication in computer games and training products. The push was on for a new generation of high-capacity CD-ROM drives. The result of this development is the DVD drive (also called digital video disc or digital versatile disc).

DVD technology

At its core, DVD technology is identical to classical CD-ROMs. Data are recorded in a spiral pattern as a series of pits and lands pressed into a plastic substrate. The actual size and dimensions of a DVD are identical to our current CDs. However, there are some key differences which give DVD its advantages. First, data are highly compressed on the DVD—where classical CDs use spiral tracks that are 1.6 μm apart, DVD tracks are only 0.74 μm apart. A typical pit on a classic CD is 0.83 μm, but DVD pits are just 0.4 μm. In short, the data on a DVD are much denser than on a regular CD. In order to detect these smaller geometries, the laser used in a DVD operates at a much shorter wavelength.

Second, DVD can employ multiple "layers" of pits and lands (each in their own reflective layer), so one physical disc can hold several layers worth of data. The laser focus control can select which layer to read. Finally, a regular CD only uses one side of the disc, but *both* sides of the DVD can be used. Combined with this multilayer technique, the DVD can supply up to four "layers" of data to a DVD drive. In actual practice, computer DVDs will likely only use one side of the disc...at least for a while. What all this means is that a DVD can offer up to 8.5 GB of storage for a single-sided DVD, or up to 17 GB of storage for a double-sided DVD. In addition, the DVD drives are backward-compatible with ordinary CDs, so your new system equipped with a DVD drive will be able to use all of your existing CDs.

The DVD "books"

As with ordinary CDs, DVD technologies are specified through a series of "books." For the DVD, the books are listed as A through E—each related to different applications of DVD. Book A focuses on DVD-ROM (read-only discs for computer data). Book B outlines DVD-video which includes descriptions of MPEG compression techniques. Book C covers DVD-audio and audio compression methods. As you probably imagine, Books B and C are of particular interest to the entertainment industry. Book D handles DVD-WO (write-once) drives, so DVD recorders are certainly in the near future. Finally, Book E deals with DVD-E which is erasable (a.k.a. rewriteable) medium. There is a discussion of DVD-RAM covered by Book E, which is intended to function essentially as a removable hard drive.

In actual practice, the disc data format used for Books A, B, and C is referred to as the Universal Disc Format (or UDF). The UDF was created by OSTA (Optical Storage Technology Association), and is referred to as the ISO/IEC 13346 standard. The UDF defines DVD data structures like volumes, files, blocks, sectors, CRCs, paths, records, allocation tables, and partitions—everything needed to allow DVD to serve as a computer data medium. The UDF is intended to be backward-compatible with the existing ISO-9660 standards used to define CD-ROMs.

There are other standards related to emerging DVD technologies. For video, you will probably see MPEG-1 (ISO/IEC 1117-2) video at 30 frames per second at 352×240 resolution, and MPEG-2 (ISO/IEC 13818-2) video providing 60 frames per second at 720×480 resolution. For audio, you will encounter MPEG-1 (ISO/IEC 1117-3) stereo, MPEG-2 (ISO/IEC 13818-3) 5.1 and 7.1 surround, and Dolby AC-3 5.1 surround.

10
CHAPTER

Other Drives

When you think about "PC drives," you probably think about the four classical types of drives: floppy drives, hard drives, tape drives, and CD-ROM drives. These are the most widely accepted and supported drives available today. However, drive designers are always looking for ways to provide better and faster storage solutions, and pack ever-more data onto smaller, more efficient media. As a result, the PC industry often deals with a number of "nonstandard" drives—devices which utilize existing magnetic and optical technologies, but do not easily fit the mold of other drives. Nonstandard drives are also traditionally after-market or add-on devices that are attached through a parallel port or external SCSI interface. Iomega and SyQuest are perhaps the two largest and best-respected makers of nonstandard drives, and this chapter will look at the background and troubleshooting of the four most popular nonstandard drives: the Iomega Zip drive, the Iomega Ditto drive, the Iomega Bernoulli drive, and the SyQuest drive.

Iomega Zip Drive

In order for a "removable medium" to be popular, it must follow three basic guidelines: it must record quickly, it must hold a lot of data on a single cartridge (or other medium), and it must be portable between drives. Floppy drives are very portable, but they hold only a little data. Tapes hold a lot of data, but they are slow and are not very portable between drives. Hard drives are quite fast and hold a great deal of data, but they are simply not portable. CD-ROM drives are relatively fast, they also hold a lot of data, and they are very portable, but you need specialized drives to "burn" a CD—and the disk can be used only once. The search for a reusable, high-capacity medium that is transportable between inexpensive, readily available drives has led Iomega to produce their Zip drive.

The Zip drive has become perhaps the single most popular nonstandard drive in production today. Zip drives offer relatively fast seek times at 29 ms and can sustain data rates of 300 kB/s across the parallel port, or 1 MB/s via SCSI or IDE interfaces. Each cartridge can hold up to 100 MB which is large enough to hold huge illustrations, CAD layouts, and even small multimedia presentations. When used with a SCSI interface and a properly configured Adaptec SCSI controller, you may even boot from the Zip drive. Zip drives are available in both internal and external versions.

Zip drive troubleshooting

Symptom 1: An Iomega Zip drive displays a floppy disk icon under Windows 95   However, the drive appears to operate properly. This is almost always due to the use of a real-mode DOS driver to support the Iomega drive and adapter. You will need to update the real-mode driver to an appropriate protected-mode driver for Windows 95. For SCSI adapters, you need to find the protected-mode SCSI driver for your particular SCSI adapter and install it through the Add New Hardware wizard in the Control Panel. After the protected-mode driver is installed, you can remove the obsolete real-mode driver from CONFIG.SYS. For native Iomega SCSI adapters, get the protected-mode drivers directly from Iomega. For parallel-port Zip drives, uninstall the old drive software and install the new Windows 95 driver software.

Symptom 2: There is no drive letter for the SCSI Zip drive under Windows 95   The drive does not appear to respond. In virtually all cases, the SCSI driver has not loaded properly. First, open the Device Manager and expand the SCSI Controllers entry, then check the Iomega Adapter line beneath it. If there is a yellow symbol with an exclamation mark on it, the Windows 95 driver did not load. Check the controller next by highlighting that Iomega Adapter line, then select Properties. Click on the Resources page, then verify that your I/O Range and IRQ options are set correctly—they *must* match the jumper settings on your adapter board. If you must update the resource settings manually, make sure the Automatic Settings box is *not* checked (and remember to save any changes). If you allocated new resources, you may have to shut off the PC and change jumper settings on the controller board itself to match the resources allocated in the Device Manager. Restart the computer—once the system reboots, the Windows 95 driver should load normally.

If problems persist, check the signal connector (especially for SCSI adapters). Make sure the SCSI cable is intact and connected to the drive properly. If problems continue, your SCSI adapter is probably installed correctly, but the bus may be terminated improperly. Make sure that you terminate both ends of the SCSI bus properly.

Symptom 3: There is no drive letter for the parallel-port Zip drive under Windows 95   Parallel-port drive problems can almost always be traced to faulty connections, port configuration issues, or driver problems. Check the external power connector first. Parallel-port drives are powered externally. Make sure that the power pack is working, and see that the power cable is connected properly to the drive. If the drive does not appear to power up, try a different power pack or drive. Check the signal cable next, and make sure that you are using a good-quality, known-good parallel-port cable which is attached securely at the PC and drive. The Zip drive is very sensitive to devices such as copy-protection modules (or "dongles"), and other "pass-through" devices. Try connecting the drive directly to the parallel port. Also disconnect any printers on the parallel port.

The parallel-port setup may be incorrect. Reboot the PC and enter CMOS Setup. Check to see that the parallel port is configured in EPP or bidirectional mode. If the problem continues in the EPP mode, try configuring the parallel port for "compatibility mode." Check the SCSI host controller. There is a known incompatibility between the Iomage Zip drive and the Adaptec 284x adapter. The Iomega PPA3 driver does not work with the Adaptec 284x controller. Check with Iomega for an updated driver.

There may be a problem with your driver(s). Open the Device Manager and find the SCSI Controllers entry (even though it is a parallel-port device). If there is no such entry, the driver is not installed. If you expand the SCSI Controllers section, there should be an entry for the Iomega Parallel Port Zip Interface. If not, the driver is not installed. Check for hardware conflicts. If the Device Manager entry for the Iomega Parallel Port Zip Interface has a yellow circle with an exclamation mark on it, the interface is configured improperly and is conflicting with other devices. Also check for device properties. Highlight the Iomega Parallel Port Zip Interface entry, click on Properties, then select the Settings page. Find the box marked Adapter Settings, then type

```
/mode:nibble /speed:1
```

Save your changes and reboot the system. If that fails, try reinstalling the drivers. Highlight the Iomega Parallel Port Zip Interface and select Remove. Then reinstall the drivers from scratch. Next, try running in DOS. Start the PC in DOS mode (command prompt only), then install the Iomega installation disk and type

```
a:\guest      <Enter>
```

If the Zip drive still does not receive a drive letter, the parallel port may be faulty or incompatible with the drive. Try the drive on another system. If this tactic works on another system, the problem is definitely related to your original PC hardware. If the problem follows the drive, the fault is likely in the drive. Try another drive.

Symptom 4: The system hangs when installing drivers for Windows 95
System hangups during installation are usually the result of hardware conflicts or problems. Check the signal cable first, and make sure that you are using a good-quality, known-good cable which is attached securely at the PC and drive. Open the Device Manager and find the SCSI Controllers. If there is no such entry, the driver is not installed. If you expand the SCSI Controllers section, there should be an entry for the Iomega Parallel Port Zip Interface. If not, the driver is not installed.

Check for hardware conflicts. If the Device Manager entry for the Iomega Parallel Port Zip Interface has a yellow circle with an exclamation mark on it, the interface is configured improperly and is conflicting with other devices. Highlight the Iomega Parallel Port Zip Interface entry, click on Properties, then select the Settings page. Find the box marked Adapter Settings, then type

```
/mode:nibble /speed:1
```

Save your changes and reboot the system. If problems continue, try running in DOS. Start the PC in DOS mode (command prompt only), then install the Iomega installation disk and type

```
a:\guest     <Enter>
```

If the Zip drive still does not receive a drive letter, the parallel port may be faulty or incompatible with the drive. Try the drive on another system. If this tactic works on another system, the problem is definitely related to your original PC hardware. If the problem follows the drive, the fault is likely in the drive. Try another drive.

Symptom 5: The Zip drive takes over the CD-ROM drive letter in Windows 95   You may simply need to switch drive letters between the Zip drive and CD-ROM drive.

- Open Device Manager and double-click on the Disk Drives entry.
- Highlight the Iomega Zip drive entry and click on Properties.
- Click on the Settings page.
- In the Reserved Drive Letters section, there is a Start Drive Letter and an End Drive Letter setting. Enter the desired drive letter for the Zip drive in both start and end drive entries (be sure to use the same drive letter for both start and end). Click on OK.
- Double-click on the CD-ROM entry.
- Highlight your CD-ROM Drive entry and click on Properties.
- Click on the Settings page.
- In the Reserved Drive Letters section, there is a Start Drive Letter and an End Drive Letter setting. Enter the desired drive letter for the CD-ROM drive in both start and end entries (be sure to use the same drive letter for both start and end). Click on OK.
- Click on OK to close Device Manager, then shut down and restart the computer.

Symptom 6: You encounter duplicate ZIP drive letters   You notice that the Zip drive (or another drive) has been assigned a duplicate drive letter. In most cases, the problem can be traced to a third-party SCSI adapter and drivers which conflict with Iomega SCSI drivers. *Do not use any drive before correcting this problem.* Open your CONFIG.SYS file and examine each driver that scans the SCSI bus to assign drive letters. Chances are very good that you have a third-party driver which is assigning a letter to the Zip drive, as well as an Iomega-specific driver assigning another letter to the Zip drive. Use a command line switch with the third-party SCSI driver to limit the number of IDs that will be assigned.

Symptom 7: A Zip guest locks up or cannot locate the drive or adapter
Chances are that an ASPI manager referenced in the GUEST.INI file is conflicting with hardware in the PC. This often happens in systems with two SCSI adapters (and parallel ports). Try editing the GUEST.INI file. Open the GUEST.INI file on your Iomega install disk and specify *which* ASPI manager needs to load in order to access the Zip drive. Remember to make a backup copy of the GUEST.INI file before

editing it. As an alternative, choose the Iomega SCSI adapter driver. If you are using a native Iomega SCSI adapter, choose the ASPI manager that applies to the adapter as shown in Table 10-1. Once you have identified the proper ASPI manager for your adapter, REMark-out all of the other ASPI lines in GUEST.INI except for the one that you need.

If you are using a non-Iomega SCSI adapter, you will need to add the complete path and filename for the driver to GUEST.INI, and REMark-out all of the other ASPI drivers. Once the GUEST.INI file is updated, save your changes and reboot the system, then run GUEST from the drive and directory containing the updated GUEST.INI file. If problems persist, try the drive on another system, or try a new drive on the suspect system.

Symptom 8: You encounter Zip drive letter problems under DOS   The drive letters following C: may change unexpectedly when Iomega drivers are installed to support a new device. This can interfere with applications that look at specific drives or access to network resources. You will need to relocate the drives before installing Iomega software. Since the GUEST.EXE utility loads at the end of AUTOEXEC.BAT, the Iomega drive will be assigned the last drive letter. DOS assigns letters to network drives alphabetically after assigning letters to any internal or external drives connected to the computer. When a new drive is added, the network drive may be "pushed down" one letter (i.e., from E: to F:). Applications that reference specific drive letters may then fail to work correctly unless they are reinstalled or adjusted for the drive letter change. If you use a batch file to connect to a network, it will need to be updated to the new drive letter. A network log-in script may also need to be revised.

Use the DOS LASTDRIVE = command to relocate your first network drive letter further down the alphabet. This insulates your network drive letter assignment from future changes should you add other drives to your system. For example, you can make your network drive N: by adding the following line to the end of CONFIG.SYS. This would allow you to add ten drives (D: through M:) to a system without pushing down your network drive letter.

```
LASTDRIVE=M
```

Table 10-1. A Listing of Native Iomega ASPI Drivers

Iomega adapter	ASPI manager
Zip Zoom SCSI accelerator	ASPIPC16.SYS
Jaz Jet SCSI accelerator	ASPI2930.SYS
Parallel-Port Zip drive	ASPIPPA3.SYS or ASPIPPM1.SYS
PPA-3 adapter	ASPIPPA3.SYS
PC1616	ASPIPC16.SYS
PC800	ASPIPC8.SYS
PC2	ASPIPC2.SYS
PC4	ASPIPC4.SYS

Note: Do not set your last drive to Z: or you will be unable to access any network drive. If you use multiple network drives, do not set your last drive to a letter late in the alphabet (such as X: or Y:) since that will limit the number of network drives you can use simultaneously.

Check your CD-ROM drive letters. CD-ROM drives have a specific drive letter determined by the /L option of MSCDEX in AUTOEXEC.BAT (e.g., /L:E assigns the CD-ROM as drive E:). When a new drive is installed, DOS may assign the CD-ROM drive letter to the new drive, and the CD-ROM drive may seem to disappear. Change the drive letter for the CD-ROM to a letter not assigned to another drive. You may want to relocate your CD-ROM drive several letters down the alphabet so that you do not have to relocate it each time you add a new drive to your system. You must have a LASTDRIVE statement in CONFIG.SYS which sets the last drive equal to or later than the CD-ROM letter. Finally, check the overall system configuration. When DOS *does* reassign drive letters, be sure to check each of the points below:

- Edit the PATH statement in AUTOEXEC.BAT to correctly reference new drive letter.
- Edit any batch files (including AUTOEXEC.BAT) to correctly reference new drive letters.
- Edit all Windows .INI files and Windows groups to correctly reference new drive letters.
- Check other application setup files and rerun the application's setup if drive letters cannot be edited.
- For networks, check your user log-in script for references to specific network drive letters.
- Reboot the computer and check major applications—those that do not work with the new drive letter may need to be reinstalled.

Symptom 9: The GUEST utility cannot find an available drive letter   If all drive letters are in use, GUEST will not be able to assign a drive letter to the Zip drive. Change the last drive designation. Use the DOS LASTDRIVE command in the end of CONFIG.SYS to increase the number of available drive letters. Do not use a letter near the end of the alphabet.

Symptom 10: System recovery fails after the Zip Tools setup process is complete   If the Zip Tools software for your Zip drive fails to install properly (or if the system hangs or was powered down), the Windows Startup group will have a Zip Setup icon that will attempt to run each time Windows is started. Delete the Zip icon in your Startup group, then reinstall the Zip software.

Symptom 11: You see error messages such as `Can't Find Zip Tools Disk` **or** `No Drive Letters Added` **when using Zip parallel-port drives**   In most cases, you will have to assign the proper ASPI driver by editing your GUEST.INI file manually. Open the GUEST.INI file on your Iomega install disk. Highlight the ASPI driver line that reads ASPIPPA3.SYS, then add the following commands; /MODE=1 /SPEED=1. Remember to make a backup copy of the GUEST.INI file before editing it. The final command line should appear such as

```
ASPI=ASPIPPA3.SYS SCAN /INFO SL360=NO SMC=NO /MODE=1 /SPEED=1
```

Save your changes to GUEST.INI, then run GUEST from the drive and directory that contains your edited GUEST.INI file. GUEST should now assign a drive letter to the Zip drive. Reboot the PC, start Windows, then run the Iomega Setup routine from the drive and directory which contains your edited GUEST.INI file. The Windows installation should now proceed normally.

Next, check the signal connector and make sure that the parallel-port or SCSI cable is connected properly between the drive and system. Try a known-good working signal cable. If problems persist, boot the system from a "clean" diskette and try running GUEST. If a drive letter is assigned properly, then there is a driver loading in CONFIG.SYS or AUTOEXEC.BAT which conflicts with the Zip drive. You will have to systematically locate the offending driver. Finally, try the Zip drive on another PC. If GUEST works on another PC, the original PC is using an incompatible parallel port. If the drive still refuses to work, try another Zip drive.

Symptom 12: Windows 3.11 allows network drive letter to conflict with Zip drive letter You may see this as a No Zip Tools Disk Detected message. The drive may also no longer be accessible from the File Manager or DOS prompt. The problem is that Windows for Workgroups allows GUEST to assign a drive letter that is already used by a network drive. Remap the shared volume. Since GUEST is typically run first, you will need to alter the network drive letter under Windows for Workgroups.

Symptom 13: The Zip drive setup could not find a Zip Tools disk for Zip parallel-port drives This is usually an issue with the GUEST.INI file which needs to be edited for proper operation. Start the system from a clean floppy diskette, insert the Iomega installation disk, then try running the GUEST utility. If a drive letter is assigned, there may be a driver in CONFIG.SYS or AUTOEXEC.BAT conflicting with the Zip drive. If GUEST fails to assign a Zip drive letter from a clean boot, open the GUEST.INI file in a text editor, locate the ASPI=ASPIPPA3.SYS line, then add the switches; /MODE=1 /SPEED=1 which makes the complete command line appear like

```
ASPI=ASPIPPA3.SYS SCAN /INFO SL360=NO SMC=NO /MODE=1 /SPEED=1
```

Reboot the PC and run the GUEST utility again. If GUEST does run, but you still cannot read the Zip Tools disk, make sure that the signal cables are secure between the drive and system. If problems persist, try the Zip drive on another PC. If GUEST works on another PC, the original PC is using an incompatible parallel port. If the drive still refuses to work, try another Zip drive.

Symptom 14: You cannot print while using a ZIP drive The Iomega parallel port Zip drive works as a "pass-through" device, and the software allows the drive to share a parallel port with printers. However, some printers require two-way communication between the printer and parallel port which conflicts with the Zip software. This can cause data corruption and system lockups. In many cases, disabling the bidirectional communication features of the printer will clear the problem.

Canon BJ-610/Canon BJC 610   These printers use drivers that are incompatible with the Zip drive. The drivers reserve the parallel port exclusively for the operation of the printer, and the Zip drive is unable to access the port (and will usually result in a system lockup when the drive is accessed). The drivers for the Canon printers must be removed. The installation program for the printers will add the following lines to the [386Enh] section of your SYSTEM.INI file. These entries must be removed

```
DEVICE=WPSRCOM.386
DEVICE=WPSCREM.386
DEVICE=WPSRBND.386
```

The following line in WIN.INI will also have to be removed:

```
LOAD=WPSLOAD.EXE
```

At this point, the Zip drive will function, but the printer will not (at least not in its high-resolution modes). To restore full printer operation, you will need to reinstall the Canon drivers.

Canon Multi-Pass 1000   You cannot use this printer and the parallel-port Zip drive at the same time. The only way to make this printer and drive compatible is to change the output of the printer to "File" when you need to use the Zip drive, then back to "LPT1" when you want to use the printer. Use the following procedure to toggle the output from File to LPT1 under Windows 95:

- Double-click on My Computer.
- Double-click on Properties.
- Right mouse button click on the Canon Printer.
- Click on Details.
- Click the down arrow button in the window labeled "Print to the following port."
- Click on FILE (to switch back, choose LPT1).
- Click on OK at the bottom of your screen.

Hewlett-Packard 4S, 4+, 4V, 4SI, 4L, 4P, and 5P   You need to disable the bidirectional communication between the printer and system. This can be accomplished by executing the following command from the RUN command line;

```
c:\windows\dinstall -fdinstall.ins
```

You can also use the procedure outlined below:

- Bring up the WIN.INI file through either SYSEDIT (in Windows) or EDIT (in DOS).
- In the first section of this file, you should see a line that reads LOAD=HPSW.EXE. You need to disable this line by inserting a semicolon (;) at the beginning of the line.
- Now scroll down to the section labeled [Spooler] and insert a semicolon (;) at the beginning of the line that reads; QP.LPT1=HPLJ4QP.DLL.
- Save the WIN.INI file, exit Windows, and restart the system.

You can now use the HP printer and Zip drive together. These changes will not affect the printer—they just disable the status windows that may pop up telling the current status of the printer.

Hewlett-Packard 5l   If you installed your printer using the HOST option, you will need to uninstall the printer then reinstall it using the PCL option. In your WIN.INI file, disable the line that reads LOAD=HPLJSW.EXE by placing a semicolon at the beginning of the line. You will need to do the same with the line that reads QP.LPT1=??? in the [Spooler] section of your WIN.INI file.

Symptom 15: You encounter problems installing a Zip SCSI drive   In virtually all cases, SCSI problems can be traced to hardware problems or driver issues. Make sure that power is provided to the drive (see that the drive power light comes on). See that the SCSI signal cable is intact and connected securely between the drive and SCSI adapter. Try a new signal cable. Both ends of the SCSI bus must be terminated properly. Make sure that terminators are installed in the correct places. Ensure that the Zip SCSI drive is assigned to a SCSI ID that is not in use by any other SCSI device. Finally, check the drivers. The drivers for your SCSI adapter and drive must be correct. Use the right command line switches and the very latest versions. Also check for conflicts between SCSI drivers or other drivers in the system.

Symptom 16: The drive letter is lost each time the PC is turned off   In many cases, the GUEST utility does not load properly because it is at the end of AUTOEXEC.BAT. Relocate the GUEST command line—open the AUTOEXEC.BAT file and move the GUEST command line to a point earlier in the file. Ideally, the GUEST command line should be the entry immediately *following* the MSCDEX command line. Save your changes and reboot the computer. The GUEST utility should now load each time the system is rebooted.

Iomega Ditto Drive

Tape drives have generally come to be seen as a necessary evil in the computer industry. We all know that backups are vitally important to protect our valuable data and system setups, yet we cringe when considering the time required to execute a backup. As a result, Iomega has taken great lengths to develop a tape drive that can be set up and used as quickly and easily as possible. The result is their Ditto drive. There are several versions of the Ditto, providing 420-MB, 800-MB, and 2-GB backups, respectively. According to Iomega, the Ditto can be installed in just 5 minutes, and the Ditto software makes backup operations almost intuitive (it will even accomplish backups in the background while you work on other things).

Ditto demands

There are two reasons why the Ditto tape drive is in this chapter (instead of Chap. 8). First, the Ditto 2-GB drive *requires* a high-performance floppy drive interface in order to function properly. If you are using an ordinary 500-kB/s floppy interface, you will need to install the Ditto Dash accelerator card. Second, the 2-GB tape is a *proprietary* tape manufactured exclusively for Iomega. The Ditto 2-GB tape cartridge uses a slightly wider tape (0.315-in) than the QIC-80 and QIC-40 minicartridges (note that the uncompressed capacity for Ditto 2-GB tapes is only 1 GB). The 2-GB tape drive can read and write to the 2-GB cartridge, but cannot format this cartridge, so all Ditto 2-GB tapes are preformatted.

Ditto drive troubleshooting

Symptom 1: The internal Ditto tape drive is not detected when running from a floppy disk controller   In most cases, the drive is not powered or is not connected properly. Check the power connector first. Internal drives are powered by a standard 4-pin mate-n-lock type connector. Make sure that +5- and +12-V supply levels are adequate, and see that the connector is securely attached to the drive. Next, make sure that the signal cable is attached properly to the drive, and see that the orientation of pin 1 is correct at the drive and controller. Try a new signal cable if possible.

Check the tape cartridge itself. Make sure that you have inserted a known-good tape properly into the drive. If the tape does not initialize after it is inserted, the drive may be defective. Try a new drive. Make sure that the backup software is installed and configured properly on your system. Try reinstalling the software. Finally, try the drive on another computer. If the drive works on another computer, the original floppy drive controller may be inadequate. Try the Ditto Dash accelerator card. If the drive does not work on another computer (or does not work properly with the accelerator card), the drive may be defective. Try a new drive.

Symptom 2: The internal Ditto drive is not detected when running from a Ditto Dash accelerator card   In most cases, the drive is not powered or is not connected properly. Check the power connector first. Internal drives are powered by a standard 4-pin mate-n-lock type connector. Make sure that +5- and +12-V supply levels are adequate, and see that the power connector is securely attached to the drive. Make sure that the signal cable is attached properly to the drive, and see that the orientation of pin 1 is correct at the drive and controller. Try a new signal cable.

Check the tape cartridge next, and see that you have inserted a known-good tape properly into the drive. If the tape does not initialize after it is inserted, the drive may be defective. Try a new drive. Check for hardware conflicts—the Ditto Dash accelerator board may be using an IRQ, DMA, or I/O setting in use by another device in the system. Reconfigure the accelerator card if necessary. Make sure that the backup software is installed and configured properly. Try reinstalling the software. Finally, you should be concerned with the card slot. Make sure that the Ditto Dash accelerator card is located in a slot away from modem/fax boards, or video boards. Try the accelerator in a new slot.

Symptom 3: You notice that the internal Ditto drive takes longer to back up than expected, and the drive regularly spins back and forth   Regular "back-and-forth" movement is known as *shoeshining*, and is usually accompanied by several corrected errors. The drive is probably running from a floppy controller, and the data transfer rate of your backup software is set too high. Check for any backup software settings that control the data transfer rate, and set the rate to 500 kB/s. Save the changes and try another backup. You should see an improvement. If the PC is in its "turbo" mode, try disabling the turbo mode and try another backup. Finally, try a different drive controller such as a Tape Accelerator II card (or a Parallel Port II tape drive) to improve data transfer rates.

Symptom 4: The Ditto parallel-port drive is not detected under DOS or Windows 3.1x This is usually caused by interference with the parallel port. Check the power connector first—parallel-port drives are powered externally. Make sure that the power pack is working, and see that the power cable is connected properly to the drive. If the drive does not appear to power up, try a different power pack or drive. Check the signal cable next, and make sure that you are using a good-quality, known-good parallel-port cable which is attached securely at the PC and drive. Parallel-port drives are very sensitive to devices such as copy-protection modules (or dongles), and other pass-through devices. Try connecting the drive directly to the parallel port. Also disconnect any printers on the parallel port.

Reboot the PC and enter CMOS Setup. Check to see that the parallel port is configured in EPP or bidirectional mode. As a rule, do *not* set the port for ECP mode. Hardware conflicts can also present a problem. Make sure that no other device in the system is using IRQ 7 (for LPT1) or IRQ 5 (for LPT2). If your soundboard is using IRQ 7 or IRQ 5, you may need to reconfigure the device. Make sure that you have inserted a known-good tape properly into the drive. If the tape does not initialize after it is inserted, the drive may be defective. Try a new drive. If problems persist, add the following two lines to AUTOEXEC.BAT:

```
set port_delay=20
set ppt_flags=16
```

Try the drive on another system. If it works on another system, the original parallel port cannot support the Ditto drive. Try adding a second parallel port to the system. If the drive does not work on another PC, the drive is probably defective and should be replaced.

Symptom 5: The internal Ditto drive does not find any catalogs during a restore The tape's catalog has been lost or corrupted. Use the steps below to rebuild a tape catalog with Iomega backup software.

- Choose the Restore option from the main menu.
- Choose the Catalog pull-down menu, then click on Rebuild.
- A screen will appear listing all the catalogs on the tape. Choose the catalog that you wish to rebuild, then choose the OK button (in DOS) or start Rebuild (in Windows).
- The software will then rebuild the catalog and write it automatically to the hard disk. The catalog will then appear in the appropriate box to select files to restore.

Symptom 6: The Ditto drive encounters many corrected errors during a compare If a tape file does not match the same file on a hard disk, the backup software logs a read error. The software then performs a series of rereads to compare the file. If the rereads match, the software corrects the logged error. If a full tape backup exceeds 50 corrected errors, there may be a system configuration problem. First, the drive may be dirty. Clean the R/W tape heads and try the tape again. You can also use the backup software to retension the tape. The tape itself may also be bad. Try a known-good tape. If a known-good tape works properly, the original tape may need to be reformatted. If problems persist, try another tape.

Try booting from a clean diskette, then try the DOS backup software again. If the problem disappears, there may be a driver or TSR which is interfering with the Ditto drive's operation. Check the signal connector. Try a new parallel-port (or internal floppy drive) cable to connect the drive and system. Also check for local electrical interference. The parallel-port drive may be positioned too close to monitors or high-power multimedia speakers. Try moving the drive away from strong magnetic sources. Internal drives may be positioned too close to CD-ROM drives or hard drives. Try relocating the internal Ditto drive to a more remote drive bay. Finally, the DMA operation of your computer may be too fast. Try slowing down DMA operation through the Iomega software.

Symptom 7: You see a `Fatal Exception Error` **with the Ditto drive** The configuration files for the drive are set up incorrectly. You will need to correct the proper entries.

Internal Ditto configurations For the internal Ditto drive, you will need to edit the TAPECTRL.CFG filr located in the QBWIN directory. Delete the following lines:

```
DRIVER_TYPE:5,1 "PARALLEL Port Tape Drive," "qbwppqt.dll"
MANUFACTURER: "IOMEGA"
MODEL: "PARALLEL PORT TAPE DRIVE,"FFFF
DRIVER: 5
FEATURES: 0
I/O ADDRESS: 278, *378, 3bc
IRQ NUMBER: 5, *7
DMA NUMBER:
```

and

```
MANUFACTURER: "IOMEGA"
MODEL: "PPT (MSO chip),"FFFF
DRIVER: 5
FEATURES: 0
I/O ADDRESS: 278, *378, 3bc
IRQ NUMBER: 5, *7, 10, 11, 12, 15
DMA NUMBER:
```

Save your changes, restart the system, then run the tape backup software again.

External Ditto configurations For the external Ditto drive, you will need to add the following two lines to the AUTOEXEC.BAT file:

```
set port_delay=20
set ppt_flags=16
```

Save your changes, reatart the system, then run the tape backup software again.

Symptom 8: The Ditto drive is not restoring selected files The backup software is probably claiming that no files are selected—even though you have selected files. Take the following steps with Iomega backup software:

- Make sure there are marks next to the files listed.
- Select all files (go to the File command and use the Select All Files option).
- If the backup software still claims that no files are selected, go back into the Select Files option, then select the Special option and take the check mark out of the box that says Exclude Read-Only Files.
- Read-only files are excluded by default. This should solve the problem.

Note: It is very important that you perform a compare after a backup. This ensures that the data on your tape are intact. If you do not compare, data integrity cannot be guaranteed (and a restore may not be possible).

Symptom 9: You encounter the error The Drive Received an Invalid Command **when using a Ditto drive** In most cases, the drive is experiencing communication problems with the controller. Change the backup software configuration. Go into the Configure menu of the Iomega backup software. Click on the Settings button, then change the Transfer Rate option to 500 kB/s. Press <Alt>+<F10> and set the option Cntr Card to "bidirectional". Click on the OK button, and run another backup. If problems persist, add the following line to AUTOEXEC.BAT:

```
set port_delay=20
```

Restart the system and try another backup.

Iomega Bernoulli Drives

Perhaps the single most important complaint about hard drives has been that they are not portable—you can't just slide out one drive and pop in a new one. Hard drives are traditionally permanent installations. When that drive fills up, you must physically add another hard drive or replace the existing hard drive with a larger model. Both options require an invasive and time-consuming upgrade procedure. The idea of high-capacity removable media overcomes this limitation. With a removable-medium drive such as the Iomega Bernoulli (or their current Jaz) drive, you can finally achieve limitless storage simply by exchanging data cartridges. If you need to use files on another PC, you can just pop out a cartridge then take it with you to another PC with a Bernoulli drive. Bernoulli drives are not quite as fast as hard drives, but they are close, and you can usually start programs right from the drive.

Bernoulli notes

The Bernoulli disk is a variation of fixed-disk technology. Conventional hard drives rotate rigid disks which force R/W heads to ride on the resulting cushion of air. By comparison, the Bernoulli disk uses a flexible platter which is forced to flex beneath a fixed R/W head. At first glance, you probably would not know the difference between a fixed-platter cartridge (such as a SyQuest cartridge), and a Bernoulli cartridge.

Bernoulli disks have been around for years, and have been through 20-, 35-, 44-, 65-, 90-, 105-, 150-, and 230-MB incarnations. The Iomega Bernoulli 230 drive will operate with all of the previous disk sizes (except 20 and 44 MB) with only a negligible performance penalty. Bernoulli drives are traditionally SCSI devices, but Iomega offers a parallel-port-to-SCSI adapter to allow operation with a PC parallel port. When used on a SCSI system, you can use the Iomega PC2x, PC4x, PC90, PC800, PC1600, and PC1616 SCSI adapters. Other SCSI adapters can also be used as long as they are ASPI-compatible, and an ASPI driver is provided by the adapter vendor.

Bernoulli drive troubleshooting

Symptom 1: The Iomega Bernoulli drive has a floppy icon in Windows 95 This is usually the result of running a real-mode driver to support the Iomega drive and adapter under Windows 95. Check the Iomega driver—you may need to disable the real-mode driver and install the protected-mode driver under Windows 95. The Iomega software provides protected-mode drivers for Jaz Jet, Zip Zoom, PC1600, PC1616, PC800, PC2x, PPA-3, and parallel-port devices. If you are using a different adapter, you may need to upgrade and update the driver accordingly. If you are using a non-Iomega adapter (such as a SCSI adapter), you will need protected-mode drivers from the particular SCSI vendor. However, Windows 95 does have a comprehensive library of protected-mode drivers already available.

Symptom 2: The Iomega Bernoulli SCSI drive does not have a drive letter in Windows 95 The drive does not appear to respond. In virtually all cases, the SCSI driver has failed to load. Check the driver first. Open the Device Manager and expand the SCSI Controllers entry, then check the Iomega Adapter line beneath it. If there is a yellow symbol with an exclamation mark on it, the Windows 95 driver did not load. Highlight that Iomega Adapter line and select Properties. Click on the Resources page, then verify that your I/O Range and IRQ options are set correctly—they must match the jumper settings on your adapter board. If you must update the resource settings manually, make sure the Automatic Settings box is not checked. Remember to save any changes. If you allocated new resources, you may have to shut off the PC and change jumper settings on the controller to match the resources allocated in the Device Manager. Restart the computer. Once the system reboots, the Windows 95 driver should load normally.

If the driver checks out properly, you'll need to check the device connections. Check the SCSI signal connector first, and make sure the SCSI cable is intact and connected to the drive properly. If problems persist, your SCSI adapter is probably installed correctly, but the bus may be terminated improperly. See that you terminate both ends of the SCSI bus properly. Finally, make sure that the SCSI ID for your drive does not conflict with the ID of other SCSI devices in the system.

Symptom 3: The parallel-port (or PPA-3) adapter does not have a drive letter in Windows 95 Parallel-port drive problems can almost always be traced to faulty connections, port configuration issues, or driver problems. Check the power connector first. Parallel-port drives are powered externally, so ensure that the power pack is working, and see that the power cable is connected properly to the drive. If the drive does not appear to power up, try a different power pack or drive. Also make sure that you are using a good-quality, known-good parallel port cable which is attached securely at the PC and drive.

Remove any other devices on the parallel port. Parallel-port drives are often very sensitive to devices such as copy-protection modules (or dongles), and other pass-through devices. Try connecting the drive *directly* to the parallel port. Also disconnect any printers on the parallel port. Reboot the PC and enter CMOS Setup. Check to see that the parallel port is configured in EPP or bidirectional mode. The controller may also be presenting a problem. There is a known incompatibility between the Iomega Bernoulli drive and the Adaptec 284x adapter—the Iomega PPA3 driver does not work with the Adaptec 284x controller. Check with Iomega for an updated SCSI driver.

Open the Device Manager and find the SCSI Controllers entry (even though it is a parallel-port device). If there is no such entry, the driver is not installed. If you expand the SCSI Controllers section, there should be an entry for the Iomega Adapter. If not, the driver is not installed. If the Device Manager entry for the Iomega Adapter has a yellow circle with an exclamation mark on it, the interface is configured improperly and is conflicting with other devices in the system. Device properties may also be a problem. Highlight the Iomega Adapter entry, click on Properties, then select the Settings page. Find the box marked Adapter Settings, then type

```
/mode:nibble /speed:1
```

Save your changes and reboot the system. You could also try reinstalling the drivers. Highlight the Iomega Adapter and select Remove. Then reinstall the drivers from scratch. Finally, consider the drive itself. Try the drive on another PC. If the drive works on another system, the parallel port is incompatible (or the PPA3 is not configured properly). If the drive does not work on another PC, try a new Bernoulli drive.

Symptom 4: The Bernoulli drive takes over the CD-ROM's drive letter in Windows 95 You may simply need to switch drive letters between the Bernoulli drive and CD-ROM drive.

- Open Device Manager and double-click on the Disk Drives entry.
- Highlight the Iomega Bernoulli drive entry and click on Properties.
- Click on the Settings page.
- In the Reserved Drive Letters section, there is a Start Drive Letter and an End Drive Letter setting. Enter the desired drive letter for the Bernoulli drive in both start and end drive entries (be sure to use the same drive letter for both start and end). Click on OK.
- Double-click on the CD-ROM entry.
- Highlight your CD-ROM Drive entry and click on Properties.
- Click on the Settings page.

- In the Reserved Drive Letters section, there is a Start Drive Letter and an End Drive Letter setting. Enter the desired drive letter for the CD-ROM drive in both start and end entries (be sure to use the same drive letter for both start and end). Click on OK.
- Click on OK to close Device Manager, then shut down and restart the computer.

Symptom 5: You encounter an `Invalid Drive Specification` **error after installing an Iomega SCSI drive** Your system automatically boots into Windows, and it will not return to the installation program. The error occurs when you try to access the Iomega drive. In most cases, you need to install the Iomega SCSI software from the DOS prompt. Boot the system from a clean diskette, then try installing the Iomega SCSI software again.

Symptom 6: You encounter an `Invalid Unit Reading Drive, x.` **error** Software drivers appear to load fine, and the Bernoulli drive is assigned a drive letter as expected. In virtually all cases, there is a problem with the SMARTDRV statement in AUTOEXEC.BAT. Check the drive controller BIOS first—there may be a conflict with the BIOS on your PC1616 controller card. If you are *not* booting from the PC1616, try disabling the PC1616 BIOS with the ISACFG.COM utility accompanying the PC1616 adapter (you can also obtain the utility from Iomega at http://www.iomega.com/). Reboot the PC; the error should be corrected.

If you *are* booting from the PC1616 controller (the Bernoulli drive), leave the controller's BIOS enabled, but try loading SMARTDRV high (i.e., into the upper memory area). If you cannot load SMARTDRV high, disable its command line in AUTOEXEC.BAT and reboot the system, then load SMARTDRV from the DOS command line once the PC initializes. If problems persist, try the new GUEST program from Iomega (make sure you're using the latest version). Once you install the GUEST.EXE and GUEST.INI files to your PC, enter the path and command line for GUEST near the end of AUTOEXEC.BAT (before Windows starts) such as

`c:\zinstall\guest.exe`

If these solutions fail to correct the error, then SMARTDRV cannot be loaded and will need to be remarked out of the AUTOEXEC.BAT file entirely.

Note: If you use the GUEST program, you cannot compress the disks using DISKSPACE. Also, GUEST does not support the PC80 or PC90 adapter cards.

Symptom 7: You encounter problems using the Iomega parallel port interface (PPA-3) with a Bernoulli drive Problems with the PPA3 are usually related to installation issues, but drivers can also prevent the PPA3 from responding. Check the power connector first—the external device *must* be turned on before powering up the computer. If the device refuses to power up, check the power pack and its connection to the Bernoulli drive. Make sure that the signal cable is the proper length and is connected securely to the drive and system. Unusually long cables may cause R/W errors. Try disconnecting the printer or other parallel-port device from the system, and try the PPA3 as the only parallel-port device attached to the parallel port.

Check the drive termination next. The PPA3 board is terminated, and the last drive attached to the PPA3 cable must also be terminated. If the Bernoulli drive is the last device attached to the PPA3, make sure it is terminated properly.

Check the driver installation. You need either OAD 1.3 (and higher), or Iomega SCSI 2.0 (and higher) to use the PPA3 board. Once the drivers are installed, you should see several lines in CONFIG.SYS such as

```
REM OAD 1.3 or later:
DEVICE=C:\OADDOS\ASPIPPA3.SYS /L=001
DEVICE=C:\OADDOS\DOSCFG.EXE /M1 /V /L=001
DEVICE=C:\OADDOS\DOSOAD.SYS /L=001
```

or

```
REM Iomega SCSI 2.0 or later:
DEVICE=C:\IOMEGA\ASPIPPA3.SYS /L=001
DEVICE=C:\IOMEGA\SCSICFG.EXE /V /L=001
DEVICE=C:\IOMEGA\SCSIDRVR.SYS /L=001
```

Try some ASPIPPA3.SYS command line options. The ASPIPPA3.SYS driver provides several important command line options in Table 10-2 that can be employed to streamline its operation. If the ASPIPPA3.SYS command line generates any errors, you can decipher the errors with Table 10-3.

Symptom 8: The Iomega PPA3 locks up on installation   Chances are that the ASPIPPA3.SYS driver is causing the computer to lock up or is causing a "Divide

Table 10-2. Command Line Options for ASPIPPA3.SYS

/MODE=n
　　/MODE=1 is the most compatible mode.
　　/MODE=2 is the bidirectional transfer mode—your PC must have a bidirectional parallel port.
　　/MODE=3 is enhanced mode, which requires an Intel SL series microprocessor (i.e., 80386SL, 80486SL, or 82360SL).
/SL360=Yes/No
　　This tells the ASPIPPA3.SYS driver whether or not the computer uses an Intel SL microprocessor chipset. If you're not sure (or a divide overflow occurs during loading), set to /SL360=No
/SPEED=n
　　Values 1 to 10 are available. Start by setting /SPEED=1. If that solves the problem, continue to increase the value until the problem recurs, then use highest value that functioned properly. If you are still not sure which value to use, set /SPEED=1
/SCAN
　　Forces the ASPIPPA3.SYS driver to check all parallel-port addresses—there are three addresses possible; 278h, 378h, and 3BCh.
/Busy_Retry=Yes
　　This option forces the driver to retry several times when a device is busy (instead of just reporting an error).
/Port=<Address>
　　Used to manually specify the port address of the parallel port.

Table 10-3. ASPIPPA3.SYS Error Messages

Error code	Possible cause
4001	Command line syntax error.
4002	Adapter initialization failed—possible problem with the adapter or the parallel port.
4003	User specified a port address and there was no adapter there.
4004	No adapter found.
4005	User pressed both SHIFT keys to bypass this driver.
4006	Current DOS version is not supported by this driver.
4100	Conflicting port address was detected in command line.
4107	Improper speed value. Acceptable range is 0 to 10 decimal.
4108	Bad value—value outside limits.

by zero overflow" error. Check the power connector first. The external device *must* be turned on before powering up the computer. If the device refuses to power up, check the power pack and its connection to the Bernoulli drive. Also, make sure that the signal cable is the proper length and is connected securely to the drive and system. Unusually long cables may cause R/W errors. Termination may be an issue—the PPA3 board is terminated, and the last drive attached to the PPA3 board must also be terminated. If the Bernoulli drive is the last device attached to the PPA3, make sure it is terminated properly by setting the termination switch on the back of the drive to "I." If the switch is set to "O," turn off the drive, set the switch to "I," turn the drive on, and reboot the PC. Update the ASPIPPA3.SYS driver. Try adding the /SL360=NO switch to the command line such as

```
DEVICE=C:\IOMEGA\ASPIPPA3.SYS /SL360=NO
```

Save your changes to CONFIG.SYS and reboot the computer.

Try the PPA3 board and Bernoulli drive on another PC. If they work on another system, the original parallel port is probably incompatible. If the PPA3 and drive do not work on another system, try another set of cables. If problems persist, try the Bernoulli drive directly on a SCSI adapter. If the drive works directly, the PPA3 has probably failed. If the drive does not work, it has probably failed.

Symptom 9: You encounter SCSI communication problems In virtually all cases, SCSI problems can be traced to hardware problems or driver issues. Check the power connector first, and see that power is provided to the drive (the drive power light should be on). Make sure that the SCSI cable is intact and connected securely between the drive and SCSI adapter. Try a new signal cable if possible. Termination may also be a problem. Both ends of the SCSI bus must be terminated properly. Make sure that terminators are installed in the correct places on your SCSI chain. The Bernoulli SCSI drive must be assigned to a SCSI ID that is not in use by any other SCSI device. Finally, check the drivers. Make sure that the drivers for your SCSI adapter and drive are correct, that you are using the right command line switches, and that you are using the very latest versions. Also check for conflicts between SCSI drivers or other drivers in the system.

Symptom 10: Your IDE Bernoulli drive receives two drive letters Your plug-and-play (PnP) BIOS is detecting the Bernoulli drive as a fixed drive and assigns one drive letter, but the Iomega drivers detect the Bernoulli drive again—assigning a second drive letter. PnP support for the Bernoulli drive may be a problem. Enter your system CMOS Setup and disable the PnP support for the Bernoulli drive. Save your changes and reboot the system. If you cannot disable BIOS support for the Bernoulli drive, power up the system with the Bernoulli disk removed. This causes BIOS to overlook the drive, but the Iomega drivers will still assign the drive letter properly.

SyQuest Drives

SyQuest is another drive manufacturer which has capitalized on the popularity of removable-medium drives. Rather than using the flexible disk medium of Bernoulli technology, SyQuest chose to employ the rigid platter/floating head approach used by more conventional hard drives. As a result, SyQuest drives are a bit closer to being "real" hard drives than Bernoulli drives. The traditional 44- and 88-MB SyQuest drives of years past have been replaced by products such as the EZ-Drive (135-MB) and EZ-Flyer (230-MB) drives. SyQuest has just recently released the dual-platter 1.5-GB SyJet drive which places the SyJet in direct contention with Iomega's 1.0-GB Jaz drive.

SyQuest drive troubleshooting

Symptom 1: You encounter problems with SyQuest drives and Future Domain SCSI adapters Although SyQuest drives should perform properly with Future Domain SCSI adapters, there are some issues that might cause problems. Inspect the SCSI ID first. Future Domain SCSI adapters install drives from the higher SCSI ID (6) to the lowest (0). This is opposite from the majority of HBA (host board adapter) manufacturers which assign drives from ID 0. Make sure any hard disk drives have a higher SCSI ID number than the SyQuest drives when you install a removable drive on the SCSI bus. That way, the hard drives will be assigned the lower DOS drive letter (i.e., C: then D:).

Future Domain controllers will not allow the SyQuest drive to serve as a boot device. If you must make the SyQuest drive bootable, contact Future Domain for a firmware upgrade. Cartridge preparation can also be a problem. Future Domain PowerSCSI software works with cartridges prepared and used on the same PC. When exchanging the cartridge with one of a different format, size, or partition, the PowerSCSI driver will not handle the new cartridge properly. You might need different SCSI drivers. Check your SCSI drivers. In order for the SyQuest utilities to work properly with Future Domain adapters (and handle nonnative cartridges), the CONFIG.SYS file must contain the following drivers:

```
DEVICE=C:\PWRSCSI!\DCAM18XX.EXE
DEVICE=C:\PWRSCSI!\ASPIFCAM.SYS
DEVICE=C:\SYQUEST\SCSI\SQDRIVER.SYS
```

The correct CAM.EXE driver for your particular adapter must be used in the CONFIG.SYS file (such as CAM950.EXE). Do not use FDBIOS.SYS or INT4BCAM.SYS with SQDRIVER.SYS (only one driver can be used to control the SyQuest drive). The SyQuest DOS formatting program SQPREP will partition and Format DOS cartridges with Future Domain adapters if the drivers are correctly installed in CONFIG.SYS as shown above.

Symptom 2: You encounter problems with SyQuest drives and NCR SCSI adapters   SyQuest drives work well with NCR (now part of AT&T Global Systems) adapters, but you must be using version 3.12 or later SyQuest utilities. The SCSI drivers may be causing problems. To make the SyQuest cartridges removable under DOS, the following three entries must be present in CONFIG.SYS:

```
DEVICE=C:\SDMS\DOSCAM.SYS      (10-08-93 or later)
DEVICE=C:\SDMS\ASPICAM.SYS     (10-08-93 or later)
DEVICE=C:\SyQuest\SCSI\SQDRIVER.SYS
```

If you choose to use the NCR driver SCSIDISK.SYS instead of SQDRIVER.SYS, the ability to remove cartridges and use nonnative cartridges will be lost. Make sure that both drivers are *not* loaded together, or data corruption will result. Also suspect an issue with the SCSI ID. Typical NCR SCSI priority is from lowest (0) to highest (6), and the NCR adapter is SCSI ID 7. The SyQuest DOS partition and format utility (SQPREP) works well with NCR adapters as long as the drivers are loaded in CONFIG.SYS as shown above.

Symptom 3: You encounter problems with SyQuest drives and Rancho Technology SCSI adapters   SyQuest SCSI drives work properly with Rancho Technology SCSI adapters, but there are some issues that you must be aware of. First, Rancho Technology SCSI BIOS requires that a cartridge be installed in the SyQuest drive at *boot time* (the Rancho Technology BIOS will hang if no cartridge is installed and the drive is ready). SCSI drivers can also be an issue. SyQuest utilities will work through the ASPICAM driver supplied with Rancho Technology adapters. To make the cartridges removable under DOS, the CONFIG.SYS file must have drivers loaded in this order:

```
REM For the Rancho Technology 1600:
DEVICE=C:\RT1600\DOSCAM.SYS            (12-14-94 or later)
DEVICE=C:\RT1600\ASPICAM.SYS           (12-14-94 or later)
DEVICE=C:\SyQuest\SCSI\SQDRIVER.SYS
```

     or

```
REM For the Rancho Technology 1000:
DEVICE=C:\RT1000\RTASPI10.SYS          (01-26-93 or later)
DEVICE=C:\SyQuest\SCSI\SQDRIVER.SYS
```

If you choose to use the Rancho Technology driver SCSIDISK.SYS instead of SQDRIVER.SYS, the ability to remove cartridges and use nonnative cartridges will be lost. Make sure that both drivers are *not* loaded together or data corruption will result. Check the SCSI ID—typical Rancho Technology SCSI priority is from lowest (0) to highest (6), and the Rancho Technology adapter is SCSI ID 7. The SyQuest DOS partition and format utility (SQPREP) works well with Rancho Technology adapters as long as the drivers are loaded in CONFIG.SYS as shown above.

Symptom 4: You encounter problems with Packard-Bell multimedia PCs and SyQuest drives   Packard-Bell systems often use unusual IRQ assignments which may interfere with the default settings of many SCSI adapters. Check the hardware settings—many Packard Bell PCs use IRQ 11 and IRQ 12 for the CD-ROM drive, soundboard, and mouse. When installing a SCSI adapter, make sure to use IRQ 10 and the I/O address of 340h. If there is any other 16-bit card (especially a network card) in the system, use IRQ 15 instead.

Symptom 5: You encounter problems using BusLogic SCSI adapters and SyQuest drives   The BusLogic ASPI driver (BTDOSM.SYS) will operate with the SyQuest device driver SQDRIVER.SYS, but the order of installation can be very important. Install the BusLogic driver first, then install the SyQuest software. Once the drivers are installed, the CONFIG.SYS file should be in this order:

```
DEVICE=C:\BUSLOGIC\BTDOSM.SYS /D
DEVICE=C:\SYQUEST\SCSI\SQDRIVER.SYS
```

Remove the BusLogic disk driver BTMDISK.SYS:

```
REM DEVICE=C:\BUSLOGIC\BTMDISK.SYS
```

Relocate any other Buslogic device drivers *after* SQDRIVER.SYS. Reboot the system after making any changes to CONFIG.SYS. Finally, check the driver dates. Make sure that you are using SQDRIVER.SYS version 7.72 or higher, or the SyQuest software release 3.12 or higher (01-27-95 or later).

Symptom 6: You encounter problems using Qlogic SCSI adapters and SyQuest drives   While SyQuest SCSI drives will operate properly with Qlogic SCSI adapters, there are some issues that can cause problems. First, Qlogic FastSCSI software does not support SyQuest cartridge exchange without installing the SyQuest SQDRIVER.SYS driver. Install the two Qlogic drivers, *then* install the SyQuest drivers. Make sure that the QL00DISK.SYS driver is *not* installed in CONFIG.SYS. A typical CONFIG.SYS file will appear such as

```
DEVICE=C:\QLOGIC\QL41DOS.SYS
DEVICE=C:\QLOGIC\QL00ASPI.SYS
DEVICE=C:\SyQuest\SCSI\SQDRIVER.SYS
```

Make sure to use the correct QLxxDOS.SYS driver for your particular Qlogic SCSI adapter. CorelSCSI software is often shipped with Qlogic SCSI adapters. If a CorelSCSI driver is installed to support a SyQuest drive, do *not* install the SQDRIVER.SYS driver. Finally, disable or REMark out the QL00DISK.SYS driver if it is entered in the CONFIG.SYS file. If the QL00DISK.SYS driver is allowed to coexist with SQDRIVER.SYS, data corruption will result.

Symptom 7: You encounter problems using an IBM MicroChannel SCSI controller and SyQuest drive   This note applies to the /A and /2A MicroChannel SCSI adapters. The IBM ASPI driver (ASPI4B.SYS) will only operate with the SyQuest driver SQDRIVER.SYS under DOS—not under Windows. The MSDRVR.ZIP shareware has been known to circumvent this incompatibility. For current pricing and availability, contact the shareware maker:

Micro Staff Co., Ltd.
1-46-9 Matsubara, Setagaya-ku, Tokyo, Japan 156
Tel: 011-81-3-3325-8128
Fax: 011-81-3-3327-7037

CompuServe ID: 100157,1053

Symptom 8: You encounter problems using Data Technology Corporation (DTC) SCSI adapters and SyQuest drives The DTC SCSI adapters will operate with SyQuest drives, but there are several points that can cause problems. Install the DTC ASPI driver first, *then* install the SyQuest utility software. Once all the drivers are installed, the CONFIG.SYS file should appear in this order:

```
REM For the DTC 3280AS ISA version and the DTC 3290AS EISA version:
DEVICE=C:\DTC\ASPI3xxx.SYS
DEVICE=C:\SYQUEST\SCSI\SQDRIVER.SYS
```

Remember to remove the DTC device driver ASCSI.SYS in the CONFIG.SYS file

```
REM DEVICE=C:\DTC\ASCSI.SYS
```

Also, in the AUTOEXEC.BAT file

```
REM C:\DTC\ASCSI.EXE
```

Load any other DTC device drivers after SQDRIVER.SYS, or

```
REM For the DTC 3130 PCI version:
DEVICE=C:\DTC\DOSCAM.SYS
DEVICE=C:\DTC\ASPICAM.SYS
DEVICE=C:\SYQUEST\SCSI\SQDRIVER.SYS*
```

Remember to remove the DTC device driver SCSIDISK.SYS in the CONFIG. SYS file:

```
REM DEVICE=C:\DTC\SCSIDISK.SYS
```

Load any other DTC device drivers *after* SQDRIVER.SYS. Remember to reboot the PC after making any changes to your CONFIG.SYS or AUTOEXEC.BAT files. Finally, check the driver dates. Make sure that you are using SQDRIVER.SYS version 7.72 or higher, or the SyQuest software release 3.12 or higher (01-27-95 or later).

Symptom 9: The lights on the SyQuest drive are blinking in a regular pattern The drive has suffered a fault, and generally must be replaced. Use Table 10-4 to find the specific error code. In most cases, you will have to replace the drive outright.

Table 10-4. SyQuest Error Codes for SQ555, SQ5110C, and 5200C Drives

Green flashes	Amber flashes	Problem	Action
0	3	Microprocessor problems	Replace drive
1	1, 2, 3	FCBA (drive circuitry) failure	Replace drive
2	1, 2, 3, 4, 5, 6	FCBA (drive circuitry) failure	Replace drive
3	0, 3	Microprocessor problems	Replace drive
3	1, 2, 4, 5	PCBA (drive circuitry) failure	Replace drive
4	1, 2, 3	Drive motor problem	Replace drive
4	4, 5	Drive motor speed problem	Replace cartridge
4	6	Cannot find servo	Reinsert cartridge
5	1	Power failure	Check power supply
5	2	Drive motor speed problem	Replace cartridge
5	3, 4, 5, 6, 7, 8, 9	Power-up initialization incomplete	Reinsert cartridge / Replace cartridge
6	0, 1, 2, 3	PCBA (drive circuitry) failure	Replace drive
6	4	Drive motor speed problem	Replace cartridge
6	5	Excessive run-out failure	Reinsert cartridge / Clean spindle motor / Replace cartridge
6	6	Incompatible cartridge	Use proper cartridge
6	7	PCBA (drive circuitry) failure	Replace drive
7	1, 2, 3, 4, 5	PCBA (drive circuitry) failure	Replace drive
OFF	Solid ON or flashing light	Power fault	Replace drive
		Defective cartridge	Replace cartridge
		Head loading failure	Replace drive
Solid ON	Solid ON	Microprocessor problem	Reinitialize the drive / Replace the drive

Appendix
Troubleshooting Charts

Chapter 4: Solid-State Memory Devices

Installation symptoms

1. New memory is not recognized.

    a. Configure DIP switches (XT) or CMOS Setup (AT).
    b. Check that a complete bank is filled.

Classic (AT) memory errors

1. 164 (memory size) error.

    a. Check/correct RAM size in CMOS system setup.
    b. Check/replace CMOS backup battery.

2. Incorrect Memory Size error.

    a. Check/correct RAM size in CMOS system setup.
    b. Check/replace CMOS backup battery.
    c. Locate/replace defective RAM IC(s).

3. ROM Error message.

    a. Replace system BIOS ROM(s).

4. Parity Check or 200-series error.

    a. Locate/replace defective RAM IC(s).

Contemporary memory errors

1. Optional ROM BAD Checksum.

    a. Isolate/replace defective peripheral device/adapter board.

2. General RAM error.
   a. Isolate/replace defective RAM IC(s) or SIMM(s).
   b. Replace the defective motherboard.

3. `Cache Memory Failure` error.
   a. Isolate/replace defective cache memory IC(s) or SIMM(s).
   b. Replace the defective motherboard.

4. `Decreasing Available Memory` error.
   a. Isolate/replace defective RAM device(s).

5. `Memory Parity Interrupt` error.
   a. Check/reseat each system SIMM.
   b. Isolate/replace defective RAM IC(s) or SIMM(s).

Chapter 5: Floppy Disk Drives

Troubleshooting floppy disk systems

1. The drive is completely dead.
   a. Check diskette and disk insertion.
   b. Check all signal connectors and wiring.
   c. Check drive power levels and wiring.
   d. Replace floppy drive.
   e. Replace the floppy controller board.

2. The drive does not seek.
   a. Inspect the mechanical assembly.
   b. Check drive power levels and wiring.
   c. Check interface for controller/drive failure.
   d. Check/replace head stepping motor.
   e. Replace the floppy drive.

3. The drive does not spin.
   a. Inspect the mechanical assembly.
   b. Check drive power levels and wiring.
   c. Check interface for controller/drive failure.
   d. Replace the floppy drive.

4. The drive will not read or write.
   a. Check/replace the diskette.
   b. *Gently* clean the R/W heads.
   c. Check interface for controller/drive failure.
   d. Replace R/W head assembly.
   e. Replace the floppy drive.

5. Drive writes to write-protected disks.
   a. Check the diskette's write-protect tab.
   b. Check/replace the write protect sensor.

6. Drive *only* recognizes HD or DD disks.
    c. Check physical interface signals.
    d. Replace drive control circuit IC.
    e. Replace drive PC board.
    f. Replace the floppy drive.

6. Drive *only* recognizes HD or DD disks.
    a. Check/replace disk sensor.
    b. Check physical interface signals.
    c. Replace drive control circuit IC.
    d. Replace drive PC board.
    e. Replace entire floppy drive.

7. DD disks won't work as HD disks.
    a. Do *not* use DD disks as HD disks.

8. `Cannot Read From Drive A:` error.
    a. Try a known-good diskette.
    b. Clean the floppy drive heads.
    c. Check the drive mechanics for obstructions.
    d. Check/replace the floppy signal cable.
    e. Replace the floppy drive.
    f. Replace the floppy drive controller.

9. Directory from previous disk appears.
    a. Check/replace the floppy signal cable.
    b. Check the floppy drive jumpers.
    c. Replace the floppy drive.
    d. Replace the floppy drive controller.

10. Drive cannot format 3.5 in HD disks.
    a. Upgrade BIOS to support 3.5 in HD floppy drives.
    b. Use the DOS DRIVER.SYS utility.

11. Cannot get 3.5 in disk to work in XT.
    a. Check DOS version (3.3 or higher).
    b. Use 8-bit floppy controller w/on-board BIOS.
    c. Check floppy DIP switches on motherboard.

12. Unable to successfully "swap" drives.
    a. Check/replace the floppy signal cable.
    b. Check floppy drive jumpers.
    c. Check drive entries in CMOS Setup.

13. Trouble using a "combo" drive.
    a. Check the floppy power levels and wiring.
    b. Replace the combo drive.

14. You encounter a "jumperless" drive.
    a. Know the default settings of the floppy.
    b. Replace the drive with a "jumpered" version.

15. Floppy activity LED stays on.
    a. Check/replace the floppy signal cable.
    b. Replace the floppy drive controller.

Chapter 6: Hard Disk Drives

Drive testing and troubleshooting

1. The hard drive is completely dead.
   a. Check the drive power levels and wiring.
   b. Check/replace the hard drive signal cable.
   c. Check the CMOS Setup.
   d. Replace the hard drive.
   e. Replace the hard-drive controller.

2. The hard drive will not boot the system.
   a. Check/replace the hard-drive signal cable.
   b. Check the CMOS Setup.
   c. Boot from a floppy disk.
   d. Check/restore the hard drive's MBR.
   e. Repartition and reformat the hard drive.
   f. Replace the hard drive.
   g. Replace the hard-drive controller.

3. Subdirectories lost or damaged.
   a. Boot system from floppy drive.
   b. Run fix utilities.
   c. Reformat and reload drive.

4. Hard-drive read/write errors.
   a. Boot system from floppy disk.
   b. Run fix utilities and check disk.
   c. Replace any corrupted files.
   d. Reformat and reload drive.
   e. Replace the drive.

5. Hard drive formatted accidentally.
   a. Rebuild the formatted drive with disk utilities.
   b. Reformat and reload drive.

6. File accidentally deleted.
   a. Undelete the file with DOS utilities.
   b. Recopy the file(s) manually.

7. Hard-drive root directory damaged.
   a. Boot system from floppy drive.
   b. Run drive fix utilities.
   c. Reformat and reload drive.
   d. Replace the drive.

8. Drive performance slows over time.
   a. Boot system from floppy drive.
   b. Check for computer viruses.
   c. Run a defragment utility.

9. HDD OK, but activity LED remains on.
   a. Check for drive activity jumpers on drive or controller.
   b. Check LED error codes for the drive (if any).

10. HDD failure, activity LED remains on.
   a. Check/replace the hard-drive signal cable.

11. `No Fixed Disk Present` error.

    b. Replace the hard drive.

    c. Replace the drive controller board.

    a. Check the hard-drive power levels and wiring.

    b. Check/replace the hard-drive signal cable.

    c. Check the CMOS Setup.

    d. Check for drive controller hardware conflicts.

    e. Check termination (for SCSI systems).

    f. Replace the hard drive.

    g. Replace the hard-drive controller.

12. Drive spins up, but is not recognized.

    a. Check/replace the hard-drive signal cable.

    b. Check the hard-drive jumper assignments.

    c. Check termination (for SCSI systems).

    d. Check the CMOS Setup.

    e. Check/correct drive partitions.

    f. Replace the hard drive.

    g. Replace the hard-drive controller.

13. Drive spins up, then spins down.

    a. Check the drive power levels and wiring.

    b. Check/replace the hard-drive signal cable.

    c. Check the hard-drive jumper assignments.

    d. Replace the hard drive.

14. `Sector Not Found` error.

    a. Try a file recovery utility or restore from backup.

    b. Check the drive medium.

    c. Low-level format (if possible).

    d. Repartition, reformat, and restore the drive.

    e. Replace the hard drive.

15. "1780 or 1781" error.

    a. Boot the system "clean."

    b. Check for computer viruses.

    c. Try a drive fix utility to restore boot files.

    d. Repartition and reformat the drive.

    e. Replace the hard drive.

    f. Replace the hard-drive controller.

16. "1790 or 1791" error.

    a. Check/replace the hard-drive signal cable.

b. Check/restore partitions.

c. Repartition and reformat the drive.

d. Replace the hard drive.

e. Replace the hard-drive controller.

17. You see a "1701" error.

a. Check the hard-drive power levels and wiring.

b. Check the CMOS Setup.

c. Low-level format (if possible).

d. Repartition, reformat, and restore the drive.

18. Random data, seek, or format errors.

a. Check the hard-drive power levels and wiring.

b. Check/replace the hard-drive signal cable.

c. Check the drive orientation and location.

d. Check the system's "turbo" mode.

e. Try a new hard-drive controller board.

f. Check/fix the drive medium.

g. Check expansion boards and other drives.

h. Check/replace the motherboard.

19. Bad or Missing Command Interpreter.

a. Check DOS versions.

b. Boot the system "clean."

c. Check for computer viruses.

d. Repartition and reformat the drive.

20. Error Reading Drive C: error.

a. Check/replace the hard-drive signal cable.

b. Boot the system "clean."

c. Check for computer viruses.

d. Check the drive's orientation and location.

e. Check/fix the drive medium.

f. Repartition, reformat, and restore the drive.

g. Replace the hard drive.

21. Track 0 not found error.

a. Check/replace the hard-drive signal cable.

b. Boot the system "clean."

c. Check the drive's partition(s).

d. Repartition, reformat, and restore the drive.

e. Replace the hard drive.

22. Access time longer than expected.

a. Double-check drive specifications.

b. Defragment the drive.

c. Check the drive benchmark software.

d. Replace the hard drive.

23. Data transfer slower than expected.

    a. Double-check drive specifications.

    b. Check the PIO mode in CMOS Setup.

    c. Defragment the drive.

    d. Check the drive benchmark software.

    e. Make sure LL format *not* performed.

    f. Check termination (for SCSI systems).

    g. Replace the hard drive.

24. LL format taking too long.

    a. Check the DEBUG string or LL format utility.

    b. Check drive parameters in CMOS Setup.

    c. Check/replace the hard-drive signal cable.

    d. Check the system's "turbo" mode.

    e. Replace the hard-drive controller board.

25. Cannot LL format from DEBUG.

    a. Check the DEBUG string or LL format utility.

    b. Check the drive parameters in CMOS Setup.

    c. Replace the hard drive controller board.

26. LL format hangs at a certain place.

    a. Check/correct the "hard error" list.

    b. Check the drive parameters in CMOS Setup.

    c. Replace the hard-drive controller board.

27. FDISK hangs up or fails.

    a. Check/replace the hard-drive signal cable.

    b. Check the drive parameters in CMOS Setup.

    c. Check FDISK version.

    d. Clear any existing partitions.

    e. Check/fix the drive medium.

    f. Replace the hard drive.

28. `Hard disk controller failure` error.

    a. Check the drive parameters in CMOS Setup.

    b. Replace the drive controller.

    c. Replace the hard drive.

29. DOS FORMAT takes too long.

    a. Check FORMAT version.

30. IDE drive prepares below capacity.
   a. Check the drive parameters in CMOS Setup.
   b. Try a suitable "translation geometry."
   c. Check the DOS version.

31. EIDE drive prepares below capacity.
   a. Check drive system for EIDE (LBA) support.
   b. Check the drive parameters in CMOS Setup.
   c. Try another hard-drive controller.
   d. Install drive management software (if necessary).

32. `Disk boot failure` error.
   a. Check/replace the hard-drive signal cable.
   b. Boot the system "clean."
   c. Check for computer viruses.
   d. Check the drive parameters in CMOS Setup.
   e. Check/fix the drive partitions with FDISK.
   f. Replace the hard drive.
   g. Replace the hard-drive controller.

33. HDD breaks down frequently.
   a. Check/replace the PC power supply.
   b. Add system RAM.
   c. Keep the drive(s) defragmented.
   d. Check/optimize the PC environment.

34. `Hard disk failure` error.
   a. Replace the hard-drive controller.

35. New HDD will not boot properly.
   a. Check the drive power levels and wiring.
   b. Check/replace the hard-drive signal cable.
   c. Check the drive parameters in CMOS Setup.
   d. Check/fix the drive partition(s) with FDISK.

36. DOS formats back below 528MB.
   a. Install Disk Manager to boot diskette.

37. ScanDisk cannot map out bad sectors.
   a. Use a surface analysis utility for your drive.

38. Drive works as primary, but not secondary (or vice versa).
   a. Check drive jumper assignments.
   b. Reverse primary/secondary relationship.
   c. Replace one of the drives.

39. Cannot get 32-bit access (Win 3.1x).
   a. Install the correct 32-bit driver.

40. A lot of wasted space is suggested.
   a. Create several smaller logical partitions.

41. "Y" power adapter fails to work.   a. Check/replace the Y adapter.
42. Drive spins up and produces noise.   a. Check/upgrade the motherboard BIOS.
                                            b. Replace the drive controller.
                                            c. Replace the hard drive.
43. Problems opening folder (Win 95).   a. Problem with FAT 32 file system.
                                            b. Place extra files in different folders.

Disk Manager (DM) troubleshooting

1. DM won't install from drive B:.   a. Install Disk Manager from A:.
2. Windows 95 fails with DM.   a. Use the latest version of DM.
3. Windows 95 uses "compatibility mode."   a. Check the drive parameters in CMOS Setup.
                                            b. Check/replace real-mode disk drivers.
                                            c. Use the latest version of DM.
4. 32-bit driver won't work (Win 95).   a. Disable 32-bit manufacturer-specific disk drivers.
5. DM fails with disk compression.   a. Use the latest version of DM.
                                            b. Check compression software for use with DM.
6. DM doesn't identify HDD correctly.   a. Disable BIOS on hard-drive controller.
                                            b. Replace the hard-drive controller.
7. Cannot remove DM.   a. Boot the system "clean."
                                            b. Repartition, reformat, and restore the drive.
8. DM conflicts with other programs.   a. Change how DM loads into memory.
9. Installing DOS over DM limits 528MB.   a. Load DM before booting from floppy to install DOS.
10. DDO Integrity Error.   a. Boot the system "clean."
                                            b. Check for computer viruses.
                                            c. Check/replace the PC power supply.
                                            d. Reinstall DM.
                                            e. Replace the hard drive.
11. 16-bit file access only under WFWG when using DM on secondary drive.   a. Install DM to your primary HDD.
12. DM "rescue disk" changes drive letters. a. Allow HDD to start DDO, then boot from diskette.
13. Data on DM drive corrupted.   a. Software on system is not using DOS or Int 13.
                                            b. Disable/remove offending utility software.
14. DM cannot identify a HDD.   a. Select proper HDD from available list.
                                            b. Disable HDD controller's on-board cache.

EZ-Drive (EZ) troubleshooting

1. EZ interfering with VL IDE controllers.
   a. Check IDE chipset for compatibility.

2. Keyboard or mouse trouble with EZ.
   a. Check your mouse driver.
   b. Install a new mouse driver.

3. QEMM 7.5 Stealth fails with EZ.
   a. Add XSTI switch to QEMM command line.

4. EZ causes Win 95 to crash.
   a. Check/update motherboard BIOS version.

5. Cannot remove EZ-Drive.
   a. Disable MBR virus protection in CMOS.
   b. Boot the system "clean."
   c. Repartition, reformat, and restore the drive.

6. EZ says `No IDE Drive Installed`.
   a. Check the drive parameters in CMOS Setup.

7. Cannot remove EZ from an LBA setup.
   a. You must correct the installation of EZ-Drive.

8. `Hold down the CTRL key....`
   a. Boot the system "clean."
   b. Check for computer viruses.

9. PC hangs after booting w/nonsystem disk.
   a. Boot the system "clean."
   b. Check for computer viruses.

10. `Unrecognized DBR` error.
    a. Try a known-good diskette.
    b. Check the HDD boot files.

11. MH32BIT.386 won't work in block transfer mode.
    a. Update the 32-bit driver for better performance.

12. MH32BIT.386 won't work with Win 95.
    a. Disable the MH32BIT.386 driver under Windows 95.

13. EZ won't run on PS/1, PS/2, or MCA systems.
    a. Remove EZ from the system (do not use EZ).

14. HDD no longer usable after removing EZ.
    a. Upgrade system to support EIDE.
    b. Check the drive parameters in CMOS Setup.

15. Cannot recover data after using EZWIPE.EXE.
    a. Repartition, reformat, and restore the drive.

Drive Rocket (DR) troubleshooting

1. `Disabling Stealth ROM` under QEMM.
   a. Add the XSTI switch to the QEMM command line.

2. `Inconfigurable Driver` error.
   a. Use the latest version of DR.
   b. Remove DR from the system.

3. Cannot remove DR.
   a. Disable the ROCKET.BIN device from CONFIG.SYS.

4. DR cannot identify HDD correctly.
   a. Use a generic version of DR (not OEM version).

5. DR cannot load into UMA.	a. Try a different memory manager (i.e., EMM386).
6. "Negative" performance increase.	a. Remove DR from the system.
7. DR causes GPF under Win 3.1x.	a. Adjust DR command line with /w switch.

Chapter 7: PC Cards

Troubleshooting PC Card problems

1. SRAM or flash card looses its memory.	a. Check/replace any backup batteries.
	b. Replace the memory card.
2. Cannot read (or write) the card.	a. Verify card compatibility.
	b. Check the write-protect switch.
	c. Check the card's insertion.
	d. Inspect card connector(s).
	e. Replace the memory card.
	f. Replace memory card controller IC.
3. PCMCIA card is not recognized.	a. Check for device driver conflicts or loading problems.
	b. Reconfigure offending drivers (if possible).
4. You are asked to insert a card, even though the card is already installed.	a. Reinsert the PC Card carefully.
	b. Enable the PCMCIA socket through BIOS.
	c. Check/correct your PC Card application(s).
	d. Adjust device driver configuration(s).
5. Card service errors when running antivirus software.	a. Load antivirus software after card services.
	b. Try a more compatible antivirus software.
	c. Disable the antivirus software entirely.
6. No pop-up displays when a PC Card is inserted or removed.	a. Configure the card software to enable "pop-ups."
	b. Free as much space as possible in the UMA.
	c. Replace or update the card services software.
7. Application fails when card is inserted or removed.	a. Insert the card before starting application.
	b. Shut down application before removing the card.

8. Fax/modem PC Card fails under Win95.

   c. Replace/upgrade the offending application.

   a. Check for hardware conflicts with the PC Card.

9. Mouse acts up after PC Card installed.

   a. Check for hardware conflicts with the PC Card.

10. Peripheral fails after PC Card installed.

   a. Check for hardware conflicts with the PC Card.

11. CardSoft enabler won't install.

   a. Check to see if a compatible enabler is already installed.

   b. Replace/upgrade the enabler software.

12. COM port not available for a card.

   a. Check for hardware conflicts with the PC Card.

   b. Reassign PC Card resources.

13. Don't hear the right beeps when installing a PC Card.

   a. Reinsert the card in its socket.

   b. Check the card software for proper configuration.

14. Card doesn't accept I/O addresses.

   a. Check for hardware conflicts with the PC Card.

   b. Reassign PC Card resources.

15. Programs stop working after a PC Card is installed.

   a. Check for updated .DLL files or other files.

   b. Correct/upgrade the offending software.

   c. Uninstall the PC Card and restore the original file(s).

16. `Client registration failed` error.

   a. Remove and reinstall the client driver.

   b. Check for hardware conflicts with the PC Card.

   c. Upgrade the client driver to the newest version.

17. PC Card cannot configure properly.

   a. Check for hardware conflicts with the PC Card.

   b. Check/disable point enablers.

   c. Reconfigure card drivers if necessary.

18. System hangs when card services are loaded.

   a. Load only one copy of card services software.

   b. Check PC Card software configuration.

   c. Check the card services software configuration.

19. `Invalid command line switch` error.

   a. Check that command line switches are used correctly.

20. Xircom combo card won't work with card manager software.
    a. Card may not use full PC Card standards.
    b. Install Xircom custom software.

21. `Abort, Retry, Ignore` error.
    a. Install proper client driver for ATA PC Card.

22. PC Card sound device not working.
    a. Use the proper client driver for the sound card.

23. Modem not initialized after insertion.
    a. Modem hardware may need to be upgraded.

24. SRAM card refuses to work.
    a. Use the proper client driver for the SRAM card.
    b. Disable point enablers driving the SRAM card.

25. `No PCMCIA Controller Found.`
    a. Upgrade PC Card software to the latest version.
    b. Enable the PCMCIA controller.
    c. Replace the PCMCIA controller.

26. System hangs after card is checked.
    a. Disable PC Card power-saving functions.
    b. Shut down offending program before card idles.

27. PC restarts after ejecting card from CardBus slot.
    a. Shut down PC Card software before removing the card.
    b. Upgrade to more robust PC Card software.

28. PCMCIA device not assigned properly in Device Manager.
    a. Get an updated .INF file to get around the problem.

29. PC disables a CardBus card socket after a second boot.
    a. Run the PCMCIA Wizard to configure the CardBus slot.

30. CardBus PCMCIA controller starts conflicting after OSR2 (Win 95) is installed
    a. Manually remove PCIC entry from Device Manager.

31. Xircom card not recognized when used together with e 3COM card.
    a. Insert Xircom card first, then insert 3COM card.

32. Suspend command allows batteries to continue draining.
    a. Upgrade laptop BIOS to correct the problem.

33. Hayes PCMCIA modem not recognized.
    a. Upgrade the PCMCIA modem to a later version.

34. Compression Agent continuously restarts at 10% finished.
    a. Configure the ATA drive card as "nonremovable."

35. PCMCIA HDD not recognized under Windows 95.
    a. Restart Windows 95 without the card, then insert it.

36. PCMCIA HDD is recognized, but is not available under Windows 95.
    a. Check for hardware conflicts with the PC Card and IDE drive controller(s).

The following items appear at the top of the right column:
b. Check the PC Card configuration file(s).

37. PC hangs when ISDN dialing.

    a. Upgrade to a later version of the ISDN PC Card.

38. Fax doesn't work via cellular link.

    a. Edit Registry to configure modem for cellular support.

39. PC Card not available on Dell Latitude.

    a. Configure the PC Card before adding the port replicator.

40. The computer failed to undock.

    a. Remove all PC Cards before undocking the PC.

41. SRAM or flash card does not get a drive letter.

    a. Check the installation of each PC Card driver.

    b. Reconfigure the PC Card drivers as necessary.

42. You log on without a password.

    a. Configure Windows 95 to use a password other than null.

    b. Disable password caching.

43. NDIS drivers are incompatible.

    a. Update all NDIS drivers.

    b. Set up the PC to multiboot.

44. Can't set up PCMCIA slot in AT&T Globalyst laptop.

    a. Enable the PCMCIA socket using the correct driver.

45. Cannot repeat-dial using a PC Card modem.

    a. Edit the proper .INF file to disable staged dialing.

46. PCMCIA Token Ring adapter does not work.

    a. Check for 10-bit I/O allocations.

    b. Remove the system sound card.

47. You restart the PC improperly after installing PCMCIA drivers.

    a. Perform a cold reboot of the system.

48. Check was stopped because of an error.

    a. Delete the ScanDisk task, or run it manually.

49. Zenith PC hangs when Win 95 starts.

    a. Change the driver order to load sound drivers first.

50. PCMCIA devices do not restart when ending a Suspend function.

    a. Do not use the laptop's Suspend feature.

    b. Upgrade the laptop's BIOS for better power management.

51. You cannot use two identical cards together.

    a. Use two similar but *different* cards.

52. PC CD-ROM adapter fails with the 32-bit Win 95 drivers.

    a. Disable the 32-bit drivers.

53. Win 95 cannot setup new PC Card if original card using Win 95 files.

    a. Manually install the new card with Add New Hardware wizard feature.

54. Cannot format SRAM card using Win 95.

    a. Upgrade the SRAM card driver.

55. PC Card may stop working after Compaq undock.

    a. Upgrade the laptop's BIOS version.

    b. Remove any incorrect PCMCIA devices.

56. Win 95 won't install more than one PCMCIA network adapter.

    a. Install the Win 95 32-bit PCMCIA socket drivers.

57. Can't view resources after connecting to network with IBM Token Ring PC Card.

    a. Use a different Token Ring adapter.

58. ScanDisk shows drives that don't exist.

    a. Update the drive list by restarting ScanDisk.

59. Xircom PCMCIA card may not work.

    a. Try loading real-mode card and socket services.

60. PC Cards do not configure properly on a Compaq.

    a. Update the laptop's BIOS version.

61. `Divide Overflow` starting Win 95.

    a. Review and install current drivers for Win 95.

62. PC Card client driver(s) won't load.

    a. Disable any real-mode card drivers.
    b. Run PCMCIA wizard to install 32-bit drivers.

63. PC Cards won't load on IBM ThinkPads.

    a. Update the BIOS on the IBM ThinkPad.

64. `Device cannot be removed` error.

    a. Check for hardware conflicts with the PC Card.

65. Win 95 doesn't recognize PC Card disk parameters.

    a. You will need to prepare the card disk like an HDD.

Chapter 8: Tape Drives

Tape drive troubleshooting

1. Drive does not work at all.

    a. Check power to the drive.
    b. Check interface wiring and connector(s).
    c. Check backup software configuration.
    d. Check host controller setup and configuration.
    e. Check tape insertion.
    f. Check interface signals.
    g. Isolate drive/controller by substitution.

2. Drive does not read or write.

    a. Check/replace tape cartridge.
    b. Check/correct tape insertion.
    c. Check/replace R/W head assembly.
    d. Check/replace drive control PC board.
    e. Check/replace the host controller PC board.
    f. Replace the tape drive.

3. Drive heads do not step properly.

    a. Check/replace BOT/EOT sensor pair.
    b. Check head stepping signals.

       c. Check/replace drive control PC board.
       d. Check/replace R/W head seek assembly.
       e. Replace the head stepping motor.
       f. Replace the tape drive.

4. Tape does not move at all.
       a. Check reel motor voltage(s).
       b. Check/replace drive control PC board.
       c. Check/clear obstructions.
       d. Replace both reel motors.
       e. Check/adjust speed encoder roller.
       f. Replace speed encoder roller.
       g. Check/replace speed encoder.
       h. Replace the tape drive.

5. Tape does not load/eject properly.
       a. Check/replace the tape.
       b. Check mechanical load/unload mechanisms.
       c. Check/clear obstructions.
       d. Replace any worn mechanical parts.
       e. Replace the tape drive.

6. Drive writes to write-protected tapes.
       a. Check tape's write-protect tab.
       b. Check/replace write-protect sensor.
       c. Check/replace drive control PC board.
       d. Replace the tape drive.

7. Drive fails to recognize the BOT/EOT.
       a. Check/replace the tape.
       b. Check/replace EOT/BOT sensor pair.
       c. Check/replace drive control PC board.
       d. Replace the tape drive.

8. Dongle causes parallel-port problems.
       a. Remove the copy-protection device.
       b. Put tape on different parallel port.

9. `Too many bad sectors` on tape.
       a. Clean the tape drive heads.
       b. Use a known-good tape cartridge.
       c. Check/replace the drive signal cable.

10. `Tape drive error XX`.
       a. Check the specific fault code with your software.

11. Drive is not detected by software.
       a. Make sure backup software works with the drive.
       b. Check the drive installation.
       c. Check the drive controller configuration.
       d. Check for hardware conflicts with the parallel port.

12. Drive fails in Windows 95.

   e. Check parallel-port mode in CMOS Setup.
   a. Check Win 95 backup software compatibility.
   b. Check for Win 95 driver conflicts.

13. `Overlay Error` in backup software.

   a. Check the number of BUFFERS in CONFIG.SYS.

14. Older PP backup software fails.

   a. Upgrade the backup software to the newest version.

15. Various tape drive "system errors."

   a. Check and reinsert the data cartridge.
   b. Reinitialize the data cartridge.
   c. Try disabling data compression in software.

16. `An ASPI drive was not found.`

   a. Disable the driver's EPP test.

17. Drive won't save or restore reliably.

   a. Reformat the tape properly.
   b. Check the parallel port mode in CMOS Setup.

18. Backups take longer than expected.

   a. Increase available RAM in the system.
   b. Close all other applications in the background.
   c. Make sure no drives are in Compatibility Mode.
   d. Check disk compression software performance.
   e. Check/defragment the hard drive.
   f. Try a new tape cartridge.

19. Can't format one tape in another drive.

   a. Drive may not be compatible with tape for writing.

20. `Serious error in memory manager.`

   a. Check for TSR or driver conflicts.
   b. Try running backup from Win 95 Safe Mode.
   c. Try disabling swap file.
   d. Remove and reinstall backup software.
   e. Try a known-good tape cartridge.
   f. Replace the tape drive.
   g. Check/replace system RAM.

21. QIC-3020 tape not recognized.

   a. Check tape drive controller performance.
   b. Try a high-performance tape drive controller.

22. Busy files not "autoskipped."

   a. Upgrade the backup software to the latest version.

23. Can't connect tape drive to floppy controller.
   a. Check/replace floppy signal cable.

24. DMA setting is incorrect.
   a. Check floppy accelerator hardware settings.
   b. Try different hardware settings.
   c. Check for TSR or driver conflicts.
   d. Disable High-Speed Burst Mode.
   e. Disable other tape drive software.

25. Drive does not initialize tape.
   a. Check power levels and wiring to the drive.
   b. Replace the tape drive.

26. File not found in file set directory.
   a. Upgrade the backup software to the latest version.
   b. Turn off file compression.
   c. Deselect the Registry.

27. Formatting takes 7–18 hours.
   a. Use a high-performance tape controller.

28. Slow reading or writing.
   a. Clean the tape drive heads.
   b. Use a high-performance tape controller.
   c. Check the disk files with ScanDisk.
   d. Defragment the disk.
   e. Check for TSR or driver conflicts.

29. Parsing or logic error.
   a. Upgrade the backup software to the latest version.

30. Running out of memory during DOS backups.
   a. Free additional conventional memory.
   b. Check the number of BUFFERS in CONFIG.SYS.

31. Excessive "shoeshining."
   a. Close any open windows.
   b. Shut down open applications.
   c. Take PC out of "turbo" mode.

Chapter 9: Optical Drives

Troubleshooting CD-ROM drives

1. Drive has trouble handling a CD.
   a. Check/clear obstruction(s).
   b. Replace any damaged linkage(s) or mechanism(s).
   c. Replace entire load/unload assembly.
   d. Check/replace geared motor assembly.
   e. Check/replace geared motor unit.
   f. Check/replace drive control PC board.

2. Read head does not seek.

    g. Replace the CD-ROM drive.
a. Check/clear obstruction(s).
b. Check/replace linear actuator.
c. Check/replace drive control PC board.
d. Replace the CD-ROM drive.

3. Disc cannot be read.

a. Check/clean the CD.
b. Try a different CD.
c. Clean read head optics if possible.
d. Clean/replace interface cable.
e. Check/replace host interface controller board.
f. Check/replace drive control PC board.
g. Replace optical read assembly.
h. Replace the CD-ROM drive.

4. Disc does not turn.

a. Check/correct drive installation or configuration.
b. Clean read head optics if possible.
c. Check/replace the spindle motor assembly.
d. Replace the drive control PC board.
e. Replace the CD-ROM drive.

5. Laser beam will not focus.

a. try a different CD.
b. Check/replace the optical head.
c. Replace the drive control PC board.
d. Replace the CD-ROM drive.

6. No audio is produced by the drive.

a. Check/replace speakers or headphones.
b. Check audio volume on drive.
c. Check/correct audio driver software.
d. Check/replace volume control.
e. Check/replace audio amplifier.
f. Replace headphone PC board.
g. Replace the CD-ROM drive.

7. No audio is produced by the sound card.

a. Check/replace the CD audio cable.
b. Check/adjust the soundboard mixer applet.
c. Replace the soundboard.
d. Replace the CD-ROM drive.

8. `Wrong DOS version` error.

a. Check the version of MSCDEX vs.DOS.
b. Upgrade MSCDEX to the latest version.
c. Use SETVER if necessary.

9. Cannot access CD-ROM drive letter.

a. Check that MSCDEX has loaded properly.

b. Check/replace the drive signal cable.

c. Check your version of MSCDEX.

d. Replace the CD-ROM drive controller.

10. Error when loading low-level driver.

a. Check that you are using the correct driver.

b. Check that you are using the latest driver.

c. Check for hardware conflicts with the CD-ROM controller.

d. Replace the CD-ROM drive controller.

11. `Not ready reading from drive D:.`

a. Check that a known-good CD is installed.

b. Clean the CD.

c. Check that the drivers are loaded properly.

d. Check/replace the drive signal cable.

e. Check the drive power levels and wiring.

f. Replace the CD-ROM drive controller.

12. SmartDrive is not caching CD-ROM.

a. Use the version of SmartDrive with DOS 6.2x.

b. SmartDrive command line should follow MSCDEX.

c. Optimize use of BUFFERS in CONFIG.SYS.

13. Drivers fail with compression software.

a. Boot from compressed drive first.

14. CD-ROM drive is not found.

a. Check the drive power levels and wiring.

b. Check/replace the drive signal cable.

c. Check for hardware conflicts with the drive controller.

d. Check the CD-ROM drivers.

e. Check termination (for SCSI drives).

15. Much less RAM with CD installed.

a. Adjust caching with CD-ROM driver.

b. Upgrade the CD-ROM driver.

16. Proprietary driver fails to load.

a. Check the CD-ROM controller configuration.

b. Check the driver command line for needed switches.

17. `CDRxxx Drive Not Ready` error.

a. Upgrade your low-level CD driver to the latest version.

b. Try a generic low-level driver.

18. Cannot set up more than one CD.

   c. Upgrade your MSCDEX to the latest version.
   a. Check the CD-ROM controller.
   b. Check for proper instance of low-level driver.
   c. Modify MSCDEX with /D switch.

19. CD won't work with IDE port.

   a. Ensure drive is actually "true" IDE.
   b. Replace the IDE controller board.
   c. Use a proprietary CD controller if necessary.

20. CD will not run mounted vertically.

   a. Check with the drive maker for proper mounting.

21. CD won't work with Adaptec interface.

   a. Update SCSI drivers to the latest version.
   b. Turn off "Sync Negotiations."

22. `No drives found` error.

   a. Check low-level driver command line switches.
   b. Check MSCDEX command line switches.
   c. Check the SmartDrive command line.
   d. Check for hardware conflicts with the drive controller.
   e. Replace the CD-ROM controller.

23. LCD displays an error code.

   a. Refer to the drive's documentation to identify the code.

24. System hangs when SCSI BIOS starts.

   a. Try disabling SCSI BIOS.
   b. Update the SCSI BIOS.
   c. Check for corrective SCSI drivers.

25. `Unable to detect ATAPI CD-ROM....`

   a. Check the EIDE/IDE controller configuration.
   b. Check/replace the IDE signal cable.
   c. Check for hardware conflicts with the controller.
   d. Check the low-level driver command line.

26. CD-ROM drive door won't open.

   a. Check the drive power levels and wiring.
   b. Check/replace the IDE signal cable.
   c. Replace the CD-ROM drive.

27. Can play CD audio, but not data.

   a. Make sure all necessary drivers are installed.
   b. Check the drive controller's resource settings.
   c. Replace the CD-ROM drive.

28. CD front panel controls don't work under Windows 95.

   a. Disable CD-ROM polling under Windows 95.

29. Can't change CD drive letter (Win 95).

   a. Use the Device Manager to change resource settings.

30. CD fails after disabling real-mode drivers.

   a. Use the Add New Hardware wizard to install the protected-mode drivers.

31. PP to SCSI interface won't work under Windows 95.

   a. Check the parallel port mode in CMOS Setup.

   b. Update MSCDEX to the latest version.

   c. Cold boot the system.

   d. Check the low-level driver command line switches.

32. `Results may not be as expected.`

   a. Install the latest protected-mode CD drivers.

33. CD sound and video is choppy under Windows 95.

   a. Install the latest protected-mode CD drivers.

   b. Shut down real-mode applications under Win 95.

   c. Shut down background Win 95 applications.

   d. Cold boot the system.

Chapter 10: Other Drives

Zip drive troubleshooting

1. Drive displays floppy disk icon.

   a. Use protected-mode drivers for Zip drive.

2. No drive letter for SCSI Zip drive.

   a. Check the SCSI driver.

   b. Check the resource settings of the SCSI adapter.

   c. Check for hardware conflicts with the SCSI adapter.

   d. Check/replace the SCSI signal cable.

   e. Check termination.

3. No drive letter for PP Zip drive.

   a. Check drive power and wiring.

   b. Check/replace the parallel port cable.

   c. Remove any dongles.

   d. Check the parallel-port mode in CMOS Setup.

   e. Check the SCSI host controller.

   f. Check the Zip drivers.

   g. Replace the Zip drive.

4. System hangs when installing drivers.

   a. Check/replace the signal cable.

   b. Check for hardware conflicts with the Zip drive controller.

   c. Replace the Zip drive.

5. Zip takes on the CD-ROM letter.
   a. Switch drive letters as required.
6. Duplicate Zip drive letters.
   a. Check for driver conflicts.
7. Zip GUEST locks up.
   a. Edit GUEST.INI for the proper ASPI manager.
   b. Use a more appropriate SCSI driver.
   c. Replace the Zip drive.
8. Zip drive letter problems under DOS.
   a. Use the LASTDRIVE command.
   b. Change the CD-ROM drive letter.
   c. Reinstall applications as necessary.
9. GUEST cannot find a drive letter.
   a. Use the LASTDRIVE command.
10. System fails after Zip Tools installs.
   a. Delete Zip icon from Startup group.
   b. Reinstall Zip Tools software.
11. "No drive letters added" error.
   a. Edit GUEST.INI for the proper ASPI manager.
   b. Check/replace the signal cable.
   c. Boot the system "clean."
   d. Check for TSR or driver conflicts.
   e. Replace the Zip drive.
12. Network drive letter conflicts with Zip drive letter.
   a. Remap the shared drive volume.
13. Zip drive cannot find Tools disk.
   a. Boot the system "clean."
   b. Edit GUEST.INI for the proper ASPI manager.
   c. Check/replace the signal cable.
   d. Replace the Zip drive.
14. Cannot print while using Zip drive.
   a. Check parallel-port mode in CMOS Setup.
15. Cannot install Zip SCSI drive.
   a. Check the drive power.
   b. Check/replace the signal cable.
   c. Check termination.
   d. Check SCSI ID.
   e. Check for TSR or driver conflicts.
16. Drive letter lost when PC turned off.
   a. Relocate the GUEST command line.

Ditto drive troubleshooting

1. Internal Ditto not detected (w/floppy).
   a. Check the drive power.
   b. Check/replace the signal cable.
   c. Check the tape cartridge.
   d. Replace the drive.
   e. Reinstall the backup software.
   f. Try a drive accelerator card.
2. Internal Ditto not detected (w/dash).
   a. Check the drive power.
   b. Check/replace the drive signal cable.
   c. Check the tape cartridge.
   d. Check for hardware conflicts with accelerator card.

3. Backups take a long time.

    e. Reinstall the backup software.
    a. Check controller data transfer rate.
    b. Disable the PC "turbo" mode.
    c. Try a different drive controller.

4. Ditto PP drive not detected in DOS.

    a. Check the drive power.
    b. Check/replace the drive signal cable.
    c. Remove any dongles.
    d. Check the parallel-port mode in CMOS Setup.
    e. Check for hardware conflicts with the parallel port.
    f. Replace the drive.

5. Ditto doesn't find any catalogs.

    a. Rebuild the tape's catalog.

6. Ditto encounters many corrected errors.

    a. Clean the drive heads.
    b. Retension the tape.
    c. Try a known-good tape.
    d. Boot the system "clean."
    e. Check for TSR or driver conflicts.
    f. Try a different parallel port.
    g. Check for local electrical interference.

7. Fatal exception error.

    a. Correct the drive's configuration files.

8. Drive not restoring selected files.

    a. Adjust the backup software configuration.

9. Drive received an invalid command.

    a. Adjust the backup software configuration.

Bernoulli drive troubleshooting

1. Drive has a floppy icon in Win 95.

    a. Use the protected-mode driver for Windows 95.

2. SCSI drive letter not assigned in Win 95.

    a. Check for hardware conflicts with the SCSI controller.
    b. Check that the proper drivers are loaded.
    c. Check/replace the signal cable.
    d. Check termination.
    e. Check the SCSI ID.

3. PP drive letter not assigned in Win 95.

    a. Check the drive power.
    b. Check/replace the signal cable.
    c. Remove any dongles.
    d. Check the parallel-port mode in CMOS Setup.
    e. Check the controller type.
    f. Check the drivers.
    g. Replace the drive.

4. Bernoulli takes on the CD-ROM letter.   a. Switch drive letters as required.
5. `Invalid drive`   a. Try reinstalling the drive software.
   `specification` error.
6. `Invalid unit reading`   a. Update the controller BIOS.
   `drive <x>`.   b. Check the loading order for
   SmartDrive.
   c. Update your version of GUEST.
7. Bernoulli won't work with PP.   a. Check the drive power.
   b. Check/replace the signal cable.
   c. Remove any dongles.
   d. Check termination.
   e. Check drivers.
8. PP adapter fails on drive installation.   a. Check the drive power.
   b. Check/replace the signal cable.
   c. Check termination.
   d. Check the drivers.
   e. Replace the drive.
9. SCSI communication problems.   a. Check the drive power.
   b. Check/replace the signal cable.
   c. Check termination.
   d. Check the SCSI ID.
   e. Check the drivers.
10. Drive assigned two drive letters.   a. Disable PnP support for the
    Bernoulli drive.
    b. Power up drive with disk removed.

SyQuest drive troubleshooting

1. Future Domain adapter problems.   a. Check the SCSI ID.
   b. Upgrade SCSI controller BIOS.
   c. Check cartridge preparation.
   d. Check drivers.
2. NCR adapter problems.   a. Check the drivers.
   b. Check the SCSI ID.
3. Rancho Technology adapter   a. Check cartridge installation.
   problems.   b. Check drivers.
   c. Check the SCSI ID.
4. Packard Bell system problems.   a. Check for hardware conflicts with
   the SCSI adapter.
5. BusLogic adapter problems.   a. Check drivers.
6. Qlogic SCSI adapter problems.   a. Check cartridge installation.
   b. Check drivers.
7. IBM MCA SCSI adapter problems.   a. Check drivers.
   b. Try corrective driver.
8. DTC SCSI adapter problems.   a. Check the drivers and driver versions.
9. Lights on drive are blinking.   a. Match the blinking with the
   appropriate error code.

Glossary

Access time The time required to locate and begin transfer to or from a specific sector, track, or frame of medium.

Actuator The mechanism which moves a set of R/W heads. Stepper motors and rotary voice coils are two common disk actuators.

ADC (analog-to-digital converter) A device used to convert analog information (usually sound) to words of digital information.

Address A unique set of numbers that identifies a particular location in solid-state memory.

AFrame The subdivision of time (seconds) from the beginning of an optical disk. One second of elapsed time is 75 frames.

Allocation The process of assigning particular areas of a disk to contain specific files.

Allocation unit A group of sectors on a particular disk that are reserved to hold a specific file (also called a *cluster*).

Anode The positive electrode of a two-terminal semiconductor device.

ANSI (American National Standards Institute) An organization that sets standards for languages, database management, etc.

Architecture Describes how a system is constructed and how its components are put together. An "open architecture" refers to a nonproprietary system design that allows other manufacturers to design products that work with the system.

ASCII (American Standard Code for Information Interchange) A set of standard codes defining characters and symbols used by computers.

Asynchronous Circuit operation in which signals can arrive at any point in time. A coordinating clock is not required.

Attribute memory PCMCIA cards provide fixed memory space to hold basic card information and configuration data.

Azimuth The angle (usually measured in angular minutes) of twist of a R/W head to the plane of the medium.

Bad block An area of a disk (usually about a sector) that can not reliably hold data because of bad format data or medium damage.

Bad track table A listing of tracks that are damaged and cannot hold data.

Base   One of the three leads of a bipolar transistor.

Batch file   An ASCII file that combines several DOS commands into a single file.

Baud   The rate at which bits are transferred between devices.

BCD (binary-coded decimal)   The number system used commonly with compact disks.

BIOS (basic input/output system)   A series of programs that handle the computer's low-level functions.

Bit (binary digit)   The basic unit of digital information written as a 0 or a 1.

Block   A sector or group of sectors on a disk, or a fixed length of bytes in a memory card.

Boot   The process of initializing a computer and loading a disk operating system.

Boot device   A drive containing the files and information for a disk operating system.

Boot sector   A section of a hard disk that holds information defining the physical characteristics and partitioning of the drive, as well as a short program that begins the DOS loading process.

bpi (bits per inch)   The number of bits placed in a linear inch of disk space.

Buffer   A temporary storage place for data.

Bus   One or more collections of digital signal lines.

Byte   A set of 8 bits. A byte is approximately equivalent to a character.

Cache memory   Simply called "cache." Part of a computer's RAM operating as a buffer between the system RAM and CPU. Recently used data or instructions are stored in cache. RAM is accessed quickly, so data called for again are available right away. This improves overall system performance.

Caddy (or caddie)   A two-part protective case used with some CD-ROM drives.

Capacitance   The measure of a device's ability to store an electric charge. The unit of capacitance is the farad.

Capacitor   An electronic device used to store energy in the form of an electric charge.

Capacity   The amount of information that can be held in a particular storage device.

Cassette   The protective outer housing of a tape or optical disk.

Cathode   The negative electrode of a two-terminal semiconductor device.

CD audio   An optical drive capable of playing compact disks based on the Red Book (IEC 908) standard.

CD-ROM   Optical medium containing digital data formatted to Yellow Book (ISO/IEC 10149) standards.

Chip carrier   A rectangular or square package with I/O connections on all four sides.

CIRC (Cross-Interleaved Reed-Solomon Code)   An error-detection and -correction process used with small frames of audio or data. The detection and correction algorithm is implemented in hardware.

Cluster   The smallest unit of disk storage defined as one or more contiguous sectors.

CMOS (complementary metal-oxide semiconductor)   A type of MOS transistor commonly used in digital integrated circuits for high-speed and low-power operation.

Collector   One of the three leads of a bipolar transistor.

Configuration   The components that make up a computer's hardware setup.

Contiguous All together, or one right after another. Usually refers to files that are not fragmented or on separate sectors of a hard disk. Contiguous files can be accessed more quickly than fragmented or noncontiguous files.

Continuous composite A type of format that describes the physical, optical, and data formats of a magnetooptical disk.

Control characters ASCII characters that do not print out but are used to control communication.

CPU (central processing unit) The primary functioning unit of a computer system. Also called a microprocessor.

CRC (cyclical redundancy check) An error-checking technique for data recording typically used by systems that perform hardware error checking.

Cylinder A collection of tracks located one above the other on the platters of a hard drive.

DAC (digital-to-analog converter) A device used to convert words of digital information into equivalent analog levels.

DAT (digital audio tape) A high-density helical tape format used for digital audio and data recordings.

Data separator A drive circuit that extracts data from combined data and clock signals.

Dedicated servo A medium surface separate from the surface used for data which contains only disk timing and positioning information.

Deemphasis Decreasing the level of high-frequency audio signals relative to low-frequency audio signals prior to recording or playback. This helps to suppress hiss noise.

DIP (dual in-line package) The classical "caterpillar-looking" IC package style.

DMA (direct memory access) A method of moving data from a storage device directly to RAM without the direct intervention of the CPU.

DOS (disk operating system) A program or set of programs that directs the operations of a disk-based computing system using command-line instructions.

DOS extender Software that uses the capabilities of advanced microprocessors running under DOS to access more then 640 kB of RAM.

Drain One of the three leads of a field-effect transistor.

DVD (digital video disk or digital versatile disk) An emerging high-density optical disk system capable of storage capacities up to 17 GB on a disk the same size as an ordinary CD-ROM.

ECC (error-correction code) A method used to recover a block of data during data playback.

Eccentricity Rotating out of round.

EDC (error-detection code) A method used to ensure data integrity such as the cyclic redundancy check (CRC-32).

EIA (Electronics Industry Association) A standards organization in the United States which develops specifications for interface equipment.

EIAJ (Electronic Industries Association of Japan) A Japanese standards organization which is the equivalent of the U.S. Joint Electronic Device Engineering Council (JEDEC).

EISA (Extended Industry Standard Architecture) A popular expansion bus architecture used on older file server systems.

Embedded servo Timing or location information placed on surfaces which actually contain data. Servo data allows R/W heads to achieve precise positioning.

Emitter One of the three leads of a bipolar transistor.

EMS (extended memory system) A highly integrated IC controller used to access extra RAM.

Encoding The protocol defining how data patterns are changed prior to being written to the disk surface.

ESD (electrostatic discharge) The sudden, accidental release of electrons accumulated in the body or inanimate objects. Static charges are destructive to MOS ICs and other semiconductors.

ESDI (Enhanced Small Device Interface) A popular physical interface for large-capacity hard drives which replaced the ST-506 interface. ESDI can transfer data up to 10 MB/s.

FAT (file allocation table) A table recorded on disk which keeps track of which clusters and sectors are available, which have been used by files, and which are defective.

File A collection of related information which is stored together on disk.

File attributes The DOS identification which denotes the characteristics of a file: copy-protected, read-only, or archival.

Firmware Program instructions held in a permanent memory device such as a PROM or EPROM.

Flatpack One of the oldest surface-mount packages with 14 to 50 ribbon leads on both sides of its body.

Flux density The number of magnetic flux transitions that can be written along a given length of disk surface.

Flying height The distance between a R/W head and a disk surface caused by a cushion of moving air.

Format The predefined pattern of tracks and sectors that must be written to a disk before the disk will retain information.

Form factor A reference to the general size class of a system or device such as a hard drive.

Fragmentation The state of a hard disk where files are stored in two or more small pieces across a disk rather than contiguously.

Gate One of the three leads of a field-effect transistor.

Head A device consisting of tiny wire coils which moves across the surface of floppy or hard disks. Heads are used to read or write information to disks.

Head actuator The mechanism that moves a R/W head radially across the surface of a hard or floppy disk.

Head crash Damage to a R/W head due to collision with a disk surface of other foreign matter such as dust, smoke, or fingerprints.

High memory The RAM locations residing between 640 kB and 1 MB.

Host adapter The circuit board used to interface the host CPU to the CD-ROM, hard drive, floppy drive, tape drive, or other peripheral.

Hot insertion/removal The ability to insert or remove a memory card from a system with the system power turned on.

Hysteresis The ability of a R/W head to reach the same track position when approaching from either radial direction.

ICMA (International Card Manufacturers Association) A consortium of PC card manufacturers.

Index A subdivision of a CD-ROM track.

Inductance The measure of a device's ability to store a magnetic charge. The unit of inductance is the henry.

Inductor An electronic device used to store energy in the form of a magnetic charge.

IDE (Integrated Drive Electronics) A physical interface standard commonly used in medium to large hard drives. IDE control electronics are housed in the drive itself instead of an external control board.

Interface The hardware/software protocol contained in the drive and controller which manages the flow of data between the drive and host computer.

Interleave The arrangement of sectors on a track. The common 1:1 arrangement places the sectors in consecutive order around a track.

ISA (Industry Standard Architecture) The classical IBM AT expansion bus architecture.

ISO (International Standards Organization) An international body responsible for establishing and maintaining a wide variety of electrical and electronic standards.

JEDEC (Joint Electronic Device Engineering Council) The U.S. standards organization that handles packaging standards.

JEIDA (Japanese Electronics Industry Development Association) The Japanese equivalent of JEDEC.

Landing zone A location in a drive's inner cylinder where R/W heads can land during power-down. No data are recorded in the landing zone.

Laser A narrow, intense beam of single-wavelength light used to read and write data to an optical disk.

Latency The time required for data to rotate in front of properly positioned R/W heads. Latency usually measures a few milliseconds. Also called rotational latency.

LCC (leadless chip carrier) An IC package whose leads sit on the package edges.

Lead-in area The area on a CD-ROM disk prior to track one which usually contains null data.

Lead-out area The area on a CD-ROM disk beyond the last information track which usually contains null data.

Lead spacing The distance (usually measured in mils) between adjacent leads on the sides of a package.

LEC (Layed Error Correction) An error-correction technique used CD-ROM systems.

LIF (low insertion force) A term used to describe sockets which require only a minimum force to insert or extract an IC.

Load The process of pressing R/W heads onto or toward the surface of a magnetic disk.

Logic analyzer An instrument used to monitor signals of an integrated circuit or system.

Magnetooptical Rewriteable optical technology using a plastic disk with a magnetic layer.

MCP (math coprocessor)   A sophisticated processing IC intended to enhance the processing of a computer by performing floating-point math operations instead of the CPU.

Medium   The physical material which actually retains recorded information. For floppy and hard drives, the medium is a coating of magnetic oxide.

MFM (modified frequency modulation)   The most widely used method of encoding binary data on a disk.

Mil   One-thousandth of an inch (0.001 in).

Motherboard   In a small computer, the major PC board containing the CPU, core memory, and most of the system's controller ICs (also called the main logic board).

MPU (microprocessor unit)   Another term for a CPU.

OC (open collector)   A circuit configuration where transistor outputs are left unconnected.

Operating system   The interface between the hardware and software running on your PC.

Overwrite   To write data on top of existing data, thereby erasing the original data.

Page   A reference to a block of memory in a computer.

Parallel port   A physical connection on a computer used to connect output devices. Data are transmitted as multiple bits sent together over separate wires. Typically used to connect a printer.

Parity   A means of error checking using an extra bit added to each transmitted character.

Partition   The portion of a hard disk devoted to a single operating system and accessed with a single logical letter.

PCMCIA (Personal Computer Memory Card Industry Association)   The leading international industry group sponsoring the development and standardization of PC card technologies.

Permeable   The ability of a material be magnetized.

Pit   A microscopic depression in the surface of a compact disk.

Platter   An actual disk inside a hard disk drive which carries the magnetic recording material.

PLCC (plastic-leaded chip carrier)   A popular plastic IC package style resulting in square ICs with small metal "contacts" along each of the four sides.

Positioning time   The radial component of access time.

POST (power on self-test)   A program in BIOS which handles the computer's initialization and self-test before loading DOS.

PQFP (plastic quad flat pack)   A popular plastic IC package style resulting in thin square or rectangular ICs with small metal "tabs" along each of the four sides (typically soldered to the PC board).

QFP (quad flat pack)   A popular IC package style (usually ceramic) resulting in thin square or rectangular ICs with small metal "tabs" along each of the four sides (typically soldered to the PC board).

Reed-Solomon Error Code   A linear algebraic formula used for error correction. See CIRC.

Resistance   The measure of a device's opposition to the flow of current. The unit of resistance is the ohm.

Resistor   A device used to limit the flow of current in an electronic circuit.

RLL (run length limited)   A technique for encoding binary data on a hard disk which can pack up to 50 percent more data than MFM recording.

RS-232   A standard interface for transmitting serial data.

SCSI (Small Computer System Interface)   A physical interface standard for large to huge (up to 9 GB) hard drives, as well as other devices such as CD-ROM drives, tape drives, scanners, and so on.

Sector   The smallest unit of storage on the surface of a floppy or hard disk.

Seek   The radial movement of a head along a disk.

Serial port   A physical connection on a computer used to connect output devices. Data is transmitted as individual bits sent one at a time over a single wire. Typically used to connect a modem or mouse.

Settle time   The time required for a head to stop reliably after it has been stepped.

SIMM (single in-line memory module)   A quantity of extra RAM mounted onto a PC board terminated with a single, convenient connector.

SMT (surface-mount technology)   The printed circuit fabrication approach of soldering components to only one side of the printed circuit.

SOIC (small outline integrated circuit)   A small, low-profile surface-mount IC style used to package simple ICs.

SOJ (small outline "J" lead package)   A small, low-profile surface-mount IC style using pins that fold up under the IC body in a J shape.

Source   One of the three leads of a field-effect transistor.

Spindle   The part of a hard or floppy drive which rotates the disks.

Spindown   The process of removing power and decelerating a hard drive to a halt.

Spinup   The process of applying power and accelerating a hard drive to running speed.

ST-506   The oldest physical interface standard for small hard drives (under 40 MB) with a data transfer rate of only 5 MB/s.

Synchronous   Circuit operation where signals are coordinated through the use of a master clock.

Track   The circular path traced across the surface of a spinning disk by a read/write head. A track consists of one or more clusters.

Transfer rate   The speed at which a hard or floppy drive can transfer information between its medium and the CPU, typically measured in megabytes per second.

TSOP (thin small outline package)   A very low-profile IC package style often employed where height is at a premium (i.e., PC cards).

TSR (terminate and stay resident)   A program residing in memory that can be invoked from other application programs.

TTL (transistor-transistor logic)   Digital logic ICs using bipolar transistors.

Tuple   A small block of memory in solid-state memory cards.

WORM (write once read many)   An optical technology which allows data to be permanently written to a disk.

Trademarks and Servicemarks

Commodore and VIC-20 are trademarks of Commodore Corporation.

IEEE is a trademark of the Institute of Electrical and Electronic Engineers, Inc.

Weller and XCELITE are trademarks of Cooper Industries, Inc.

Iomega is a trademark of Iomega Corporation.

Floptical is a trademark of Insite Peripherals, Incorporated.

ThinCard and ThinCardDrive are trademarks of Databook, Inc.

CleanSphere is a trademark of Safetech Limited.

FileSafe SideCar, FileSafe, and Mountain are trademarks of Mountain Network Solutions, Inc., Campbell, CA.

ST, SensaTemp, Cir-Kit, and PACE are trademarks of PACE Incorporated.

AlignIt is a trademark of Landmark Research International Corp.

DriveProbe and HRD are trademarks of Accurite Technologies Incorporated.

Elan is a trademark of Elan Digital Systems Ltd. U.K.

PCMCIA is a trademark of The PCMCIA, Sunnyvale, CA.

Windows, MS, MS-DOS, Microsoft, and Windows for Pen Computing are trademarks of Microsoft Corporation.

PenPoint is a trademark of GO Corporation.

Toshiba and Satellite are trademarks of Toshiba America Information Systems, Inc.

Tri-State is a trademark of National Semiconductor Corporation.

IBM, PC/XT, PC/AT, and PS/2 are trademarks of International Business Machines, Inc.

HP and Kitty Hawk Personal Storage Module are trademarks of Hewlett-Packard Company.

TI, Texas Instruments, and Travelmate are trademarks of Texas Instruments, Incorporated.

GRiDPAD, PALMPAD, and GRiD are trademarks of GRiD Systems Corporation.

Tandy and Radio Shack are trademarks of the Tandy Corporation.

ProDrive ELS, ProDrive LPS, HardCard EZ, GoDrive, Quantum, and ProDrive are trademarks of Quantum Corporation.

AMP is a trademark of AMP, Inc.

QuadClip is a trademark of ITT Pomona.

Innoventions, RAMCHECK, and SIMCHECK are trademarks of Innoventions, Incorporated.

Seagate is a trademark of Seagate Technology, Inc.

SunDisk and SDP are trademarks of SunDisk Corporation.

Maxtor is a trademark of Maxtor Corporation.

Intel, 8088, 80286, 80386, 80486, x286, x386, and x486 are trademarks of Intel Corporation.

Lotus 1-2-3 is a trademark of Lotus Development Corporation.

Bibliography

Alting-Mees, Adrian. *The Hard Drive Encyclopedia.* San Diego, CA: Annabooks, 1991.

Bigelow, Stephen J. "Cleaning and Aligning Floppy Disk Drives." *The PC Troubleshooter,* March, 1993.

Brenner, Robert C. *IBM PC Advanced Troubleshooting & Repair.* Indianapolis, IN: Howard W. Sams & Company, 1988.

Buell, Jim. "Floppy Drive Test Media Technology." *MSM.* April: 47–49, 1991.

"Card Related Terms and Abbreviations." *Memory Card Systems & Design* 2(1): 38–40, 1992.

Greenfield, Joseph D. *Practical Digital Design Using ICs.* New York, NY: Wiley Books, 1983.

GRiDPAD-HD/GRiDPAD-RC Computer Technical Reference Manual. Fremont, CA: GRiD Systems Corporation, 1991.

GRiDPAD-HD/GRiDPAD-RC Computer Service Manual. Fremont, CA: GRiD Systems Corporation, 1991.

Hall, V. Douglas. *Microprocessors and Digital Systems.* New York, McGraw-Hill, 1980.

Howard, Bill. "High-End Notebook PCs." *PC Magazine.* April 14: 113–143, 1992.

Hughes, Allan. "Duplicator Drive Maintenance." *Software Manufacturing News.* November 15: 28–31, 1992.

Johnson, Jim. *Laser Technology.* Benton Harbor, MI: Heath Company, 1985.

Leach, Donald P., and Malvino, Albert P. *Digital Principles and Applications,* 3d ed. New York, Gregg/McGraw-Hill, 1981.

Margolis, Art. *Troubleshooting and Repairing Personal Computers,* 2d ed. Blue Ridge Summit, PA, Windcrest/McGraw-Hill, 1991.

Matzkin, Howard. *Palmtop PCs: Power By the Ounce. PC Magazine.* July: 197–226, 1991.

Methuin, Dave. "Adding Memory: A Step-by-Step Guide." *PC Computing.* June: 152–154, 1991.

Negrino, Tom. "Fast Forward Storage." *MACWorld.* November: 177–185, 1991.

1992 Arrow Systems Product Guide. Melville, NY: Arrow Electronics Corporation, 1992.

Osborne, Adam. *An Introduction to Microcomputers,* vol. 1, 2d ed. Berkeley, CA: Osborne/McGraw-Hill, 1980.

ProDrive 40S/80S Product Manual. Milpitas, CA: Quantum Corporation, 1989.

Product Manual for the Stingray 1842. Boulder, CO: Integral Peripherals, Inc., 1992.

Prosise, Jeff. "Tutor" [monthly column]. *PC Magazine.* April 28: 359–362, 1992.

Rosch, Winn L. "Choosing and Using Hard Disks." *PC Magazine.* December 31: 313–331, 1991.

Rosch, Winn L. "Minicartridge Tape Backup." *PC Magazine.* April 14: 185–224.

Rosch, Winn L. *The Winn L. Rosch Hardware Bible,* 2d ed. New York: Brady Publishing, 1992.

Service Manual: Tandy 1500HD Laptop Computer. Fort Worth, TX, Tandy Corporation, 1990.

Sharp Service Manual OZ/IQ-8000 & OZ/IQ-8200. Yamatokoriyama, Nara (Japan): Sharp Corporation, Information Systems Division, 1990.

Smith, Jan. "Tape Backup." *PC Computing.* April: 206–208, 1992.

TAPE250 Technical Description Manual. Iomega Corporation. EN067300. December, 1992.

Tillinghast, Charles. "IC DRAM Technology and Usage." *Memory Card Systems & Design* 2(1):28–31, 1992.

Index

About the Author

Stephen J. Bigelow is an experienced electronics engineer and the author of more than 100 books and articles. Among his many previous books are *Troubleshooting, Repairing, and Maintaining PCs; Bigelow's Computer Repair Toolkit; Troubleshooting and Repairing Computer Monitors;* and *Troubleshooting and Repairing Computer Printers,* all published by McGraw-Hill. Bigelow is the founder and president of Dynamic Learning Systems, Inc. (http://www.dlspubs.com), and publisher of *The PC Toolbox*™ troubleshooting newsletter. A member of *Who's Who Worldwide,* Bigelow is a graduate of Central New England College. He lives and works in Jefferson, Massachusetts.

The PC Toolbox™

Use this form when ordering *The PC Toolbox*™. You may tear out or photocopy this order form.

YES! I'm tired of fixing computers in the dark! Please accept my order as shown below: (check any one)

_____ Please start my *one year subscription* (6 issues) for $39 (USD)

_____ Please start my *two year subscription* (12 issues) for $69 (USD)

PRINT YOUR MAILING INFORMATION HERE:

Name: Company:

Address:

City, State, Zip:

Country:

Telephone: (   )   Fax: (   )

PLACING YOUR ORDER:

By FAX: Fax this completed order form (24 hrs/day, 7 days/week) to 508-829-6819

By Phone: Phone in your order (Mon-Fri; 9am-4pm EST) to 508-829-6744

By Web: Complete the online subscription form at http://www.dlspubs.com/

___ MasterCard   Card: ___ ___ ___ ___ ___ ___ ___ ___ ___ ___ ___ ___ ___ ___ ___ ___

___ VISA   Exp: ___/___   Sig: _____

Or by Mail: Mail this completed form, along with your check, money order, PO, or credit card info to:

Dynamic Learning Systems, P.O. Box 282, Jefferson, MA 01522-0282 USA

Make check payable to Dynamic Learning Systems. Please allow 2-4 weeks for order processing. Returned checks are subject to a $15 charge. There is a 90 day unconditional money-back guarantee on your subscription.